PIMLICO

703

THE ITALIAN BOY

Sarah Wise is a freelance journalist and has written for the *Guardian*, the *Independent on Sunday Review* and the *Observer*. She completed an MA in Victorian Studies at Birkbeck College in 1996. This is her first book.

'Written with flair and plentifully illustrated ...has all the melodrama, plot twists and pathos of Victorian fiction...History at its most shamefully entertaining.'
Michel Faber, *Guardian*

'A gruesome and gripping study...contains a wealth of information.'
Mark Sanderson, *Sunday Telegraph*

'Wise handles her sources with delicacy and rigour...she can take credit for the least smug and self-congratulatory book ever written on 19th century slum life.'
Matthew Sweet, *Sunday Times*

'E...
an
Cl

THE ITALIAN BOY

Murder and Grave-Robbery in 1830s London

SARAH WISE

PIMLICO

Published by Pimlico 2005

11

Copyright © Sarah Wise 2004

First published in Great Britain by
Jonathan Cape 2004

Pimlico edition 2005

Pimlico
Random House, 20 Vauxhall Bridge Road,
London SW1V 2SA

Addresses for companies within The Random House Group Limited
can be found at:
www.randomhouse.co.uk/offices.htm

Random House UK Limited Reg. No. 954009

A CIP catalogue record for this book
is available from the British Library

ISBN 9781844133307

Penguin Random House is committed to a sustainable future for
our business, our readers and our planet. This book is made from
Forest Stewardship Council® certified paper.

Printed and bound in Great Britain by Clays Ltd, St Ives plc

For Peter

'Of the common folk that is merely bundled up in turf and brambles, the less said the better. A poor lot, soon forgot.'
Stony Durdles, funerary stonemason, in Charles Dickens's
The Mystery of Edwin Drood (1870)

We are not concerned with the very poor. They are unthinkable, and only to be approached by the statistician or the poet.
E.M. Forster, *Howards End* (1910)

The real central theme of history is not what happened but what people felt about it when it was happening.
G.M. Young, *The Portrait of an Age: Victorian England* (1936)

CONTENTS

List of Illustrations   ix

Acknowledgements   xii

Preface   xv

Chapter 1   Suspiciously Fresh   1

Chapter 2   Persons Unknown   30

Chapter 3   The Thickest Part   54

Chapter 4   Houseless Wretches   71

Chapter 5   Systematic Slaughter   92

Chapter 6   Houseless Wretches Again   102

Chapter 7   Neighbours   118

Chapter 8   Meat – an Interlude   127

Chapter 9   Whatever Has Happened to Fanny?   142

Chapter 10   A Horrid System   158

Chapter 11   At the Bailey   183

Chapter 12   A Newgate Stink   212

Chapter 13   'I, John Bishop . . .'   223

Chapter 14   Day of Dissolution   229

Chapter 15   The Use of the Dead to the Living   235

Chapter 16   How Many?   252

Epilogue   273

Notes   290

Bibliography   328

Index   337

List of Illustrations

1. An Italian Boy, or Image Boy, from J.T. Smith's *Etchings of Remarkable Beggars*, 1815 (*by permission of the British Library, shelfmark 1259b3*).

2. *The Watch House, Covent Garden, c.* 1830, unsigned oil painting (*Museum of London*).

3.–5. Two court sketches of John Bishop, James May and Thomas Williams, and the *Sunday Times* court portrait of John Bishop (*Tower Hamlets Local History Library and Archive*).

6. Field Lane (*Wellcome Library, London*).

7. Holborn Bridge over the Fleet River (*Guildhall Library/Corporation of London*).

8. Edward Tuson's anatomy school in Little Windmill Street (*City of Westminster Archives*).

9. The King of Denmark pub in Old Bailey (*Guildhall Library/Corporation of London*).

10. The river frontage of King's College/Somerset House (*Guildhall Library/Corporation of London*).

11.–12. Sketches of Covent Garden market by George Scharf (*British Museum*).

13. *The Bodysnatcher* by Morris Meredith Williams, 1913 (*City Art Centre: City of Edinburgh Museums and Galleries*).

14. The Fortune of War pub (*Guildhall Library/Corporation of London*).

15. Aquatint of Old Bailey by Thomas Hosmer Shepherd, 1814 (*Guildhall Library/Corporation of London*).

16. Coldbath Fields Prison (*Museum of London*).

17. Nova Scotia Gardens in 1831 (*Guildhall Library/Corporation of London*).

18. Millbank Penitentiary sketched in 1828 (*Guildhall Library/Corporation of London*).

19. Millbank Penitentiary photographed in 1903 (*London Metropolitan Archives*).

20. The Bow Street police office/magistrates' court, exterior (*British Museum*).

21. Inside Bow Street police office/magistrates' court (*Guildhall Library/Corporation of London*).

22. Bishop, Williams and May in the Bow Street dock (*Wellcome Library, London*).

23.–24. William Burke and William Hare as they appeared in court in Edinburgh in December 1828 (*Wellcome Library, London*).

25. Clerkenwell New Prison (*Museum of London*).

26. A Charley is removed from his place of watch, unsigned engraving of 1825 (*Guildhall Library/Corporation of London*).

27. Pages of the *Police Gazette, or Hue and Cry* (*British Library Newspaper Library*).

28.–32. Caravan shows and puppet booths (*British Museum; Guildhall Library/Corporation of London*).

33. Italian musicians (*Guildhall Library/Corporation of London*).

34. Sketch of Carlo Ferrari (*Tower Hamlets Local History Library and Archive*).

35. The Quadrant, Regent Street (*Museum of London*).

36. Police officers search Nova Scotia Gardens (*Tower Hamlets Local History Library and Archive*).

37.–40. Black Joe Johnson, Charles Wood and his Learned French Dog Bob, an aged 'sledge beggar', and The Dancing Doll Man of Lucca, from J.T. Smith, *Etchings of Remarkable Beggars*, 1815, and *Vagabondiana*, 1817 (*by permission of the British Library, shelfmarks 1486gg10 and 1259b3*).

41. Samuel Horsey (*Wellcome Library, London*).

42. Dancing doll man, sketch by George Cruikshank, 1835 (*Guildhall Library/Corporation of London*).

43.–45. Street characters as captured by George Scharf (*British Museum*).

46. Smithfield Market (*Guildhall Library/Corporation of London/Bridgeman Art Library*).

47.–48. Two contemporary views of the Friday horse market at Smithfield (*Museum of London*).

49. George Cruikshank's *The Knackers Yard, or the Horse's Last Home*, 1830 (*British Museum*).

50. Tudor/Stuart housing in Cloth Fair, Smithfield (*British Museum*).

51. Sightseers at Nova Scotia Gardens (*Guildhall Library/Corporation of London*).

52. King's College (*Wellcome Library, London*).

53. Herbert Mayo (*Wellcome Library, London*).

54. Joshua Brookes (*Wellcome Library, London*).

55. The Brookesian (*Wellcome Library, London*).

56. The Brookesian Vivarium (*London Metropolitan Archives*).

57. Richard Partridge as a young man (*Wellcome Library, London*).

58. The lecture theatre at King's College (*British Museum*).

59.–60. Two Old Bailey court-room sketches of Bishop, Williams and May (*Wellcome Library, London*).

61. Newgate Prison (*Guildhall Library/Corporation of London*).

62. Debtors Door, Newgate Prison (*London Metropolitan Archives*).

63. A sketch of the Newgate Press Room (*London Metropolitan Archives*).

64. Deadman's Walk (*Museum of London*).

65. Theodore Williams (*with kind permission of London Borough of Barnet Archives, from the collection of the Mill Hill Historical Society*).

66.–67. The true likenesses of John Bishop and Thomas Head, sketched by William Clift of the Royal College of Surgeons (*Royal College of Surgeons of England*).

68. Great Windmill Street School of Anatomy (*Guildhall Library/Corporation of London*).

69. 'The Bethnal-Green Tragedy' (*St Bride Printing Library/Corporation of London*).

70. 'An Italian Boy' (*Tower Hamlets Local History Library and Archive*).

71. 'Trial and Sentence of Bishop, May & Williams' (*Tower Hamlets Local History Library and Archive*).

72. *Carlos Ferriers*, engraved by J. Thomson, from a painting by John Hayes (*Wellcome Library, London*).

73. Sketch of Carlo by Mr Tillotson (*Guildhall Library/Corporation of London*).

74. *Figaro In London* (*by permission of the British Library, shelfmark PP5264*).

75. The *Grampus* hospital hulk (*Wellcome Library, London*).

76. Richard Partridge's examination of Garibaldi (*The Lancet*).

77. Sketch of Nova Scotia Gardens by George Godwin, from *Town Swamps and Social Bridges* (*Tower Hamlets Local History Library and Archive*).

78.–79. Columbia Market and Columbia Square (*London Metropolitan Archives*).

80. Sightseers queue outside the Old Red Lion Tavern in Smithfield (*Guildhall Library/Corporation of London*).

81. Fleet Ditch (*Guildhall Library/Corporation of London*).

82. Lodging house in Field Lane, above the Fleet (*Wellcome Library, London*).

Acknowledgements

This book would probably not have been written had I not enrolled on the Victorian Studies postgraduate degree course at London University's Birkbeck College, in 1994. There, I had the immense good fortune to be taught by three inspirational tutors: Dr David Feldman, of Birkbeck's History Department, Professor Michael Slater of the English Faculty, and Professor Clive Emsley – co-opted from the Open University to teach Birkbeck's Crime and Victorian Society course.

Ever the best of friends: Debbie Millett and Wanda Opalinska read an early draft of the book and gave me detailed feedback that was both wise and kind; they, along with Anne-Marie Collins, Prue Jeffreys, Liz Tames, Katie Matthews and Helen Woolston, cheered me up whenever my spirits or energy were flagging.

I am grateful to Phil Daoust and Caroline Roux, both of the *Guardian*, and to Dominic Lutyens, for giving me stimulating and enjoyable commissions which helped to keep my writing life from being exclusively devoted to early nineteenth-century slumlife.

The staff of the following libraries/archives were never less than friendly and knowledgeable: the British Library at St Pancras; the British Library's Newspaper Library at Colindale; the Public Record Office at Kew; the library of the Wellcome Institute for the History of Medicine; the Guildhall Library; the Corporation of London Records Office; the London Metropolitan Archives; the City of Westminster Archives Centre; the Hackney Archives; the Shropshire Records and Research Centre in Shrewsbury.

My thanks also to Malcolm Barr-Hamilton, David Rich and Chris Lloyd at the Tower Hamlets Local History Library and Archive; Mark Annand, author of the Greenwood's Map website (http://users.bathspa.ac.uk/greenwood/), hosted by Bath Spa University College; Jeff Gerhardt of the Haringey Museum and Archive Service; Hugh Petrie, Heritage Officer at Barnet Archives, and Bridgnorth local historian Robert Davies. Marion Rea at St Bartholomew's Hospital allowed me to riffle through that institution's archives, while Tina Craig of the Royal College of Surgeons of England's Library allowed me to consult items in the College's manuscript collection, and Chris Reed of the RSPCA supplied me with suggestions for further reading on the life of animal-cruelty campaigner Richard Martin. Duncan Broady of the Greater Manchester Police Museum helped me track the later life of Joseph Sadler Thomas, while Ray Seal and Steve Earle at the Metropolitan Police Museum, and Roger Appleby of the City Police Museum, allowed me access to documents and exhibits, which, sadly, remain inaccessible to the general public. John Ross, curator of Scotland Yard's Black Museum, allowed me to visit his gruesome archive in the hope that I would find Bishop and Williams on his shelves of nameless, dateless phrenological casts of criminals; they weren't there, but the visit was unforgettable nevertheless.

Thank you John Saddler, my wonderful agent, and Will Sulkin and Jörg Hensgen, my wonderful editors.

Last but foremost, Peter Neish has read – and proof-read – various early versions of this story and put up with hours of talk about long-dead strangers; our life together has been peopled by a cast of pretty unpleasant characters for longer than I care to remember. For this and for much more, many thanks.

Old Money

One guinea = 21 shillings = 252 pennies (*d*) = £1.05
One pound = 20 shillings = 240*d* = £1
One crown = 5 shillings = 60*d* = 25p
Half a crown = 2 shillings and 6*d* = 30*d* = 12½p
One florin/guilder = 2 shillings = 24*d* = 10p
One shilling (bob) = 12*d* = 5p
One farthing = ¼*d*

Some London prices/wages, early 1830s

Hackney cab fare, Old Bailey to Shoreditch Church (1½ miles): 2 shillings
Charles Dickens's weekly factory wage as a 12-year-old in 1824: 6–7 shillings
Weekly wage of an East End silk-weaver in 1831 (12-hour day): 5–10 shillings
Weekly wage of a skilled, 'master', tailor or carpenter: 30 shillings
Glass/pint of Blue Ruin gin: 3*d*/1 shilling
Glass/pint of cheap gin: 2*d*/10*d*
A quartern loaf of bread: 9*d*
A pint of porter: 2*d*
10lb potatoes: 4*d*
1lb cheese: 2*d*
Average cost of an Old Bailey prosecution: £3 10*s*
Average cost of a fresh corpse in 1831: 8–12 guineas

Preface

Towards the end of 1831, London's Metropolitan Police were alerted to a series of crimes that appeared to be imitations of the notorious Burke and Hare killings-for-dissection in Edinburgh three years earlier. I first came across the 'London Burkers', or the 'Italian Boy', case when I was writing a newspaper article about the Boundary Street estate in Bethnal Green, London's first council housing, which had been built on the site of one of the nineteenth century's most notorious slums. During my research I stumbled upon a claim that the surrounding district had been tainted for decades by the events that had occurred just north of what is now Arnold Circus, London E1. That area, Nova Scotia Gardens, had comprised a number (no one knows how many) of tiny, odd-looking cottages, probably (their origins are unknown) built as homes cum workshops for weavers, of whom there were around 15,000 in Bethnal Green/Spitalfields at the start of the nineteenth century. In the late autumn of 1831, Number 3 Nova Scotia Gardens had infamy thrust upon it by its residents, John Bishop and Thomas Williams, and an associate, James May – all of them body-snatchers, or 'resurrection men'.

The London Burkers have been eclipsed by their Edinburgh counter-parts, whose story has survived many retellings and film and stage inter-pretations; but in fact it was the London case, not Burke and Hare, that speeded up the passing of controversial legislation to make the unclaimed bodies of paupers legally available to surgeons for dissection. The Anatomy Act was passed by parliament within ten months of the investigation into the events at Nova Scotia Gardens, heralding the beginning of the end of bodysnatching in Britain. The case also revealed some extremely unpleasant aspects of life in London – a city that had increased in size by one-third between 1801 and 1831 to over one and a half million inhabitants: the largest and most diverse population to be found anywhere on earth.

The London Burkers/Italian Boy case occurred on one of recent history's fault-lines: the Regency was over – those years of roistering dandies and beaux; of newly gaslit streets and shopping arcades, and the heroics of the Napoleonic Wars; but also of political oppression and economic collapse; of sclerotic institutions unable to adapt to the new industrial era; high levels of petty crime and the remnants of the vicious Bloody Code that punished them; and a governing elite still reeling from the implications of the murderous overthrow of the *ancien régime* in France. The revolutionary year of 1789 felt like very recent history to many in Britain. Victoria was yet to ascend the throne, and her new age of moral certainty and love of order – the era when statistics, bureaucracy, a highly professionalised civil service and legal and medical elite came to dominate – was not in place. Not yet. Not quite. William IV ruled from 1830 to 1837 – a short reign, but a mighty turbulent one for all that. There is no mistaking the flavour, the dominant mood, of the late 1820s/early 1830s in the writings that have survived. Everywhere is heard an insistent, articulate call for change in every aspect of British life: parliament, the judiciary, the church, medicine, gaols, schooling, public and private manners and mores, architecture, street-planning – all were loudly condemned for being outmoded, inefficient, unworkable, 'old'. Britain was felt to be tottering to the point of collapse because of an inability to embrace and implement change.

In this Era Without a Name, the Reform Act of 1832 would see the middle classes begin to wrest power from the aristocracy and the church; yet the newly enfranchised tradesmen, industrialists and administrators were also seeking to separate themselves off from the poor. If the common man – labourer, artisan or pauper – had expected to benefit from the advance of democracy, he was to be badly disappointed. The 1832 Act gave the vote to just one-seventh of the adult male population; the Poor Law Amendment Act of 1834 would see those who sought parish relief incarcerated in institutions that were prisons in all but name, while the living conditions of 'the submerged tenth' (the phrase belongs to William Booth, founder of the Salvation Army, writing in 1890) were to remain a source of shame and disgrace to the richest nation on earth for the rest of the century.

As I followed the reports of the Italian Boy investigation in the newspapers of the day, I became curious about the type of people who had fallen into the path of the accused on their nightly prowls around the metropolis. What sort of city was London in 1831 – what sort of country was England? – that children and young adults could seemingly be picked off by anyone who chose to prey on their fellow man: desperate resurrectionists, brothel-keepers, Fagin-style gang-leaders, sex-offenders, press gangs? What sort of people could simply disappear unnoticed from the city's streets? Why, even in death, did their identities remain mysterious? How much of the history of the very-poor – the destitute – has come down to us? What sorts of evidence could be trusted to give a reliable picture of their lives? What did they think of themselves?

The Italian Boy case also seemed to provide a rich archival source to learn of how *non*-destitute, ordinary lower-class Londoners perceived themselves, and perceived those both poorer and wealthier than themselves, and to examine their notions of community and criminality in this strange new society that was forming in their city. The story appeared to me to be a window on the lives of the poor at a period of great change: a window that is badly damaged – opaque in places, blacked out or shattered in others – but offering a glimpse of those who have left little authentic trace of themselves.

Before the advent of oral history the poor were able to tell us little about themselves directly; the very-poor could tell us even less. Everything in their lives has fallen to pieces: the coarse paper of the broadsheets they read, the hovels they lived in; while the majority of their songs, stories and sayings have passed unrecorded. They are persons unknown – an enigma for the social historian; a deafening silence that roars down the centuries. Those working-class people of the 1820s and 1830s who were literate (around half of poor Londoners were) had, ordinarily, little access to writing materials and publishers/printers, still less time to write. Committing thoughts and feelings to paper – making oneself the object of investigation – is a strange act for anyone to undertake; if you have little time and money, it is a quite bizarre undertaking. And while a number of British working-class autobiographies have been discovered by historians, these were almost all written in later years by people who had been able to change their social status, or who had become part of an organised labour force, or a religious movement, with which their own personal identity had merged.

What we know of the lives of the very-poor in the first half of the nineteenth century is mediated to us by those outside their culture; we hear their stories filtered through people who, even with the most sympathetic of hearts and imaginative of minds – even William Cobbett; even Thomas De Quincey; even Henry Mayhew – were strangers travelling in a strange land. I have had to rely on such sources far more than I would have liked. The journalist, the polemicist, the magistrate, the prison official, the parliamentary enquirer, the charity official all allow us to see the very-poor over their shoulders; but they edit, paraphrase, pass comment on and even overtly criticise the object of their interest. Poverty, then as now, was often presented as a moral failing. Despite these reservations, I still believe the greatest commentator on the London very-poor remains Charles Dickens, who was able to draw on personal experience when he wrote *Oliver Twist* in 1837–8. As a twelve-year-old, left to fend for himself in central London, he had felt himself to be in danger of falling into destitution; he had observed the vagrant children of Covent Garden at first hand, and with his creation of Jo, the street-crossing sweeper in *Bleak House* (1852–3), he seems to have climbed inside the mind of one of the hordes of urban outcast infants. For these reasons, and for one other, explained in a lengthy footnote to Chapter 11, Dickens weaves in and out of the following pages.

Researching this book took me down many blind alleys as I tried to piece together the criminal careers of John Bishop, Thomas Williams, James May and other London bodysnatchers. Official records were not obliged to be kept of cases heard in magistrates' courts (which is where anyone arrested for possession of an illegally disinterred body would be examined), and JPs habitually failed to supply the higher courts with the required returns of those they had convicted – an oversight that was as infuriating to the Home Office of the day as it is to the modern historian. Bodysnatching cases were reported in the national newspapers, but coverage of such hearings is patchy; worse still, most snatchers had aliases – some of them had several – and it was not always clear who, exactly, was on trial. (To compound the problem for the researcher, the 1820s and 1830s registers of the London gaols where snatchers would be confined if convicted – primarily Coldbath Fields Prison and Clerkenwell New Prison – have for the most part failed to make it to the twenty-first century.) In an age when guilt was often established by eyewitness evidence, and sentences decided on the notion of good or bad repute, it was in the criminal's interest to keep his or her identity as fluid as possible. As one penal reform campaigner wrote in despair, in 1832: 'No man goes into Newgate twice with the same name, trade, or place of nativity.' So Bishop, Williams and May could well be lurking in the records under assumed names.

Five more things spoke out from the archive sources: the deference shown by many in the case towards the judiciary and other authority figures; the central role of drink in the lives of the protagonists; the increasing tendency in the city towards the identification of its citizens through badges, uniforms, registers, licences and permits; allied to this, the growing urge to tie things down, to lash people to their 'proper' place and put a stop to urban nomadism; and finally, the sense that, in these years before the laying of London's great drains, people were living within a giant cesspit – picking their way between faecal matter and pools of piss. Physically this was quite a different city to today's capital; many of the most famous structures and the broadest, most-travelled roads had yet to be constructed; populous, densely built areas were yet to be razed. To many in authority in 1831 it seemed that London's topography – its sinuous streets and unlit warrens – connived at criminality: there were calls for the lanes and alleys to be illuminated, straightened out or flattened altogether. Nova Scotia Gardens itself was such an obscure destination that its name never appeared on any map. The Italian Boy case reminded citydwellers, rich and poor, that at this town's heart lay unknown, unknowable mysteries.

ONE

Suspiciously Fresh

George Beaman, surgeon to the parish of St Paul's, Covent Garden, turned back the scalp of the corpse lying before him. Beneath the skin he found evidence of internal bleeding, and, peeling away the flesh along the length of the neck, he saw similar minor haemorrhages at the top of the spinal column. He concluded that death had been caused by a sharp blow to the back of the neck.

The body was that of a boy of around fourteen years of age, 4 feet 6 inches in height, with fair hair and grey eyes that were bloodshot and bulging. Blood oozed from an inch-long wound on his left temple, and his toothless gums were dripping blood. At the time of his killing, a meal – which had included potatoes and a quantity of rum – was being digested. A large, powerful hand had grasped the boy on his left forearm – black bruises from the finger marks were plainly visible – and earth or clay had been smeared across the torso and thighs. The chest appeared to have caved in slightly, as though someone had knelt upon it. The heart contained scarcely any blood, which Beaman took to indicate a very sudden death, but all the other organs were found to have been unremarkable and perfectly healthy. The most perplexing thing about the corpse was its freshness: it had been alive three days earlier, Beaman felt sure; and it was also clear to the surgeon that this body had never been buried, had never even been laid out in preparation for burial – and yet it had been delivered to King's College's anatomy department as a Subject for medical students to dissect.

It was late evening, Sunday 6 November 1831, and Beaman was anatomising the corpse in the tiny watch-house in the graveyard of St Paul's Church, Covent Garden, at the request of local magistrates. He and a number of fellow surgeons had been probing and exploring the body in the first-floor room since early afternoon. A sunny winter's day had turned into a chilly evening by the time the medical men had made up their minds about the cause of death. As Beaman and four colleagues left, two young trainees, by now feeling faint with tiredness and nausea, were left in the cold, stuffy room to sew up the corpse. Working alongside Beaman had been Herbert Mayo and Richard Partridge, respectively professor and demonstrator of anatomy at King's College, just a few streets away in the Strand. The day before, Partridge had sent for the police when one of the bodysnatching gangs that supplied disinterred corpses to medical schools had tipped this body out of a sack on to the stone floor of the dissecting-room at King's. It had looked suspiciously fresh. Partridge tricked the bodysnatchers into waiting at King's while police officers were summoned, and at three o'clock in the afternoon, John Bishop, James May, Thomas Williams and Michael Shields were arrested on suspicion of murder.

'We are proceeding in the dark,' complained a member of the coroner's jury at the inquest on the King's College body two days later. The hearing was under way at the Unicorn public house, Henrietta Street, Covent Garden, which backed on to St Paul's watch-house. It appeared to the jury that no one in authority was able to rebut or confirm the various rumours about the identity of the dead boy; speculation about who the child had been had even reached the national newspapers. But as soon as any goings-on at hospitals were mentioned, or any surgeon looked likely to be named, the coroner and the parish clerk of St Paul's would go into a huddle to discuss between them whether the inquest should proceed or be adjourned. How – the jury asked – can we be expected to arrive at a verdict when we don't even know who has died?

On Sunday the 6th, worried parents of missing sons had been admitted to the watch-house to view the body, having read a description of the boy circulated in police handbills and notices posted on walls, doors and windows throughout the parish. Among the visitors had been several Italians. Signor Francis Bernasconi of Great Russell Street, Covent Garden, 'plasterer to His Majesty', had wondered whether the deceased was a boy from Genoa who had made his living as an 'image boy' – hawking wax or plaster busts of the great and the good, past and present, about the streets of London. Bernasconi was a plaster figurine-maker, or *figurinaio*, and he employed a number of Italian child immigrants to advertise and sell his wares in this way. Another *figurinaio* said the dead boy had sometimes helped to paint the plaster figures, and that his 'master' had left England at the end of September. The minister at the Italian Chapel in Oxendon Street, off the Haymarket, claimed that the boy had been a member of his congregation, but was unable to name him. Two more Italians identified the dead boy as an Italian beggar who walked the streets carrying a tortoise, which he exhibited in the hope of receiving a few

VERY FINE VERY CHEAP

1. An Italian Boy, or Image Boy, from J.T. Smith's *Etchings of Remarkable Beggars*, 1815.

pennies; while Joseph and Mary Paragalli of Parker Street, Covent Garden, said the boy was an Italian who wandered the West End exhibiting white mice in a cage suspended around his neck. (Joseph was a street musician, playing barrel organ and pan-pipes.) The Paragallis had known the child for about a year, they said, but neither of them suggested a name for him. Mary Paragalli claimed she had last seen him alive shortly after noon on Tuesday 1 November in Oxford Street, near Hanover Square.

Charles Starbuck, a stockbroker, had come forward to tell the Bow Street police officers that he believed the boy to be an Italian beggar who was often to be seen near the Bank of England exhibiting white mice in a cage; Starbuck had viewed the body and was in 'no doubt' about it being the same child. He had seen the boy looking tired and ill, sitting with his head sunk almost to his lap, on the evening of Thursday 3 November between half-past six and eight o'clock. Starbuck was walking with his brother near the Bank and said, 'I think he is unwell,' but his brother replied, 'I think he's a humbug. I've often seen him in that position.' A crowd gathered round, concerned at the boy's condition, and one youth told the boy he ought to move along as police officers were heading that way. The Starbucks walked on. On Wednesday the 9th, however, Charles Starbuck wrote to the coroner to say that he had subsequently seen this boy near the Bank, and retracted his identification.

The newspapers seized on the possible Italian connection remarkably swiftly, with *The Times* reporting the first day of the coroner's hearing as 'The Inquest on the Italian Boy', when no such identity had been confirmed. In fact, *The Times* reporter seems to have been quite carried away with emotion by the death of 'the poor little fellow who used to go about the streets hugging a live tortoise, and soliciting, with a smiling countenance, in broken English and Italian, a few coppers for the use of himself and his dumb friend.' The report continued:

We saw the body last night, and were struck with its fine healthy appearance. . . . The countenance of the boy does not exhibit the least contortion, but, on the contrary, wears the repose of sleep, and the same open and good-humoured expression which marked the features in life is still discernible.[1]

This was a fantastical statement, since only someone able to make a positive identification could possibly know how the child had looked when alive. The following day, the Thunderer thundered thus, in an extraordinary editorial:

If it shall be proved that he was murdered, for the purpose of deriving a horrible livelihood from the disposal of his body – if wretches have picked up from our streets an unprotected foreign child, and prepared him for the dissecting knife by assassination – if they have prowled about in order to obtain Subjects for a dissecting-room – then we may be assured that this is not a solitary crime of its kind.

In such a way, rumour was being reported as fact – a matter that was not lost on the coroner's jury. Their exasperation compelled vestry clerk James Corder, who was overseeing proceedings, to state that he understood 'from inquiries he had made' that the dead boy was called Giacomo Montero, a beggar who had been brought to London a year earlier by an Italian named Pietro Massa, who lived in Liquorpond Street, in the area of Holborn known colloquially as Little Italy.[2] But here, Joseph Paragalli spoke up to say that he had made his own inquiries at the Home Office's 'Alien Office', near Whitehall, and that the description held there of Montero did not fit the dead boy in the least. Perhaps then, said Corder, the boy had been Giovanni Balavezzolo, another Italian vagrant boy who was said to be missing from his usual haunts. Corder told the jury they ought simply to return a verdict of wilful murder against some person or persons unknown. The jury remained unimpressed.

It was at this awkward point for Corder that the prisoners were summoned from their underground cells in the Covent Garden watchhouse to give their account of how they had come to be in possession of the boy's body. They entered the crowded room at the Unicorn to be viewed by a fascinated public; the memory of the crimes committed by William Burke and William Hare in Edinburgh just three years earlier was fresh. Had similar events been occurring in the English capital? And what would these monsters look like? Very ordinary indeed; your common or

2. *The Watch House, Covent Garden*, circa 1830, unsigned oil painting. St Paul's Church is to the right, the Unicorn tavern to the left, an 'image boy' just right of the arch.

garden Londoner. John Bishop was thirty-three, stocky, slightly sullen-looking but with a mild enough expression; he had a long, slender, pointed nose, high cheekbones, large, slightly protruding grey-green eyes and thick, dark hair that continued down into bushy, mutton-chop sideburns which covered a good deal of his cheeks. James May, thirty, was tall and good-looking, with a mop of unruly fair hair and dark, glittering eyes; he looked pleasant enough – like Bishop, he was still wearing the yokel smock frock in which he had been arrested, which perhaps made him seem even more

BISHOP   WILLIAMS.   MAY.

THE MURDERERS OF THE ITALIAN BOY.

London - Published by Kelly, Chancery Square.

3.–5. John Bishop, James May and Thomas Williams as they appeared to two court sketch artists; and the *Sunday Times* court portrait of John Bishop. While Bishop's appearance changes comparatively little from sketch to sketch, depictions of May and Williams vary dramatically, and in fact the sketch at the top of the page has mislabelled May and Williams in its caption.

6. Field Lane, one of the districts of London where second-hand
clothing was bought and sold.

guileless; his left hand was bandaged. Thomas Williams, in his late twenties,
was shorter than the other two, with deep-set hazel eyes and narrow lips
that gave him a slightly cunning appearance, but mischievous rather than
malevolent; his hair was mousey, his face pale, and he could have passed
for someone much younger. Michael Shields just looked like a frightened
old man.

The accounts of Bishop, May and Williams of the events of Friday
4 November and Saturday 5 November, given at the coroner's inquest
and at hearings yet to come, differed remarkably little from those offered
by the various eyewitnesses also called to testify. There were a few

7. Holborn Bridge over the Fleet River/Fleet Ditch; the houses to the right are in Field Lane.

discrepancies, but these would appear small and insignificant. The following train of events, at least, was not in dispute.

John Bishop and Thomas Williams awoke in Number 3 Nova Scotia Gardens, the cottage they shared in Bethnal Green, at about ten o'clock on Friday morning, breakfasted with their wives and the Bishops' three children and set off for the Fortune of War pub in Giltspur Street, Smithfield – opposite St Bartholomew's Hospital, and the regular meeting place, north of the river, for London's resurrection men. Here, they began their day's drinking and met up with James May. May had known Bishop for four or five years, and was introduced to Williams, whom May knew only by sight, having seen him in the various pubs around the Old Bailey and Smithfield. The three men drank rum together and ate some lunch. May admired a smock frock that Bishop was wearing, and asked him where he could buy a similar one. Bishop took May a few streets to the west, to Field Lane, one of the districts given over to London's second-hand clothes trade. Field Lane was also known colloquially as Food & Raiment Alley, Thieving Lane and Sheeps' Head Alley, and Charles Dickens was to add to its notoriety six years later by siting one of Fagin's dens here, in *Oliver Twist*. A steep, narrow, undrained way, Field Lane comprised Jacobean, Stuart and early-Georgian tenements that were largely forbidding, rotting hovels; those on its east side backed on to the Fleet River – often called the Fleet Ditch, since it was by 1831 almost motionless with solidifying filth, though when it flooded its level could rise by six or seven feet, deluging the surrounding area with its detritus. By weird contrast, the windows in Field Lane were a dazzling display of brightly coloured silk handkerchiefs ('wipes'); if the commentators of the day are to be believed, the vast majority of these were stolen, by gangs of young – often extremely young – 'snotter-haulers', who would soon be incarnated in the popular imagination as the Artful Dodger (though Dickens used the more polite slang term, 'fogle-hunters'). Here, in Field Lane, James May bought a smock frock from a clothes-dealer, then decided he wanted a pair of trousers too, and turned the corner into West Street, where he attempted to bargain with the female owner of another cast-offs shop.[3] Already pretty drunk, May was unable to agree a price with the woman, but, feeling guilty at having wasted her time, insisted on buying her some rum, which the three enjoyed together in the shop. May and Bishop then went back to the Fortune of War to have more drink with Williams, before Bishop and Williams set off for the West End, to try to sell the corpse of an adolescent boy lying trussed up in a trunk in the wash-house of 3 Nova Scotia Gardens.

Their first call was made at Edward Tuson's private medical school in Little Windmill Street, off Tottenham Court Road, where Tuson told Bishop that he had waited so long for Bishop to come up with a 'Thing' that he had bought one from another resurrection gang the day before. So they walked a few streets south to Joseph Carpue's school at 72 Dean Street, Soho. Carpue spoke to the pair in his lecture theatre with several

8. Edward Tuson's anatomy school in Little Windmill Street, near the Middlesex Hospital.

students present who all wanted to know how fresh the Thing was. Carpue offered to pay eight guineas and Bishop agreed to this price, promising to deliver the boy the next morning at ten o'clock.

Bishop and Williams got back to the Fortune of War at a quarter to four, and shared some more drink there with May. Bishop now began to wonder whether he could get more than the eight guineas Carpue had offered – the boy was extremely fresh, after all. Bishop called May out on to the street to ask him – away from the ears of other resurrectionists –, what sort of money he was achieving for Things. May told Bishop that he had sold two corpses at Guy's Hospital for ten guineas each just the day before, and that he would never accept a fee as low as eight guineas for a young, healthy male. Bishop told May that if he were able to help sell the body for a higher price, May could keep anything they earned over nine guineas. They went back into the Fortune of War for a drink to seal the bargain, and then, leaving Williams drinking, set off to procure a coach and driver in order to collect the body.

This was not easy. At around a quarter past five, as dusk was falling, they approached hackney-coach driver Henry Mann in New Bridge Street – the approach road to Blackfriars Bridge – but Mann refused to take them, because, as he later said, 'I knew what May was'; he hadn't spotted Bishop, who was standing behind his cab in the increasing gloom.

James Seagrave had just given his horse a nosebag of corn and was taking tea in the King of Denmark – a pub cum cab-men's watering house in Old Bailey, 200 yards south of the Fortune of War – when Bishop and May asked Thomas Tavernor, who helped out at the nearby cab-stand, to call Seagrave out to the street. (Tavernor later claimed that it had been so dark in the street, he could not clearly make out the features of the men addressing him.) Seagrave came out, and May, leaning against the wheel of a nearby cart while Bishop hovered near Seagrave's cab, asked if he would be willing to do a job for them. Seagrave, suspicious, replied that there were a great many jobs, long ones and short ones – what kind did they mean? May said it was to be 'a long job' carrying 'a stiff 'un' from Holloway (Seagrave misheard; May actually said 'Holywell', a district of Shoreditch, near Bethnal Green), for which trip they would 'stand' one guinea. The driver was intrigued and allowed May to buy him tea in the King of Denmark to discuss the journey – but also to find out more about the resurrection world. Seagrave had no intention of letting them hire him, intending to 'do them', as he later told the coroner's court.

The King of Denmark combined the operations of inn, tea-house for cab- and coach-drivers and booking office for errand carts. (It was also the best spot in London for watching public hangings, since it stood immediately opposite Newgate's Debtors Door, where the scaffold was erected on execution days.) Inside, closely observed by a barman, May, Bishop and Seagrave sat down to talk. During their discussion, May poured gin into Bishop's tea from a pint bottle and Bishop protested, laughing, 'Do you mean to hocus, or burke me?' Seagrave did not know what this meant.[4] A man sitting close by nudged Seagrave and muttered to him that Bishop and May were well-known snatchers. His curiosity about them satisfied, Seagrave went out into the street while Bishop and May's attention was distracted and drove off. 'It won't do,' he muttered to Tavernor on his way out. 'They want me to carry a stiff 'un.' As he pulled away, he looked back and spotted Bishop and May walking up and down the Old Bailey cab-rank, trying to hire a driver. No one would take them.

They had better luck in nearby Farringdon Street, where they found someone willing to drive them to Bethnal Green and then south of the river to the Borough for ten shillings – more than double the going rate for such a journey. But there was yet more drinking to fit in first, and Bishop and May took the driver to the George pub in Old Bailey (where Williams had arranged to meet them) and then on to the Fortune of War for another round, before the trip to Nova Scotia Gardens.

They arrived at the Gardens at around half-past six, observed by several neighbours: the doors of their hired vehicle were bright yellow, and it was a 'chariot' – a rather more salubrious version of the hackney coach. Bishop and May jumped out and went up the path that led to Number 3, leaving Williams standing up on one of the chariot's front wheels, chatting to the driver; the chariot door was left wide open. They were watched by George Gissing, the twelve-year-old son of the owner of the Birdcage pub, which stood opposite the Gardens (and still does). Gissing, from the doorway of the Birdcage, had a good view of the men. He recognised both Bishop and Williams, though not May; he saw that Bishop and May were in smock frocks and that May was smoking a pipe. Another youth, Thomas Trader, observed the three men too, recognising Bishop and Williams, as did a local girl, Ann Cannell (though, unlike Gissing and Trader, Cannell later claimed not to know who Bishop and Williams were). Cannell's mother

9. The King of Denmark pub in Old Bailey, opposite Newgate's Debtors Door.

passed by and started to watch as well, saying to Trader, 'This looks strange. See where they are going so quick.' But Trader replied, 'I'm sure I won't go after them. If I did, they wouldn't mind giving me a topper.'⁵ But the boy did try to note the licence number of the chariot, though this was obscured by its open door and he gave up when he saw the driver staring at him. After ten minutes or so, Williams went down the path to the cottage, and shortly afterwards returned with Bishop and May. May was carrying a sack and Bishop was helping to hold it up. They placed it in the chariot, all three men got in and drove off westwards in the direction of Shoreditch High Street.

At seven o'clock the chariot arrived at the main gate at Guy's Hospital, over the river in the Borough, where Bishop and May were allowed in

by the porter of the gate, John Chapman, Williams staying outside in the chariot. Chapman noticed that the sack – carried by Bishop – appeared to contain something heavy; he knew the two men by sight but later claimed that he had not known their names. ('Now John, are you certain it was I who carried the sack?' Bishop called out when Chapman gave his evidence to the magistrates. 'Yes, I am,' said the porter. At which May said, 'Why, it was I who carried the sack, not Bishop! It is a matter of no moment, but it only shows how careful men ought to be when they are on their oaths.') Chapman showed Bishop and May through to James Davis, the porter of the medical school's dissecting-room. Davis noted that a human foot was protruding from the sack and concluded from its size that the corpse of a woman or boy was inside; but Davis was in no need of a Subject since he had bought two corpses from May just the day before. Bishop asked if he could leave the Thing there until the next morning and Davis agreed, locking it in a small chamber off the dissecting-room. Bishop took Davis's assistant, James Weeks, aside to tell him not to allow the body to be taken away from Guy's unless Bishop was present; May overheard this, and took Davis aside to say that the Thing belonged to Bishop but that it should not be handed over without May being present, otherwise May would end up out of pocket. May had bought all the drinks that day, including James Seagrave's in the King of Denmark, and he had also agreed to pay the cab fares.

Before discharging their driver, May and Bishop dashed to Richard Grainger's private anatomical school in nearby Webb Street and tried to make a sale of the Thing – telling the porter there that it was 'a rare fresh Subject' – but without success. Then they rejoined Williams, May paid the driver his ten shillings and the three went to a nearby pub before hiring another coach to the Fortune of War for more drink – May insisting on treating this coachman to a drink too.

Thomas Wigley, a porter at the Cross Keys Inn in Wood Street, Cheapside, was a regular drinker at the Fortune of War. He watched as Bishop entered the pub at about half-past seven, followed a short while later by May. Wigley had been at the pub since about half-past six, sitting in a corner of the tap-room drinking beer. He knew both Bishop and May by sight, but not to speak to. Bishop came and sat down next to Wigley, and May sat opposite Bishop – both with a glass of 'rum hot'.[6] Wigley heard Bishop say to May, 'What do you think of our new one? Didn't he go up to him well? I told you he was a stanch one – don't you think he's a stanch one now? Do you stick by me and I will stick to you. I know the other one is all right, he's nothing but a good one.'[7] (Stanch/staunch meant

trustworthy, loyal. It had a secondary meaning: close, private, tight-lipped, and it could be that Bishop was indicating Williams's ability to be discreet – essential for successful bodysnatching.)

About an hour later, Williams came into the pub, proclaiming that he had just 'had a ride'. As he entered, Bishop said to May, 'There he is. I knew he would come. I knew he was a game one,' to which May replied, 'I don't know what you mean.' Bishop said, 'That's all right then.'[8] Bishop, who appeared to Wigley to be more drunk than either May or Williams, then said, 'You know what I mean,' and May replied, 'I am going home.' Bishop said, 'We are all going the same road,' to which May said, 'I shall stop a bit,' and picked up a newspaper and began to read as Bishop and Williams left the room. It's likely that Bishop and Williams did not leave the Fortune of War at this point, but simply left the tap-room of the pub, which appears to have been a separate area, since May did share part of the journey home with Bishop and Williams.

(Wigley would later explain that he had not understood the conversation he had overheard. Bishop's face reddened when Wigley had repeated before a magistrate Bishop's praise of Williams, and Williams laughed heartily on hearing it. Wigley, however, had been close to tears as he gave his account of the evening at the Fortune of War; he had been named as an important witness by the publican, a Mr Farrow, and had not come forward of his own volition.

Wigley was asked by the magistrate, 'Did you know what they were?', and Wigley said yes.

'And you drank with them?'

'I did, sir, but it was through fear. I knew their calling and I was uneasy whenever I was with them, and dreaded their vengeance if I should affront them and meet them elsewhere.' Wigley claimed that he had seen resurrection men in the Fortune of War 'knock a man down with a pot'.

Wigley lived next door to the Fortune of War and, as a porter, may even have been one of the carriers for the bodysnatchers who met there; it may have been this fact, and a sense of shame about it, that kept Wigley on the point of tears in the magistrates' court. Or perhaps it was pure terror. He appeared to collapse as he came to the end of his evidence and was helped down from the stand. As he passed James May, he sighed deeply as he looked up into May's face.)

Later in the evening, shortly before nine o'clock, May went up to the bar of the Fortune of War, poured some water over something he was holding in a handkerchief and began rubbing it. Henry Lock, the barman, took a look and saw that May was clearing blood and flesh from a set of human teeth. Lock remarked to May that they looked like the teeth of a young person, and would no doubt be worth something, and May boasted that he expected to get two pounds for the set.

(Lock was asked by the magistrate how May had been dressed that night, and the barman replied that he hadn't noticed. May called out to him: 'Then how can you tell the hour when you first saw me in the Fortune of War?' Lock had claimed that on the Friday morning, May, Bishop and Williams had all entered the pub together, which all three men denied. Lock replied, 'Although I cannot speak to your dress, I am certain as to the hour.' Then he recalled that when May showed him the teeth, May had been wearing a smock frock.)

Bishop, May and Williams left the Fortune of War together, some time after nine, stopping off for another drink in Golden Lane – a few streets to the east – May treating this coachman to a drink too. Further east, in Old Street, at 'the Star Corner' (a pub of that name stood at the south-east corner of the junction with City Road), May got out of the coach and said he was going home – home was south of the river – handing over a loan of three shillings to Bishop and three to Williams. The three men agreed to meet up the next morning at Guy's Hospital. Bishop and Williams took the coach on to the corner of Union Street and Kingsland Road in Bethnal Green, paid the driver and walked the rest of the way home – not a great distance, but it is possible Bishop and Williams did not want their address to be known to the coachman, who may well have deduced how they made their living. There's another, more mundane, explanation: they may have been attempting to save a few pennies; while the fare from Old Bailey to Kingsland Road was two shillings, to proceed any further east would have pushed it up to three.

James May, meanwhile, was meeting up with one of several sweethearts, Mary Ann Hall, joining her outside the Alfred's Head pub – a large inn that faced the Elephant and Castle – at around half-past eleven, before going back to the lodgings they shared nearby.

At around nine o'clock the next morning, James May entered the premises of dentist Thomas Mills in Bridge House Place, on the north side of Newington Causeway, not far from May's rooming-house. He showed Mills a set of twelve teeth that still had portions of gum attached; a small piece of jawbone clung to the lower set. Mills pointed out that one of the front teeth had a chip in it and did not look as though it belonged to the others, but May swore that all the teeth had been taken from the same mouth, and that, furthermore, the body had never been buried. Mills thought they looked like a woman's teeth but May replied, 'The fact is, they belonged to a lad about fourteen or fifteen years of age. Upon my soul to God,

10. The river frontage of King's College/Somerset House.

they all belonged to one head not long since.' May said he was looking to receive a guinea, but Mills – though he considered them a fine and fresh set – would pay only twelve shillings.

('May seemed to be in no hurry,' Mills told the magistrate. 'We were some time cheapening.')

At around the same hour, Bishop and Williams were at the Fortune of War, hiring Michael Shields, over pints of beer, to carry a heavy load between various hospitals for a fee of half a crown. Shields had known Bishop for eight or nine months; he did not know Williams. Bishop asked Shields to go and get hold of a hamper, but Shields refused, so Bishop went across the street himself to take a hamper from just inside the gates of St Bartholomew's Hospital. This was not an act of theft; one of several matters that were to embarrass the medical profession during these hearings was the fact that hospital staff would 'leave' hampers lying around their precincts where resurrection men could easily pick them up in order to deliver their produce.

Bishop, Williams and Shields set off for Guy's Hospital – crossing the second, brand-new London Bridge – where they met May, as arranged. Williams and Shields went to a pub while Bishop and May again unsuccessfully tried to persuade the dissecting-room porters at Guy's and Grainger's school in Webb Street to buy the boy. Bishop and May joined Williams and Shields for more drink (May having stopped a passer-by and asked, politely, for money for drink, whereupon the stranger handed him 6*d* from his purse); then the pair set off to try to strike a bargain at King's College, crossing the Thames by ferry to the imposing new building at the eastern end of Somerset House in the Strand – so new, a bricklayer was still at work as they rang the bell of dissecting-room porter William Hill, shortly before noon. They asked Hill whether King's professors and students needed a body. Hill replied, 'Not particularly,' but asked, 'What have you got?' and, on hearing the reply, went to fetch anatomist Richard Partridge to double-check on the medical school's supply. Hill told Bishop and May that there was a good fire blazing in the grate downstairs, why didn't they come down and warm themselves? Partridge entered the room where Bishop and May were warming up, and told them he didn't need a Thing; but Partridge took Hill aside and told him to offer them nine guineas for the body. When Hill did so, May, visibly drunk, shouted at Hill, 'I'll be damned if it should go under ten guineas!' Bishop murmured to Hill, when May stepped outside to urinate, that he would be able to persuade May to accept nine guineas. 'He is tipsy,' explained Bishop. 'I'll bring it in for nine.' Then Bishop and May left by cab for the pub near London Bridge where Williams and Shields were still drinking, and the four men had lunches of steaks and beer.

There seems to have been a desperation about Bishop's attempts to sell the corpse – this relentless traipsing from school to school as the produce became less and less desirable. He was about to earn only one more guinea than Joseph Carpue had offered the day before, and from that additional guinea, deductions for fares and drink would have left him worse off than if he had delivered to Carpue as arranged. Back at Guy's once more, the four men packed the sacked-up body into the hamper and placed this on the porter's knot on Shields's head. Bishop warned Shields to be careful not to stumble and fall; like the others, Shields had been drinking since nine o'clock in the morning. Williams and Shields walked together, Bishop and May following slightly behind, sometimes slightly ahead, in a cab. They reached King's at around a quarter past two, Shields carried the hamper into an ante-room to the anatomy theatre and May clumsily tipped the body out of the sack and on to the floor. Shields and Williams loitered outside in the courtyard, and Bishop and May told Hill that he should make out to Williams that just eight guineas was being paid for the body – that Bishop and May would split the remaining guinea between them, giving Hill half a crown as reward for his part in the deceit.

('Is it customary for persons in your station to receive such presents?' Hill was asked by the magistrate.

'Yes, sir, sometimes,' he replied.

'He gets many a guinea in that way!' Bishop called out.)

Hill noted that the body appeared to be that of a boy between fourteen and sixteen years of age, and unusually fresh; its left arm was awkwardly twisted above its head and the left hand was clenched. Bishop and May told Hill this body was 'a good 'un', and Hill agreed that it was. He asked what the child had died of, and May replied, 'I neither know nor care,' and said it was no business of either May's or Hill's.[9] Bishop said, 'It is quite indifferent what he died of, for here he is, stiff enough.' Pointing out a cut on the boy's forehead, Hill was told by Bishop that the wound had just occurred as the body was tipped from the sack. Hill did not believe this.

(Bishop and May both laughed when Hill told the coroner of his worries about the body's freshness, and Bishop interjected, 'The fact is, you are not in the habit of seeing fresh Subjects and you don't know anything about it!')

The body didn't look to Hill as though it had ever been buried, despite the marks of clay on its thighs and torso, which would indicate resurrection.

('You know nothing about raising bodies! Is there not a difference in the soil? Besides, clay could have got into the coffin.' John Bishop was a man who knew his soils.

Bishop and May were warned that they were not helping their case by jeering and laughing, and Bishop muttered, 'I can do myself no harm, at all events.')

Some of Partridge's pupils came down to the dissecting-room to take a look at the body, having read a notice about a London youth of around fourteen who had recently gone missing from his home in Oxford Street.

Hill revealed his suspicions about the state of the body to Richard Partridge, who came to the dissecting-room to inspect it. Hill and Partridge noted that blood had dripped on to the boy's chest.

(May called out, before the magistrate: 'Didn't the blood come from the mouth – wasn't it caused by the teeth having been removed?'

Hill: 'It certainly might be so.'

May: 'Oh it might, might it!')

Partridge told the resurrectionists that as he had only a £50 note, they should wait at King's while he went to get this changed into smaller tender with which to pay them. Bishop said he would take what change Partridge had and collect the rest on Monday; May said he would take the £50 note and get it changed himself, at which Partridge smiled strangely and said, 'Oh no,' and left the room. Twenty minutes later he returned with Police Superintendent Joseph Sadler Thomas and several officers from Division F, Covent Garden's branch of the Metropolitan Police, and the four men were taken into custody, May putting up a violent struggle in Catherine Street, Drury Lane, when one of the constables refused to allow him to speak to Bishop. It took a number of officers to restrain May, and he entered the station-house on all fours, with his smock frock over his head.

Superintendent Thomas told May that he was being charged on suspicion of 'improper' possession of a Subject. May replied, 'The Subject is the property of that gentleman,' pointing at Bishop. 'I only came with him to get the money.' Turning to Bishop, Superintendent Thomas asked how he had come by the body, and Bishop replied that he was simply

11.–12. Porters loading vegetables (*left*) as Covent Garden's new market building (*above*) approaches completion, in 1829, sketched by artist George Scharf.

moving it from Guy's to King's. When asked whose body it was, Bishop replied, 'It's mine.' Asked what his trade was, Bishop told Thomas, 'I'm a bloody bodysnatcher.'

Only Michael Shields's testimony was at odds with this narrative, with regard to his role in the story, but he crumbled easily each time he was pressed on various points. He told the coroner's court, 'I can't say that I never worked for a resurrectionist before. . . . If I was to speak my last words, I did not know what the hamper contained. . . . I don't know how Bishop got his livelihood. I don't know as he dealt in dead bodies before this.' Shields even claimed to be unaware that the Fortune of War was a house of call for resurrectionists. In fact, Shields had carried bodies for Bishop on at least one other occasion, and was highly involved in the resurrection trade. After being dismissed from his position as watchman-caretaker at Moorfields Roman Catholic chapel for stealing silverware, Shields worked partly as a porter at Covent Garden market, partly as a gravedigger at St Giles-in-the-Fields' churchyard and partly as a sack- or hamper-carrier for resurrectionists.[10] He knew very well what sort of pub the Fortune of War was.

He told the coroner's court that he had accidentally met Bishop in Covent Garden on the Saturday morning. Shields denied being in the Fortune of War that day and was warned by vestry clerk James Corder, 'Take care – the pot-boy is present. Don't you recollect having any egg-hot at the Fortune of War that morning?' (presumably picking up on a detail given by the helpful barman Henry Lock), and immediately Shields admitted that the meeting in Covent Garden on the Saturday was a lie – at which a murmur of astonishment passed around the upstairs room at the Unicorn pub.

Shields claimed that when they reached King's College, he had stood outside while Bishop, May and Williams took the hamper into the dissecting-room; but Hill had already told the coroner's court of how he had greeted Shields as an acquaintance, even mentioning that it had been a while since the two men had met. (Hill knew Bishop and May well too; they had, acting separately, been among his most prolific suppliers in one of Hill's earlier jobs, at George Dermott's private anatomy school in the West End.)

When asked if he knew anything about the death of the boy, Shields replied, 'Bishop said that the body was got from the ground, and that he knew where it was got from. He smiled as he said so, saying that if he were brought before the jury, he would give them ease about it.'

After Shields stepped down, Bishop was brought forward and, with James Corder scribbling down every word, said:

'I cannot account for the death of the deceased. I dug the body out of the grave. The reason why I decline to say the grave I took it out of is that there were two watchmen in the ground, and they intrusted me, and being men of family, I don't want to deceive them. I don't think I can say any more. I took it for sale to Guy's Hospital, and as they did not want it, I left it there all night and part of the next day. And then I removed it to the King's College. That is all I can say about it. I mean to say that this is the truth. I shall certainly keep it a secret where I got the body. I know nothing as to how it died.'

The coroner was not impressed by Bishop's explanation, and warned him that a higher court was likely to interrogate him far more closely. The coroner said it was impossible for someone to be in possession of a body that was almost warm without knowing how it had died. Facetious in the face of pomposity, Bishop replied that it was impossible for it to have been warm – it had passed a night at Guy's Hospital. Bishop offered to sign his statement, though in law, he was not obliged to sign; by withholding his signature, he would have been able to make subtle alterations to his version of events, to counteract any new information that might come to light during the investigation. But he chose to sign; it looked more honest.

Next, May in his smock frock confidently explained that he wished to tell the court everything he knew – that he would speak only the truth.

'I live at 4 Dorset Street, Newington. I went into the country last Sunday week and returned on the following Wednesday evening. I brought home a couple of Subjects with me. I took them to Mr Grainger's in Webb Street the same evening, and on the following morning, which was Thursday, I removed them to Mr Davis at Guy's and after receiving the money, went away. I went to the Fortune of War in Smithfield and I stayed there, I dare say, for two or three hours. Between four and five o'clock, to the best of my recollection, I went to Nag's Head Court, Golden Lane, and there I stopped with a female till eleven or twelve the next day, Friday. From Golden Lane I went to the Fortune of War again, and there I stopped drinking till six o'clock, or half past. Williams and Bishop both came in there. They asked me if I would stand any thing to drink, which I did. Bishop then called me out and asked me where I could get the best price for Things. I told him where I had sold two at Guy's and he told me he had got a good Subject, and he had been offered eight guineas for it. I told him I could get more for it. He said all I could get over nine guineas I might have for myself, and I agreed to it. We went from there to the Old Bailey and we had some tea at the watering house in the Old Bailey, leaving Williams at the Fortune of War. After we had tea we called a chariot off the stand and drove to Bishop's house. When we came there, Bishop showed me the lad in a box or trunk. I then put it into a sack and took it to the chariot myself, and took it from thence to Mr Davis at Guy's. Mr Davis said, "You know, James, I cannot take it, because I took two off you yesterday, and I have not got names enough down for one, or else I would." I asked him if I might leave it there that night and he said, "Certainly." Bishop then desired Mr Davis not to let any person have it but himself, for it was his own Subject, which Mr Davis said he would not, and told his man James not to let any person have it besides himself. I told Mr Davis not to let it go until I came as well, for I should be money out of pocket if it went before I came. I went home that evening, where I slept, and in the morning I went to Mr Davis and had not been there many minutes before Bishop came in, and Shields with a hamper, and took it from thence to King's College, and there I was taken into custody.'

May was happy to sign his statement. There was no mention here of the clothes-buying and rum-drinking in Field Lane/West Street. But he did own up to the selling of the teeth:

'I admit all that, and what does it amount to? I did use the brad awl to extract the teeth from the boy, and that was in the regular way of business, and in doing so, I wounded my hand slightly – there is nothing very wonderful in that.'

For his part, Thomas Williams claimed that he had only gone along to King's to see what the new building was like – perhaps not such an unreasonable claim: the Robert Smirke-designed college was considered a glorious new addition to the capital.

'I live at Number 3 Nova Scotia Gardens and am a glass-blower. In the first place, I met with Bishop last Saturday morning in Long Lane, Smithfield. I asked him where he was going. He said he was going to King's College. We then went to the Fortune of War public house. Instead of going to King's College, we went to Guy's Hospital and he came out of there and went to the King's College. Then May and the porter met us against the gate, then Bishop went in, and I asked him to let me go in with him. A porter took a basket from the Fortune of War to Guy's Hospital, and I helped him part of the way with it. That is all I have got to say.'

Williams declined to sign.

Richard Partridge and George Beaman explained to the coroner and his jury their findings at the post-mortem. Although they disagreed on the detail, both men found that death had been caused by a blow to the back of the neck, probably with a stick or some other implement. The wound on the forehead was superficial, they agreed.

At half-past ten on the evening of Thursday 10 November, the foreman of the coroner's jury returned the verdict: 'We find a verdict of wilful murder against some person or persons unknown, and the jury beg to add to the above verdict that the evidence produced before them has excited very strong suspicion in their minds against the prisoners Bishop and Williams, and that they trust that a strict inquiry will be made into the case by the police magistrates.'

A juror stood up to praise Superintendent Thomas; the jury foreman added his praise for the policeman and also praised vestry clerk James Corder; the coroner praised Corder, and Corder thanked the jury and praised the coroner.

The apparent similarities to the Burke and Hare case, and the deep embarrassment that had caused the medical and legal professions, had prompted Home Secretary Viscount Melbourne to request James Corder to forward the verdict and a report of the coroner's hearing to him as quickly as possible. This Corder did, at eleven o'clock at night in a hand-delivered letter, apologising for disturbing his lordship at such a late hour, but saying that his urgency was due to the fact that 'the enquiry into the present case has been the means of eliciting the fact that several boys of a similar age to the deceased have recently been missed by their friends, and there is too much ground for justifying the conclusion that they have, with him, been the victims of a horrid system carried on for some time past by wretches whose business it is to supply the hospitals.'[11] Outside Corder's office, in the dark and the freezing fog of November, beneath the stalls and in among the fruit and vegetable baskets of Covent Garden's market building, around one hundred destitute boys and girls were bedding down for the night.

TWO

Persons Unknown

John Bishop had been a resurrection man for twelve years; James May had started to disturb the dead in 1825, acquiring the nickname Jack Stirabout (slang for 'prison', after the maize and oatmeal staple gaol diet, much as we call it 'porridge') and a string of convictions for grave-robbery; Thomas Williams was new to the trade, having recently emerged from a prison sentence for theft; Michael Shields was a familiar face around the graveyards of central London. Resurrection was a revolting but potentially highly lucrative trade, with earnings way beyond those of even the most highly skilled worker. In 1831, a silk weaver in the East End of London could earn as little as five shillings a week working a twelve-hour day, six days a week;[1] a well-paid manservant to a wealthy London household could expect to earn a guinea a week (there were 21 shillings to a guinea; and 20 shillings to a pound), which was also the starting wage for the first constables recruited to the Metropolitan ('New') Police force in 1829. (The predecessors of the New Police, the old parish watchmen, earned 16s 5d a week for a winter night shift lasting from seven in the evening to seven in the morning.) By contrast, a disinterred body could bring in between eight and twenty guineas, depending on its freshness and on how many Things were being hawked around London's hospital medical schools and seventeen private anatomy schools in any given week.[2] It was a speculative trade, and John Bishop himself missed out on more than one occasion by failing to procure promptly a corpse for a surgeon, who went ahead and bought from a rival who had delivered more quickly. There were periodic gluts, and it was largely seasonal work, since the hospital schools ran courses between October and April (though many private lecturers held summer classes).

Male corpses were more highly prized than female, since they offered greater scope for the study of musculature, while a fresh, well-developed limb could be worth more than a whole body that was on the verge of putrefaction. Other offcuts – a woman's scalp with long, thick hair attached;

unchipped teeth ('grinders'), either singly or as whole sets – were profitable sidelines for the resurrectionist since the living paid well to patch themselves up from parts of the dead. Infant mortality levels were high, and there was a brisk trade in children, either as 'big smalls', 'smalls' or foetuses. Speciality corpses achieved higher than average prices: in the autumn of 1827, when a young female inmate of an insane asylum succumbed at last to a long illness, William Davis, a member of the notorious Spitalfields Gang of snatchers, was offered twenty guineas by surgeons keen to anatomise her brain; but Davis was arrested by a parish watchman as he was digging up the corpse in Wigginton's private burial ground in Golden Lane.[3]

There were around 800 medical students in London in 1831, of whom 500 dissected corpses as part of their anatomical education; each student was said to require three bodies during his sixteen-month training – two for learning anatomy; one on which to practise operating techniques.[4] The only legal supply of flesh came from the gallows, with the corpses of those executed for murder being made available to the nation's surgeons. But the number of murderers being executed was far too low to meet the needs of an expanding, research-hungry medical profession. Death sentences for any crime were increasingly unlikely to be carried out as the Bloody Code of the eighteenth century was diminished by wave upon wave of legislation abolishing the death penalty for various property crimes.[5] However, the numbers of those executed had held steady because of the rise in arrests and convictions. While, for example, 350 death sentences were passed in England and Wales in 1805, only 68 people were executed (10 for murder); in 1831, 1,601 people were condemned to death, yet only 52 were executed (12 for murder).[6] And so the anatomists and their students relied on the 'snatchers', 'grabs', 'lifters', 'exhumators' or 'resurgam homos' to make up the numbers.

Digging up the dead in over-full city graveyards was physically arduous, but an exhumation could be completed in as little as half an hour by the well-practised. Resurrection men would also travel to outlying villages to retrieve corpses. Just as livestock, vegetables, herbs and milk were imported daily into the capital, and touted around the streets by itinerant sellers, the country dead were regularly ferried into town on covered 'go-carts'. A network of informers passed details to the London gangs of an impending death or recent burial in villages and hamlets, with corrupt sextons, gravediggers, undertakers and local officials taking a cut of the sale price. James May had just got back from the country on the Wednesday before his arrest, where he had been disinterring the rural dead; on the Thursday he had failed to make a sale of his two dead rustics at Grainger's, but Guy's took them off his hands for ten guineas each.

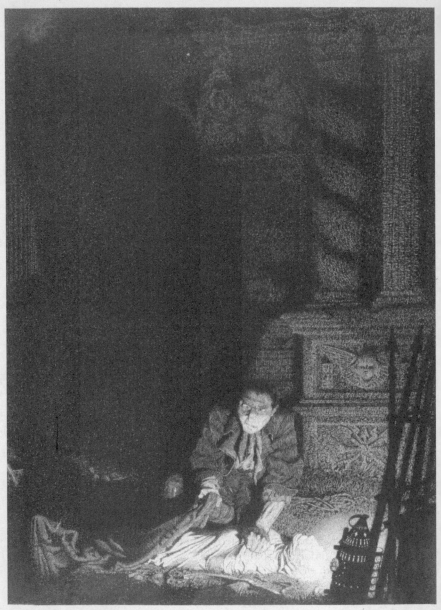

13. *The Bodysnatcher* by Morris Meredith Williams, 1913; in fact, disinterment was just one of several ways in which resurrectionists obtained corpses.

Another, increasingly popular, method of obtaining Things – and one that could involve the womenfolk of resurrectionists – was to pose as the friend or relative of a dying pauper, one who was too ill to alert work-house or hospital staff to an impostor; the corpse would then be signed over for private burial (the institution being glad to be free of the cost of interment). This grotesque vigil could last for days, but after the pauper's death, the resurrectionist could take possession of the body with every appearance of respectability and peddle it to a surgeon for dissection. A variation on this theme occurred in March 1830 in Walworth, then a village in south London. One Miss Christy had been unwell for some time and her health was deteriorating rapidly. As she lay in her sickbed a gang of known resurrectionists could be spotted lurking around her home. When she died Miss Christy was buried in the graveyard of St John's chapel, West Lane, Walworth. But a day later a police officer stopped a man carrying a sack in a street near the chapel, and it was found to contain Miss Christy. An inquest was held at a local inn, and here another pair of resurrectionists waited at the back of the room, trying to pass them-selves off as relatives waiting to claim Miss Christy's body when the coroner had finished with her remains. Enraged locals had them ejected from the hearing, and when Miss Christy was again laid to rest, her friends pledged to keep vigil at the grave until such time as she would be too putrid to be saleable.[7]

Even more opportunist, or impatient, snatchers would simply sneak-thieve a corpse that was known to be in a family home awaiting burial. On Saturday 15 October 1831 Thomas Williams used a crowbar to open the door of a house in Red Lion Court, off Hackney Road – very near to Williams's Nova Scotia Gardens home – and made off with the body of fourteen-year-old William Sullivan, who had died, after a long illness, a day or two before. The boy's mother, a widow, had gone out on an errand, leaving him lying in his coffin on the kitchen table. Neighbours saw a man passing through the court carrying a large, stinking basket; because of the smell, they took particular care to note the man's face (though it is interesting that none had the temerity to challenge him). When Mrs Sullivan returned and raised the alarm, the neighbours' description was so precise that a police officer arrested Williams the next day. He was identified by the witnesses, but since the boy's body could not be found, and no other evidence was offered, the local magistrate dismissed the charge.[8] Dissection disfigured and eventually destroyed corpses, a process that provided resurrectionists with their best chance of avoiding prosecution. No body, no evidence; no evidence, no case to answer.

Some snatchers were so confident that they felt no need to be circum-spect. On the afternoon of 29 December 1828, at the funeral of a dustman at St Andrew's church, Holborn, snatchers mingled with the large crowd of white-jacketed fellow dustmen. The deceased, who had lived in Battle Bridge (today's King's Cross) and had died in an accident, had been a very popular man; the white jackets were a sign of respect. His widow had already been approached by resurrectionists offering to buy the body from her; since she had refused to sell, they determined to 'izzey' (steal) it in a stunningly brazen manner. They staggered drunkenly into the church and swore and blasphemed throughout the service; they then hovered by the graveside as the coffin was lowered. None of the crowd attacked or remonstrated with the resurrectionists, but one friend of the dead man jumped down on to the coffin, calling to another, 'Come, Bill, let's squeeze the bugger down tight, and then he von't be fit for the knife.' Another declared, 'Ve'd better stop up at night and votch,' since they did not trust St Andrew's 'votchman'.[9]

So the resurrection man could expect to be reviled and ostracised by those he lived amongst, and shunned, too, by strangers – shopkeepers, publicans, coachmen – who suspected his profession. Knowing this, resur-rectionists wishing to take revenge on a rival would leave disfigured corpses or body parts festooned around the rival's home to arouse the fury of the neighbours and possibly the attentions of the police.[10] From the mid-1820s the work itself became more dangerous, with armed guards posted at many London graveyards as popular revulsion at the increasing incidence of bodysnatching grew. However, in the eyes of the law, resurrection was only a misdemeanour, not a felony. What was considered by the public to be one of the worst crimes was, to law-makers, comparatively trivial. The misdemeanour was 'unlawful disinterment', an act that breached 'common decency', according to a legal judgement of 1788, and was punishable by a fine or up to six months in gaol. The human body was deemed to belong to no one and therefore did not constitute property. For this reason, resur-rection men were scrupulous about replacing shrouds and coffin lids, in order to avoid the more serious charge of theft.

Magistrates in some parts of London were said to be becoming more likely to convict and imprison resurrectionists towards the end of the 1820s, though there was a wide range of attitudes among even senior, long-serving JPs. Records of cases heard before magistrates are rare for this period, just before the boom years of bureaucracy; newspaper reports and anec-dotal evidence of magistrates' hearings give a colourful though incom-plete picture, so it is difficult to ascertain whether there really was a crackdown. In 1828, the parliamentary Select Committee on Anatomy reported that London magistrates had been coming down harder on the resurrection community. However, none of the JPs who gave evidence to the Committee corroborated this statement: Thomas Halls, a JP at Bow Street, said he could remember presiding at only two resurrection cases in the previous seven years; Samuel Twyford of the Worship Street police office, near Shoreditch, was able to recall six in as many years, while the representative of the Thames police office claimed that he had never had a resurrectionist before him.

A number of contemporary newspaper reports suggest that from 1829 the newly formed Metropolitan Police were responsible for an increasing number of apprehensions – many of which, nevertheless, did not result in conviction.[11] But if there really was greater vigilance by the police and a rise in the number of arrests, this may have reflected the apprehension of part-time resurrectionists for perfectly ordinary thieving. Dr James Somerville stated to the Select Committee on Anatomy that the majority of 'resurrection' carts that were stopped by police were found to be carrying not exhumed corpses but the proceeds of house-breaking.[12] Increasingly, resurrection was becoming a specialist field, where only the best-informed, most fearless, physically strong, discreet and level-headed would be able to farm the dead on a full-time basis. The ageing, the drunk, the boastful and the careless would have a much tougher time of it.

Resurrection was one of the most covert underworld activities of the day, and tantalisingly little about it has ever come to light: the researcher continually finds herself in a blind alley. A handwritten index card in St Bartholomew's Hospital Archives states baldly that 'since obtaining bodies from resurrectionists was surreptitious, there are no written records of this process'; the minutes of King's College council meetings refer to various sums granted to the medical school, including £50 to Richard Partridge on 31 October 1831 'received on account of the anatomical department' – its destiny not accounted for, unlike all other sums of money mentioned in the minutes; and in a biography of surgeon Sir Charles Bell is a typical admission: 'That Bell did business with these blackguards may be accepted, but with regard to that side of his affairs, information is scanty.'[13] The Select Committee on Anatomy conducted interviews with three resurrection men – identified as 'AB', 'CD' and 'FG' – and a number of the surgeons they supplied, and the Committee's report and evidence form a major plank of what is known of the trade.[14] Other glimpses of resurrection culture appear in the recollections, reminiscences and memoirs of various medical men of the day – though such references are always hostile, with little interest shown in the everyday working lives of 'the most iniquitous set of villains who ever lived'.[15] It is not even clear how many resurrection men were at work in London in 1831. There may have been as many as seven London gangs, but with infighting a common feature of resurrection life, gangs were likely to have been constantly breaking up, re-forming and disintegrating again – so a 'gang' could have comprised two men or as many as fifteen. The Select Committee, considering all that it had been told, believed that while there were around 200 London resurrectionists, the vast majority of these were part-timers – making most of their living through more orthodox theft, and dealing in bodies only if these came their way with ease. 'They get a Subject or two and call themselves resurrectionists,' complained 'AB' to the Select Committee, bitterly regretting the influx of men who were no more than 'petty common thieves' and who were ruining the business. The specialists – the men that a number of anatomists grudgingly admitted they could trust not to overcharge, cheat, blackmail or turn informer to magistrates – were thought to number around ten. It is quite possible, though unprovable, that John Bishop and James May were among this elite.

It is also possible, and equally unprovable, that 'AB' was Bishop himself: there is a similarity between the intelligent, sardonic and saturnine replies to Committee questions and the syntax and flavour of Bishop's answers in his court hearings. The Select Committee report reveals that 'AB' started snatching at roughly the same time that Bishop is thought to have become a full-time resurrectionist. 'AB' worked with one partner; Bishop worked with just one accomplice for seven years, between 1821 and 1828, the date of the Select Committee's hearings. 'AB' claimed to know the Spitalfields Gang; Spitalfields is just south of Bethnal Green. 'AB' had been shot at by a graveyard guard from two yards' distance; Bishop had scars on his chin and had broken both legs at some point. 'AB' had served a six-month sentence in gaol; so had Bishop. 'AB' had in his best year lifted 100 corpses; Bishop had lifted 500 to 1,000 by 1831.

The Committee's hearings were described years later, in 1867, in *All the Year Round*, the journal that Charles Dickens 'conducted' and contributed articles to. In a piece entitled 'Old Stories Re-Told: Resurrection Men' an unnamed writer recalled:

> For several days in the summer of 1829, a certain committee room of the House of Commons, as well as all the passages leading to it, were thronged by some of the vilest beings that have perhaps ever visited such respectable places. Sallow, cadaverous, gaunt men, dressed in greasy moleskin or rusty black, and wearing wisps of dirty white handkerchiefs round their wizen necks. They had the air of wicked sextons, or thievish

14. The Fortune of War resurrectionist pub shortly before demolition; the Golden Boy cherub commemorates the Great Fire of London.

gravediggers; there was a suspicion of degraded clergymen about them, mingled with a dash of Whitechapel costermonger. Their ghoulish faces were rendered horrible by smirks of self-satisfied cunning, and their eyes squinted with sidelong suspicion, fear and distrust. They had been raked together from their favourite house of call, the Fortune of War in Smithfield. There were terrible rumours that when 'subjects' ran short, they had a way of *making* dead bodies.[16]

This has the smack of eyewitness remembrance, and it is possible that Dickens himself was co-author (though no Dickens authority has made such an attribution). However, the Select Committee on Anatomy sat in the summer of 1828, not 1829 (which would have been an unusual error for Dickens himself to have made); and there is something rather fanciful about the notion of a 'throng' of London resurrectionists coming to parliament by invitation. Certainly, only three men's evidence was used. If the *All the Year Round* story is correct, some kind of truce seems to have been arranged between the authorities and the landlord of the Fortune of War – a pub that sorely needed official indulgence. In its day the pub, which stood until 1910 at the north corner of the junction of Giltspur Street and Cock Lane, was said to have been such a safe house for snatchers that they would stash their stolen corpses, with tickets of ownership attached, on or under the pub's benches while they went off to strike a bargain. But by 1828 it is likely that the trade had become so shameful, so vulnerable to public distaste and police action, that no produce was actually kept on site; certainly John Bishop made no attempt to bring his wares to the pub.

The Fortune of War had originally been called the Naked Boy. In the seventeenth century a tailor had run the pub, and his shop sign depicted a lad with no clothes on, with the inscription: 'So fickle is our English nation/I would be clothed if I knew the fashion.' But the Naked Boy himself was inherited from an earlier age: shortly after the Fire of London, the Golden Boy of Pye Corner, a corpulent gilded wooden cherub, was 'in Memmory Put up for the late Fire of London Occasion'd by the Sin of Gluttony'. (A version of him still dangles from the office block that stands on the site today.) In 1721 the Naked Boy pub was bought by a man who had lost both legs and one arm in a sea battle: the fortune of war was mutilation.'[7] How the pub became the haunt of the resurrection community is not known, though its proximity to St Bartholomew's Hospital is likely to have played a role in its transformation.

At once close-knit and highly volatile, the resurrection trade had a tight network of such meeting places. Certain pubs and inns operated as unofficial guild halls, where bodies could be stored, and tips and warnings exchanged, and as houses of call for those indirectly involved in the trade (such as Michael Shields and, possibly, Thomas Wigley – the porter at the Cross Keys Inn). The hub of London resurrection culture north of the river was the Old Bailey thoroughfare and its northern continuation, Giltspur Street. South of the river the Bricklayer's Arms (where Old Kent Road became New Kent Road) and the Rockingham Arms (at 1 Newington Causeway, next to St Saviour's workhouse and very near James May's home) were both handily situated for south London's two large hospital medical schools – Guy's and St Thomas's – and their private competitor, Grainger's school in Webb Street. Such pubs were comparatively safe places for resurrection men – where they would not be subjected to the scorn of other working people. When John Bishop and James May took tea in the King of Denmark, a non-resurrection pub, their presence caused something of a frisson.

But it is likely that John Bishop had, to some extent, become inured to this kind of treatment – notoriety having come to him at a fairly early age. He was born in Highgate in 1797, the son of a hard-working, locally respected, 'plain, plodding man',[18] also called John, who ran a successful errand-cart business from the family home on North Hill, Highgate, transporting goods to and from the city 350 feet below and 4 miles to the south. Transportation was one of Highgate's biggest trades; some eighty coaches a day stopped at the village's Red Lion inn on the route to and from the north. Highgate also had a formidable drinking culture, with around twenty licensed taverns within its parish boundaries.[19]

John Bishop the son, the second of five children, lost his mother when he was eight years old. His father remarried and had more children, including a daughter, Rhoda, born in 1813; his second wife died and Bishop married for a third time. In November 1816 John Bishop the father was run over by a Pickfords van in Tunnel Road (now Archway Road) and both his legs had to be amputated at the hip; he died two weeks after the operation. The people of Highgate collected the considerable sum of £300 for his widow, Sarah, who was eight months' pregnant. But within weeks it became apparent that John Bishop the son and Sarah were living as man and wife. The locals tried to recoup their money, but most of it had already been obtained from the trustees and spent – on what, it is not known.

John Bishop took over his father's carting business and began three other money-making activities: informing on local criminals to the parish constables to secure reward money (his favourite Highgate drinking den was the Green Dragon, where informers congregated); hiring himself out as a witness/alibi man in court cases – committing perjury for a fee; and ferrying bodies around in his cart for a resurrection gang. Old Bailey – as well as being a gathering place for resurrectionists – was the centre of London's carting trade, and the Bailey's dual role is likely to have played a part in drawing Bishop further and further into resurrection and away from legitimate carting. (Many, perhaps most, resurrectionists had a prior and/or simultaneous connection with conveying goods, as carters or as porters.) Bishop teamed up with a noted resurrectionist – identity unknown

15. Thomas Hosmer Shepherd's 1814 aquatint of Old Bailey – the street that gave its name to the Sessions House (seen on the right). Newgate Prison is the building to the left of the courthouse; out of view on the far left is the King of Denmark; and hidden by the covered wagon is the Fortune of War. The cattle, sheep and drovers have walked down from Smithfield, which lies beyond.

– and between them they were reputed to have emptied the churchyard at the nearby village of Holloway. Some time before 1820 Bishop sold his father's business to a neighbouring rival firm, Cokeham's of North Hill, and sold off a small piece of Highgate Common inherited from his father, raising £80 – more than a year's wages for a skilled working man. Sarah continued to receive fifteen shillings a week, an annuity paid out by the Duchess of St Albans (Highgate's local aristocrat, who had pitied Sarah and had been unable or unwilling to stop the payments on hearing the scandalous talk of the widow's relationship with her stepson). Whatever else they were, John Bishop and his stepmother-wife did not start their life together poor. They married at St Leonard's Church, Shoreditch, on 2 August 1818, and it is likely that Highgate residents' disapproval of their liaison had contributed to their decision to abandon the north London village for the east of London; in the mid-1820s the family was living in Pitfield Street, Hoxton, a relatively impoverished area.[20]

By 1831, according to his own estimate, Bishop had sold between 500 and 1,000 bodies to the surgeons of London. He had always been confident of his talents; on one occasion, after being released from Bow Street when a charge against him was dropped, he passed the police office the next day, pulled a handful of sovereigns from his pocket and called across to one of the officers standing outside, 'You see! You cannot keep me from it. I got another stiff 'un last night and had nine guineas for it.'[21] According to a report in the *Morning Advertiser*, Bishop's success as a snatcher was the result of his patience and stealth, rather than any feats involving daring or physical strength; the newspaper claimed that among resurrectionists, he was considered something of a coward. As graveyard security tightened, Bishop became a prolific stealer of corpses from coroners' and undertakers' premises and from parish 'bone houses' after bribing the watchman or splitting his fees with him. He was also said to be adept at playing the relative of a vagrant dying in a workhouse, often accompanied, the same report claimed, by Sarah or 'a friend'. He must have operated on tip-offs, for it is said that on more than one occasion in the Old Street/Hoxton area he took lodgings, posing as a travelling carpenter and carrying a large basket, in a house where a corpse was lying in wake, absconding on his first night and taking the body with him. Bishop was once double-crossed by a watchman at Shoreditch workhouse, who had promised to sell him six pauper bodies; the authorities were alerted by the watchman but Bishop and his accomplices of the time ran off when they spotted the trap. He would not always be so lucky, and spent several stretches in 'sturbon' ('prison', from the German *sterben*, meaning 'to die' – a rival etymology for today's 'stir').

16. Coldbath Fields Prison stood on the site of today's Mount Pleasant Royal Mail depot; John Bishop served more than one sentence in this gaol for bodysnatching.

Bishop appears in the records of Clerkenwell New Prison in October 1825, serving two months for having possession of an illegally disinterred corpse,[22] and – as a result of a later stretch, in Coldbath Fields Prison – he makes an appearance in Captain George Laval Chesterton's book *Revelations of Prison Life*. Chesterton was the governor of Coldbath Fields from 1829 (and later became a friend of Charles Dickens) and Bishop passed through Chesterton's gaol some time in 1829, 1830 or 1831. Writing in 1856, Chesterton recalled Bishop as 'without exception, the most finished ruffian within my memory' with a 'powerful frame, of repulsive countenance, and of brutal address and manners. . . . He entered the prison uttering oaths and execrations, and indulging in the grossest language, while he assailed the subordinates, and even myself, with menace and defiance. He had received no provocation, but gave vent to the irrepressible brutality of his nature.' However, fourteen days of solitary confinement (a treatment being pioneered by Chesterton) wrought an extraordinary change in the man: 'That iron-souled miscreant became so meek and subdued, so prone to tears, so tremulous and agitated . . . he could hardly be recognised as the same coarse and blustering bully.' Nevertheless, claimed Chesterton, when Bishop passed from Coldbath Fields to Newgate, where he was free to mingle with other prisoners, 'I found, on inquiry, that renewed association with lawless men had revived the brutality so inseparable from his nature.'[23]

Bishop narrowly escaped being transported for perjury in December 1827, when, for a fee of £3, he gave a false alibi for two horse-thieves, Thomas Chapman and William Johnson. The jury at Chapman and Johnson's Old Bailey trial did not accept Bishop's story that the pair had been drinking with him in the Plough Inn, Windmill Court, Smithfield (directly opposite the Fortune of War in a lane that terminated in St Bartholomew's dissecting-rooms and burial ground) on the afternoon of 5 October, believing instead that they had been stealing two mares 120 miles away in Marshfield, Gloucestershire. Bishop was hopelessly evasive in the witness box and attempted to pass himself off as a general carrier ('I move any goods – it does not make much odds to me'),[24] refusing to name the crime for which he had twice been arrested. Instead of being transported, Bishop was gaoled for a brief time for lying to the court; Chapman and Johnson were executed.

In April 1831 he was involved in a perplexing case which was heard at Guildhall magistrates' court. Bishop and co-defendant Joseph Taylor were accused of stealing the body of an elderly man called Gardner from St Bartholomew's Hospital. Gardner's daughter-in-law deposed that she had given Gardner – who had been suffering with 'a spinal complaint' – a meal on the evening of Friday 18 March and sent him off with a shilling to find a bed for the night in a lodging house. The next day Taylor and Bishop called at Mrs Gardner's house in Dorset Street, just south of Fleet Street, and said that they had met the old man in the street, that he had been feeling very ill, and that if Mrs Gardner would give them a shilling, they would see that he gained free admittance to the casual ward at St Bartholomew's; they would swear to the medical staff that Gardner had no friends within 100 miles of London, which would, they said, guarantee him free treatment. Mrs Gardner agreed to this, and on Sunday 20th, Taylor came to her to say that he had indeed had the old man admitted as a charity patient, but that she should not visit him in hospital as this might jeopardise his free treatment. However, one week later Taylor turned up again to tell her that Gardner had died in hospital on Thursday 24th and had been quickly buried within St Bartholomew's own burial ground. When Mrs Gardner checked with the hospital, she was told that Bishop and Taylor had called for and removed the corpse themselves, saying that they would pay for a private burial, outside the hospital's ground.

Did Bishop and Taylor hasten the old man's death somehow, before his admission to St Bartholomew's? (Mrs Gardner's behaviour seems odd, too

The Cottages of Bishop and Williams The Resurrectionist in Nova Scotia Gardens

supposed Burkers of the Italian Boy

17. Nova Scotia Gardens in 1831. Number 3 is on the right. The cottages lay just north of Crabtree Row in the north-west corner of the map opposite.

– giving money to a stranger to assist her frail father-in-law.) There is no suggestion that anything other than bodysnatching was suspected by the Guildhall magistrates, and indeed, all charges against Bishop and Taylor were eventually dropped.[25]

It may be indicative that Bishop, disinterrer of hundreds, was, by 1831, losing his touch to such a degree that he needed to ask James May's advice on prices. It is also strange that, even with his past connections to the carting trade, he no longer had any access to a horse and cart – equipment that many a full-time snatcher relied on. Perhaps Bishop had made himself so unpopular within the resurrection world that he was becoming isolated and ill-informed; perhaps he had had to sell off his transportation to raise cash.

In July 1830, Bishop and his family had moved to a rented cottage in a semi-rural, semi-slum part of Bethnal Green; their landlady was Sarah Trueby, who lived nearby with her husband and grown-up son. This relocation suggests that the Bishops had come down in the world – reasons unknown, though the proportion of his income that Bishop was spending on drink is likely to have been a factor. Despite a generous inheritance, the funds raised locally, the earnings from resurrection and from Sarah's work as a seamstress/laundress, the Bishops and their children were reduced to living in one of the most squalid areas of East London. Nova Scotia Gardens was a stretch of land just north of St Leonard's Church in Shoreditch High Street, bordered to the west by Hackney Road and to the south by Crabtree Row (today's Columbia Road); its level was slightly below that of the surrounding streets, and some referred to it as the Hackney Road Hollow. A map of 1703 shows the area to have been called Goodwell Garden, on the fringes of the Huguenot settlements of Spitalfields, to the south; and maps of the 1740s and 1750s indicate that it remained largely unbuilt-upon open space. By 1810, the older horticultural and food-related street names (Crabtree Row, Birdcage Walk, Orange Street, Cock Lane, Bacon Street) were being joined by the martial/naval/colonial references of the brick-built terraces that were springing up in the vicinity. The Gardens had become Nova Scotia Gardens and nearby was Virginia Row, Nelson Street, Gibraltar Walk and Wellington Street.

The Gardens comprised a number of cottages which by 1831 were noticeably quaint; they were interconnected by narrow, zig-zagging pathways. Numbers 2 and 3, both of which were owned by the Trueby family, formed a semi-detached unit and were not in among the labyrinth of Nova Scotia Gardens, but close by Crabtree Row and near to the main entrance into the Gardens. The garden of Bishop's house, Number 3, had a side gate, opening on to a path known locally as the Private Way, and the house was entered by a back door, close to a coal-hole. Number 2 opened directly on to the largest path, connecting the Gardens to Crabtree Row. A four-inch-thick brick wall separated the dwellings. Each cottage had two upstairs rooms, a downstairs parlour, eight feet by seven, a smaller room housing the staircase, and a wash-house extension. The downstairs window overlooked the back garden. The roof of Numbers 2 and 3 was unusual in sloping sharply down from the front of the building to the back, and this may indicate that the cottages had been built – like so much housing in Bethnal Green, Shoreditch and Spitalfields – as homes for weavers: the lack of an overhanging front gable would allow light to pour into the upper rooms, which may once have contained looms. Each cottage had a thirty-foot-long, ten-foot-wide garden, divided from its neighbour by three-foot-high wooden palings, in which was a small gate. At the end of each garden was a privy. In the garden of Number 3 was a well to be shared by numbers 1, 2 and 3, though in fact, the residents of many of the cottages could have reached it easily; it was halfway down the garden and consisted of a wooden barrel, one and a half feet in diameter, sunk into the soil.

The generous size of these back gardens may reflect an earlier use as tenter grounds, to stretch and dry silk. The ground was described as 'former waste – slag and rubbish',[26] and it is possible the cottages had been built on the site of a brick-field, of which there had been a great many in Bethnal Green in the eighteenth century. Another theory is that the Gardens had once been allotments, and that the cottages had developed from a colony of gardeners' huts or summer-houses.[27] However, John Stow's *Survey of London* (1603) refers to some houses recently built in the area upon 'the common soil – for it was a leystall' (dunghill), which would make the development much older.

The Gardens and their surrounds had, during the 1664/5 plague visitation, seen some of the highest mortality figures in the capital. In 1831, the district's old reputation for poverty and despair was returning. The 1825 collapse of the English silk trade – the result of a surge of cheaper textile imports from France – proved calamitous, since weaving and cloth-working had provided thousands of households in Bethnal Green, Shoreditch and Spitalfields with an income. In 1829, wages among skilled workers in the silk trade of the East End, which employed an estimated 15,000 people, were half what they had been between 1815 and 1825. The governor of the Bethnal Green workhouse revealed that admissions had risen from 498 in 1821 to 1,160 in 1831.[28] One eyewitness wrote of 'the dwarfish and dwindled weavers of Spitalfields'; any man over 5 feet 2 inches tall was not a native of Spitalfields, he claimed. These men rarely made it to the age of sixty, and proved too weak and broken by their fourteen-to-sixteen-hour working days to say more than a few sentences at a public meeting convened to discuss the issue of free trade, which had opened English markets to foreign imports. At twenty, the commentator noted, Spitalfields men looked thirty; at forty, they looked sixty, with 'squalor and misery etched into their faces'.[29] Letters from Londoners concerned about conditions in this part of the East End – unpaved, undrained, unlit – were starting to appear in the newspapers. The *Morning Advertiser* printed a complaint about the filth outside the violin-string factory in Princes Street, just south of Nova Scotia Gardens – a mess (mainly consisting of offal) that was 5 feet wide and 1 foot deep; while 'An Observer' wrote to the same paper to report the level of filth in Castle Street – 200 yards from the Gardens, and home to the Feathers, one of the local beer-houses patronised by John Bishop.[30]

In July 1831, one year after the Bishops arrived, the house adjoining theirs was leased by the Truebys to Thomas Williams. Williams was born Thomas Head in Bridgnorth, Shropshire, on 28 February 1803. Although Bridgnorth was a thriving town, at the start of its long and lucrative association with the carpet-weaving industry, George and Mary Head moved with their children to London, to Highgate, at some point in the second decade of the century, and from there to the less salubrious Smithfield district. Thomas tried and failed at more than one trade, having been apprenticed to a bricklayer, then taking up carpentry before turning to working as a porter for local glass-manufacturers. As an adolescent, he had started to drink heavily and steal, despite coming from what appears to have been a comparatively stable and loving family. His mother was reportedly devoted to her son and watched with dismay his decline into crime.

He went by at least four different, though similar, names – his own, Thomas Williams, William Jones, and John Head – the name of a younger brother of his, born in 1805, who died in 1807.[31] He also tampered with his date of birth, perhaps to take advantage of looking younger than his years in order to receive more lenient treatment from magistrates and constables. He gave his age as twenty in 1827 – shaving off four years. It was a well-known ruse for those who were under arrest or in prison to adopt combinations of common christian and surnames; one lawyer counted fifteen prisoners at Newgate who were using the same combination of aliases. In this way, it was harder for police, magistrates and judges to identify 'known criminals' with any certainty, and a case could be lost if a jury felt that the accused had not been securely identified. 'No man goes into Newgate twice with the same name, trade, or place of nativity,' wrote the author of the book *Old Bailey Experience*.[32]

Head/Williams was in and out of court from an early age, and his luck ran out in February 1827, when he was found guilty at the Old Bailey of the theft of a 20-shilling copper bath-tub from the kitchen of his parents' landlord at 46 Turnmill Street, Smithfield. He had attempted to sell the vessel at Pontifex's copper and brass foundry at the northern end of Shoe Lane and was convicted on the eyewitness evidence of a chimney-sweep (who saw him leaving the house with the tub) and of Henry Pontifex.[33] He was sentenced to seven years' transportation, though, in the event, he served four years in Millbank Penitentiary – the controversial 'Panopticon' prison on the banks of the Thames, where Tate Britain stands today.

Head passed through Newgate on his way to Millbank, and the ledger book noting the physical description, 'character' and conviction of each prisoner shows that, as prisoner number 489, he gave his age as twenty, as he had at the Old Bailey. His trade was noted as bricklayer, his religion Church of England, and he was found to have two intertwined lovehearts shot through with arrows tattooed on to his right forearm; and the characters THNA on his left forearm – 'NA' presumably being his sweet-

18.–19. Millbank Penitentiary sketched in 1828, and photographed shortly before demolition in 1903. Thomas Williams served four years here for theft.

heart. He was 5 feet 4 inches tall, had hazel eyes, was in good health and was 'stoutish', with a 'fresh' complexion and a 'good' character – which in prison parlance tended to mean tractable.[34]

Received at Millbank in the same month was one Thomas Williams of Eaton in Buckinghamshire, a twenty-two-year-old who had been sentenced to seven years for the theft of a looking-glass. It is possible that Head borrowed the name and date of birth of this fellow convict; but Thomas Williams was also the name of a prolific East End bodysnatcher – he lived just off the Commercial Road – and in giving this name upon his arrest at King's College, Head may have been trying to fool the authorities that he was nothing more sinister than a regular resurrectionist.

Millbank Penitentiary had opened in 1816, closed down and reopened in 1824: not only had its buildings proved substandard, sinking into the marshy site, but in 1823 there had been outbreaks of scurvy and dysentery that had affected almost every inmate. The rehabilitation of the prisoner was to be paramount at Millbank. It was intended that both male and female inmates would be taught a skill (this may be where Williams learned the glass trade) and subject to an aggressively proselytising form of religious instruction. There was also a new emphasis on seclusion, in order to bring the prisoner to a closer relationship with God and to minimise the chances of moral 'contamination' from other villains; under 'the separate system', Millbank prisoners were allowed no contact with each other – a treatment that was said to have resulted in soaring rates of insanity among inmates of the gaol. Millbank pioneered the use of surveillance, and the building (the Panopticon comprised six pentagons abutting a central hexagon containing a chapel) was designed so that prisoners would be visible at all times. However, this failed to prevent outbreaks of rioting in 1826 and 1827 by a group of around twenty-five, who called themselves the Friends of the Oppressed. In March 1827 they hanged a warder's pet cat as part of their campaign to get themselves transferred to the hulks – normally the most dreaded of all penal institutions, which may reflect how appalling conditions were felt to be at Millbank.[35]

Upon his early release from Millbank, Williams rented Number 2 Nova Scotia Gardens, which had a large fireplace that Williams intended to adapt as a furnace, in order to manufacture glass. But his new start lasted just a month. Williams failed to register his trade with Customs and Excise (under an act of 1825, glass manufacture required an annual licence, costing £20; there had been a recent clampdown on unlicensed traders), who raided his home on 6 August, confiscated his equipment and large quantities of glass, cullet and iron and mounted a prosecution, which was still unheard at the time of his arrest for murder. Williams had walked in and found the confiscation in progress and called the Excise officer 'an oppro-brious name'.[36] Now without an income, he began to join his next-door neighbour, John Bishop, in supplying Subjects to the private anatomy schools. The new term was about to start at the hospital medical schools, and Bishop seems to have been happy to take on an apprentice. If Bishop had indeed been attached to the Spitalfields Gang, who were infamous for their feuds and fallings out, it could be that he had suddenly found himself without a partner; if there really had been some sort of crack-down on snatchers, many potential accomplices may have been in prison. Perhaps Bishop felt he could trust this new neighbour who was so down on his luck, yet so enterprising, with new ideas on how to obtain bodies; perhaps the friendship was helped along by their both having grown up in Highgate. Whatever the case, Williams had so smitten Rhoda, Bishop's seventeen-year-old half-sister/stepdaughter, that on 26 September he married her at St Leonard's Church, Shoreditch.[37] After the service, cele-bratory beers were drunk at the Birdcage pub, then there was a small family celebration in the back garden of Number 2, and Williams moved into Number 3 with his bride, John and Sarah Bishop and their children. Number 2 would remain empty for three more weeks.

James May was also a married man, and a father too, though he never let that stop him. He shared his lodgings at 4 Dorset Street[38] with Mary Ann Hall ('We do not live together exactly, but I think he is more with me than with anybody else') – a woman so devoted she had stayed up until three in the morning of Thursday 3 November trying to dry his soaking-wet jacket as he slept.

Like both Bishop and Williams, May had tried and found wanting more than one trade before becoming a resurrectionist. He was the illegitimate son of a barrister at New Inn – one of London's smaller inns of court – and the Inn's laundress. May's mother doted on her only child, to the extent that he was known locally as something of a mother's boy. He was educated at a boarding school, had fine handwriting and his father found him a post as a lawyer's clerk at New Inn. But he quickly became bored, preferring to try his hand as a butcher's assistant in Clare Market, the tiny seventeenth-century market square that was just around the corner from the Inn.[39] But before long he was finding this dull too and was unable to settle with any of his various employers in the meat trade. Despite the concerns of his parents and friends, he began to mix with thieves and resurrectionists and bought himself a horse and cart with which he helped them to transport corpses. Then he became a grave-robber himself.

May took lodgings in Clement's Lane overlooking the burial ground of St Clement Danes Church. This ground, called the Green Ground by locals, was also the graveyard of the workhouse in nearby Portugal Street and was notoriously overcrowded, with new burials often lying just a foot beneath the surface. The walls of the Clement's Lane houses backing on to the Green Ground ran with stinking slime, and the stench from the graveyard was so bad that windows were kept shut all year round. The children who attended Sunday school just across the lane in the Enon Chapel learned their lessons as 'body bugs' (mayflies) buzzed around them, while during services parishioners often passed out because of the smell emanating from the chapel's own crypt, where around 12,000 bodies lay packed on top of each other (the coffins having been broken up for fire-wood) in a space just 60 feet by 29 by 6.[40] From his Clement's Lane room, May kept watch for imminent and recent interments in the Green Ground: at last he had found a trade at which he could stick, although when asked by the authorities he would always give his trade as 'butcher'. But he couldn't keep quiet about the excitement and high earnings of his new job, and would brag around the streets of Clare Market. He soon found himself shunned in the district in which he had grown up, so he moved south of the Thames, to Elephant and Castle.

He was well used to the attentions of the police, having been arrested on a number of occasions for being in possession of an illegally disinterred body. In April 1825 he and fellow snatcher John Jerrome were caught by two watchmen, accompanied by a number of local residents, in the graveyard of St Leonard's, Shoreditch, with a body in a sack, a spade and a pickaxe close to a newly refilled – empty – grave. In court, May and Jerrome's attorney attempted the audacious defence that the pair had simply been two among the concerned crowd of locals attempting to apprehend those who had robbed the grave and fled. This defence caused much laughter in court but, astonishingly, the jury acquitted May and Jerrome.

So despite putting the arresting officers to great trouble on the afternoon of 5 November 1831, May was not taking this latest run-in very seriously. He felt sure the New Police's mistake would soon be cleared up.

THREE

The Thickest Part

On Friday 18 November, eight days after the verdict of the coroner's jury, Bishop, Williams, May and Shields were brought to the bar at Bow Street magistrates' court for the first of a series of hearings. George Rowland Minshull JP was in charge of proceedings; James Corder would present the evidence against the prisoners. The office was packed with spectators; the bench, where the magistrates sat facing the accused across the room, was crowded with 'gentlemen', many of them London surgeons, which gave the impression that they, too, had some authority over the prisoners and were on the side of right.

It was a small room, formerly the parlour of what had once been a private house, and Charles Dickens was shortly to describe it thus: 'The room smelt close and unwholesome; the walls were dirt discoloured; and the ceiling blackened . . . [There was] a thick greasy scum on every inanimate object.'[1] Minshull himself had written to the commissioners of the New Police protesting that the cess-pools in the adjoining lock-up rooms were in urgent need of emptying, since the 'soil' was oozing through the cell walls.[2] Moreover, wrote Minshull, 'The water closet is so situated as to open immediately upon the entry appropriated to the whole public, including prisoners and paupers, and we can only reach it by passing through the crowd. This has always been a source of inconvenience and discomfort and in some respects endangers the health of the magistrates, and we are now more than ever desirous of having a water closet placed in an accessible and safe position.' He went on to point out that the magistrates were obliged to sit in front of the fireplace, 'a damp and gusty spot' that 'attracts the smell of the whole room'.[3]

Into this foetid environment walked witness Margaret King, heavily pregnant and described in reports of the hearings as 'a decent-looking woman'. She told the court that at about one o'clock in the afternoon of 'the Thursday before Guy Fawkes Night' (she also called it 'Thursday the 4th' – Thursday was in fact the 3rd; the *Morning Advertiser* quotes her as

20. The Bow Street police office/magistrates' court.

giving the time as 'between ten and eleven o'clock in the morning') she was walking with her children near Nova Scotia Gardens when she saw what she described to the magistrate as 'an Italian boy' standing about 30 yards from her, with a small box or cage slung around her neck and resting on his chest. He had his back to her. King lived with her husband, son and daughter at Number 3 Crabtree Row, near to the Birdcage pub, and she claimed that she had often seen the same boy in the area. On that day she had refused to let her children go across to the boy to see what

21.–22. Inside Bow Street police office/magistrates' court; and another representation of Bishop, Williams and May, in the Bow Street dock.

MAY. WILLIAMS. BISHOP.
A Sketch taken at Bow Street.

was in his box. No, she had not seen his face. She went on to say that the following week, 'I heard some gentlemen speaking about the awful murder that had been committed on the body of a poor Italian boy, and I immediately said, "Dear me! I saw a boy such as is described standing at the end of Nova Scotia Gardens a short time ago."' On that day, she said, the boy had been standing with his back to her, but nevertheless she was sure it was 'the poor Italian' she had seen so often. And she had never seen him since that Thursday.

Before Margaret King had spoken, John Bishop had been smiling and James May appeared nonchalant; when King mentioned the cage, both sat up, leant forward, stared and began to listen carefully.

Mary Paragalli now repeated the evidence she had given to the coroner – that the dead boy was the Italian she used to see displaying a cage of white mice, that she had last seen him just after noon in Oxford Street, near to Hanover Square, on Tuesday 1 November, and that she had seen his corpse on Sunday 6th at the Covent Garden watch-house.

From across the room, John Bishop asked her. 'Are you quite certain that the boy you saw in Oxford Street was the same boy whose body lay at the watch-house?'

'I have no doubt of it,' she replied, adding, 'and at a distance, the cage might appear like a box,' as though to explain away Margaret King's confusion about the contraption in which the boy had kept his mice. Quite how Mrs King could have seen it at all when the boy had his back to her was a matter the magistrate did not pursue.

Minshull appears to have been generous in allowing Bishop, Williams, May and Shields to ask questions and to call out contradictions. But since the prisoners were not yet on trial – this was simply an 'examination' to discover whether there was any case to be answered before a higher court – they had no attorneys to guide them or to pick up on discrepant statements made by witnesses. Minshull's courtesy in allowing them to speak so freely could invite the men to incriminate themselves, and it is possible the magistrate was stretching the rules in order to pick up anything at all that would assist the inquiry.

James Corder announced to the court that its task – and the task of the New Police – was 'to fill up the links in the chain of evidence already brought forward'.[4] Corder had given his private opinion to Home Secretary Lord Melbourne that Shields and May were probably only accessories after the fact, and might therefore be persuaded to turn King's Evidence;[5] but none of the prisoners had offered to assist the prosecution in return for immunity. This had been the only way in which any sort of justice had been achieved in the Burke and Hare case; if Hare

WILLIAM BURKE.
(From a Sketch taken in Court)

WILLIAM HARE.
(From a Sketch taken in Court)

23.–24. William Burke and William Hare as they appeared in court in Edinburgh in December 1828.

had not turned King's Evidence, it was quite possible that a jury would have acquitted both the Edinburgh killers, or brought in the unique Scottish-law verdict 'not proven'. It was at Hare's lodging house that an aged Highlander, Donald, had died in his bed, owing £3 in back rent; and it was Hare, who, like Burke, had never been a resurrectionist, who struck upon the idea of imitating the bodysnatchers. Donald was sold to Dr Knox for £7 10s. When another old and feeble lodging-house inmate, a miller called Joseph, was taking too long to die of a fever, he was suffocated by Burke and Hare, and sold to Knox for £10. With the next murder, probably of aged street pedlar Abigail Simpson (the precise order of the killings is unknown), Burke and Hare perfected their *modus operandi* of holding shut the victim's nose and mouth. This method was to be used on prostitutes Mary Paterson and Mary Haldane (and Mary Haldane's retarded daughter); eighteen-year-old 'Daft Jamie' Wilson; Burke's cousin by (common-law) marriage Ann M'Dougal; an unnamed Englishman suffering from jaundice; and a number of beggars and pedlars whose names never came to light. Hare is also alleged to have dispatched at least one victim by himself. The killers were arrested on 1 November 1828, when guests at the lodging house discovered the body of beggarwoman Mary Docherty in bedding straw. One month later,

Hare betrayed Burke and escaped the gallows, laughing openly in court at finding himself a witness for the prosecution in the trial of his colleague.

This was the sort of treachery that James Corder was hoping for from Bishop, Williams, May or Shields. The investigation would be easier if somebody snitched: if they didn't, establishing the order of events that converted an unidentified boy into the Subject that was tipped on to the floor at King's College would require the tracking down and bringing together of witnesses and physical evidence in order to create a plausible narrative for an Old Bailey jury to consider. But the concept of objects being able to tell tales and supply solutions to mysteries was in its infancy; observation, deduction, analysis and 'scientific' forensics were only on the verge of taking over from traditional English approaches to criminal cases. In the 1830s guilt was still established by eyewitness accounts, being caught in the act, having a bad reputation, or simply looking and sounding the part of a criminal.

Upon arrest, John Bishop had sneered at the question put by Police Superintendent Joseph Sadler Thomas, of Covent Garden's F Division, about how he had come by the boy's body: 'If you want to know how I got it, you may find it out if you can,' the resurrectionist had said. Superintendent Thomas intended to rise to this challenge. The eyes not just of the capital but of the whole nation were focused on these proceedings. Melbourne himself had told Thomas 'to employ his men without reserve as to labour or expense' and had offered a King's pardon 'under the usual limitations' to any accomplice, and a £200 reward for anyone who came forward with evidence that would secure the conviction of the suspects in the case of the Poor Italian Boy – for even Whitehall had taken to referring to the victim in this way.[6] This, Thomas's first murder case, shows the fumbling beginnings of a methodical analysis of a crime scene and possible weapons, the checking of alibis and the testing of eyewitness evidence. As with any new science, the experiments, to later ages, can appear ludicrous.

Item number one was a tortoise. Following newspaper reports that the dead boy was being tentatively identified as an Italian beggar who exhibited white mice and/or a tortoise, an anonymous letter was received at Bow Street. The writer stated that there was a 'similar-looking' tortoise for sale in a shop in Middle Row, Holborn.[7] Superintendent Thomas wasted no time in going to the shop, where the owner's wife told him that her husband had purchased the creature in Leadenhall Market. Nevertheless, Thomas took the tortoise into custody, and when he showed it to Joseph Paragalli, the Italian claimed that, yes, it certainly looked like the dead boy's tortoise.

Next, Thomas flourished before Minshull and the court the hamper and bloodstained sack that had been used to transport the body to King's College; and – presented in a small box – the teeth that May had sold to the dentist, Mills. At this point in the hearing James May was thrown from his usual facetiousness when Mills gave his evidence; he was perhaps realising how a jury might choose to interpret the fact that he had told Mills that all the teeth had come from the same body and that the body had never been buried. *The Times* reporter noted that May now began to stare wildly, compressing his lips tightly as he took in every word the dentist said: 'May appeared for the first time to lose that hardness of nerve that distinguished him.'[8] Then May self-consciously attempted to compose his features, and laughed a rather hollow laugh, before starting and staring again, muttering, 'You bloody rascal,' at Mills.

May was also alarmed to learn that his lodgings had been searched by Thomas's men and a number of items retrieved. The officers had found a waistcoat with marks of clay on it, some metal implements, and a pair of trousers – bloodstained; there was also blood on the floor near where the trousers had lain. May protested, telling the court that after his arrest, a jackdaw had hopped on to his trousers after injuring its leg; he knew, because one of the other tenants had visited him in prison and told him so. Superintendent Thomas said that he was inclined to believe this story, since the search had taken place a full week after May's arrest and the bloodstains were 'entirely too fresh and glutinous' to have had any connection with the murder, though Constable Joseph Higgins pointed out that in carrying the clothing back to the police station, a shower of rain may have been responsible for making the blood look fresh. In his evidence, Higgins made no mention of the jackdaw story, although he knew of it, and May picked up on this attempt to implicate him, saying, 'Now Mr Policeman, do you remember the jackdaw having hurt his leg? You did not state that to the worthy justice when you ought to have done.' The bloodied jackdaw was no bizarre invention; Charlotte Berry, one of the residents at the lodging house, admitted that she had been playing with the bird – which was kept as a pet by the landlady, Mrs Carroll – on the first-floor landing at 4 Dorset Street and had accidentally injured it by pinching its foot in the door; the bird had then hopped into May's room, which was next to Berry's.

The police had also been investigating May's alibi and had examined Rosina Carpenter, 'a young woman with whom one of the prisoners had occasionally co-habited'. May claimed that he had spent the night of Thursday 3 November with Carpenter, from late in the afternoon. Carpenter was a childhood friend of May's with whom he was now intimate; she lived in Nag's Head Court, at the northern, Old Street, end of Golden Lane. Whatever Carpenter had told the authorities was withheld from the press, however, on the grounds that 'it would be very imprudent to publish at present'.[9]

A Jewish clothes-dealer who lived in Saffron Hill had come forward to tell Superintendent Thomas and Minshull that four men came into his shop in West Street, Smithfield, at half-past two on the afternoon of Friday 4 November to exchange a pair of bloodstained corduroy breeches and a waistcoat for clean versions of the same, and had bought a smock frock with unusual stitching; two of the four men were already wearing smock frocks. The clothes-dealer was escorted to see the prisoners in Clerkenwell New Prison,[10] where they were being held on remand, on Saturday 12 November, in an attempt to identify the four men he had served; he was able to pick out May and Bishop though not Williams or Shields. If indeed two other men had come to his shop, their identities would never be established: Bishop and May had made no mention of them in their statements about their movements on the Friday. For reasons that are not clear, James Corder told Minshull that the prosecution did

25. Clerkenwell New Prison, where Bishop, Williams and May were detained during the police investigation.

not intend to investigate further this clothes-exchanging episode, despite the identification that had been made. This promising line of inquiry may have been abandoned in order to protect the clothes-dealer from attacks from the accused on their acquittal, or from their associates in the event of their conviction. And with two unknown men entering the story, the case was perhaps becoming too convoluted to be put convincingly before a jury. Minshull put it thus: 'They were now in the thickest part of the horrid affair.' Yes, 'the facts certainly thickened upon them,' replied Superintendent Thomas.[11]

An unsigned letter was sent to Thomas stating that John Appleton, the dissecting-room porter at Grainger's medical school in Webb Street, had told a postman that the body offered to him by Bishop and May on Friday 4 November was still warm. Thomas brought Appleton before Minshull, but the porter indignantly denied having said any such thing to anyone – that he had never even seen the body.

Turning to the cause of death, Thomas announced to Minshull that he believed the cut on the forehead of the dead boy was probably the fatal blow; in saying this, he was contradicting the unanimous evidence of the anatomists who had studied the corpse. Thomas also saw significance in the fact that James May's left hand was poulticed and bandaged, and he asked Richard Partridge to step across the Bow Street office to examine the wound. This Partridge did, and announced that there was an injury to the top of the forefinger, which had probably occurred just before the arrest. May said he had received the wound as he punched out the dead boy's teeth with a brad awl at 3 Nova Scotia Gardens.

Every word the accused spoke was seized upon by Superintendent Thomas. Bishop had said shortly after his arrest that the body had come from Guy's Hospital. (This wasn't strictly a lie, since Bishop and May had collected it from there on the morning of Saturday the 5th.) Thomas immediately sent a message to Guy's with a request to know whether any boy had died there lately. Guy's sent back a slip of paper stating that since 28th October three people had died at the hospital – a woman, and two males, aged thirty-three and thirty-seven.

Thomas was also proud to reveal that while the four men were waiting to be taken to the coroner's hearing at the Unicorn pub, Bishop had leaned over Williams and muttered to May, 'It was the blood that sold us.' They were sitting beneath a police notice about the murder for which they were being held. Bishop stood up and read the notice, gave a forced laugh and told his colleagues, 'This states that there were "marks of violence". The marks of violence were only breakings-out on the skin.' He sat down smiling. These comments were overheard and written down by a plain-clothes officer sitting nearby. Before Minshull, Bishop denied having made them.

Minshull was profoundly impressed by the energy and diligence with which Thomas was amassing clues and memorising possibly telling exchanges. Reading the various published accounts of the committal proceedings, it is striking how throughout, Thomas pops up at crucial points like a *deus ex machina*, revealing his latest 'information received', producing physical evidence, conjuring up new witnesses. However, just in case his confidence was misplaced, Minshull also called upon one of the oldest of the Bow Street Runners, Samuel Taunton, to make inquiries around Bethnal Green and Shoreditch, a move not calculated to please Thomas. Or perhaps it was to prove a spur to even greater efforts on the part of the New Police superintendent. London's New Police were not detectives, after all: they had been created to prevent crime happening in the first place. Such clearing up of mysteries that did take place was still the work of the Bow Street Runners – the small, plain-clothes force set up by Henry Fielding in 1749 that worked alongside the New Police until being disbanded in August 1839. The Runners relied heavily on informants to solve crimes, and anyone contributing to a conviction received a sum from the court in recognition of their evidence; the payments were called 'keeping them sweet'. The Runners received a retaining fee from the authorities and relied on rewards for their real earnings. While idolised by many, the Runners achieved their success by mixing with the very thieves, fences and procurers they were supposed to be thwarting; pure analysis had little to do with it. Later in the century, Dickens would puncture their reputation, claiming they were 'far too much in the habit of consorting with thieves and the like . . . they never lost a public occasion of jobbing and trading in mystery and making the most of themselves. . . . As a detective police they were very loose in their operations.'[12]

The Runners were among the most sceptical about the New Police's ability to bring wrongdoers to justice. Robert Peel's new force faced enormous opposition, and contempt for Peel's Bloody Gang, Peel's Private Army, The Blue Devils, The Plague of Blue Locusts permeated the whole of London society. But the 'Old' system of policing – much of it dating back to Tudor times – was perceived by Peel to be not simply incompetent and inadequate for modern society, but inherently corruptible: in 1816, six Runners were transported after being found guilty of setting up robberies and claiming the proceeds of the crime by then acting as prosecutors.

Before 1829, London was policed by a ramshackle medley of parish constables, the Bow Street Night Patrol, the Day Patrol, the Horse Patrol (to protect the highways), the River Police and the Runners, as well as the much-mocked Charleys – widely reputed to be elderly men who dozed the night away in their sentry boxes while stealing and brawling went on all around.[13] That there had also been popular dissatisfaction with the Bow Street Patrol officers is suggested by a report of an angry meeting of the parishioners of St Paul's, Covent Garden, in September 1828, who alleged that the patrol officers had been too drunk to be of any assistance when two houses fell down in Exeter Street, off the Strand, killing a woman and a child. According to those trying to free the injured from the debris, only the St Paul's parish constables were sober and came immediately to help.[14]

However, not every metropolitan parish was as fortunate in its constables. In St Pancras eighteen rival watch-trusts divided up the policing of the parish without any common system; Lambeth, Fulham and Wandsworth were said to have no night watchmen at all, while at one point, Kensington was said to have had just three parish constables. If a

26. A Charley is removed far from his place of watch as he dozes, in this unsigned engraving of 1825.

crime were taking place in front of a parish constable on the other side of the street – and that other side was in another parish – he was unable to intervene.

Despite all the evidence of a need for change, Peel's Metropolitan Police Act faced ethical objections: widespread hostility was expressed towards attempts to put any Englishman under state surveillance – a distinctly foreign concept, it was believed, that would imperil the freedom of the individual. There were fears that his New Police would be a militaristic body, placing the country at the mercy of thousands of uniformed petty despots, acting as they wished with full governmental backing. Many property-owners and tradesmen were angered by the imposition of a centralised body over a set of local men – no matter how corruptly these may have been elected: the New Police answered to the Home Office, via Scotland Yard, while the Old Police – though ultimately overseen by the Home Office – were answerable to the local magistrate at London's nine police offices. On a more mundane level, parish authorities resented the new police rate (not to exceed 8*d* in the pound) that was levied in place of the old watch rate, which had brought the additional benefit of keeping old men in employment and thus off the parish poor rate; some London parishes withheld their police-rate payments for as long as possible.

The government under Wellington's premiership passed a watered-down version of Peel's controversial bill, excluding the City of London, which was permitted to continue with its own ancient system of policing. On the morning of Saturday, 26 September 1829, the new force, numbering over 1,000 men (2,000 men had applied for the positions), was sworn in, in the grounds of Thomas Coram's Foundling Hospital.

The antipathy towards them was as deeply felt in the drawing rooms of the West End as it was in the capital's 'flash-houses' – pubs and taverns where stolen goods were fenced and new robberies plotted. When Lord Melbourne took over from Robert Peel as Home Secretary in the new Whig government of Earl Grey in November 1830 he tended to side with chief London magistrate Sir Richard Birnie (who once stated, 'I never saw a constable who was perfectly competent') in his relentless criticisms of the Metropolitan Police's first, joint commissioners, Charles Rowan and Richard Mayne. Rowan and Mayne spilt a great deal of ink mollifying newspaper editors, refuting the notion that there was to be any increase in the numbers of Metropolitan Police officers.[15] George IV himself made a point of very loudly praising the manager of the Drury Lane Theatre after a performance for refusing to allow any New Police into the building. (The Runners were to retain their exclusive role of keeping an eye on pickpockets within the theatre for ten more years.)[16]

Members of the new force were to be drawn from the 'respectable' sections of the working class: an ingenious stroke – using the poor to police the poor. Rowan and Mayne advised recruits to the New Police against cultivating informers and mixing with villains, and officers were expressly forbidden to enter the pubs and lodging houses in which thieves were said to meet. So the Runners were kept on in their capacity of infiltrating the underworld of thieves and receivers. In a sense, they were containing crime, by keeping a close eye on the men-most-likely-to and the premises where such people congregated. (Various Newgate prisoners were, together, able to name 200 London flash-houses.) However, the much-loathed figure of the 'common informer' also continued to play a significant role in policing and the punishment of crime in the 1830s. This ancient facet of English social life had increased in scope during the eighteenth century to become crucial to the detection and prosecution of criminals. Every trial for a property crime required a private prosecutor, and the real victim of the loss was often unable or unwilling to institute proceedings. The common informer mounted the action against a suspected thief and filled the role of prosecutor in the courts; upon a conviction, a portion of the value of the goods stolen was passed to the informer as a reward. In addition, an informer who brought to the attention of the authorities any citizen who committed a broad range of nuisances – short-changing, food adulteration, the dumping of refuse in the highway, Customs and Excise abuses, for example – received cash payments. So unpopular was this role, an act of parliament was passed specifically to outlaw physical attacks on common informers.

An informer did not have to be a professional snitch, though. Any member of the public was entitled to tell tales and be paid for it – a privilege that was just one way in which the community was deemed capable of policing itself. However, juries were known to take into consideration the fact that 'information received' had often been paid for, and could choose to treat such purchasable evidence with scepticism.

There were to be no rewards for a Metropolitan Police officer who solved a crime or returned stolen goods to their rightful owner; and no justice-evading, out-of-court deals were to be done by the new force. But if an officer was not close to the source of criminality – mingling with thieves, fences, procurers, swindlers and forgers; keeping the channels open between himself and the common informers – how could he realistically find out what he needed to know? If, as seemed to be the case, criminals were becoming increasingly well organised, what strategies could be put in place to discover their networks and thwart their plots?

The age of the detective-as-hero was imminent; in 1841 Edgar Allan

Poe would introduce the sleuth to English-language fiction with Auguste Dupin in 'The Murders in the Rue Morgue'. But in 1831, detection was a phenomenon as new and experimental as railway travel, gallstone-removal, the omnibus, phrenology, Catholics in parliament, the concept of votes for all. The notion of one man exploring the mechanisms and milieu of urban crime had been introduced to London in 1828 with the publication of the English translation of the memoirs of Eugène-François Vidocq (1775–1857) – a criminal turned police informer who went on to head Napoleon's police department. Ghostwritten and unreliable, Vidocq's *Mémoires* nevertheless enjoyed huge success in Britain, and reached poorer homes through plagiarisms and stage adaptations. Vidocq's appeal was that he could penetrate seemingly alien strata of urban society, bring back tales of the speech and habits of these worlds and provide solutions to crimes and mysteries.[17] That was the sort of man it would take to crack the Italian Boy case, since none of those in the know was talking.

Joseph Sadler Thomas was, in many ways, the model of the new type of policeman – but could he also be a London Vidocq? He was already something of a local legend when he became the first superintendent of Covent Garden's Division F at its formation in September 1829, having lived in the parish since 1813. If 'zealous' could have been his middle name, so too could histrionic, lachrymose, prudish, self-pitying and outspoken. Since October 1827 Thomas had been the parish constable (that is, one of the 'Old' police) of St Paul's, Covent Garden – an unpaid post that he combined with his paid job as cashier at the box office of Covent Garden Theatre. Thomas's aim, he told the 1828 Select Committee on the Police of the Metropolis, was 'to correct the many evils with which my neighbourhood abounds. . . . In consequence of my interference, I have reason to believe that a very great change has taken place for the better.'[18]

Superintendent Thomas's opinions ('I perceived, as anybody else does, a wonderful apathy in the police officers')[19] and activities (applying to magistrates to have cab-stands removed, coffee-stalls shut down, pub-licence applications denied) had made him enemies. Because of his high arrest rate, which cast doubt on the competence of other officers, Thomas received threats to harm his wife and three children, and once he was physically assaulted and dragged through the streets by two Runners and two officers of the Bow Street Day Patrol, who, tired of his criticism of their indolence, decided to arrest him for loitering outside Drury Lane Theatre: 'I was struck and dragged through the streets like a felon . . . past an exulting set of blackguards,' he told the 1828 Police Select Committee. Magistrate Sir Richard Birnie dismissed the charge of loitering that the Runners and Day Patrol had brought against Thomas; but many other London magistrates had little patience with him.

Those even higher up the line of authority frequently belittled Thomas and lost no opportunity to trip him up – a task he made much easier for them by his habit of speaking before thinking. The 1828 Select Committee had quite a deal of fun questioning him, playing on his moral certainty which combined rather disastrously with a lack of knowledge of basic law. Thomas asserted to the Committee that it was well known that the two pubs that stood opposite the Bow Street police office – the Brown Bear and the Marquis of Anglesey – were flash-houses. When pressed on this matter, he backed down, saying that they probably weren't flash-houses after all, but that they certainly didn't keep to their licensing hours.[20] At a later Select Committee hearing, Thomas was accused of relying on 'defective evidence', showing 'weak and childish conduct' and being 'weak and pusillanimous and childish. . . . For in fact, he shed tears,' sneered Middlesex magistrate Sir John Scott Lillie.[21] Even Commissioners Rowan and Mayne wrote him frequent reprimands when he failed to adhere to the new, post-1829 way of doing things:

> The Commissioners of Police notice in *The Times* of this morning that Mr Thomas asked advice from the magistrates at Bow Street, respecting the state of dogs in the street. The Commissioners have more than once had occasion to notice the irregularity of such a course, and acquainted Mr Thomas that he was to apply to them in all cases when he required any advice for the guidance of the police. The Commissioners now desire Mr Thomas to understand that if they find him again repeating this practice they will consider it a wilful disobedience of their orders.[22]

And so on.

But Thomas had two well-placed allies: George Rowland Minshull seems to have been cut from similar cloth. The magistrate was often derided for being unworldly, and the phrase he frequently let slip when hearing evidence, 'Oh! How shocking!', was a source of fun to his detractors.[23] He was one of the few London magistrates who wanted to see the New Police succeed; and he saw that Thomas was, apart from anything, an effectual officer, who, two days after the New Police was formed, organised the break-up of a mass brawl in Seven Dials, Covent Garden, arresting thirty drunken, fighting men by marshalling forty F Division officers.[24] Then, on Wednesday 27 April 1831 in the Strand, Thomas had gone into the middle of a group of between 2,000 and 3,000 angry Londoners – a crowd that included many women and children – who were protesting at the defeat of the Reform Bill in the House of Lords and persuaded them not to riot as they marched through the West End. The Bill was intended to widen male suffrage by lowering the property-value threshold, thereby enfranchising certain sections of the merchant class for the first time. Many (perhaps most) working men believed this step would bring them the vote too. It was also a measure to end the phenomenon of 'rotten' or 'pocket' boroughs – seats with few constituents, which were in the control of wealthy landowners and which had a representation in parliament that was disproportionate to their small populations. Wednesday 27 April was the night of the General Illumination, on which Londoners lit every available light, lamp or candle and placed them in their windows to show their support for parliamentary Reform. In addition to homes, shops and pubs, the boats and barges on the Thames, theatres, banks, newspaper offices and even the Mansion House were all ablaze with light. Although the majority of protestors were peaceful, and some even sang 'God Save the King', a number had stoned darkened windows, and missiles were thrown at Thomas and his men in the Strand. He was struck twice by staves, but he stood his ground, and some in the crowd even shouted 'Bravo Police!' By the end of the protest, at four o'clock in the morning, 168 stone-throwers had been arrested – almost all later being acquitted, bailed or receiving a small fine, which seems to indicate either the lack of seriousness of the offences or the tacit sympathy of the magistrates.[25]

Thomas also had the support of influential London Radical and political reformer Francis Place (1771–1854), who consulted the superintendent on policing matters. Place thought Thomas 'very useful and intelligent', and between them, at Place's Charing Cross home, Britain's first-ever baton charge was worked out in theory. Eager that the government should find no excuse to deploy troops on the streets – Peterloo Massacre-style – to deal with Reform unrest (or any sort of unrest), Place and Thomas decided that if an unruly mob should assemble in London and appear intent on looting and damage to property, sound thrashings should be meted out, but not until the police were certain that they were about to be attacked. Only 'sufficient' violence, as Place termed it, was to be used; just enough to disperse the large groups that Place believed had no interest in political or social issues, merely 'a vague hope of plunder'. These London mobs, he wrote, had no genuine 'bond of union' and 'were composed of idle and miscreant people' and were 'remarkably cowardly'.[26]

The baton-charge theory was put into practice on 9 November 1830, when a large crowd armed with staves (in fact, pieces of wood stolen from a building site in Chancery Lane) poured through the Temple Bar heading west along the Strand, shouting 'Down with the police'. The origins of this disturbance are complex: Reform Bill unrest had been fomenting for some time; there was a degree of anti-New Police feeling; William IV had been scheduled to ride through town in state to the Mansion House – a parade that was cancelled because of fears that it would spark a riot; and in the East End on the 9th there had been a march in support of the unemployed Spitalfields weavers. Thomas and a large body of policemen were waiting in Catherine Street, close to Drury Lane, and fanned out across the Strand to block the crowd's progress. The police, also armed with staves, rushed towards the crowd, who scattered instantly. Place claimed that this rout marked the end of that particular type of 'mobbing' in London.

Thrashings and military-style manoeuvres aside, Superintendent Thomas was also capable of kindness and empathy. He often returned runaway children to their parents when he came across them sleeping in Covent Garden market. One of these was the son of a surveyor from Marylebone whom Thomas had found at three o'clock in the morning asleep under a market stall; the child had taken his father's watch and said he was planning to stow away on board a ship when dawn came.[27] Although he was compelled by threat of a fine to arrest anyone sleeping in the open air, he admitted to the 1828 Police Select Committee that he never arrested the dozen or so paupers who bedded down every night at the King's Entrance to the Drury Lane Theatre when the actors and audience had departed. As Thomas put it, 'in many of those instances, they are very unfortunate people who have seen better days.'

FOUR

Houseless Wretches

The number of anxious parents who had come to see the young boy's body in the Covent Garden watch-house, and the tales of loss they told, had amazed the coroner, his jury, the magistrates and the parish authorities of St Paul's. It had also surprised the Home Secretary. Viscount Melbourne was indolent and indecisive, where his predecessor, Robert Peel, had had a horrified curiosity about the new urban society that was emerging and had effected measures to confront it. (Typical of Melbourne's effete manner was his response on being offered the premiership, later, in 1834: 'He thought it was a damned bore and he was half inclined to turn it down.')[1] But James Corder's letter accompanying the report of the coroner's findings had elicited an uncharacteristically vigorous reply from Melbourne in which he asked Corder to see if he could find out why it was that so many young people appeared to have gone missing in the city.[2]

In addition to the various Italians who had come forward, eight sets of parents had notified the Bow Street magistrates that their sons had recently disappeared and had asked to see the dead child. The mother and father of a deaf-mute boy told Bow Street magistrate George Rowland Minshull that they feared their child had been abducted, killed and sold to the surgeons for dissection, since they had heard that the men being held in custody were known resurrectionists. Mr Hart, a linen-shop-owner of Oxford Street, 'a most respectable tradesman, in affluent circumstances', according to the *Morning Advertiser*, wept as he told Minshull that his fourteen-year-old son had gone missing on Tuesday 1 November, and that he had placed a notice of this, with a full description of the boy, in the newspapers; it may have been this advertisement that Richard Partridge's pupils had read when their suspicions were aroused about the corpse delivered to King's. According to local solic-itor James Isaacs, Hart's son 'was well-educated, of moral pursuits, and could not be suspected of a roving inclination, and yet he had disap-peared all at once, and no trace could be obtained of him.'[3] (The body of Hart's son was pulled from the Regent's Canal at Lisson Grove one week later, fully clothed and decomposing. The cause of his death was never to be established, but the newspapers nevertheless decided that it was likely he had been 'burked'.)

Perhaps what had been most startling was the nature of the families reporting lost children – ordinary working people, many of them in trade, whose predicament presented an unsettling glimpse of the fragility of family life in the world's largest, wealthiest city. If children from settled, reasonably well-off families could simply disappear, what chance the orphans, the offspring of the desperately poor or the imprisoned? 'I know that I have lounged about the streets insufficiently and unsatisfactorily fed. I know that, but for the mercy of God, I might easily have been, for any care that was taken of me, a little robber or a little vagabond. . . . It is wonderful to me how I could have been so easily cast away at such an age.' This was Charles Dickens, towards the end of his life. At twelve years old, Dickens had found himself living alone in a boarding house in Camden Town and working in a small factory just off the Strand when the rest of his family moved into the debtors' prison, the Marshalsea, following his father's bankruptcy. Dickens earned six or seven shillings a week, but he felt that shockingly little separated him from the fate of the vagrant children he saw all about him in the streets around Covent Garden; and he never forgot the vulnerable condition into which he had been plunged.[4] Dickens's parents teetered in and out of genteelly distressed circumstances; the step into destitution was a short one. They were rescued by family connections, who gave Dickens's father the chance to make a living as a journalist (and John Dickens would later sponge off his successful son for many years). In households less blessed with skills and contacts, even contentedly married couples could find themselves with little time to devote to their children, since many families were able to subsist only if both parents worked virtually every hour they were awake. Other parents, though, may have been too attentive: the governor of Newgate Prison claimed that many of the child thieves in his care were the children of 'decent working tradesmen' but had fled their homes because parental discipline was too harsh.[5]

A thirteen-year-old boy called Williams was found starving, diseased and fast asleep in a doorway in Bedford Street, Covent Garden, by a parish constable in March 1826. Though he claimed that he was an orphan from Devizes in Wiltshire, come to town to seek his fortune, it transpired that Williams's parents lived just a mile away, in a street off Fitzroy Square, and that the boy had run away from them at least twenty times. The magistrates ordered Williams to be looked after at the St

Martin's-in-the-Fields watch-house until an apprenticeship could be arranged for him.[6]

The ten-year-old son of an army surgeon named Macher was inveigled away from the family home in Knightsbridge in 1824 by a former shoemaker turned vagrant variously known as Thomas Wood, Thomas Buxton and Thomas Cox, whose speciality was to chalk poems on the pavement and await contributions from passers-by. Seven months after the boy's disappearance, constables spotted Wood/Buxton/Cox sitting begging in Keppel Street, off Gower Street in Bloomsbury, with an 'attractive little boy' alongside him – this was Master Macher. The boy 'strenuously denied' that he was Macher, and was seen waiting patiently for hours for his abductor to be released from police questioning; however, he eventually and reluctantly admitted his identity 'and he was, to the utmost joy of his disconsolate parents, delivered over to them.' It is not quite the picture of happy family life that this newspaper report wished to convey.[7]

Police and magistrates also heard many stories of parents who would send their children into the streets telling them not to come home until they had earned a certain sum, either through begging or theft; those children who were too afraid to return empty-handed were frequently reported to be among those found sleeping rough in London's more secluded spots – under the stalls of the various markets; in the shrubs of Hyde Park; in the shells of houses under construction; in summer curled up in the haystacks of Marylebone; in the coopers' barrels of Whitechapel; among the warm kilns of East End brick-fields.[8] Some vagrant children took it upon themselves to live entirely outside the realm of adult supervision. One gang of Covent Garden vagabond boys formed itself into the Forty Thieves, and its members identified themselves by a primitive form of tattoo: a needle dipped in gunpowder pricked the gang-membership number into the skin of the palm. In September 1828 numbers 5 and 8, both around the age of twelve, were arrested by the parish constable, possibly Joseph Sadler Thomas, and committed for trial on theft charges.[9]

Children under the age of seven were not criminally liable under the 1824 Vagrancy Act; they were not deemed to be capable of any crime. Yet London's prisons had plenty of older children serving sentences for begging. In 1827, according to the 1828 Police Select Committee Report, seventeen boys and twenty-seven girls under the age of twelve served sentences in the Bridewell prison for begging. (Newgate Prison even had a schoolmaster to teach the gaol's under-fourteens.) Elizabeth Butler, imprisoned in the Tothill Fields bridewell on a charge of vagrancy in January 1828, was, in fact, seven years old, as the Select Committee's own tables showed.[10]

He was traced to a public house at Banstead, near Epsom, where he told the landlord that he had been stripped and maltreated by Irishmen. When at Godstone he put on a frock coat given to him by a brother, of the name of Ross, out of charity. The colour of this had been blue, but from washing and wear, had faded to nearly a drab. He also begged a hat, which had a piece cut or torn out of the back part of the brim.

On Saturday, the 2d of February, about eleven o'clock, an Elderly Man, nearly sixty, who speaks broken English, and is apparently a Jew, hired a horse and gig of Mr. Fagg, of Cheltenham, for three days, which not being returned at the appointed time, suspicion arose that he has taken the gig off. The horse is about fourteen hands high, of a brown colour intermixed with white, white face, with two white legs behind, and a bay mane. The gig is a green Stanhope, lined drab, mail-coach boxes; the driving-box had some grey cloth at the back of it.—Whoever will give information, so that the offender may be brought to justice, shall receive Five Guineas reward, on application to Mr. H. Fagg, of Cheltenham, aforesaid.

On Thursday night the 7th instant, or early on Friday morning, some person or persons, having a horse and cart, entered a turnip-field belonging to Mr. Taylor, of Broomhall Manor, in the parish of Windlesham, and stole therefrom seven sheep; viz., six Welsh sheep, and one Lincoln ditto.—Twenty Pounds reward. The skins are marked, and would be easily known.

Stolen from the sheds of Mr. James Coleman, at Upper Holloway, in the county of Middlesex, on Tuesday night, or early on Wednesday morning, the 6th instant, a dark brown, strong, useful horse, short tail, aged, having a white blaze on his forehead, fifteen hands high, and two white heels behind, and was some time since marked 'I. C.' on the hoofs, but may not now be visible.

Stolen from a stable of Mr. J. Partridge, of Hunnington, Halse Owen, near Birmingham, on the night of the 29th January, a black waggon gelding, rising four years old, between fifteen and sixteen hands high; a large white star on the forehead, two Wolfs' teeth, one of them is cut, and has a black spot near the gum, the other is only just visible, full black main, long tail, and the near hind leg a little white from the hoof.—Ten pounds reward upon conviction, on application to Mr. Partridge, as above.

Stolen from a stable of Mr. Wyley, High Onn, near Stafford, on the 16th of October last, a very dark brown hackney mare; six years old, fifteen hands high, tan-muzzle, cut tail, two or three white spots on the side; worth about forty pounds. And an old saddle, and double reined bridle. The mare is supposed to have been sold in Smithfield, on Friday the 19th October. Fifty pounds reward upon conviction, on application to Mr. Wyley, or H. Crockett, Esq., Proctor to the Church-Eaton Association for the prosecution of Felons. A reward of five pounds will be given to any person who will give information to whom the said mare was sold.

Stolen, in the night of Monday, the 4th instant, a Bay Mare, the property of Mr. James Butler, of Hawberry Farm, near Erith, Kent, from his stable there. Also a saddle, nearly new; maker's name, 'Snowden, Dartford,' and a bridle and halter. The Mare was aged, and about fifteen hands high; has black legs, one white fetlock behind; a particularly dark mark on her off side, a star to her forehead, a nag tail; has been fired in her off fore leg; has a very small head and ears, and many white hairs in her mane. Whoever will give information which may lead to the conviction of the offender or offenders, shall receive a reward of Ten Pounds, from the Dartford Association for the Protection of Property; and a further reward of Ten Pounds, from the said James Butler.

Stploaen Friday or Saturday night, 2d last, from Horning-ton Court, near Hereford, a Brown Filly, of the Nag kind, rising three years old, nearly fourteen hands high, has a large blaze of white down the face, with white on the hind legs, which reaches, on one leg, above the fetlock joint; a cut tail; was recently broken in and shod.

Whoever will give information of the offender or offender so as to lead to his or their conviction, shall receive Ten Guineas Reward, by applying to Mr. W. Vevers, Dorning-ton Court, near Hereford.

From the filly being very low in condition, and not able to travel many miles, it is likely she may be turned up by the person who stole her. Should that be the case, any person giving information where she may be found, shall be handsomely rewarded for his trouble.

From the premises of Mr. J. Coleman, of Upper Holloway, on Tuesday night, the 5th last, a strong dark-brown Horse, aged, short tail, white blaze on the forehead, both hind heels white, hind's marked J. C.—Twenty Pounds Reward on conviction, from the Smithfield Association.

Stolen from the Rectory Farm, Hayes, Middlesex, late on the night of the 31st of January, or early in the morning of the 1st of February, a black gelding, aged; about fifteen hands three inches and a half high; had, when stolen, a long mane and large bushy tail; the tail has been docked, but the hair was been suffered to grow long. The horse was, when stolen very fat, and had no shoes on his feet.

WAR OFFICE,
A List and Description of

NAME.	CORPS.	PARISH.	COUNTY.	TRADE.	AGE.	SIZE.	PERSON.	HEAD.	FACE.	EYES.	EYEBROWS.	NOSE.	NECK.	HAIR.
John Wragg	84th Foot	Bradfield	York	grinder	20	5 3	stout	prop	oval	grey	light	prop	long	fair
John Bryden	Royal Staff	Glenholm		bellhanger	21	5 10	well m.	common	oval	blue	brown	common	long	brown
Richard Holleman	87th Foot	Rock Hill	Limerick	labourer	21	5 11	stout	long	long	hazel	dk. brown	long	dk. brown
Duggan Pat	84th Foot	Ballyclancers	Limerick	labourer	20	5 9½	stout	large	long	grey	dk. brown	long	brown
Robert Sutherland	92d Highlanders	Dysluchroth	Edinburgh	lather	19	5 5	slender	large	round	grey	fair	short	brown
Richard Nuxan	57th Foot	Kilhelan	Cork	labourer	22	5 6½	stout	large	oval	blue	light		brown
Peter Cossens	45th Foot	Ballylooby	Tipperary	labourer	21	5 7½	stout	small	round	grey	light	long	brown
Robert Parkins(?)	71st Highlanders	Barney Glasgow	Lanark	moulder	27	5 5	stout	common	oval	blue	brown	long	grey
William Kyle	ditto	Eastwood	Renfrew	weaver	20	5 5	stout	common	oval	blue	brown	long	brown
Daniel Sirvin	ditto	Dumbarton	Dumbarton	locksmith	24	5 5	stout	round	round	grey	dk. brown	common	dk. brown
Joseph Pierce	ditto	Bannockbron	Pollon		23	5 7	stout	round	long	black	dark	large	black
George Davrse	60th Rifles	Newington	Montgomery	plumber & glaz.	20	5 5	slender	large	oval	grey	common	long	brown
James Dale	ditto	Stoke Damoral	Devon	labourer	21	5 5½	slight	large	round	grey	light	large	brown
Abraham Chanson	60th Foot	Tiverton	Devon	cooper	22	5 5	stout	round	long	grey	heavy	large	stout
Brice Holyoak	4th Light Drag.	Kilby	Leicester	weaver	23	5 11	stout	large	oval	grey	heavy	prop	brown
Peter M'Naughten	79th Foot	Foetagil	Perth	labourer	19	5 8	stout	prop	oval	hazel	brown	short	dark brown
Peter Coosey	41st Foot	Sladish	Sligo	tailor	22	5 5	stout	round	oval	grey	dark brown	sandy	brown
George Sturges	61st Foot	Macclesfield	Chester	silk weaver	19	5 6	slender	large	oval	grey	dark brown	large	common
Alexander Snodgrass	77th Foot		Donegal	weaver	19	5 5½	slender	prop	round	grey	prop	short	light brown
Patrick Smith	98th Foot	Lurgan	Cavan	weaver	19	5 3	stout	large	broad	grey	fair	common	brown
Thomas Madden	37th Foot	Ballophakana	Tipperary	labourer	20	5 6½	stout	round	long	grey	sandy	common	red
Paul M'Mullen	67th Foot	ditto	Derry	weaver	19	5 4	stout	round	oval	brown	brown	long	brown
James M'Kienou	67th Foot	Sallness		weaver	12	5 8	stout	oval	oval	grey	brown	short	brown
John Dunkinson	68th Foot	Kilrendich	Middlesex	labourer	18	5 2	slender	long	round	grey	brown	long	light brown
Timothy Leary	23d Foot	Kilbritton	Cork	labourer	20	5 9	slender	prop	oval	grey	rather dark	prop	brown
Robert Scott	19th Foot	Rottendale	Lancaster	tailor	21	5 8	stout	large	round	grey	brown	prop	brown
John Grady	1st Foot	Arghlogeen	Galway	carpenter	23	5 7½		prop	oval	grey	brown	prop	brown
William Cameron	1st Foot	Crunekil	Inverness	labourer	19	5 6	slender	prop	oval	grey	brown		brown
Robert Wallace	41st Foot	Newborough	Isle	weaver	26	5 5	stout	prop	oval	grey	dark	common	prop
John Hankins	47th Foot	Barbage	Leicester	knitter	22	5 5½	slender	round	oval	hazel	dark	prop	long
Daniel Reardon	27th Foot	St. Finn Barrs	Cork	labourer	21	5 5	stout	round	oval	grey	brown	common	long
George Townley	88th Foot	Lower Darwin	Lancaster	spindle maker	16	5 3	stout	large	round	grey	fair	common	short
Patrick Griffiths	88th Foot	St. Berry's	Cork		16	5 5	stout	common	oval	grey	sandy	common	short
Charles Todd	49th Foot	St. Andrew's	Fife	painter	20	5 5	stout	round	oval	grey	light	common	prop
George New	1st Dragoons	Gillingham	Dorset	farmer	18	5 4½	stout	prop	round	hazel	light	common	prop
Rowland Long	68th Foot	Yarlow	Carlow	labourer	20	5 5½	stout	round	oval	brown	brown	common	prop
John N. Webb	4th Light Drag.	Dunkfield	Dumbarton	confectioner	20	5 4	stout	round	comely	grey	light	prop	prop
James Carroll	4th Light Drag.	Dunlaw	Galway		21	5 5	slender	prop	round	grey	brown	prop	prop
Francis Nelson	66th Foot	Beresford	Dublin	fowler	21	5 4½	stout	large	round	grey	dark	brown	long
William Johnston	Royal Horse Gds.	Dorchester	Dorset	carpenter	19	5 5½	stout	long	round	hazel	light brown	aquiline	long
Charles Smith	Royal Horse Gds.	All Saints	Derby	musician	17	5 5	good fig	com men	round	hazel	dark	common	long
Thomas Lewis	69th Foot	St. Peter's	Hereford	musician	18	5 9	stout	prop	round	grey	brown	long	long
William Mills	80th Foot	Barfam	Suffolk	labourer	30	5 8	slender	round	round	hazel	dark	prop	short
Michael Avons	87th Foot	Dunmanha	Galway	labourer	19	5 8	slender	long	oval	grey	fair	prop	short
James Wilson [al. Carroll]	5th Foot	All Saints	Galway	labourer	18	5 8	stout		smell	brown	brown	aquiline	long
C.CoaringNamadinaSlater	89th Riflemen	St. Mary's	Dublin	cabinet maker	21	5 6½	stout	large	long	grey	brown	aquiline	short
Martin Burke	Rev. African Col.	Limerick	Limerick	carpenter	24	5 6½	stout	round	round	blue	dk. brown	prop	short
William Croker	42d Foot	Stoke Damoral	Devon	labourer	18	5 5½	stout	common	broad	grey	light	aquiline	short
Thomas Lees	17th Foot	Stoke-upon-Trent	Stafford	miller & brewer	27	5 6½	stout	prop	oval	grey	dark	prop	short
James Rain	35th Foot	Christ-town	Meath	labourer	22	5 7	stout	large	long	grey	dark	long	dark
Michael Sweeney	49th Foot	Drumcree	Westmeath		24	5 5	stout	round	round	hazel	light	short	long
James Tully	12th Foot	Navy	Sligo	labourer	20	5 9½	stout	small	round	hazel	brown	short	brown
William Johnson	66th Foot	Naughton	Suffolk	labourer	20	5 11	stout	common	oval	grey	dark	common	black
James Madding	90th L. Infantry	Wednesill	Cumberland	labourer	21	5 7	common	long	prop	grey	dark	common	auburn
John Fackinbottom	1st Foot	Abbey	Galway	labourer	22	5 8	slender	round	round	blue	brown	long	dk. brown
Walter S. Fenwick	56th Foot	Croft	York		23	5 9	stout	prop	long	grey	dark	prop	light
Robert Grant	24th Foot	Methlick	Aberdeen	labourer	27	5 10	stout	prop	round	grey	light	common	prop
George Powell	50th Foot	Preson	Shropshire	labourer	21	5 8	small	oval	long	grey	fair	common	brown
John Roseph	58th Foot	Donlany	Dublin	stone mason	20	5 11½	stout	prop	oval	grey	brown	aquiline	dk. brown
	SERVICES.												
	Artillery	Carrick	Waterford	saddler	50	5 10	well m.	small	short	grey	heavy	short	long	brown

Whoever will give information of the same, at either the public office, Bow-street, or Hatton-garden, shall, upon conviction of the offender or offenders, receive the above reward.

LARCENY.

On Tuesday morning some person broke into the premises of James Aston, White's-yard, Whitecross-street, a turner, and therein stole a steel collar and iron mandril, with an iron head to it, being the principal parts of a lathe. Information was immediately spread among the pawnbrokers, and, about half past ten, a man was stopped by Mr. Roberts, pawnbroker, Cow-cross, offering to him the stolen articles in pawn; the pawnbroker gave charge of him to a constable, whom he called in for the purpose, from whom the man escaped. His name is Thomas Clarke, formerly living in Ironmonger-row, St. Luke's; he is about twenty-one years of age, five feet seven inches in height, and generally wears a blue coat and white apron, clean and smart in appearance. The property was retained by the pawnbroker.

On Monday night, or early on Tuesday morning, 1 pair of gold earrings, 1 silk handkerchief, 1 cotton handkerchief, with red and white stripes; a leather purse containing 17 or eighteen shillings, and another leather purse containing two-crown halfpenny, were stolen from the vessel Joachim Wohlenberg, lying in the London Docks.

Stolen last night, the premises of Messrs. Reid, Wainwright, and Co. in East Smithfield, were stripped of a quantity of gutter lead.

Information has been received, that in the course of last week two large gun springs, one cased with wrought iron,

and having brass lids; and the other cased with brass, were stolen from the premises of Mr. Hallahan, in Fore-street, Lambeth.

On Tuesday night, or Wednesday morning, from the passage of the house of Mrs. Harris, No. 22, Arundel-street, Strand, a drab great coat with covered buttons, and a grey cloth dressing-gown with waistcoat.

Stolen from the apartment of Margaret Stokes, in Church-street, St. Giles's, on Wednesday, one black bombazine gown, two shifts, several caps and frills, one black silk bonnet, one pair of shoes nearly new, one pair of pattens, two checked aprons, and one pair of white cotton stockings.

Stolen from Mr. James Truscott, a red gold chased seal, set with a yellow stone; a yellow gold plain seal, set with a white cornelian stone; and a yellow gold chased key, set with white cornelian and amethyst stones.

ROBERT COLVILL, a person charged with being concerned with others in a felony, on board the ship Waterloo, lying in the West India Dock, is not yet in custody.

Stolen on Wednesday, from the lower room of the house of Mary Williams, No. 3, Park-street, Lambeth-hole, a white-coloured cloak, and a cotton gown. The above articles were pawned at Mr. Harris's, Commercial-road, by a thin woman, who gave her name, Mary Kale, No. 7, Jamaica-street, Commercial-road. A false address.

MISCELLANEOUS INFORMATIONS

Information has been received, that the real name of GEORGE WHITEHEAD, alias STANTON, advertised in "The Hue and Cry," of the 8th instant, is GEORGE ALMOND; that he is a native of Sheffield, and a very bad

character: in the year 1817 he was tried at Rotherham Sessions for uttering base coin; he was tried and convicted once after that, and imprisoned; he was again tried on the 25th of October, 1820, and transported for seven years, and returned to Sheffield.

On the 9th instant, about 10 at night, two women, one short and stout, about eighteen years old, red cloak, willow bonnet and black ribbons; the other taller, about thirty, light-coloured shawl, Leghorn bonnet, trimmed and lined with pink, and thin face, came to the shop of Ann Cox, of No.0, Phoenix-row, Blackfriars-road, and passed a bad sovereign.

ESCAPED.

Description of Prisoners who escaped from the Gaol of the City of Hereford, on Sunday night, the 10th instant.

JEREMIAH MORGAN, labourer, aged 19, five feet ten inches high, fair complexion, light brown hair, grey eyes; had on a smock frock, a hat, and corduroy small clothes; from Radnorshire; a recruit, and a deserter from the 2d Fusileers.

JAMES PREECE, mason, aged 22, five feet four inches high, dark complexion, dark brown hair, dark eyes; had on a slate coat, dark waistcoat, and fustian trowsers; from St. Owen's, Hereford; committed for an assault.

THOMAS BRACE, painter, aged 30, five feet six inches and a half high, fresh complexion, dark brown hair, hazle eyes; had on a blue coat, trowsers, and waistcoat; from St. Owen's, Hereford; committed for an assault.

JAMES DAVIES, mason, aged 19, five feet five inches and a half high, fair complexion, light brown hair, grey eyes; had on a short smock frock, fustian jacket under, and blue trowsers; from St. Martin's, Hereford; committed for an assault.

[See last page.]

FEBRUARY 15, 1828.
Deserters from His Majesty's Service.

REGIMENT.	ARMS.	HANDS.	LEGS.	FEET.	MOUTH.	MARKS AND REMARKS.	TIME.	PLACE.	COAT.	WAISTCOAT.	TROWSERS.
						has marks of punishment, D on his left side; took reg. nec.	11 Sep. 27	Jamaica	white		blue
						took his regimental great coat, marked D—R. C. No. 40.	19 Jan.	Hythe			regimental
						slightly pock-marked	14 Jan.	Cork		old black	corduroy
						2d foot desertion	10 Jan.	Cork	regimental		blue grey
						stained in white-coat and trowsers, bears mks. of punishment	14 Jan.	Edinburgh	great coat		tartan
						took cab-belt and whole of regimental necessaries	13 Jan.	Castlebar	regimental		blue grey
						a Catholic	12 Jan.	Clonmell	flannel jacket		brown
							12 Nov. 27	Montreal	reg. grt. coat	red jacket	blue grey
							12 Nov.	Montreal	reg. grt. coat	red jacket	blue grey
							12 Nov.	Montreal	reg. grt. coat	red jacket	blue grey
						marks of punishment	14 Jan. 28	Cork	regimental	white	blue grey
						a little stoppage in his gown	14 Jan.	Cork	regimental		regimental
						marks of punishment	14 Jan.	Gosport	regimental		green
						stole a pair of green cloth trowsers, and silver chain	24 Jan. 28	Gosport	regimental		grey
						has served in the Chatham Division of Royal Marines	14 Jan.	Maidstone	undress jac.	flannel	white
						deserted from a recruiting party at Stirling	14 Jan.	Stirling	regimental		tartan
						absconded before attesting; cut off his hair	24 Jan.	Gosport	blue	black	black
						deserted when on guard duty	24 Jan.	Dublin	regimental		blue grey
						2d time desertion; took his regimental necessaries	14 Jan.	Belfast	red		grey
						took side-arms	21 Jan.	Clare Castle	regimental		blue grey
						should have rejoined his regt. from Furlough 23d Dec. 27.	23 Dec. 27	Tipperary	red		blue grey
						should have rejoined his regt. from Furlough 23d Dec. 27.	23 Dec.	Gallowgate	red		blue grey
						should have rejoined his regt. from Furlough, 23d Dec. 27.	23 Dec.	Baltinask, Ayr	regimental		blue grey
						off Furlough	23 Dec.		brown jacket		reg. grey
						a Catholic	23 Jan. 28		white jacket	yellow	white duck
						a recruit who has never been attested	14 Jan.	Leeds	blue	blue	black
						deserted when on Furlough	16 Jan.	Limerick	blue	dark striped	corduroy
						escaped from a party of the 23d on his way to Carlisle	24 Jan.	Strathspey	regimental		regimental
						supposed to be at Trim; took his side-belt	24 Jan.	Langtown	blue	black	black
						supposed to be gone to Galway; took all his necessaries	24 Jan.	Trim, off part	regimental		grey
						off Furlough	24 Jan.	Templemore	regimental		grey
							24 Jan.	Manchester			
							24 Jan.	Portsmouth	white		grey
							24 Jan.	Chatham	regimental		grey
							24 Jan.	Salisbury	Rifles	coloured	blue grey
							24 Jan. 27	Gosport	regimental		corduroy
						bears marks of punishment, and marked with the letter D.	24 Dec. 27	Gosport	regimental		green
							24 Jan. 28	Maidstone	undress	flannel	white
							25 Jan.	Maidstone	undress	flannel	white
						a scar on the inside of the ancle, left foot	23 Jan.	Sunderland	green		grey
						born in the army; supposed to be on board ship in Thames	23 Jan.	Reg. b. London	blue		dark overalls
						born in the army; supposed to be on board ship in Thames	23 Jan.	Reg. b. London	blue		dark overalls
							23 Jan.	Canterbury	white		regimental
						took side-belt and bayonet, marked Pa. No. 53. 55th Regt.	17 Jan.	Portsmouth	red		corduroy
						absconded after having enlisted	24 Jan.	Trim	brown fustian	striped	corduroy
						enlisted head, supposed deserter from the 91st.—A. Watson	13 Jan.	Dublin	regimental		black
						supposed present at a review, and followed Chanson. 2d inst.	30 Jan.	Gosport	regimental		blue
						3d time desertion; sent on board the Maria at Portsmouth	24 Jan.	Devonport	red regulated	linen	blue
						pock-pitted	24 Jan.	Templemore	blue jacket		blue grey
						2d time of desertion; took his necessaries; wore woollen cap	2 Feb.	Gravesend	red reg.jacket		blue grey
						took his great coat and regimental cap—character good	12 Dec. 27	Dublin	reg. coatee	white	white
							28 Jan. 28	Gibraltar	reg. coatee	white reg.	blue grey
						well situated	13 Jan.	Aughnacaugh	regimental		regimental
						thick side-arms	13 Jan.	Carlisle	blue	striped	fustian
						deserted from furlough	13 Jan.	Glasgow	regimental		regimental
						stole the coloured clothes he had on, and a watch	21 Jan.	Newcastle Ty.	regimental		blue grey
						not attested	21 Jan.	Aberdeen	blue dress	light coloured	dark
						hands much cut; supposed to be comp. at new London bridge	21 Jan.	Nottingham	slate		Russia duck
						genteel appearance	25 Jan.	London	blue jacket		cord
							23 Jan.	Clonmell	black	striped	grey

A number of factors contributed to the heightened vulnerability of young people in British cities, and one of the biggest of these was the strain placed on the family. Divorce was not to be available to anyone outside the aristocracy until 1857, but common-law marriages – 'living tally' – increased in number from the end of the eighteenth century, with step-parents becoming more notable in descriptions of the make-up of urban families. Abandoned wives figure large in any data, descriptive or numerical, on the urban poor of these times, and while many women were widowed by the Napoleonic Wars (1799–1815), or saw their husbands rendered unfit for work through injury, some men had found conscription a handy exit from family life. Other men decamped for the cities to find work and never called for their wives and children to join them. Absconding fathers could be arrested and gaoled for one month under the Vagrancy Act for failing to maintain their dependants, and adverts were placed for them in the London publication the *Hue and Cry* (from 1828 renamed the *Police Gazette*), a twice-weekly compendium of recent court hearings, notices of stolen property, escaped prisoners, deserting soldiers, wanted criminals and, from time to time, notices about missing children.

Another destabilising factor for young people was the end of 'living-in' apprenticeships. Traditionally young males who were apprenticed to learn a trade moved in with the 'master's' family, and received board and lodging as well as training. These formal apprenticeships lasted seven years – the years of adolescence/early manhood. The master took over the role of paterfamilias as long as the apprenticeship lasted, and many contracts stipulated that the apprentice was to abstain from drink and fornication. The signing of these 'indentures' was witnessed by a senior figure in the parish, or even by a magistrate. (Their importance in a young man's life is indicated by the fact that John Bishop's own signed indenture had his birth caul attached to it.) In 1814 the Statute of Apprentices was repealed by parliament in a move to free up the labour market and enlarge the pool of semi-skilled workers who could take up jobs without needing highly specialised training. The practice of shorter 'out-apprenticeships' began, which removed the board, lodging and moral supervision elements; when the day's training was over, young men had more time on their hands, unsupervised by either family or master. Some police officers and magistrates claimed this rise in the amount of leisure hours brought greater opportunities for youths to be led into 'juvenile depravity', as it was coming to be termed.

Only about one in eight cases heard at the Old Bailey involved any kind of violence (although this figure is unlikely to reflect the true level of violence – particularly in the home), and, in fact, London was a safer place for the person (though not for property) in the early decades of the nine-teenth century than it had been in the eighteenth. But it didn't seem so. Though the highwaymen and footpads of the Hanoverian age had been largely eradicated, vaguer, less easily located anxieties about urban evil remained. There began to be voiced, from the early 1820s, a suspicion that an organised, systematic layer, or web, of criminality existed that was becoming harder and harder for the authorities to penetrate as the classes began to separate out from each other culturally while at the same time living in ever closer physical proximity. Such matters did not appear to be measurable, quantifiable, governable; and the aspects of city life that were evading the tables and lists began to prey on official minds precisely because of their refusal to be knowable.

What the statistics did show was that around 30,000 babies were born in London each year in the first decades of the nineteenth century; yet the rising ranks of Londoners were not merely the result of the city's birth rate but reflected the phenomenon of urbanisation. In 1801, the year of the first English census, just over one-third of the population lived in rural areas; by 1831, this proportion had dropped to just below one-quarter. In 1801, London's population had passed the one million mark; in 1831, it had risen to 1,646,288, representing almost one-eighth of the population of England and Wales. But people were coming to towns and cities from the country not so much to seek their fortune as to subsist. Internal migra-tion had swelled from a steady stream to a torrent after 1815 – an increase that was, arguably (and many historians have argued about it), acceler-ated by the process of 'enclosure', by which 740,000 acres of farmland were amalgamated into large agricultural estates between 1802 and 1815. Some 5 million acres of common had been enclosed between 1760 and 1810, removing a livelihood from those who made a humble living from grazing on commons and 'waste' land. (These livings were a long-held custom, not a legal right.) The flight to the cities was the only reasonable prospect for the landless, propertyless and unskilled; but it coincided with an economic collapse following the end of the Napoleonic Wars which had demobilised half a million men on to a contracted employment market, sending them home to a land where food prices fluctuated wildly and bread prices were kept artificially high in order to protect the incomes of landowners and owners of large farms.[11] Then, in 1825, came another, sudden, economic depression.

Edward Pelham Brenton, a retired naval captain and philanthropist, noticed the saddest results of the mass migration on the streets of London every day. In addition to setting up refuges for the destitute, Brenton urged the wealthy, in a series of open letters, to remember their traditional, pater-nalistic duties to the poor in this rapacious new age of industrial and agrarian capitalism:

> There are in the streets of this great Metropolis about 15,000 poor boys who gain their bread by lying, cheating, thieving, sweeping the streets and holding gentlemen's horses, and they are all perishing for want of our care. . . . We found them in the streets without food and clothes, or house, or friend, the objects of persecution and punishment, alternately the inmates of workhouses, of prisons, of dark cells, of tread mills, pursuing an uninterrupted course through all the gradations of misery and infamy, to the hulks and the gibbet.[12]

But destitution, like crime, was proving hard to catalogue. London's transient population fell outside the scope of the census, and London's 153 parish vestries were under no obligation to collect such information.[13] The various charities, the police and a number of select committees attempted headcounts that were heavily reliant on anecdotal evidence. The London Society for the Suppression of Mendicity reported that over 40,000 people had come to its office in 1828; Edward Pelham Brenton put the figure for vagrant children in London at 15,000; the Society for Relieving the Houseless Poor admitted more than 6,500 individuals to its three London refuges in the bitter winter of 1830–1 (providing bread, water and clean straw to sleep in), with a total of 55,000 visits recorded. Police and judicial statistics are difficult to interpret, since JPs habitually – either through carelessness or for reasons of humanity – failed to supply the sessions courts with details of convictions for vagrancy, as they were legally obliged.[14] (Vagrancy was an offence that was tried summarily before a JP.) One glimpse of such humanitarian feeling is caught in a report in the *Morning Post* in which Bow Street magistrate Thomas Halls lamented having to gaol twelve vagrant men who had been found asleep in a prison van that was stored at night-time in the vaults under the Adelphi Terrace, between the Strand and the Thames. Halls handed out one-month sentences to the reoffenders among the group, and seven-day sentences to the first-time offenders, saying that he disliked having to imprison men 'without their committing any other crime than that of having no place to go'.[15]

Vagrancy, and child vagrancy in particular, was one of the most urgently discussed topics of the time, both at parish level and in parlia-ment. Select committees convened to discuss the destitute in 1816, 1821 and 1828; there was a lively pamphlet debate about the best way to rescue

street children and train them up for 'useful' lives; a variety of philan-
thropic societies – some harshly disciplinarian, others humane in intention – sprang up, supported by contributions from the wealthy. The
London Society for the Suppression of Mendicity (colloquially known
among the poor as the Dicity) was founded in 1818; the Children's Friend
Society and the Society for the Suppression of Juvenile Vagrancy were
founded in 1830; and the Nightly Shelter for the Houseless opened in
1822, with asylums in Playhouse Yard, off Golden Lane, and in London
Wall. There were specialist charities too, such as the Society for Foreigners
in Distress, the Marine Society for destitute former sailors, and the
National Guardian Society for those who had formerly been employed
as servants. Other bodies named themselves after the specific kind of help
given, and in the East End the Soup Society, the Blanket Association,
even the City of London Truss Society attempted to alleviate the suffering
of the very-poor.

This piecemeal, haphazard charitable giving had two motives:
humanity; and the need to head off the threat of revolution. What had
happened in Paris in 1789 informed much of the activity and behaviour
of the powerful and the wealthy. The year 1831 saw the formation of the
National Union of the Working Classes, a coalition of London working
men, mainly artisans in the furniture-making and weaving trades, who
sought universal male suffrage, the reform of the House of Commons,
and the passing of laws to protect the British working man from exploita-
tion. A number of independent political unions were additionally springing
up all over Britain in manufacturing towns and cities. With the shock news
in October 1831 that the House of Lords had thrown out the second
attempt to pass the Reform Bill, there was nationwide civil unrest, with
three days of rioting in Bristol (the town hall and bishop's palace were
torched) and severe disturbances in Nottingham (the castle was razed),
while in the capital the houses of prominent anti-Reform Bill figures were
stoned. The newspapers of Monday 7 November 1831 carried two major
home-news stories: the discovery of a possible Burke and Hare case in
London; and the suppression of a meeting of a body calling itself the
Eastern Division of the Political Union of the Working Classes of the
Metropolis – described by *The Times* as 'The Mob' – at White Conduit
House, Copenhagen Fields, Islington.[16] This rally, which the union itself
billed as a 'Monster Meeting', had caused so much alarm that the New
Police posted public notices declaring it illegal – many of which were flam-
boyantly torn down by Radical Londoners; however, the union leaders
called off the rally late in the day, their obedience confounding those who
painted them as irrational, bloodthirsty Jacobins.

Meanwhile, in the countryside, protest against the enclosure of farm-land, against low wages, unemployment and the corruption of many rural parochial authorities – in particular, those who administered the Poor Law – had manifested itself in outbreaks of civil unrest. The Captain Swing riots – 1,400 outbreaks of arson, livestock-maiming and damage to farm property – lasted throughout the summer and autumn of 1831, spreading across the whole of southern England, from Kent to Cornwall.[17]

But the labouring classes contained elements within their own ranks that proved the most effective means of maintaining the social status quo. Before the 1824 Vagrancy Act, anyone apprehending a beggar – including a parish constable – had been entitled to a financial reward. One of the most despised figures was the local 'vagrant collector', such as John Conway of Highgate, who turned to the trade when his stay-making business collapsed. Conway was one of the most prolific professional vagrant collec-tors, receiving ten shillings from the parish upon the conviction of every beggar he apprehended and delivered to the magistrates.[18] The new Act abolished these rewards – though many were to remain unaware of this change in the law – but introduced fines of up to £5 for any parish constable who failed to arrest a beggar. The continuing belief that an apprehender of beggars was paid for turning in vagrants meant that there were plenty of dangers in undertaking such an arrest. The London Society for the Suppression of Mendicity had, since 1818, employed a number of plain-clothes officers, recruited from the lower-middle classes, to go into the streets to arrest suspected vagrants and bring them to the Society's offices, at number 13 Red Lion Square, Holborn. (Residents of the square protested at the 'numerous and tumultuous assemblage' that gathered outside the Dicity upon the sudden onset of the very cold winter of 1830–1.)[19] Once there, the vagrant would either be handed over to the authorities (to magistrates for trial on vagrancy charges; or to the appropriate parish for relief under the Poor Law) or supplied with vouchers for cheese, potatoes, rice, bread and soup; or, for a skilled worker, a loan with which to buy the tools of his trade. If you proved up to stone-breaking or oakum-picking when put to the test in the Dicity's yard, you could be admitted to its very own poorhouse, whence around one in seven absconded. In order to qualify for relief, the claimant had to give a full account of his or her life – in effect, had to agree to be surveyed. This type of punitive, snooping activity was loathed by the London poor, and Dicity officers were often attacked as they attempted to make arrests. One day in 1829, several hundred bystanders took the side of 'MD', aged forty-two, an Irish woman who had travelled to London from Macclesfield with her four children, all of whom were visibly feverish. The Dicity had given her financial aid in the past and its officers attempted to arrest her when they spotted her begging once more, but they were prevented from taking her into custody by the crowd that gathered round.[20] (The police faced the same hostility: one autumn evening a number of officers attempted to rescue a senior London magistrate, Allan Laing, who had had to barricade himself into a shop in Lamb's Conduit Street, Holborn, when a crowd attacked him for attempting to make a citizen's arrest on an itinerant match-seller who had asked him 'for a penny or two'. 'Bonnet him! Bring him out!' shouted the crowd, as they freed the beggar from Laing, to loud cheers.)[21]

The Dicity produced annual reports, praising its deeds of the past year and providing a statistical breakdown and anecdotal evidence of the 'Objects' it had processed. The 1830 report gives the following picture of the 671 people detained by Dicity constables: twenty-one claimed to be impoverished because of old age; six cited business failure; four claimed to be foreigners who could not afford their fare home; sixty-four (mainly women) were destitute through loss – by death, desertion or imprisonment – of a husband or close relative; one had lost everything in a fire; one had been shipwrecked; sixty-one had met with an accident or had suffered a serious illness; four had had their pay or pension suspended; two were ex-convicts who could not find anyone to vouch for their good name when seeking employment; seven had no clothes in which they could decently seek work; another seven had no tools with which to carry out their trade; 493 described themselves simply as 'in want of employment'. Of the 671, some 285 had come up to London from the English countryside in search of work; 156 described themselves as native Londoners; 127 were from Ireland; twenty-eight were described as coming 'from Europe' – regions unspecified; twenty-eight were Scottish; ten were Welsh; seven were American; five were West Indian; two were from the East Indies; two were African; and a disproportionate twenty-one were Italian. The London parish most likely to be named as place of abode was St Giles, the rotting slum – in the process of becoming a national embarrassment – just north of Covent Garden. Twice as many impoverished Londoners came from St Giles as from the next two parishes on the list – St Mary's, Whitechapel, and St Andrew's, Holborn.

Since this data appeared in what was essentially a booklet appealing for funds, this attempt at categorisation and quantification may well have impressed those with the ten guineas it cost to become a lifelong governor of the Dicity. After the report's figures come some brief notes on certain of the Dicity Objects of 1830:

'JT', wife, four children, no job, good character, had sold all belongings and was begging;

'WR', 38, a failed Oxford Street linen-draper with debts, friends helped but they were in trouble too, on the streets;

'MD's husband a long-term hospital patient, he had been a manservant, Irish, good character;

'WS', 39, discharged lieutenant and now a failed artist, a wife, four children, starving in an empty garret with not even a bed;

'JG', 39, a Manchester manufactory lad, induced to seek fortune in London, abandoned by his pals, he was returned to his grateful parents in Salford;

a failed umbrella maker, 31, of Liverpool, came to London but he and his wife and two children were begging in Covent Garden, could only get casual shifts at the dock;

'JH', 27, of Birmingham, was found with a placard 'Obligation! Myself, my wife and two children are nearly starving in a land of plenty! My wife wants bread, my children pine and cry, Kind reader, pray a mite impart as you pass by.'[22]

The Dicity was a tantalising mixture of narrow-minded judgementalism punctuated by outbursts of compassion and even sentimentality; in its publications, scepticism about beggars' claims of unemployment does battle with exclamations on how dreadful the state of the labour market has been of late. The Dicity had come into being not to help the poor, but to ensure that as many vagrants as possible were apprehended and prosecuted as the law allowed. In 1830, one-third of vagrancy cases brought before London JPs were the result of arrests made by Dicity constables.[23] The term used in its literature for the activities of its members is 'clearing the streets' – that is, ensuring that public places were free from the sights, sounds and smells of extreme poverty. Removing, or at least hiding, the poor was becoming an increasingly urgent task.

That said, it seems that many vagrants did go to Red Lion Square of their own accord, to seek shelter, food or safety. One such was a twelve-year-old native of Parma, northern Italy, who had been seen around the streets of central London carrying a wax doll in a wooden box. He was in a dreadful physical condition; his skin was covered in scabs, his eyes were infected – probably a result of scurvy – and his face was bruised. In the April of 1834 he went to the Dicity and told its officers that he was too frightened to go back to his lodgings in Vine Street, off Saffron Hill, in Little Italy. He said that he had been beaten by the man he worked for, Alexander Ronchatti, because he had failed to bring back enough money from his begging; Ronchatti also 'employed' two other lads to go out into the street to beg, said the boy. When questioned through an interpreter, Ronchatti denied the boy's story, saying that the child had absconded from his lodgings with the doll, which belonged to Ronchatti. The Dicity officer on duty claimed to have witnessed such a scene before – where an Italian running a troupe of beggar boys had used an interpreter to lie and cover up for him. However, Ronchatti was discharged, after being admonished via the interpreter. The boy was given into the care of the Italian ambassador's staff. Only the doll was arrested – it was impounded by the Dicity, being worth £3.[24]

It was a telling incident. By the 1830s, a separate group of vagrant children had emerged, combining the role of entertainer and outcast and catering for that hunger for spectacle that saw people flock to the flimsiest, makeshift, unlicensed theatrical performance ('penny gaffs') and to horse-drawn caravan shows featuring midgets, bizarre animals, waxworks and people with unusual deformities; even to gawp at the oranges and pineapples and other exotic fruit when their season arrived at Covent Garden market.[25] To a population with little access to books or periodicals, with no access to parks, zoos, galleries or museums –

28.-32. Caravan shows and puppet booths attracted adults as well as children, despite a crackdown on street noise and 'nuisance' in London.

forbidden to them by price and by social exclusivity – Italian boys brought music, pathos, intriguing objects and strange animals, plus, in many cases, their own physical beauty, to some of London's grimmest streets. The imaginative life of the poor was kept from starvation by such humble food.

The economies of the Italian states had been devastated by the Napoleonic Wars, and there was even famine in some northern regions in 1816 and 1817. There was political repression in the disputed regions of Piedmont and Savoy, which bordered France. (Savoy would be ceded to France in 1860; Piedmont to Italy.) Throughout the 1820s there was large-scale migration, with many Italian artisans moving to northern European cities to pursue their trades. In London, Italians were renowned for their skill in manufacturing optical devices – spectacles, telescopes, barometers – musical instruments, puppets and waxworks; they introduced to Britain *fantoccini*, grotesque puppets in elaborate costume, at which grown men were observed to collapse into giggles at performances in booths at street corners.[26] The wax and plaster artists, the *figurinai*, came mainly from Lucca in Tuscany, and settled in Holborn and Covent Garden. While later in the century Italian street children would be known for playing instruments and dancing, until the mid-1830s their principal source of income was exhibiting small animals as well as wax and plaster figures.

There was a good trade in silk or paper flowers to which wax birds were attached; busts of literary and theatrical greats, and military and navy heroes, would be transported on large trays carried on an Image Boy's head, as a walking advertisement for the *figurinaio* who had created them, while an Image Boy's *boîtes à curiosité* included anatomical wax models, notably a copy of a pair of recently still-born Siamese twins who had been sketched and dissected by anatomists. Let the rhymester responsible for 'The Image Boy', in the January 1829 issue of the *New Monthly Magazine*, explain:

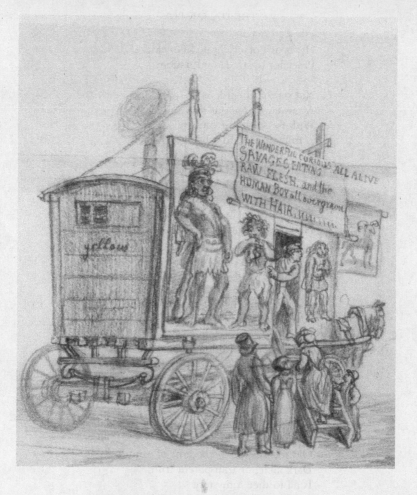

Who'er has trudged, on frequent feet,
From Charing Cross to Ludgate Street,
That haunt of noise and wrangle,
Has seen on journeying through the Strand,
A foreign Image-vendor stand
Near Somerset's quadrangle.

His coal-black eye, his balanced walk,
His sable apron, white with chalk,
His listless meditation,
His curly locks, his sallow cheeks,

His board of celebrated Greeks,
Proclaim his trade and nation.

Not on that board, as erst, are seen
A tawdry troop; our gracious Queen
With tresses like a carrot,
A milk-maid with a pea-green pail,
A poodle with a golden tail,
John Wesley, and a parrot.

No, far more classic is his stock;
With ducal Arthur, Milton, Locke,
He bears, unconscious roamer,
Alcmena's Jove-begotten Son,
Cold Abelard's too tepid Nun,
And pass-supported Homer . . .

Poor vagrant child of want and toil!
The sun that warms thy native soil
Has ripen'd not thy knowledge;
'Tis obvious, from that vacant air,
Though Padua gave thee birth, thou ne'er
Didst graduate in her College.

'Tis true thou nam'st thy motley freight;
But from what source their birth they date,
Mythology or history,
Old records, or the dreams of youth,
Dark fable, or transparent truth,
Is all to thee a mystery.

But it wasn't all poets and philosophers. Exhibiting portable creatures that were highly unusual to London eyes could prove lucrative too, and one Italian boy, 'PG', arrested by the Dicity in 1826 while entertaining a passer-by with his dancing monkey, was found to be carrying £21 7s 6d.[27] Beasts for display included white mice, guinea pigs, monkeys (uniformed or 'naked'), tortoises, porcupines – even a marmot, a groundhog native to the mountains of the Savoy region. The objects and creatures were rented out to the boys each morning by the men who ran the trade, at these daily rates:

Box of wax Siamese twins	2s
Organ with waltzing figures	3s 6d
Porcupine	2s 6d
Organ	1s 6d
Organ plus porcupine	4s
Monkey in a uniform	3s
Monkey without uniform	2s
Box of white mice	1s 6d
Tortoise	1s 6d
Monkey on a dog's back	3s
Four dancing dogs, in costume, with pipe and tabor	5s.[28]

It was said that one happy outcome of the 1824 Vagrancy Act was a reduction in the practice of beggars waving their deformities in the face of the public; what had arisen in place of this was an appeal to sympathy – with plaintive looks and an air of patient submission becoming more prevalent among those with a regular pitch. Italian boys were indeed pitiful – victims of organised child-trafficking by their fellow countrymen. The so-called *padroni* ('masters', 'owners' or 'employers'; another name for them

33. Many Italian immigrants made a living as itinerant musicians.

was *proveditori*, 'providers') paid a sum of money to impoverished peasants in rural, mainly northern, Italy in return for the services of their son – a sort of beggars' apprenticeship.[29] The parents were told that their child was being taken abroad to learn a trick or skill, usually theatrical in nature, that would earn him a living. The parents' (dialect) term for their son's fate was *È peo mondo co a commedia*, which translated as 'He is wandering the world with a theatrical troupe'; in reality, once the child had been walked through France to England, he would find himself a virtual slave to his *padrone*.

The Italian Boy trade stretched across Britain: Bristol, Birmingham, Liverpool, Manchester, Sheffield, Bradford, Glasgow, Brighton and Worthing were all home to *padroni*. In London, whole houses in the Holborn area – in Saffron Hill, Vine Street, Eyre Street, Greville Street, Bleeding Heart Yard – as well as the streets around the southern end of Drury Lane were taken over by *padroni*, and boys were packed into dormitories, for which they were charged 4*d* a night. The animals belonged to the *padroni*, often acting as syndicates who owned *una zampa per uno* – 'a paw apiece'. The boys, who often learned little English during their stay, were instructed to tell anyone who asked that the *padrone* was their uncle or much older brother, and to provide false names for themselves and the *padrone*. Procuring a child to solicit alms was a breach of the Vagrancy Act, but little action appears to have been taken against the *padroni* until certain notorious assaults and deaths later in the century.[30]

Londoners appear to have felt sentimental about Italian Boys/Image Boys/White Mice Boys, with their dark imploring eyes, sweet, melancholy expressions and picturesque destitution. In a curious little case of 1834, Lord Dudley Coutts Stuart, Whig member of parliament and 'champion of the oppressed' (according to his obituarists), announced that he would personally request the Home Secretary to secure the release of two Italian boys committed to a fortnight in prison by JPs White and Burrell at the Queen Square magistrates' office, Holborn. Metropolitan Police constables Simpson and Brockway of B division (Westminster) had arrested Antonio Loniski and Barnard Malvarham, both aged about fourteen, for begging in Wilton Street, Pimlico, at three o'clock in the afternoon of Easter Monday; one boy had a monkey, the other a cage of white mice. The magistrates had gaoled them for committing an offence under the Vagrancy Act, and the court had sold off the animals in order to help pay the boys' prison costs. On hearing this, Stuart went straight to the Queen Square justices to explain that the boys had been two of a party of nine Italian entertainers invited by him to an Easter feast at his London home, and that they had simply been waiting outside his house for the door to be answered. Stuart's footman had told the constables this, he said, but they had still taken the boys into custody.[31] It is possible that Loniski and Malvarham were arrested, while the other seven Italians were not, because they were not playing instruments; if playing could be defined as 'skilful', the Vagrancy Act did not apply – or rather, it might have made a police officer unsure of his grounds for arrest. Displaying animals involved very little skill and left the child more vulnerable to arrest, which may be why from the 1840s it was more common for Italian street children to play music and dance for money than exhibit animals. 'If they are considered vagrants, they are the most inoffensive and amusing vagrants,' declared journalist Charles MacFarlane of Italian boys. 'No offences or crimes are committed, despite their poverty and youth.' In any case, MacFarlane added, such entertainments were probably good for the lower orders, being instructive and educational: 'They propagate a taste for the fine arts . . . and [their] animals may awaken an interest in natural history.' Fellow journalist Charles Knight quite agreed, writing in 1841,

> We have some fears that the immigration of Italian boys is declining. We do not see the monkey and the white mice so often as we could wish to do. . . . What if he be but the commonest of monkeys? Is he not amusing? Does he not come with a new idea into our crowded thoroughfares, of distant lands where all is not labour and traffic? These Italian boys, with their olive cheeks and white teeth – they are something different from your true London boy of the streets, with his mingled look of cunning and insolence.[32]

All in all, Italy was providing London with a better class of vagrant. The pathos an Italian boy evoked could earn his master six or seven shillings a day. Dead – and apparently murdered to supply the surgeons – his appeal only seemed to increase.

FIVE

Systematic Slaughter

At daybreak on Saturday 19 November, the body of the dead boy was exhumed. He had been buried (described in the register of burials as A Boy Unknown) on the 11th in the graveyard of St Pancras workhouse in Cleveland Street, off Tottenham Court Road; this was the overspill burial ground for St Paul's, Covent Garden, and was where the less well-off of the parish were destined.[1] (Later, there would be criticism that the Subject of an ongoing criminal case had been buried so swiftly, the *Lancet* pointing out the decision as one more example of the incompetence of coroners.) Augustine Brun, an elderly Birmingham-based *padrone*, had been named by Joseph Paragalli as the dead boy's master, and a messenger had been sent to that town to bring him to London to view the corpse. Paragalli acted as Brun's interpreter to the magistrate.

Brun revealed that he had brought a boy called Carlo Ferrari to England from northern Italy in the late autumn of 1829; though from Piedmont, Carlo was a Savoyard, said Brun. His father, Joseph, had signed Carlo over to Brun for a fee. Brun had had charge of the boy for his first nine months in England, though Carlo had lodged at the house of another man, called Elliott, at number 2 Charles Street – the southern continuation of Bow Street itself (today it is Wellington Street).

In the summer of 1830, Brun had bound Carlo over to a new master, an Italian called Charles Henoge who played the hurdy-gurdy and exhibited monkeys, for a period of two years and one month, and, as far as Brun knew, the new master had taken Carlo to Bristol. Carlo would now be about fifteen years old, Brun believed. (The *Globe and Traveller* newspaper report has Brun additionally claiming, 'The poor boy ran away from his master about a year ago,' and that Carlo made sure that he left London whenever this particular *padrone* – presumably Henoge, though the newspaper does not make this clear – was rumoured to be coming to the capital.)[2]

As soon as the coffin lid came off at the St Pancras workhouse, Brun was reported to have exclaimed, '*Mon pauvre garçon, pauvre Carlo, mon pauvre*

34. One sketch artist's concept of Carlo Ferrari, named as the victim two weeks after the discovery of the corpse.

garçon.' This seems odd: if Brun had spoken French, Paragalli would not have been the only person who could have acted as his interpreter. Even odder was Brun's statement to the magistrate that he had been unable to identify the dead boy because of the extent to which the body had decomposed. The child was now green, and the facial features were disfigured; the attentions of the surgeons at the post-mortem had not helped matters either. Brun told the court he believed the hair colour and stature of the dead boy were similar to Carlo's. He added that Carlo had been a well-known figure in the squares of the West End of London, and that his customary phrase – in French, though he was 'an Italian boy' – was, '*Donnez un louis, signor.*' (Short for *un louis d'or*, a gold coin with a value of 20 francs. Presumably the word was used figuratively – 20 francs was a steep price to pay to look at white mice.) Superintendent Joseph Sadler Thomas now revealed that the corpse had a number of warts on its left hand, and he asked Brun whether Carlo Ferrari had had such blemishes. Brun replied that the hand had been too green for him to tell if there were any warts on it. This was not the question he had been asked.

Vestry clerk James Corder, however, was quite satisfied with Brun's evidence, telling the magistrates' court that it was clear to him that Brun had identified the boy as his former charge, Carlo Ferrari, since Brun had been unable to stop crying since viewing the corpse – itself a rather extraordinary claim. Corder added that Margaret King had also been taken to see the exhumed corpse – a pointlessly distressing exercise, since King had admitted that she had not seen the face of the boy who had been in Nova Scotia Gardens; King, sure enough, was unable to identify the dead boy.

Next, Joseph Paragalli explained that he was now able to recall that a boy called Carlo Ferrari had been living at 2 Charles Street eighteen months earlier. He stated that when he had first seen the body, he had thought that it was Carlo, whom he had last seen alive standing outside the County Fire Office in the Regent Street Quadrant in early October. On that day it had been raining hard, and the child looked cold and unhappy. Paragalli said that he had not noticed what the boy was wearing but he had seen that his mice were kept in a box that was divided into two; one half was a cage with a wheel for the mice to run round in; the other half was wooden and enclosed, and this was where the animals slept. Paragalli said he often visited Elliott's house in Charles Street and had seen Carlo there on a number

35. The Quadrant at the southern end of Regent Street, under construction in 1813; the County Fire Office is to the far right in the picture.

of occasions, and was even present when Brun had bound Carlo over to Charles Henoge. One week before seeing him in the Quadrant, Paragalli had, he claimed, spoken to Carlo in Portland Place, just north of Oxford Circus.

Proceedings in the magistrates' court were about to finish for the day when Superintendent Thomas stepped forward and asked if he could – in his capacity as a public officer – make a further charge against Bishop and Williams only. May and Shields having been escorted from the dock, Thomas charged Bishop and Williams with 'the murder of another boy, whose name for the present is unknown'. He believed much more evidence on this second case would come to light before long. Minshull told Thomas that he had acted very properly in bringing this new charge. The case could not be in better hands, said the magistrate, deeply impressed.

On Superintendent Thomas's orders, Sarah Bishop and Rhoda Head had been taken into custody. Acting on 'information received', Thomas had brought them before Minshull and they were charged with being accessories after the fact of murder. Thomas told Minshull that he expected in the near future to be able to produce evidence that proved the women had known about the killing of the Italian Boy. There was no suspicion that they had taken an active role, but Thomas was convinced that anyone living in a house as small as 3 Nova Scotia Gardens must have been aware of everything that had gone on there.

Sarah and Rhoda had been arrested by Constable Higgins at the Fortune of War at four o'clock in the afternoon. Higgins went with them to Nova Scotia Gardens, accepting that Sarah had to make provision for her children – two boys, aged twelve and seven, and a two-year-old girl. While there, Higgins searched the cottage and took away with him what he believed to be significant objects: two chisel-like iron implements, each with one end bent into a hook; a brad awl with dried blood on it; a thick metal file, and a rope tied into a noose.

Later, before the magistrate, Richard Partridge examined these tools and gave his opinion that one of the bent chisels could have been used to inflict the wound on the dead boy's forehead; that the heavy file could have dealt the blow to the back of the neck. Partridge told Minshull that he and George Beaman were certain that death had been caused by a blow to the back of the neck, repeating their evidence to the coroner's court. The two surgeons differed, said Partridge, in only one respect: Beaman believed death had been caused by blood entering the spinal column as a result of the blow, while Partridge thought death had occurred as a result of concussion of the spinal marrow. George Douchez, another local surgeon who had also been present at the post-mortem, was called and gave his opinion that the boy had been stunned by a blow to the head, and then killed by having his neck wrung 'like a duck's'. At this, a thrill of horror – gasps and murmurs – ran around the shabby Bow Street court room.

Forensic medicine was a young discipline. While celebrated surgeon and anatomist William Hunter had written his *Signs of Murder* treatise in 1783, the first coroners' guides were not published until thirty-five years later.

'Blood never coagulates after death,' announced Partridge, in reply to a query about whether the injury to the back of the neck would have had the same appearance if it had been inflicted after death.

'Could the deceased have committed suicide?' wondered Minshull.

'It is just barely possible that a person might inflict a blow on the back of his own neck which would cause death,' replied Partridge. 'It is, however, exceedingly improbable and almost impossible.'

And Beaman added, 'There was nothing to show that he died of indigestion.'

As for the blood-clotted brad awl, James May didn't wait for the medical men's opinion, calling out to the magistrates, 'I took the teeth out with that.'

In fact, all the implements found at Number 3 were the paraphernalia used to haul bodies up out of the grave. A resurrection man's work required a wooden spade – wood making less noise than metal – to dig down to the head of the coffin; two large iron hooks attached to ropes were inserted under the lid of the coffin to snap it off, and the corpse was then pulled up through the hole in the lid.[3] (It was not unlike fishing – which is the term Dickens's fictional bodysnatcher Jerry Cruncher uses to describe his work in *A Tale of Two Cities*.) These were the very objects likely to be found in the home of a bodysnatcher, and Constable Higgins recognised them as such. (Higgins had challenged Sarah about the tools in the cottage, saying, 'I know what these are for.' 'I dare say you do,' she replied, 'but do not speak before the children.' She then claimed that the brad awl was used by Bishop for mending shoes.) But Partridge and Beaman did not appear to realise the implements' functions, and decided that the collection had a more sinister purpose.

Higgins had also found that Sarah was in possession of a document that read:

The humble petition of John Bishop, and three others, most humbly showeth that your petitioners have supplied many Subjects on various occasions to the several hospitals, and being now in custody, they are conscious in their own minds that they have done nothing more than they have been in the constant habit of doing as resurrectionists, but being unable to prove their innocence without professional assistance, they humbly crave the commiseration of gentlemen who may feel inclined to give some trifling assistance in order to afford them the opportunity of clearing away the imputation alleged against them. The most trifling sum will be gratefully acknowledged, and your petitioners, as in duty bound, will ever pray . . .

It was unsigned.

Petitions such as these were also part of a resurrectionist's kit. They were a reasonably gentle form of blackmail, letting the surgeon(s) know that it might be in the interest of the good name of the medical profession to stump up bail money; to arrange and pay for the advice of an attorney; or perhaps – using connections, nods, winks – to get the misdemeanour charges dropped altogether. At worst, the resurrection man's family could be given financial help until the breadwinner was out of gaol. (Surgeon Sir Astley Cooper, created a baronet in 1821 after removing a tumour from George IV's scalp, spent hundreds of pounds in this way. His personal accounts for 1818 show that he paid £14 7s as bail for one of his main suppliers – a man called Vaughan; 6s to Vaughan's wife; and £13 on 'gaol comforts' – food, drink and tobacco – for Vaughan when he was imprisoned.)[4] It is likely that Sarah and Rhoda were in the process of applying to the various surgeons supplied by Bishop for assistance of this kind when they were arrested at the Fortune of War.

At Bow Street, Minshull advised Sarah that she was not legally obliged to say anything, but Sarah said that she was eager to defend herself. 'I have nothing to fear, sir,' she said to Minshull, 'for I have done nothing wrong.' She told Minshull that although she knew her husband had been a resurrectionist for several years, and she had visited him in prison on a number of occasions, she had no knowledge of the crime of which he was now suspected. She pointed out that she had always worked in her own right, for her own money, supplementing whatever cash Bishop brought home with the income she received from doing needlework and taking in washing. She said that Thomas Williams 'had only been out three times' with her husband and that he was a 'very respectably connected' person. She admitted that she knew her husband had been out at work the night before he was arrested because he had washed his hands in a basin, leaving a great deal of mud or clay in the bottom of it.

Rhoda also said that she knew nothing of any murder, and that while she was aware that her husband of seven weeks had been assisting Bishop with resurrection work, he was in fact a bricklayer by training, had also been a carpenter and had worked in the glass trade, too. (Rhoda referred to Bishop as 'my father'; he was, in fact, her half-brother and stepfather.)

Minshull remanded the women into custody while the case against them was investigated, and he issued an order for the Bishop children to be placed in the Bethnal Green workhouse for the time being. It was quite likely, said Superintendent Thomas, that they might say something that would incriminate their parents. A parish officer of St Matthew's, Bethnal Green, needed John Bishop to swear to his place of settlement, in order that his children could be signed over to the care of the parish. (Although Nova Scotia Gardens was very close to St Leonard's, Shoreditch, it was just north of the St Leonard parish boundary.) Bishop signed the necessary papers, 'with a very firm hand',[5] and, in an apparently sarcasm-free act of courtesy, thanked Superintendent Thomas for having made the arrangements for his family.

On the same day that the boy-corpse was disinterred – a full two weeks after the arrest of Bishop, Williams, May and Shields – men from F Division undertook a thorough examination of 3 Nova Scotia Gardens, 'it having been intimated to Mr Minshull that it would be advisable that the premises should be strictly searched,' as *The Times* put it.[6] Today, this delay would be unthinkable; in 1831, a detailed search of the home of a murder suspect, except to recover any stolen goods, was not an obvious move. But somebody in the neighbourhood had already told Thomas that before her arrest, one of the Bishop women had been seen scattering ashes in the garden – had they been burning incriminating items?

Thomas, along with Constable Higgins, labourer and gardener James Waddy, James Corder, William Cribb (the coroner's jury foreman, and with no obvious official interest in the case) and a number of F Division officers went to the deserted cottage at noon on Saturday 19 November. Thomas was very interested in that long back garden. He noticed that a pathway running its entire length, from the house to the privy, looked uneven, and in places the soil appeared to be loose; there was indeed a thin layer of ashes on the surface at one spot. Bishop's eldest son stood by during the digging, and it is possible that Thomas had asked for him to be present in the hope that the lad might let slip some damning piece of information. Indeed, as Higgins started to prod the earth near the path with an iron bar, the boy told him to take care, since there was a cesspool lying immediately beneath. This warning made Thomas suspicious, and he told Higgins to explore exactly that spot. Here, five yards from the

Bishops' back door, and one yard from the palings, Higgins's bar came up against a spongy substance. Waddy dug, and about a foot down unearthed a child's jacket, trousers and shirt. The jacket was of good-quality blue cloth with two rows of covered buttons and expertly sewn buttonholes; some gilt buttons on the jacket had a star motif at their centre. The black trousers looked as though they had been removed with force, since the buttonholes that connected them to their yellow calico braces were torn. A yard away, Waddy and Higgins dug up another set of clothes – a shabby blue coat of an unusual cut (later described in court as being like the sort of coat worn by charity-school boys) with white buttons; a pair of coarse grey trousers with patched knees; an old shirt that was ripped down the middle, and a striped waistcoat that had bloodstains on the collar and shoulder, and in its pocket, a small piece of comb. The outfit would have fitted a youth; the waistcoat had once been an adult's but had been cut down and re-stitched to fit a boy. Thomas noted that this had been done in a slipshod way, using cheap, coarse yarn. When the waistcoat was shown to Minshull, the magistrate pointed out that it could prove significant that the waistcoat had been taken in, since it might bring forward the man to whom it had originally belonged.

The floor of the coal-hole of Number 3 was dug up and nothing was discovered. But in the privy at the bottom of the garden, Thomas found a human scalp with long matted brown hair attached; down among the faeces, the officers worked to disentangle chunks of human flesh. Thomas and his men – and, later, the magistrate – assumed that this find was evidence of Bishop and Williams's resurrection work; there was a good trade in body parts if the entire corpse were not fresh, and the scalp had probably been removed for the sale of the hair to a wig-maker, and discarded once it was known that the house might be searched.

At four o'clock in the afternoon, with the garden dug to a depth of one foot and the privy thoroughly probed, the men went home. Two days later, Thomas returned and searched the inside of the house once more. The downstairs room (the parlour) contained scarcely any furniture – there was a fireplace and the remains of a small, rickety cupboard. In one corner lay a heap of old, soiled clothes, many of them children's. Sarah Bishop worked as a washerwoman, taking in washing for locals; but the women-folk of resurrectionists were known to make money by selling the clothing from pauper bodies stolen from mortuaries, hospitals or workhouses. Superintendent Thomas was particularly interested in a brown, furry cap – the colour of dark fox-fur – which was lying near the top of the heap; on his first visit to the cottage he had seen it hanging up on a nail in the parlour and had taken little notice of it, but now it intrigued. He took it to show Margaret King and her family in Crabtree Row, and then to Covent Garden to see what Joseph Paragalli made of it. The Italian told Thomas that Carlo Ferrari had worn a cap very like it when he first came to London, though he added that Carlo's cap had been larger, and that this one looked as though it had been taken in. Paragalli said that the fur crown of the cap was English, but that its green visor had been made in France.

Thomas seems to have found it hard to keep away from Nova Scotia Gardens. Number 3 was now officially in police hands, and the superintendent continued to scour it for anything that would forge links in the story he was piecing together. He had told Minshull that he found the Gardens 'remarkable'; that there was not a street lamp within a quarter of a mile of the place; and that he considered Number 3 itself to be 'in a ruinous condition', with its garden being little more than wasteground.[7] Thomas pointed out to Minshull that Bishop and Williams had access to around thirty other gardens, since they had only to step over palings to

36. Police officers begin their search of Nova Scotia Gardens, in this curiously compressed version of Bishop and Williams's cottages.

Dean & Munday Litho^{rs} Threadneedle S^t

reach the privies and grounds of their neighbours. Searching these would not be a problem, he said, since people were moving out swiftly, in horror and shame at the new notoriety of the Gardens. Minshull was pleased with the trophies the superintendent was bringing into his office from the East End and was agog to hear of his daily progress.

On Tuesday 22 November, Thomas decided to take a look at 2 Nova Scotia Gardens. It had lain empty after Williams went to live with the Bishops in the last week of September until William Woodcock, a brass-worker, his wife Hannah and their twelve-year-old son, also called William, moved in on 17 October. Thomas found nothing of significance in the house, but from the bottom of Woodcock's privy he retrieved a bundle: unwrapped, it comprised a woman's black cloak which fastened to one side with black ribbon, a plaid dress that had been patched in places with printed cotton, a chemise, an old, ragged flannel petticoat, a pair of stays that had been patched with striped 'jean' (a heavy, twilled cotton) and a pair of black worsted stockings, all of which appeared to have been violently torn or cut from their wearer. There was also a muslin hand-kerchief, a red pin-cushion, a blue 'pocket' (a poor woman's equivalent of a purse, or small, everyday bag) and a pair of women's black, high-heeled, twilled-silk shoes. The dress and chemise had been ripped up the front, as had the petticoat, which also had two large patches of blood on it. The stays had been cut off in a zig-zag manner.

Thomas then decided to search the well in Bishop's garden; it was covered over by planks of wood, on to which someone had scattered a pile of grass cuttings. From the bottom of the well he fished out a bundle that proved to be a shawl wrapped around a large stone.

During Thomas's enquiries at the anatomical schools of London he had been told by Guy's Hospital that two bodies – one of them a young female – had been bought from Bishop in the first week of November; St Bartholomew's had told him that Bishop had offered them a boy and a woman within the month before his arrest; and John Appleton – the porter at Grainger's school in Webb Street – had told him that a tall, thin, middle-aged woman had been sold to them by Bishop early in October. Several women had lately been reported missing in Bethnal Green and Shoreditch; two sets of worried relatives had already contacted Thomas. A number of local children had not been seen for months. It was dawning on the superintendent that what had been going on at Nova Scotia Gardens was not the processing of disinterred corpses into saleable Subjects, but systematic slaughter.

SIX

Houseless Wretches Again

Urban poverty, so often a disgusting and harrowing sight to the respectable, could also be a source of wonder and intrigue. A beggar with a certain look, or air, or 'act', could feed on city-dwellers' craving for novelty and display. Certain street people, moving around wealthy West End districts and the poorer locales, began to take on the status of peripatetic performers, with all the slightly unreal aura of a renowned theatrical or operatic artiste, standing out in the torrent of rush and hurry, seeping into urban popular consciousness. You rarely find them in the newspaper columns or police reports of the day; they have survived in the reminiscences of those who thought to note them down before their image faded for ever. They are described as though they were apparitions: they seem to haunt, rather than inhabit, the city, and their connections to their environment are mysterious and seemingly unfathomable. One such phantasmagoric creature was Samuel Horsey, who trundled about in a wooden cart cum sledge, and was a common sight around Charing Cross. His story was that the celebrated surgeon John Abernethy had removed both his legs at St Bartholomew's; he frequently terrified horses by rolling into their eyeline and would berate them loudly when they whinnied or reared in fear; he would erupt into pubs and gin-shops by bashing his vehicle at the doors until they burst open and he sailed in. Black Joe Johnson was a West Indian who wore a model of Nelson's ship *Victory* built on to his hat and would come up to ground-floor windows and move his head so that the ship appeared to be sailing along the sill as he sang a sea shanty. The Dancing Doll Man of Lucca played drum and flute as puppets danced upon a board in front of him, worked by strings attached to his knee (in fact, there appear to have been at least ten Dancing Doll Men of Lucca in London at the same time). Possibly in imitation of such Continental *élan*, blind Charles Wood exhibited a poodle, the Real, Learned, French Dog, Bob, who wore a frock coat and danced to the organ played by Wood ('Look about Bob, be sharp, see what you're about').[1] Tim Buc Too was

37.–40. Black Joe Johnson; Charles Wood and his Learned French Dog, Bob; an aged 'sledge beggar'; and The Dancing Doll Man of Lucca, all sketched by J.T. Smith for his compendia of street people, *Etchings of Remarkable Beggars* (1815) and *Vagabondiana* (1817).

SAMUEL HORSEY.

41. Samuel Horsey was one of London's most famous sledge beggars.

an old African street-crossing sweeper whose patch was at Ludgate Hill/Fleet Street; he arranged his profuse white hair so it looked as though he was wearing a pith helmet. In Camden Town, 'TL', a fifty-four-year-old former servant unable to find work, exhibited in the street his own scale model of Brunel's Thames Tunnel – the 'Great Bore' that was taking years longer than anticipated to complete.[2]

There was a sense that these people were unlikely to survive much longer in the type of city that London was becoming, and in the kind of society that was coming into being. For journalist Charles Knight, the fear was that the street sights were being 'shouldered out by commerce and luxury'. Writing in 1841, seventeen years after the passing of the Vagrancy Act, twelve years after the arrival of the Metropolitan Police, and seven years after the implementation of the infamous New Poor Law, Knight regretted that girls carrying pails of milk, fresh herbs and water-cress from the country were less often to be seen selling their goods in the streets. It is, he wrote, a quieter, duller London, now that the muffin man cannot scream out his wares, no bugle can be sounded to announce news and

42. George Cruikshank sketched one of the city's many rival dancing doll men, in 1835.

events, and 'chaunters' cannot sing the first few lines of a broadsheet to tempt a passer-by. The itinerant traders were being seen off as much by competition from fixed-location shopkeepers as by legal prohibitions on noise and nuisance; the introduction of plate-glass, gas lighting and the proliferation of cheaper, more diverse and increasingly exotic goods in shops and bazaars were rendering the pedlar obsolete. So perhaps it is unsurprising that attempts were made to capture in pictures and words some of the grotesques who wandered the town. J.T. Smith, keeper of the prints at the British Museum, compiled *Etchings of Remarkable Beggars* in 1815, and *Vagabondiana* in 1817 – compendia of destitute people. Smith's later work, *The Cries of London*, recorded the chants and ditties of dead, or soon sure to be dead, trades. Anatony Antonini was sketched in 1819 with a huge tray of silk and paper flowers ('All in full bloom!') with plaster birds attached to them; William Conway was an itinerant spoon-seller of Crabtree Row, Bethnal Green ('Hard-metal spoons to sell or mend') who once rescued Smith when he was surrounded and threatened by a crowd while sketching another beggar – the locals had thought Smith was an authority figure, sent to snoop on them. George Smith was a rheumatic

43.-45. Like J.T. Smith, George Scharf captured many of London's street characters throughout the 1820s and 1830s, including 'Walking Advertisements' and (*overleaf*) itinerant vendors of many nationalities – an Italian 'image boy' is second from left.

brush-maker, reduced to peddling groundsel and chickweed; Jeremiah Davies, a Welsh weightlifting dwarf, performed his tricks around Chancery Lane. Ekeing a living from the bizarrest of trades – that was typical of the city, where people subsisted on a seemingly infinite subdivision of labour; associated trades spun out of associated trades.

But 'the high and rushing tide of greasy citizenry', according to Knight, needed the colour and spectacle that the poor, the idle and even the impostor brought to city streets.[3] The architectural splendours of London were many; but most streets were notable for their monotony and dreariness (a look that the Victorians were to delight in defacing with large, florid buildings from the 1860s onwards). Away from the brilliance of the lighted streets, deep gloom pervaded: Joseph Sadler Thomas complained that after sundown, Covent Garden market was hard to penetrate and police effectively since there was just one, centrally placed lamp. He could hardly see his hand in front of his face, he said: 'I act in the dark.'[4] Ornamentation had been severely limited by the 1774 Building Act – which imposed higher standards of house construction and fire-proofing at the expense of architectural variety – and aside from the occasional flourish of stucco and Portland stone, street after street comprised brick buildings that were blackened by smoke and filth; some had even been painted black – a Georgian fancy. Houses were rarely higher than three storeys, and in many areas by the 1830s the products of the eighteenth-century building boom were proving unable to cope with the sheer numbers of people cramming into them. The squalid frowsiness of many parts of east and central London was well-known ('foetid localities . . . infected districts', proclaimed a furious Sydney Smirke, architect);[5] but the Georgian terraces of the wealthy West End were also seen as dismal regions – dark, featureless, cheerless canyons of blank brick wall.

However, against this backdrop, the tide of greasy citizenry itself could also provide a spectacle to the onlooker – a cavalcade of images not unlike the panoramas, dioramas, cosmoramas and georamas that were enjoying such popularity in new, purpose-built venues. The flickering glare of gaslight (by 1823, 215 miles of London street had been lit) brought a theatrical quality to many central streets, an effect enhanced by the presence of music (players strolled the streets of the West End, and one Italian band seems to have taken up a regular pitch in Portland Place, just north of Oxford Circus). This stage-like quality could render the crowd even stranger than it already looked. For writer Thomas De Quincey, Londoners passing along the street looked like 'a masque of maniacs, a pageant of phantoms'; in a short story, Edgar Allan Poe described the heady fascination of watching London's 'tumultuous sea of human heads' rolling by as the hero attempts to sort them into 'types'; while in 1837, a doctor writing about the effect of the city on human health described Londoners walking along the street as appearing to be constantly hurried and distracted; pallid, shattered, sallow-complexioned and 'paralytic of limb' – the crowd seemed to move like puppets or automata, ceasing to be fully human, moving to some unseen mechanical force.[6]

Who had the right to be in these streets? Who was entitled to space in the city? The well-signalled, much-discussed changes to the poor laws brought anticipation that all paupers – and thus, beggars – were to be contained behind the high walls of grim new workhouses; there was anxiety that those who were unable to give a good account of themselves would be liable to imprisonment; a further crackdown was heralded in 1839 with an act of parliament that gave the Metropolitan Police even greater powers to suppress noise and 'nuisance' created by street-sellers and the more enterprising beggars.[7]

A huge unknowable – a subject that greatly perplexed those who looked into the question of vagrancy – was the proportion of beggars who were frauds; even a central London magistrate of long standing admitted that he could rarely distinguish someone who was genuinely out of work and hungry from someone quite capable of making a living but who habitually played on public sympathy.[8] Fashion was an increasingly unreliable witness: Continental visitors noted that the English tended to wear clothes that did not necessarily reflect their class, and, from the start of the nineteenth century, the English working classes had reportedly shown a new interest in self-adornment.[9] There was a vast trade in second-hand clothing and many householders would dress their servants in their cast-offs, further eroding class distinctions in dress. Thieves were known to dress in the type of clothing that parish constables or local firemen wore, in order to loiter near or enter a house to commit a burglary unchallenged. Sometimes, only the shabbiness of a garment would mark out the pauper, say, from a tradesman or clerk, and one policeman reported that his decision not to arrest a group frequently seen loitering in the Bond Street area had been taken because 'they are too well-dressed to be apprehended under the Vagrant Act'.[10]

Journalist John Wade claimed that the city-dweller 'is everywhere pestered with clamours, and his feelings lacerated by the spectacle of real or fictitious suffering, which ought ever to be excluded from his sight'.[11] Wade believed that virtually all London beggars were fakes; many people agreed with him. Another type of compendium sprang up claiming to detail the various ruses that beggars used to fool the public, and providing a glossary of street slang used by this emerging other tribe of Londoner. The anonymous pamphlet *An Exposure of the Various Impostures Daily Practised by Vagrants of Every Description* appealed to the cynic who wanted to be bolstered in the view that all beggars were impostors; it also tapped into the apparently large market discovered by James Hardy Vaux, a twice-transported thief and fraudster whose *New and Comprehensive Vocabulary of the Flash Language* was published in 1819, and by journalist and comic author Pierce Egan, whose *Life in London* tales of high life and low life had translated the slang of the criminal/sporting fraternities.[12] *An Exposure of the*

Various Impostures, for example, reveals that 'Lurkers' have fake documentation showing loss by wreck, fire, accident, and so on; so one could try a Fire Lurk, a Sick Lurk, a Deaf & Dumb Lurk, a Weaver's Lurk, and so on. 'High-flyers' were begging-letter writers. 'Cadgers on the downright' begged from door to door, while 'Cadgers on the fly' begged from passers-by. A 'Shallow Lay' stood about in rags on cold days, and 'Screevers' would chalk on the pavement such piteous appeals as 'Hunger is a sharp thorn and biteth keen', or 'He that pitieth the poor lendeth to the Lord, and He will repay', as a mournful look was adopted, in order to fool the 'Flat' – dupe, or mug. Loud groanings and lamentations were required in order to be heard over the roar of daytime traffic. (Traffic noise could be so loud that ordinary conversation was often impossible on main streets.) Ann Taylor, in her thirties, was found groaning on a doorstep in Red Cross Street, Barbican, having apparently just miscarried; when a police officer discovered that the bloody matter in her lap was a sheep's liver, he attempted to arrest her – recognising her as the woman who had staged a fit outside the Dicity in Red Lion Square and received bread, cheese and five shillings from passers-by. Jane Weston was sentenced to three months on the prison treadmill for playing the part of a starving woman with nine children; the infants were hired, and two accomplices played the part of benevolent society ladies, to provoke others into alms-giving. James Prior spent fourteen nights in the Bridewell for dressing up as, and acting the part of, a pilgrim unable to continue his journey to Canterbury without money.[13] John Wade claimed that he had seen a beggar chewing soap in order to produce a more convincing fit, while J.T. Smith wrote scathingly of Italian boys' 'learned mice and chattering monkies', and recalled seeing an Italian throw his mice at a terrified nursery maid who had refused to give him any money.[14]

Despite widespread concerns about fraud, criminal convictions were a hit-and-miss affair, even after the passing of the 1824 Vagrancy Act. The parliamentary select committee that convened in 1828 to consider the inadequacies of the old methods of policing the capital was told that it was well-known that two of the four JPs who sat at Great Marlborough Street magistrates' court never convicted anyone of vagrancy if it was a first offence, even though they had the power to do so.[15] In 1827, the committee heard, 196 of the 429 vagrants arrested and brought to Great Marlborough Street were instantly discharged, much to the anger of the arresting constables. (Figures such as these cannot give a clear indication of the true level of vagrancy in the city since many vagrants – the majority, perhaps – were never arrested in the first place.) However, by 1832 imprisonment figures for vagrancy had risen significantly, suggesting that the New Police were more active in apprehending and/or more persuasive before the magistrates; the number of London vagrants committed to prison rose from 2,270 in 1829 to 6,650 in 1832.

Many beggars or 'disorderly' or 'suspicious' characters escaped arrest because of both Old and New Police inactivity, or officers' genuine fellow-feeling for the street poor, or their fear of attracting an angry crowd during an arrest; other beggars benefited from the territorial disputes between the New Police and the medieval watch system that would be adhered to by the Corporation of London until 1839. Metropolitan Police-loathing magistrate Peter Laurie advised the aldermen of the Corporation to keep driving any unwanted characters found on their patch through the Temple Bar in Fleet Street, across the border for the Metropolitan force to deal with, since, Laurie claimed, he had heard that West End magistrates had advised the driving of the idle and itinerant over the boundary for the City to deal with. Policing the poor had become a game of 'tennis ball', according to one City alderman; it was a spectacle that certain Londoners came to the Temple Bar to watch on a regular basis, on a mild evening – enjoying the dance of pursuit and escape performed nightly between the police and the criminalised.[16]

It was not meant to be this way. In place of the perceived chaos of the old Charleys-plus-Bow-Street-patrols method of policing, the first Metropolitan Police commissioners had divided London (except the City Corporation) into seventeen divisions; each division comprised eight sections and each section had eight 'beats' worked by ten men (one sergeant and nine constables). A beat was one to one-and-a-half miles in distance – an officer was to be able to see each part of his beat every quarter of an hour or so. This pattern was superimposed upon the ancient parochial geography of London, and its apparent regimentation, and the military overtones of having a uniformed squad on patrol, alarmed many that the arrival of the New Police was simply the first in a line of measures to restrict an Englishman's liberty; even an Englishwoman's liberty was under threat. This letter to *The Times* was a characteristic response:

Sir, I see by your paper that a few days since [magistrate] Mr Roe, of Great Marlborough Street, committed some dozen women of the town for not obeying the policemen when desired to leave the Quadrant. I have observed lately various instances of the same illegal and arbitrary conduct. I am no patroniser of disorderly persons of any class or description, but if our personal liberty is of any value, and is not to be at the mercy of every insolent policeman, I should wish to know by what legal authority this very constitutional force assumes to itself the power of seizing and imprisoning any woman, disorderly or not, who does not choose to leave the streets at their command. I should also wish to be informed under what authority that excellent magistrate Mr Roe commits women of the town by wholesale upon the bare assertion (not oath) of the constable that the said women were disorderly, when it is well known that punishment is not inflicted for any act of disorder but for presuming to remain in the streets contrary to the prohibition of the policeman.

Let a law be passed that these unfortunate persons are not to be permitted to walk the streets at all and then they will at least be acquainted with the laws to which they are subject; but at present the law stands thus, 'that any prostitute being found in the streets in a state of drunkenness, or acting otherwise in a disorderly manner, may be committed' &c. It is, therefore, clearly contrary to law to seize or imprison them for any thing short of this.[17]

The correspondent was quite right, and had clearly read the Vagrancy Act. Properly entitled *An Act for the Punishment of Idle and Disorderly Persons, and Rogues and Vagabonds, in that part of Great Britain called England*, the 1824 legislation had been intended to be a tightening-up of outmoded, unworkable statutes and the bedrock of policing the public activities of the poor; instead, it was a ramshackle collection of prohibitions of various open-air 'misdeeds'. In its strictest application, anyone who looked out of place and failed to give a plausible account of themselves could be imprisoned. Far from settling once and for all the definition of beggar, or of loiterer-with-intent, or of 'suspicious character', the Act left vast leeway for police and magistrates to decide on who was, and who was not, legally entitled to occupy public space. It conflated the concepts of idle and of disorderly – eliding unemployment with criminality – and it had the potential to circumscribe the activities of street entertainers and the sort of peripatetic sellers who provided a useful, less expensive alternative to shops and bazaars. When the Select Committee on the Police of the Metropolis gathered its evidence in 1828, Joseph Sadler Thomas admitted to being unsure whether simply sleeping out in the open constituted an offence under the Act.[18] (It did, and was punishable by three months' hard labour.) Certainly, the following were deemed to be criminal if the 1824 Act were followed to the letter, and one month's hard labour was the sentence for: anyone who could work but wilfully refused or neglected to do so and applied for parish relief; anyone applying for relief in a parish where they had no settlement; any unlicensed itinerant pedlar; any common prostitute wandering in the public streets behaving in an indecent manner; 'and every person wandering abroad . . . in any public

Place, Street, Highway, Court or Passage, to beg or gather alms, or causing or procuring or encouraging any Child or Children so to do, shall be deemed an idle and disorderly person within the true intent and meaning of this act.'

Three months' hard labour was for: anyone found sleeping in the open air with no visible means of subsistence and unable to give a good account of himself or herself; anyone asking for charity under false pretences, or showing wounds or deformities to gain alms; itinerant fortune-tellers and palmists; anyone betting or gambling in a public place; anyone selling or exposing to view an obscene picture or exhibition; any man found indecently exposing himself 'with the intent to insult any female'; any man who deserted his wife and/or family, leaving them dependent on parish relief; anyone carrying implements that could be used for burglary; and 'every suspected person or reputed thief, frequenting any River, Canal, or navigable Stream, Dock or Basin, or any Quay, Wharf or Warehouse near to or adjoining thereto, or any Street, Highway or Avenue . . . with intent to commit Felony.'[19]

Demobbed soldiers and sailors were entitled to permits to gather alms; and discharged prisoners were similarly granted certificates that allowed them to beg on their journey back to their place of settlement; certain seasonal workers, such as harvesters, might be allowed chits that exempted them from the labyrinthine strictures of two far older pieces of legislation – the Act of Settlement and the Elizabethan Poor Law. The 1662 Act of Settlement and Removal had been framed to coerce the poor into staying put – into not travelling the land in search of work or better pay and thereby causing local labour shortages or forcing the hand of local employers. Settlement meant that an individual was tied to his or her parish – usually their place of birth, though women were entitled to settlement in their husband's parish upon marriage.[20] (The 'beating of the bounds' is a medieval tradition that is still carried on as an enjoyable, redundant spectacle in certain parts of the country. On Ascension Day, a parish boy – usually an apprentice – was whipped with a willow wand at the parish boundaries, to remind him, illiterate as he probably was, of where he belonged, and of where he did not belong.) Before the Poor Law Amendment Act of 1834, parish authorities were responsible for providing help to the local poor; but this assistance was to be given only to those with a settlement in the parish. Admission to the workhouse was one way of feeding and housing those without work, the sick and the old; another was the system of 'outdoor relief', which meant that the poor could, in theory at least, receive cash payments, food and fuel, along with advances to buy work-tools, clothing and shoes, while remaining in their own home

– or out on the street.[21] The economic depressions of 1815 and 1825 pushed up the poor rates paid by householders; where the nation's poor rates had amounted to around £2 million at the turn of the century, in 1832 the figure stood at £8.6 million. One in ten Britons were wholly or partially dependent on poor relief. In 1821, parliament had debated removing the right to any kind of relief to the able-bodied; but, with memories of Paris 1789 still fresh, they baulked at such an inflammatory move.

The system of settlement was yet another antiquated, inadequate mechanism that was falling to pieces in the face of the needs of post-Industrial Revolution Britain. Casual, often factory-based, employment required a large influx of potential workers into town – though the jobs were often precarious or seasonal in nature. Moreover, settlement disputes were a notoriously complex maze for even a lawyer to negotiate, and took up an inordinate amount of time in the lower courts; the cost of such legal wrangles to the parishes of Great Britain was running at over £250,000 a year by the end of the Napoleonic Wars.[22] John Wade, writing in 1829, was amazed at the confusion and potential for abuse of poor relief that the settlement system created. A surprising number of individuals, he claimed, were unable to name the parish to which they 'belonged', something he believed to be particularly common among the London-born poor, who were 'so little acquainted with themselves' – a beautiful phrase that prefigures much later writing about the effects of urban living on the soul.

> The number of persons [wrote Wade] who, with their families, find their way to the metropolis from the remote parts of Great Britain and Ireland, in hopes of finding employment, is inconceivable. . . . Having incurred the expense and fatigue of the journey, and entertaining hopes, probably, of a change in circumstances, they are loth to apply to the parishes where accident has fixed them and thereby subject themselves to forcible removal. In this dilemma, they often linger till all they possess in the world is sold or pledged, and then falling into utter destitution, the females do not infrequently resort to prostitution, the feeble-spirited among the males to begging, those of more profligate principles to petty thefts or more atrocious offences, contributing to swell the general mass of delinquency.

Wade estimated that around 13,000 people were removed from London and 'passed back' (that is, forcibly returned by wagon to their parish of settlement, and to rural destitution) each year. Yet he conceded that there was no practical way of making someone stay where they did not want to live. Those who did remain in London were not properly dealt with by the parochial authorities, he wrote, but were passed from parish to parish, 'driven to and fro like a weaver's shuttle'.[23]

A young woman named Elizabeth Warner jumped into the New River near City Road on the morning of Wednesday 7 October 1829. Two men passing by dived in and rescued her, and when, later, she was able to speak, she explained that she had come to London from Chigwell in Essex to find a job, had not eaten for three days, nor slept in a bed for a fortnight. She said she had been denied parish relief because she did not belong to any London parish; that the Dicity would not relieve her because she had not resorted to begging; that the Blackfriars Road Magdalen Hospital for repentant prostitutes would not take her in because she had never sold her body. Warner's fate was to be taken to the hospital ward of the Islington workhouse to recover, with the aim of her being 'removed' to Chigwell at Islington's expense.[24]

Diving into a river to save a stranger is a brave act; and, like the harrying of constables arresting beggars, it rather flew in the face of the increasingly gloomy pronouncements about city life and the urban-dweller's excessive subjectivity and self-absorption. To John Wade, there was something sinister in the idea that 'in the midst of a million people the Londoner can create for himself a social solitude.' For Thomas De Quincey, 'No loneliness can be like that which weighs upon the heart in the centre of faces never-ending . . . eyes innumerable . . . and hurrying figures of men and women weaving to and fro.' And as James Grant, the editor of the *Morning Advertiser*, saw it, 'Everyone runs, as though their house were on fire, even when they have no purpose. Nobody wants to know each other's business.'[25] But the poor did not appear either to dash about or drift along withdrawn and uncommunicative – their intervention to help each other was noted with incredulity by some observers. One fact that disgusted many was that it was often those in poverty themselves who gave to beggars. J.T. Smith described a number of poor people pursuing a staggering drunk along High Holborn in order to hand coins to him because he had a piece of paper that read 'Out of Employment' stuck to his hat; Smith found this deplorable, and believed the message on the hat to be untrue.[26]

Such generosity may be evidence that the disparate groups comprising lower-class London felt something that could perhaps be described as emergent solidarity. 'Hit him hard, he has no friends' was a saying among the London poor in the 1820s – a sardonic comment on the perceived lack of social justice for the powerless and impoverished.[27] While London was one of the most heavily unionised areas of the country, with most trades having at least some sort of representative body, it is also true that most Londoners were never members of unions – whether trades bodies or organisations pressing for political reform. But class consciousness was on the rise outside of politicised groups. Friendly societies and co-operatives were developing in the capital as early as 1820, and in more settled areas, fragments of community did appear to be forming in the new enclaves that were establishing themselves. If society had been torn apart by economic change, it was also in the process of putting itself back together again. Even Viscount Melbourne had spotted it: 'I am well aware of the obstinate fidelity with which the lower classes cling to one another.'[28]

And the events of November 1831 were encouraging diverse types of Londoner to look at each other anew – to take notice of the potential fates of those around them. Where once missing children had been consigned to privately printed handbills and the columns of the *Hue and Cry/Police Gazette*, not even making its front page, but placed amid notices of absconding prisoners, deserting soldiers, absent fathers, strayed livestock (the ranks of those who had failed to keep to their proper place), the letters pages of national newspapers now throbbed with the concern of their gentleman readers. Thus in *The Times* of 29 November:

Sir, I have forwarded to you two cases of the loss of children, which I trust you will give publicity to, as the parents are too poor to pay for printing; and as it may be the means of discovery, at least in the recent case. In the month of March last, Mrs Hughes, a widow, of No 5, Paradise Place, Frog Lane, Islington, went out one morning to wash, leaving, as was her custom, her little boy at home; and on her return in the evening he was missing, and she has never heard of him since. He was seven years old; had on a blue jacket, black trousers, blue waistcoat, old brown pinafore, cloth cap and hob-nailed boots.

The other case was a boy about nine years of age, the son of a poor woman at Poplar. On the 15th of October last, he was at play with his little brother in the street, and told him that a man had promised him such lots of sugar – a great many basins full – and that he would bring him some when he came back. He then left his brother and has never returned. He had on a corduroy dress that had been washed, a good linen shirt, and half-boots.

I should be glad to render any assistance in discovering what has become of these poor children, and will satisfy any inquiries as far as lies in my power.

I am, yours, obediently, W.H.

And from the *Weekly Dispatch*:

> Among the supposed victims to the 'interests of science' who have disap-
> peared lately is a youth named Smith, about seventeen years of age, the
> son of respectable but unfortunate people in Grove Place, Camden
> Town. He was about 5ft 3in, of florid complexion, with full, dark eyes,
> and rather stout. He left his father's house on business last Tuesday
> evening, dressed in a blue coat and dark trousers, and has not been seen
> or heard of since.[29]

The *Morning Advertiser* gave regular bulletins about missing children after
the arrest of Bishop, Williams, May and Shields: Caroline Brand, eight,
of Wolverley Street, Hackney Road, sent out by her parents to sell bundles
of firewood one evening, and not seen again, just as her thirteen-year-old
brother had disappeared, five months before; and Henry Borroff, a five-
year-old, of Barton Court, Hoxton Old Town – gone.

SEVEN

Neighbours

William Woodcock was awoken in his bed at 2 Nova Scotia Gardens at around one or two o'clock in the morning of Friday 4 November by a loud noise from next door. As was his habit, he had gone to bed at half-past nine in the evening. He slept downstairs at the front of the house in a room that was next to the Bishops' parlour. The sounds he heard were a 'scuffling, or struggling', as he described it, like the sound of men's feet. The noises stopped suddenly, and he heard two sets of footsteps running from Bishop's house, slamming the gate shut. Then Woodcock heard the slow, heavy tread of one person in the parlour. 'Everything was quite still at the time and I could have heard a mouse stir. Had I known that any thing wrong was going on, I would have put my ear closer to the wall and might have heard every thing that passed.' After around a minute, the other two pairs of footsteps returned, and there was the sound of voices, though words were impossible to make out. Then all was quiet, and Woodcock fell back to sleep.

This was Woodcock's evidence to George Rowland Minshull on Friday 25 November, the final day of the magistrates' court hearings. Outside in Bow Street several hundred people had gathered and remained put all day, in spite of the heavy rain that fell for hours. Fifty persons 'of rank' had written to Minshull to request a seat alongside the magistrate for the committal hearings.

Minshull was keen to establish how many men Woodcock had heard during the disturbance.

'I can speak to the voices of two of the men, but I cannot speak as to the third,' said Woodcock.

Minshull pressed him on whether he could recognise the voices. Would he be able to confirm that they belonged to Bishop, Williams and May?

Woodcock replied that he had never heard the voices of Bishop – his neighbour of three weeks – or of May, though he believed that one of the voices had been Williams's.

Williams called out from the dock that what Woodcock had heard was a row between himself and John Bishop. The latter, said Williams, had smashed up some of Williams's belongings and was about to start on Rhoda's. Williams claimed that he had grabbed his wife's looking-glass, bonnet and shawl and left the house at about two in the morning to fetch an officer of the New Police. The constable had, however, refused to come beyond the garden gate and had walked away.

'I distinctly contradict that,' said Woodcock; that particular row, he said, had happened on the Sunday before.

No, Williams retorted; the argument had happened on the Thursday . . . or perhaps the Friday . . . 'The women can say which night it was.'

At this point, Bishop, who was sitting alongside him, whispered something urgently in Williams's ear, and Williams fell silent.

The magistrates were attempting to place May in the Bishop family home, making the cottage-sharing duo of Bishop and Williams into a well-established trio, with May.

'To the best of your belief, were there three men?' Minshull asked Woodcock.

'There must have been three,' said Woodcock.

Woodcock had moved into Number 2 with his wife and son on Monday 17 October. Despite living next door to Bishop and Williams for three weeks, Woodcock claimed to have seen only Williams, Sarah and Rhoda at Number 3; the first time he had laid eyes on Bishop had been at Bow Street magistrates' court.

Woodcock went to bed at around nine o'clock in order to rise at six in the morning to go to his job in a local brass foundry; this may explain his unfamiliarity with the men he lived next door to, who worked to a very different rhythm. Alternatively, he may have heard local talk that made him wish to shun the Bishop *ménage* altogether. On Sunday 6 November, Rhoda asked Woodcock if she could borrow a shilling; his response is not in the records.

Woodcock's son told the court that he was sure Williams was living at Number 3; he recalled seeing him smoking a pipe in the garden one evening, two or three days before Guy Fawkes Night.

Robert Mortimer, an elderly tailor who lived in Nova Scotia Gardens, testified that to the best of his belief, Williams lived at Number 3 with the Bishops. Towards the end of September, Mortimer had made Williams's wedding coat for him. He had gone to Number 3 on a number of occasions to collect the money Williams owed him for this, without success.

A local boy had told Superintendent Thomas that about four days before the arrests, he had found a cap and a bonnet, both muddy and trampled-looking, close to Bishop's house. Thomas told the court that both items tallied with those he had subsequently found on the premises.

Sarah Trueby told the magistrates' court that she had let Number 3 to Sarah Bishop in July 1830, and Number 2 to Thomas Williams in July 1831, and that he had lived there for about two months. Trueby said she had often seen Williams in Bishop's house since he had left Number 2. Of Rhoda, Trueby said, 'I have seen her without any bonnet on.'

Minshull had asked Superintendent Thomas whether it was true, as he had heard, that Bishop's house lay 'in a very lonely situation', the sort of place where evil deeds could be committed unseen. Thomas had had to reply that in fact the Gardens was 'a colony of cottages', divided from each other by low palings, and that one had only to step over these in order to have access to at least thirty other dwellings. Also, Numbers 2 and 3 were at the very entrance to the Gardens, just off Crabtree Row and within sight of the Birdcage pub.

How unnoticed could someone live in London? How little did one know about one's neighbours? It intrigued those investigating Nova Scotia Gardens.

'*There is no such thing as neighbours,*' wrote James Grant of the *Morning Advertiser*. '*You may live for half a century in one house without knowing the name of the person who lives next door.*'

George Gissing, son of the Birdcage's publican, knew both Bishop and Williams and recognised them on the night of the 4th, but he admitted that he had never seen Rhoda.

'*There is no such thing as a vicinage, no curiosity about neighbours. It is from this circumstance London affords so many facilities for the concealment of criminality. . . . The metropolis is like an immense forest,*' wrote John Wade.

'This looks strange. See where they are going so quick,' said Ann Cannell's mother, who, like her daughter, said she had not recognised Bishop or Williams.

'*In the metropolis men live for years without knowing their next-door neighbours, and an individual may there at his will maintain absolute solitude, or immediately be lost to pursuit amidst the congregated million and a half of inhabitants,*' claimed a prominent campaigner for civic reform.

'I'm sure I won't. If I did, they wouldn't mind giving me a topper,' said young Thomas Trader of Nova Scotia Gardens.

Superintendent Thomas had written up a statement for Margaret King of Crabtree Row to sign, confirming what she had already told the magistrate about seeing the Italian boy in Nova Scotia Gardens. The arrival of

King's baby was imminent, and it was unlikely that she would be able to attend an Old Bailey trial, should the case make it into the final session of 1831. But when she stood before Minshull again, King said she was unable to swear to the detail of the clothing the Italian boy had been wearing when she saw him on Thursday 3 November. She had been aware only of a 'Quaker-fashion' dark-blue coat or jacket, with a straight collar; it had seemed unremarkable. 'The boy's dress appeared to be shabby, such as other boys wear who go about the streets,' she said. It was odd in itself that she could tell the cut of the coat, when she had said that the boy had been standing with his back to her. She hadn't observed whether he had been wearing anything on his head. All the clothing that had been dug up at Number 3 was now placed in front of her, and Minshull asked King whether the poorer quality 'charity-school' coat was the one she had seen on the boy: 'The coat is, to all appearances, exactly like the one which the boy had on,' she said, 'but there is no mark about it to enable me to swear positively that it is the same coat.'

'You are not being called upon to swear positively to it, but only to the best of your knowledge and belief,' Minshull told her.

She replied, 'All I can say is, the coat is exactly like, as far as regards colour, size, and shape, and it has every appearance of the coat which the boy had on when I saw him on Thursday. And so is the cap.'

Her nine-year-old son, John, was more forthcoming. He told the court that he had seen the Italian boy too, from the Kings' first-floor window, and when he had asked his mother if he could go and see what the boy had in his cage or box, his mother had told him no. Minshull asked him to describe all he could about the Italian boy, and John recalled that the boy had been standing with his back to Nova Scotia Gardens and facing Birdcage Walk – the northern continuation of Crabtree Row; he had his right foot turned out, his arms rested on his cage, and he was wearing a brown furry cap with a visor that was lined in green fabric. Thomas then brought the cap he had found in Bishop's parlour over to John King, who told him, 'It looks exactly like the cap the Italian boy had on.' (John Bishop had smiled oddly in court as Thomas revealed that the cap had been found in his parlour.) The King family had seen all the items of clothing before, since Thomas had taken them straight round to their home after exhuming them. Despite this, much play was made in court of the fact that John had been kept out of the courtroom as his mother gave her evidence on the clothing.

Minshull asked John King if he had ever seen the same boy before, and the child said: 'I think I have seen him about before. He used to carry a doll with two heads in a glass case. I saw him about a month ago. He looked like the same boy. I have not seen him since the Thursday I saw him in the Gardens. He was then standing still, to see if anybody would come out and see what he had to show. I did not see him go away.' When asked how far the boy had been standing from Bishop's house, John replied, 'It would not take me more than half a minute to get there.'

His eleven-year-old sister Martha said that she was not sure if it was a Wednesday or a Thursday on which she saw the Italian boy at Nova Scotia Gardens. She did not remember any of his clothing except for the brown cap and the string around his neck from which his box or cage was hung. She could not see the colour of the cap's visor lining since the boy had his back to her. But when Thomas handed her the cap, she said it was like the one she had seen.

It must be supposed, since there is no evidence to the contrary, that Margaret, John and Martha King were describing the same incident; that they were all looking at the boy from either the first floor (John) or the ground floor (Margaret and Martha) of their house, which stood opposite the Birdcage and on the south side of Crabtree Row facing Nova Scotia Gardens (the Row took a sudden twist to the left as it became Birdcage Walk – today's Columbia Road makes the same movement). Both Mrs King and her daughter saw the boy with his back turned; but John claimed to have seen the boy full on, from above. And now, all three were placing themselves within their home, though in her earlier evidence, Margaret King had stated that she and the children had been out walking when they had seen the Italian boy.

Superintendent Thomas would not relinquish his grip on the two elder Bishop children. He believed they would eventually reveal damning facts about the household since, Thomas stated, and reporters duly reported, Williams had been living with them in the cottage for eighteen months. But here, the superintendent had become confused: Williams had moved into Number 2 in July 1831, not July 1830, and had lived with the Bishops for just a few weeks. It was the Bishops who had moved into Number 3 in July 1830.

The Bishop children had been brought from the Bethnal Green workhouse to be lodged at the Covent Garden watch-house in the hope that closer acquaintance with the police would encourage them to speak more openly. It had already been established that Bishop's youngest son had told another little boy who lived nearby that he had 'some nice little white mice at home' but that his father had used the cage as firewood.

A change had come over the prisoners during the past week, and, as they stood at the bar on this, their final day at Bow Street, gone were the sneering and jeering, the sarcastic comments about foolish questions and flimsy, ill-remembered evidence. On the Monday Williams had even loudly sung several songs in the prison van, handcuffed and leg-ironed as he was; he had complained to Bishop that he should not look so 'down upon his luck'. Now, though, Williams was bloodless-looking and fidgeted constantly, his mouth and nose twitching in an odd manner. Bishop looked crest-fallen, his eyes were sunk and he seemed as though he were in a trance; his weight had dropped dramatically. When Minshull told him that he could ask any questions he liked of the witnesses, Bishop bowed to the magistrate and said quietly, 'Thank you, sir, we are aware of that.' The *Sunday Times* of 13 November attempted a pun at Bishop's expense, saying that the bodysnatcher was now looking 'cut up'. The Reverend Dr Theodore Williams, vicar of Hendon, magistrate and prison visitor, had seen Bishop in gaol and asked the resurrectionist if there was anything he wished to discuss with him; Bishop had burst into tears and said no, not yet. Michael Shields looked skeletal and appeared to be in a stupor, standing rigidly at the bar and barely moving for the entire three-and-a-half-hour final hearing.

Only May's nerve appeared to hold, though he was noticeably quieter than before and listened intently to all that was said. May and Bishop had had a fight. May blamed Bishop bitterly for getting him 'into this scrape' (according to Dodd the gaoler, who listened in on conversations and reported them to Superintendent Thomas).[2] May had shouted at Bishop, 'You're a bloody murdering bastard – you should have been topped years ago.' The signs were that May would, at any moment, turn King's Evidence. What was he waiting for?

After the neighbours had had their say, the summing up began, and all the evidence that had been gathered during the inquiry was read out in court – everything that had been told to the coroner's inquest; all the witness statements given at Bow Street; all Thomas's tip-offs and 'information received'. Then James Corder revealed that proceedings against Michael Shields were being dropped, no evidence having been found against him. Shields was now officially discharged but was called round to stand in front of the bench. Minshull told Shields that he was now a witness – what did he have to say for himself? Shields repeated once again the story that had been prised from him at the coroner's inquest: that he had met Bishop on the morning of Saturday the 5th in the Fortune of War and had agreed to carry a large hamper – taken from just inside St Bartholomew's railings by Bishop – from Guy's to King's, a job for which, Shields pointed out to Minshull, he had still not been paid his promised half-crown.

Minshull said, 'Do you still persist in saying that you were not aware of what the hamper contained?' and Shields replied, 'Upon my word, your worship, I knew nothing about what the hamper contained. I carried it as I would any other job.'

'Did you ever carry any load for Bishop or May before?'

'No, your honour, never.'

A clerk warned him: 'You know, Shields, you have carried bodies repeatedly to the hospitals. You should remember you are now on your oath.'

'I mean to say that I did not know what the hamper contained that May and Bishop hired me to carry. I never saw Bishop and Williams at my house. I never gave them my address.' At which James Corder produced a piece of paper that had been found at Number 3 Nova Scotia Gardens. 'Is this paper, on which is written "Number 6 Eagle Street, Red Lion Square", in your handwriting?' Corder asked.

Shields studied the scrap for some time before saying, 'Yes, sir, it is.'

Corder turned to Minshull: 'It is quite clear that this man cannot be believed upon his oath, and therefore it would be useless to make a witness of him.'

Minshull agreed: 'Every word he has spoken goes for nothing.'

The magistrate was extremely annoyed with Shields for failing to be prosecution-witness material. But he could not quite let go of the idea of wringing from the man something that would incriminate May, Bishop and Williams – since the case against them still appeared worryingly slender. Minshull told the porter he intended to detain him for a while longer as he might want to charge him with some other offence – which he had not yet decided upon. The magistrate was going to have a think about how best to 'dispose' of Shields. 'Can you produce any security for your appearance at trial?' asked Minshull, wondering about the chances of binding him over to appear at the Old Bailey.

'I cannot,' said Shields. 'No one would be answerable for me.'

Then Minshull changed his mind again and decided to let Shields go, warning him to keep Superintendent Thomas informed of where he was living – partly for Shields's own protection. He knew how the crowd could vent its ill-feeling towards resurrectionists.

Minshull now turned to the three men remaining in the dock and said: 'If you wish to say anything, now is your time, as this is the last opportunity you will have of appearing before me.'

Bishop: 'No, sir. I have nothing to say at present. I will reserve what I have got to say for another place.'

Williams: 'Nothing, sir, but what I have already said.'

But James May had plenty to say: 'This man, Bishop, can clear me of everything, if he likes to speak the truth. He knows I am innocent of the charge. The man says he got the body from the ground, but that he doesn't like to say where because he is loath to injure the two watchmen left to guard it. Things, however, have come to such a crisis now that he ought to speak the truth, for I defy him to say anything to implicate me.' He turned to Bishop: 'I knew nothing of the body until I went to take it from your house!'

'I have said nothing against you. It's true what you say – you knew nothing of it until then.'

'That is the truth. I did not. I know that nothing you can say – if you will only tell the truth – can implicate me.'

Minshull told them: 'Prisoners, you will all be committed to Newgate to take your trial at the ensuing Sessions at the Old Bailey, commencing on 1st December, for the wilful murder of Carlo Ferrari, and there will be another count in the indictment, charging you with the wilful murder of a person unknown.'

Downstairs in the lock-up room, May burst into tears, swearing to Dodd the gaoler that he had had nothing to do with the boy's death – that the first he had seen of the lad was when he lay curled up dead in the trunk in Bishop's wash-house. Even if he were to be acquitted, wailed May, how would he ever be able to find work again? He beat his breast and railed at Bishop and Williams, who both appeared to have rallied a little. But when the door was opened to take them to the prison van that would carry them to Newgate they shrank down behind the double row of police officers who stood between them and the huge crowd that surged forward to scream insults; someone broke through and Bishop's left shoulder was injured. May, though, insisted on walking tall, as he followed them into the van amid the jostling and shouting.

Around 300 people chased the vehicle as it turned down into the Strand, along Fleet Street, and up Chancery Lane, startling horses on the roadway and causing numerous accidents; but in Chancery Lane, the van became held up by traffic and the crowd caught up and began to pelt it with mud and stones.

At Coldbath Fields Prison, just to the north of Saffron Hill, the van dropped off two prisoners, and then it went on to Newgate with Bishop, May and Williams, arriving at a quarter past five. It took a great deal of effort to move the three into the prison without letting the crowd seize them.

Back at Bow Street, Sarah and Rhoda were called from their cells before

Minshull immediately after the committal of their husbands to be told that they would not face any charges. They were too cold to speak – their teeth were chattering – but they curtseyed to the bench to show their gratitude. Superintendent Thomas had, it seems, for the time being given up hope of building a case against them. Similarly, it had now been decided – probably by Minshull and Corder – that the Bishop children were too young to be given the burden of incriminating their parents. Minshull was concerned for the women's well-being and insisted that they should not be released until it was quiet in the streets outside. Bishop had been told by Thomas of his wife's imminent release and he told the superintendent, 'I thank you, sir, and I hope you will look to her and see that she is not insulted by the mob.'

Michael Shields was allowed out of the Bow Street office near to midnight. Minshull had advised Dodd to hold him as late as possible, for his own safety. But though the hearing had ended before four in the afternoon, Shields found himself confronted by a large group still waiting in the street who hissed, hooted and groaned at him. He walked briskly northwards and turned into Long Acre, heading east towards home in Eagle Street, but the crowd pursued him. He dodged right into Drury Lane, hoping to throw them off, then ran into Vinegar Yard, a tiny thoroughfare alongside the Drury Lane Theatre. Still they gave chase and, terrified, the old man ran round to Bow Street, where the officers took him back into custody for his own protection. Here he stayed for hours, cowering in a corner of the office, gibbering and sobbing.

EIGHT

Meat – an Interlude

The Fortune of War stood where Giltspur Street meets Cock Lane – a spot known as Pye Corner. Here, on 6 September 1666, the Fire of London was stopped in its westward tracks after having destroyed four-fifths of the City. Smithfield, the Smoothe Field of twelfth-century descriptions, lying just without Newgate and Aldersgate, was largely undamaged by the flames, with the consequence that by the early part of the nineteenth century some of London's oldest buildings were to be found surrounding the large open space that was given over to the meat market. In the 1820s some one and a half million sheep, 150,000 cattle and 60,000 pigs were driven to Smithfield every year to be sold and slaughtered, even though meat consumption had been in slow decline since the final decade of the previous century. Smithfield was the 'live' market; Newgate Shambles, half a mile away and just north of St Paul's Cathedral, was the main dead-meat market. 'Prime', the best meat, cost between 8d and 9d a pound in the late 1820s, while 'seconds' sold for 5d to 7d. At Pye Corner, the poorest quality dead meat was sold off; 'cag-mag' could cost as little as 2d a pound, and supplemented the diets of the desperately poor, along with condemned fish from Billingsgate, damaged and withered fruit and vegetables, and cheap starch in the form of potatoes. Cag-mag was often meat that had simply been around too long (in summer, freshness was limited to just twenty-four hours after a kill); but in many cases it was the flesh of recently killed but worn-out, old, thin or diseased beasts. Cag-mag's etymology is uncertain, though 'cag' is likely to be derived from 'cack', meaning excrement, and a 'mag' was slang for a farthing – so, 'cheap crap' is a reasonable guess. Just how bad the quality of food sold at Smithfield could be was shown by a witness to the 1828 parliamentary Select Committee on the State of Smithfield who had entered the Bear & Ragged Staff inn on the north-east side of the market place, close to where, today, Charterhouse Street forks left into Charterhouse Square; the inn also did duty as a slaughterhouse. The witness, Adam Armstrong, told the committee he had seen hanging up in the pub a cow's carcass that was so rancid, the fat was no more than dripping yellow slime. On questioning the slaughterman, Armstrong was told that this was cag-mag that was to be sent to a nearby sausage factory, for 2*d* a pound.[1] Other campaigners claimed that the most rotten cag-mag was fed to beasts awaiting slaughter: 'Let the reader reflect on the bare possibility of having partaken of the flesh of an animal fed, perhaps, on the foetid refuse of a diseased or glandered horse,' ran one warning about feeding meat to herbivores.[2]

Beasts came to Smithfield from all over Great Britain, with drovers walking the animals in their charge for 15 to 20 miles a day. It was a skilled job to manoeuvre herds of up to 1,000 animals across the country, and drovers would frequently sleep out in the open in order to keep watch for rustlers; animal theft was common, despite still being a capital offence (in London, four rustlers were executed in 1825, one in 1826, and three in 1827).[3] An ox lost around 20lb in weight for every 100 miles it walked to market, and if the creature came from the Scottish Highlands – and many

46. A view of Smithfield Market, sketched from the Bear & Ragged Staff inn cum slaughter-house, looking south to the top of Giltspur Street, home to the Fortune of War. St Bartholomew's Hospital is the large building to the left of centre.

did – the three-week journey could affect the quality of its flesh unless it had had time to put weight back on. The cattle that were driven to the capital from the north were pastured in the 'grazing counties' of Norfolk, Lincolnshire and Leicestershire in order to fatten; the last stopping place was the meadows of Islington before the final thrust down St John Street and into Smithfield. At Islington the rural drover handed his charges over to London drovers, of whom there were around 100, appointed by the City of London and required by law to wear numbered badges on their arm. In reality, these badges were often not worn, or were pawned, or were lent out by master drovers to their apprentices for a daily fee; fake badges were regularly seized. After a sale was made, a butcher's drover would drive a beast to its place of slaughter, which was usually in Smithfield, Whitechapel, Shoreditch or Leadenhall Market in the heart of the City.

Country drovers avoided towns and turnpikes by using the 'drovers' roads' – grassy tracks where hooves would be less likely to be damaged; but in London there came a point where no roads could be given over to animals alone, and beasts had to share city space, often with calamitous consequences. In the summer of 1828 a bullock went berserk in Hatton Garden and killed a woman who was looking in a jewellery-shop window. The beast was being pursued by a gang of boys, though whether they were trying to stop it or had caused the stampede in the first place was never established. (One method of ensuring a richer haul when stealing from the person, or from a shop, was for a gang to select an ox from a passing herd, goad or terrify it into charging, then, when there was uproar, to pick pockets or snatch from window displays. Sometimes, a panic was caused simply for fun, not for gain.)[4] Around the same time, a woman who sold oranges in the streets was knocked down and badly injured when an ox charged in Lad Lane, near Guildhall.[5] Many less serious injuries caused by kicks from frightened or furious animals were seen by hospital doctors. Beasts that became separated from their herd would often panic and charge up the narrow courts and alleys of Smithfield, terrorising inhabitants, disrupting sleep and work, even entering homes and causing injuries.

Trades that had nothing to do with butchery intermingled with meat-market businesses in Smithfield and its immediate surrounds, and many shopkeepers complained that their revenues dropped on market days: it was claimed that women would not venture out to buy when beasts were being driven in town; that women would not shop where they had to pass by mounds of flesh lying on the pavement or in the gutters. (Women were frequently cited as potential or real victims of the herds, though it is quite possible that this appeal to chivalry was a calculated ploy by those who wanted to see wholesale reform of the market.) William Wilkinson, an upholsterer of Ludgate Hill, said that terrified women would often run into his shop to shelter from a passing herd; that his plate-glass windows were frequently smashed when bullocks poked their heads through. Robert Padmore of Marriott's ironmongery in Old Bailey saw a woman run down by a drove of panicking sheep, one of which ran into his shop and fell down into his cellar, on top of his workmen.[6] Some animals simply wandered off: 'Found, in Holborn, a black and white cow, which is dry, in very bad condition, and aged; she has long horns, and is supposed to be diseased. Apply at the Police Station, Covent Garden,' said a notice in the Daily Police Report of 16 November 1831.[7]

Monday was the busiest day at Smithfield; it was the main beef-trading day, with 2,000 cattle changing hands and 15,000 sheep. On Friday there was a second cattle market and, from mid-afternoon, a horse market. At eleven o'clock on Sunday night the cattle that had been held at Islington were moved down into Smithfield – an operation that lasted until four or five in the morning. Some coming in from the east were moved in along Sun Street and Chiswell Street and into Long Lane; thousands of sheep and lambs were held in Hatton Garden until their curfew ended at nine o'clock at night and they were herded eastwards into their pens. That Sundays should end with the most unholy noise of animals thundering along narrow, residential streets, with drovers' dogs barking and the habitual cursing of drovers, was felt by some to be an outrage: this was 'a shocking conclusion of the Christian Sabbath', it was claimed in an anonymous pamphlet of 1823, *Cursory Remarks on the Evil Tendency of Unrestrained Cruelty, Particularly on That Practised at Smithfield Market.*[8] At Christmas 1827 the sheer volume of cattle coming to market meant that the streets to the east of Smithfield as far as Barbican were solid with a bovine traffic-jam.[9]

Many believed that Friday's horse-trading attracted a large criminal population into the area because of the number of stolen horses that were disposed of for cash. Around 8,000 horses a year were stolen in London alone ('pladding a prig' and 'prad-chewing' were slang for stealing a horse), earning the thief around £20 a head. The *Hue and Cry/Police Gazette* was filled with advertisements for missing beasts: 'A black gelding, from Mr Thomas, at Manor Place, Kennington, Middlesex, 21st ultimo, 5 years old, near 15 hands, star on his face, switch tail, hair rubbed off his back and legs' – this was a more detailed description than those of the missing citizens who appeared in the paper's columns.[10] Horse thieves and their hangers-on, it was claimed, flooded into Smithfield – more particularly, to its fifty or sixty pubs and inns – and those who would defend the reputation of the market, and the integrity of its dealers and drovers, pointed

47.–48. Two contemporary views of the Friday horse market at Smithfield – one sedate, one wild.

to 'outsiders' as the source of much of the mischief. 'There are a great many boys who are running about the market that come there for mere wantonness,' said one beef salesman. 'Those are the persons they ought to punish.'[11] As with all London markets, many vagrants, and vagrant children, slept the night in the straw of the pens, beneath the wooden stalls, or in the doorways of surrounding houses and shops. Quite what the overlap was between these waifs and the 'wanton boys' identified by the salesman cannot be known; one man's juvenile delinquent is another man's object of compassion.

Another more alarming market was held at Smithfield from time to time; making a 'Smithfield bargain' was the sale by a husband of his wife, and was believed in many working-class communities to be a perfectly valid form of divorce (it had its roots in Anglo-Saxon common law). The sale was usually pre-arranged, and the buyer was often a friend of the family or a neighbour who, motivated by pity, wanted to help bring an unhappy union to an end. The public nature of the sale was to validate for the community the ending of the marriage. At two o'clock on the afternoon of Monday 20 February 1832, a man brought his twenty-five-year-old wife in a halter and tied her in the pens opposite the Half Moon pub, close to the gate of St Bartholomew-the-Great. A crowd gathered and the auction began, with a 'respectable-looking man' striking a deal for 10s; throughout, the woman made no complaint of her treatment.[12] Some twenty cases of wife-selling at Smithfield are on record between the 1790s and the 1830s, though the true figure is likely to be higher.

Descriptions of Smithfield challenged even the most euphemistic of writers. It is clear that offal, excrement ('filth') and urine ('steam') had to be negotiated by a pedestrian. Quite apart from the stink and refuse from the market and the slaughterhouses, associated trades helped to contaminate the nearby streets – the sausage-makers, tanners, cat- and rabbit-fur dressers, bladder blowers, tripe dressers, bone dealers, cat-gut manufacturers, neat's-foot-oil makers. Here is Charles Dickens attempting to convey the aura of Smithfield to a family readership, in *Great Expectations*: 'The shameful place, being all asmear with filth and fat and blood and foam, seemed to stick to me.' And in *Oliver Twist*:

> The ground was covered, nearly ankle deep, with filth and mire; and a thick steam, perpetually rising from the reeking bodies of the cattle, and mingling with the fog, which seemed to rest upon the chimney tops, hung heavily above. . . . Countrymen, butchers, drovers, hawkers, boys, thieves, idlers, and vagabonds of every low grade, were mingled together in a dense mass.[13]

49. George Cruikshank's *The Knackers Yard, or the Horse's Last Home* (1830) shows the appalling conditions in slaughterhouses.

Dickens did not attempt to address the issue of animal slaughter itself, which frequently took place in the cellars or back yards of ill-adapted private houses; but others, intent on reform, did not spare the detail. For the Smoothe Field that had been outside the medieval City was now right in the centre of a busy metropolis, the capital of a great and growing imperial power – and its goings-on were, frankly, not respectable.[14] They ordered these matters better in France, the select committees on Smithfield discovered, and the abattoirs of Paris were analysed and eulogised by committee witnesses. While Corporation of London bylaws forbade any emission of blood from a slaughterhouse, it was, nevertheless, a regular sight across the pathways of Smithfield, and pedestrians would get blasts of hot, stinking air through street-level gratings since animals were often kept and killed below ground.[15] Passers-by glancing left or right into a court or yard where a butcher worked could find themselves witnessing a killing. It was alleged by various witnesses before the 1828 Select Committee on Smithfield that sheep were often skinned before being completely dead; it was observed that an unskilled slaughterman could take up to ten blows with an axe to kill a bullock; and while an inspector was supposed to be notified before the slaughter of any horse, this rule was said to be broken more often than kept, and horses were observed up to their knees in the weltering remains of their fellow creatures, maimed and starving and showing obvious signs of distress as their fate dawned on them.[16]

The cruelty that was meted out to creatures was quite apparent to the passer-by. While a goad on the end of a drover or market-man's rod or staff was supposed to be no longer than one-eighth of an inch, many were longer and were seen being used on the head, eyes, genitals and shins of animals that were standing perfectly still; the 'wake-them' beatings just before daylight in winter were said to be particularly vicious. In the market place, cattle were arranged in 'drove rings' – circles of around fifteen, nose in, tail out – and were kept in that formation by beatings. Hundreds of cows and bullocks stood crowded together in this way in the wide paved area just to the north-west of St Bartholomew's Hospital;[17] this section was criss-crossed by pathways for pedestrians, with only a wooden handrail between beast and bypasser. Walking this route was a challenge, particularly with the slippery nature of Smithfield terrain and especially so in the 'black frosts of November'.[18] That Smithfield was often brighter by night than by day was confirmed by a witness to the Select Committee, who said that in winter the hand-held lamps of the drovers and the street gas lamps meant that selling could continue after dusk fell in the afternoon. The newspaper columnist who wrote under the pseudonym 'Aleph', remembering the Smithfield of the 1820s, recalled that 'if the day was foggy (and there were more foggy days then than now) then the glaring lights of the drover-boys' torches added to the wild confusion . . . . The long horns of the Spanish breeds . . . made it a far from pleasant experience for a nervous man to venture along one of these narrow lanes, albeit it was the nearest and most direct way across the open market.'[19] Road traffic continued to travel across the quarter-mile stretch between the top of Giltspur Street and the southern end of St John Street, and collisions with animals were common; beatings were used to move beasts out of the way of carts, coaches and carriages, but hind-quarters were frequently hit by passing vehicles.

It was this type of common, easy-to-spot brutality at Smithfield that was to prove a major impetus in securing the world's first legally enforceable animal-protection measures. In April 1800 a motion had been defeated in parliament to ban bull-baiting and cock-fighting; in 1809, a more broadly defined anti-animal cruelty bill was also defeated, though it had travelled further than its predecessor before being lost. In May 1821 a similar bill was passed in the Commons but lost in the Lords. Then, in May 1822, a Bill to Prevent Cruelty to Horses, Cattle and Donkeys was passed by both Commons and Lords, gaining Royal Assent in July of that year. It was always to be known as Martin's Act, after its mover, Colonel Richard

Martin, MP for Galway.[20] Martin was popularly known as Humanity Dick, a nickname thought to have been given to him by George IV, with whom he was friendly, despite the king's love of hunting and cock-fighting.[21] He was also called Hair-Trigger Dick because of his over-excitability and his readiness to fight duels (he killed no one, but inflicted and received a number of gunshot wounds). Martin was nearly seventy when his Act was passed, but he was tireless in his drive to expose brutality to animals and drag the offender before the magistrates; within a year of Martin's Act becoming law, 150 people were prosecuted in police courts for cruelty. Martin lived, like many MPs of the day, in Manchester Buildings, a court of rented rooms on the river next to Westminster Bridge,[22] and was often to be seen parading Whitehall and Charing Cross Road inspecting cabmen's behaviour and the condition of their horses. A contemporary described him as 'a meteor of ubiquity', who appeared to be all over London at the same time, seeking out the ill treatment of animals.

The first prosecution to be brought under his novel piece of legislation came about after Martin paid a visit to the Friday horse market at Smithfield and secured the arrest of Samuel Clarke and David Hyde. Clarke was a horse-dealer who had repeatedly struck a horse on the head with the butt of his whip in order to make it look more lively as it stood tethered to a rail; Hyde had severely beaten a horse as he was riding it, for the same reason. Both men were fined 20s each. (The minimum fine was 10s, the maximum £5 or up to two months in gaol.) Martin also undertook a citizen's arrest of a Smithfield butcher whom he saw breaking the leg of a sheep; Martin manhandled the man away, even though a gang of drovers appeared on the scene and threatened him. He gave eyewitness evidence at the successful prosecution at Guildhall magistrates' court of a Smithfield dealer who regularly flung calves into a van with their legs tied together and cords around their necks; the creatures piled on top of each other and many suffocated. (In his defence, the dealer said that if he was not allowed to do his job the way he saw fit, 'gentlefolk would get no veal'.)[23]

Martin was alarmed at the use of vivisection in medical research. During the 1825 House of Commons debate on a bill that would broaden the scope of Martin's Act, the member for Galway told the House how the French anatomist François Magendie ('This surgical butcher, or butchering surgeon,' Martin called him) had, on a visit to London, bought a greyhound for 10 guineas (the going rate for a dead human) and nailed the dog's paws and ears to an operating table and dissected its facial and cranial nerves one by one, severing its sense of taste, then of hearing, and saying that the next day he would perform a vivisection, if the dog was still alive.[24]

The use of live animals for medical experiment was beginning to be debated, with the majority of eminent London surgeons voicing their opposition – in public at least. The great John ('Fear God, and keep your bowels open') Abernethy saw little value in such research, believing that observation, not experiment, was the key to physiological knowledge. Whenever Abernethy did investigate animal anatomy, he insisted the beast be killed quickly and humanely before dissection. Sir Charles Bell believed that there was little of use to humans to be learned from exploring animal physiology – and he had moral scruples, too: 'I cannot perfectly convince myself that I am authorised in nature or religion to do these crudities,' he wrote in a letter to his brother George in 1822. Elsewhere Bell wrote: 'Experiments have never been the means of discovery; and a survey of what has been attempted in late years in physiology will prove that the opening of living animals has done more to perpetuate error than to confirm the just views taken from the study of anatomy and natural motions.' To which Magendie, who was determined to fathom the mysteries of muscle movement – particularly with regard to the facial muscles – replied: 'One should not say that to perform physiological experiments one must necessarily have a heart of stone and a leaning towards cruelty.'[25] In 1824, before a crowd of physicians, Magendie severed part of the brain of a dog, which fell down, stood up, ran around, then died.

Edinburgh's Dr Knox, purchaser of Burke and Hare's produce, was another who preferred to work on humans:

> I have, all my life, had a natural horror for experiments made on living animals, nor has more matured reason altered my feelings with regard to these vivisections. . . . A minute and careful anatomy, aided by observation of the numerous experiments made by nature and accident on man himself, seems to me to present infinitely the best and surest basis for physiological and pathological science.[26]

Humanity Dick was never able to bring an action against a vivisectionist, his 1825 measure to outlaw animal experiments failing in parliament. But in pursuing cases of ordinary, everyday cruelty he became legendary, and his London court appearances – as prosecutor – often found him in front of George Rowland Minshull, who obtained many contributions to the court-room swearbox (proceeds to the poor) as a result of fining Martin for his endless stream of exasperated 'By God's' and 'Oh God's'. The two men seem to have enjoyed a part-joshing, part-peevish series of exchanges in the mid-1820s, such as this, at Bow Street. Minshull had suggested that a man could judge for himself how much chastisement his own horse might require, to which Martin called out, 'By God, if a man is to be the judge in his own case, there is an end of everything!'

'I fine you five shillings for swearing,' said Minshull.

'I'll pay up,' said Martin.

'No, I was joking,' said Minshull, who went on to acquit the defendant, who had been charged with cruelty to a horse. Martin was furious, quoting Macbeth (and shouting): 'Time has been, that when the brains were out, the man would die,' as he leapt across the court room to make his point.

'My brains may be out,' said Minshull, 'but I cannot make up my mind to convict in this case.'

'Then it is time that you were relieved from the labours of your office!'

'Well that was a very kind and gentlemanly remark, I must say,' said Minshull, 'but I am going to keep my temper, whatever you do, and I dismiss the case.' And Martin flounced out.[27]

Martin was determined to extend his 1822 anti-cruelty Act to protect all animals, including domestic pets, and to ban bull- and badger-baiting, cock- and dog-fighting, and to improve conditions in knackers' yards. He failed to get further bills passed in 1823, twice in 1824, three times in 1825, and three times in 1826. On 16 June 1824, the day after the loss of Martin's Slaughtering of Horses Bill (an attempt to force knackers to keep horses well fed while they awaited slaughter), a meeting took place at the inappropriately named Old Slaughter's Coffee House,[28] in St Martin's Lane, of the Friends of the Bill for the Prevention of Cruelty to Animals – who resolved to become a more permanent body: the Society for the Prevention of Cruelty to Animals (to be given its 'Royal' prefix by Queen Victoria in 1840). Those assembled pledged to redouble their efforts in personally policing the behaviour of cab-men and drovers; and to publish tracts and write letters to the authorities on why mistreating brute beasts was immoral. Such activities could take time: one Charles Merritt told the 1828 Select Committee on Smithfield that it had taken him the best part of a day to get a drover's boy arrested and committed by a JP for injuring a bullock in Oxford Street. A growing number of anti-cruelty campaigners took to patrolling Smithfield, reflecting a growing passion for personal intervention in the face of the apparent unwillingness or inability of the constables appointed by the Corporation of London to police Smithfield Market effectively. (The Metropolitan Police had no jurisdiction in Smithfield; it was to be 1839 before the City exchanged its parochial constables for a body modelled on the Met.) Eight to ten constables were supposed to be on hand at any time during the day, recognisable by their blue jacket, buff waistcoat and Corporation badge, but there were frequent complaints that officers were never to be found, or if found, would do little to act against a cruel drover.[29]

The first twenty-five years of the century witnessed a sizeable shift in attitudes to animal cruelty. Opposition to the 1800 and 1809 anti-cruelty bills had largely focused on two issues. Firstly, it was felt that it would be a gross infringement of liberty for a man to be prohibited from doing as he saw fit with his property – living property included (the same reason that, short of murder, a man could do as he pleased with his wife). Undue interference in private lives was to be avoided as far as possible (though some private lives were to be considered more worthy of protection than others). Martin's Act cleverly got around the freedom-of-the-individual objection by framing the legislation to apply to those who had *charge* of a beast; its result, though, was a crackdown on working men, who merely had charge – not ownership – of horses, cattle and donkeys. Secondly, there was doctrinal objection to animal protection, at least when the Lords came to debate the measure. Why should animals be considered the equal of man when he was given dominion over every living thing that moves upon the earth? The concept of an animal having feelings and legal rights was seen as yet one more eccentric notion held by Methodists, Quakers, Baptists, Evangelicals and other religious non-Conformists who made up a large and vocal part of the anti-cruelty lobby. (Richard Martin, however, was the son of a Roman Catholic but had been brought up in the Protestant faith so that he might go to Cambridge and then enter parliament; Catholics were not allowed to sit as MPs until 1829.) Many of Martin's supporters conflated their attacks on animal cruelty with opposition to ancient aristocratic privilege and to arcane, outmoded civil processes and institutions, and many different threads of protest were to be interlinked in the literature of animal-cruelty campaigners. The 1823 *Cursory Remarks on the Evil Tendency of Unrestrained Cruelty* pamphlet, for example, worked itself up into a purple passage eliding all manner of social ills perpetrated in unreformed, aristocratically misruled Britain:

Man has the vanity, the preposterous arrogance, to fancy himself the only worthy object of divine regard; and in proportion as he fancies himself such, considers himself authorised to despise, oppress, and torment all the creatures which he regards as his inferiors . . . and thus the proud and voluptuous in the higher ranks of society too often regard the humble and laborious classes as beings of a different cast, with whom it would be degrading familiarity to associate, and whom, whenever they interfere with their pleasures, their interest, or caprice, they may persecute, oppress and imprison. . . . [This last was a reference to the Vagrancy Act, being debated in parliament.] Thus men in the lowest stations become, in their turn, the persecutors and tormentors of the brute creation, of creatures which they regard as inferiors.

The chain of evil passed downwards from the aristocracy to Smithfield, where the cattle appear to take on Christlike attributes, exhibiting, according to *Cursory Remarks*, 'the most patient endurance of every kind of persecution' and having 'a harmless, unresisting, uncomplaining nature'.[30]

Impassioned rhetoric such as this, combined with zealous personal intervention, appeared to be winning the day. Humanitarianism was becoming attractive to those seeking a new respectability – those who felt themselves to be on the verge of getting the vote – and increasing support was being shown for moves that would separate the new industrial/mercantile age from a past that was felt to have been barbarous. Some of the more obvious excesses were being eradicated by legislation: the slave trade was abolished in Britain in 1807, and the ownership of slaves in the Empire in 1833; the use of child labour began to be diminished with the passing of the first Factory Act in 1833. The Bloody Code was crumbling: the burning of female felons ended in 1790; hanging, drawing and quartering was abolished in 1814; the last beheadings were in 1820; the stocks, the whip, the pillory and the gibbet would all fall idle by 1837. (London's last set of stocks would stand disused for many years in Portugal Street – James May's former haunt.) One of the last public whippings in London happened in 1829, when a thirteen-year-old boy was whipped for 150 yards while tied to the end of a cart for stealing a pair of shoes; the crowd that gathered were vocal in their opposition, but it is interesting that no one attempted his rescue.[31] The old was becoming repugnant, and Smithfield offended on so many levels; everything about the place stood in direct opposition to the impulses of those bent on reforming, modernising, cleansing, ordering, making open and visible.

The very topography of 'this old field of cruelty'[32] appeared to modern eyes to embody and perpetuate the sins of ages past. Until the middle of the thirteenth century, a small wooded section of the Smoothe Field called the Elms – which lay between today's Cowcross and Charterhouse Streets – had been the place of public execution. In 1532, Henry VIII devised the spectacle of the boiling to death of offenders, to take place in Smithfield (a kitchen servant, who had been accused of poisoning, died in a vat, slowly, in this way; then a serving woman ten years later). In the next decade, Mary Tudor had forty-five Protestants burnt close to the gates of St Bartholomew-the-Great, and her sister sent Catholics to the flames. Two centuries later, the convoluted lanes running around Turnmill Street,

50. Tudor/Stuart housing in Cloth Fair, Smithfield. Considered squalid in the 1830s, its destruction at the end of the nineteenth century provoked an outcry.

West Street, Field Lane, Saffron Hill, Cow Cross and other thoroughfares near the Fleet were colloquially known as Jack Ketch's Warren, after the seventeenth-century executioner; the Warren was where gallows-fodder hid from the law and bred new sinners. These festering piles of wooden buildings cut off the south (Farringdon Street leading to Blackfriars Bridge leading down into south London and Surrey) from the north (Clerkenwell Green, St John Street, Islington and the North), while the higgledy-piggledy, queer and quaint alleys and courts, with their antique names (Black Boy Alley, Swan Inn Yard, Bread Court), were increasingly felt to be harbouring immorality, criminality, disease and civil unrest – right in the heart of the wealthiest city in the world.[33] The sinuosity and complexity of the warren confounded those who attempted to enter and investigate these ancient spaces: to the horror of one surveyor and public health campaigner Frying Pan Alley, off Turnmill Street, was found to be 20 feet long, but just 2 feet wide.[34]

But it was only the outsider who was bewildered by the twists and turns of Smithfield. Those who lived there or worked there were able to negotiate it with ease. When Thomas Williams was sought for the theft of the copper tub from his parents' lodgings at 46 Turnmill Street on 19 February 1827, James Spoor, his parents' landlord, was told that he could probably find the culprit at the Bull's Head.[35] This pub was a right, right and right again walk from Turnmill Street – and sure enough, there was Williams, and he was taken into custody. The pub was in a secluded court (Bull's Head Square off Bull's Head Court off Peter Street off Saffron Hill) within a morass of tiny streets; but to those in the know, it was simple to locate.[36]

Cleanliness, godliness and commercial progress – the Victorian trinity – would sweep much of the district away; the alleys and courts that remained were often no more than amputated stumps abutting the fine new thoroughfares that thrust through the region: Farringdon Road, Clerkenwell Road, Holborn Viaduct, Charterhouse Street, the Metropolitan railway line; the filthy Fleet would be locked into a conduit beneath Farringdon Road. Disease, the Victorians believed, was airborne; petty, and not-so-petty, criminality festered in dark, unseen quarters; trade was shackled by poor lines of communication and slowed traffic. Before the century's end, Smithfield's secrets would be laid open to the skies.

NINE

Whatever Has Happened to Fanny?

On Thursday 24 November two admission booths were set up outside Bishop's House of Murder, as Number 3 Nova Scotia Gardens was now known. The police had asked John and Sarah Trueby, owners of numbers 1, 2 and 3, if some arrangement could be made whereby visitors could enter the House of Murder, five or six at a time, paying a minimum entrance fee of five shillings – a move officers hoped would prevent the house being rushed by the hundreds who were thronging the narrow pathways of the Gardens and straining to get as close to the seat of the horror as possible. Sarah Trueby's grown-up son told Constable Higgins that he was concerned about his family's property sustaining damage and asked Higgins and his men if they could weed out the rougher element in the crowd. Somehow, Higgins did ensure that some kind of pretence of decorum was achieved, and the *Morning Advertiser* later claimed that 'only the genteel were admitted to the tour'. Nevertheless, the two small trees that stood in the Bishops' garden were reduced to stumps as sightseers made off with bark and branches as mementoes – ditto the gooseberry bushes, the palings and the few items of worn-out furniture found in the upstairs rooms, while the floorboards were hacked about for souvenir splinters. Local lads were reported to have already stolen many of the Bishops' household items, and around Hackney Road and Crabtree Row a shilling could buy the scrubbing brush or bottle of blacking or coffee pot from the House of Murder. All of which prompted journalist and historian Albany Fontblanque to ruminate on English morbidity and enterprise in the *Examiner* magazine:

> The landlord upon whose premises a murder is committed is now-a-days a made man. . . . Bishop's house bids fair to go off in tobacco-stoppers and snuff-boxes; and the well will be drained – if one lady has not already finished it at a draught – at the rate of a guinea a quart. . . . If a Bishop will commit a murder for £12, which seems the

51. Sightseers at Nova Scotia Gardens. This drawing shows a third variant impression of Bishop's House of Murder. The Gardens differed as much as the faces of the accused in the various visual representations of the day.

average market price, the owner of a paltry tenement might find it worth while to entice a ruffian to make it the scene of a tragedy, for the sale of the planks and timbers in toothpicks, at a crown each.[1]

One of the assistants of architect John Soane came to take a detailed sketch of Number 3 in order to create a scale model for use at the Old Bailey trial, while celebrated solicitor James Harmer (who had offered his services as prosecution lawyer to the impoverished parish of St Paul's, Covent Garden, for free) undertook a full survey of the cottage.[2] Both exercises were intended to show that all the inhabitants of Number 3 must have been aware of any killings that were taking place within; Sarah and Rhoda were not yet in the clear. Indeed, they never would be, in the minds of locals. In the streets of Bethnal Green, Shoreditch and Hoxton, a number of women had been jeered at and jostled by people who mistook them for Sarah or Rhoda. On Monday 28 November the real Sarah and Rhoda made an ill-advised visit to the neighbourhood, and were spotted and chased by a crowd. A Shoreditch publican hustled them into the garden at the back of his premises and helped them to escape over the back wall.

*

Reports of attempted burkings on the streets of the metropolis after dark began once again to fill the news pages of the national papers, just as they had after the Edinburgh Horrors; but it is likely that panic and paranoia were contributing to making perfectly ordinary robberies and attempted sexual assaults appear bungled efforts to supply the surgeons. William Burke had been hanged in January 1829, and in that year *The Times* carried thirteen stories of attempted or alleged burkings, ten of them in the January and February. Throughout 1830, however, just one such story appeared in the newspaper, though there had been no diminution in anatomists' need for Subjects. After the Italian Boy arrests, five supposed attempted burkings were recorded by *The Times* within four weeks. Typical is this, from the edition of 24 November 1831:

On Tuesday evening between eight and nine o'clock, Charles White, a young lad about thirteen years of age, was returning from Messrs Fowlers manufactory in the Belvedere Road, near Waterloo Bridge, to his own home at 8 James Street, Lambeth, when he was seized by two men in a place called Sutton Street, leading into the York Road. One of the ruffians held him while the other clapped a large plaster over his face and endeavoured to stifle him. The poor lad struggled violently, got one of his hands loose and took the plaster from his mouth. The boy screamed for help and the villains, finding that they could not accomplish their diabolical purpose, and again clap the plaster on his face, became alarmed. The cries of the lad were fortunately heard when one of the villains, with a ruffian's grasp, seized him by the neck and threw him over a paling into an unused plot of ground and then ran away. A number of persons came to his assistance, and he was conveyed to the station house in Waterloo Road. . . . A description of one of the men, who was dressed in a smock frock, was taken down and the constables placed on alert.[3]

The smock-frock reference is interesting; it had been widely reported that May and Bishop had been arrested wearing this common item of rural labourer's clothing, which appeared to be coming to be associated, in the London mind, with resurrection and burking. Also, at the time of the attack on White, no *modus operandi* had been suggested for the murder of the Italian Boy; but no one had forgotten the iconic woodcut images in various broadsheets of Williams Burke and Hare suffocating their victims by placing pitch-plasters over the mouth and nose – a mythical method of killing, since, by their own admission, Burke and Hare had simply pinched shut the noses and clamped closed the jaws of their victims.

There were a number of other reported attacks on south London young-sters as the Italian Boy hearings were in progress. Henry Edward, fourteen, of Felix Street, Westminster Bridge Road, was assaulted in Waterloo Road; Henry Morgan, eighteen, was being attacked in Fore Street, a street running alongside the Thames, in Lambeth, when the police arrived and scared away his assailant; Martha Allenby, sixteen, of Bronti Place, off Walworth Road, thwarted an attempt to place a pitch-plaster across her mouth; Elizabeth Turner, eight, of Waterloo Road, was lured from her doorstep by a man offering her sweets, then tied with a rope and beaten before being rescued by passers-by.[4] All these assaults were reported as attempted burkings.

The man who swept the crossing at the Stamford Street junction with Waterloo Road suddenly stopped turning up for work – unusual in one who, according to those who knew him, was of regular habits. The *Sunday Times* of 27 November stated that 'little doubt is entertained that he has been murdered'. Meanwhile, in the East End, a boy who had claimed that he was the victim of an attempted burking on open ground opposite the Salmon and Ball pub in Bethnal Green Road later admitted that he had lied – concocting the story as an excuse to his family for having stayed out late.[5]

On the evening of the Monday after the Italian Boy arrests, residents of Chalton Street, Somers Town, heard the screams of local girl Eliza Campbell as she ran from the pathway that led north through the fields to Camden Town. She told those who came to help her that on the unlit path two men had thrown her to the ground, stuffed something into her mouth and placed a noose around her neck. She fought hard and screamed so loudly that the two ran off across the fields. 'We again caution the public to be on their guard,' warned the *Morning Advertiser*, in its 10 November report of the case, stressing that there were thousands of hardened villains in London who were likely to be tempted to commit murder by the high price of bodies (in fact, prices were down to eight to twelve guineas a corpse, from an earlier high of fifteen to twenty guineas). 'It is impossible to find any excuse for persons thus imprudently placing themselves in the way of danger,' admonished the *Advertiser*. 'It is to be hoped that the publicity of this transaction, the narrow, nay miraculous, escape of this young woman, will be a warning to both sexes to avoid at night the lonely paths of the suburbs of this town.'

At twenty to ten on the night of Saturday 3 December, Mary Cane went to the public, three-seater privy that served the tenements of Hartshorn Court, between Whitecross Street and Golden Lane. Opening the latch, with a method known only to those familiar with its faulty mechanism, Cane stumbled in the dark upon a small body lying just inside the door. Her screams alerted a twelve-year-old neighbour, William

Hartshorn Court, where Mary Duffey was found dead, lay just south of the school building at the Old Street end of Golden Lane.

Newton, who took a candle and opened the privy door. A man and a woman rushed out, knocking hard against Newton and blowing out his candle; the man was wearing a long black coat, Newton later said, and the woman a light shawl and pale-coloured bonnet. Other neighbours gathered and when they entered the privy found the body of a five-year-old girl, lying on her back, with her frock pulled above her knees and her stockings removed; one of her legs was drawn up. She had been strangled.

Half a mile away in Broad Arrow Court, near the Barbican, Mary Duffey was distraught. Her five-year-old daughter Margaret had last been seen being led away by Duffey's next-door neighbour, Bridget Culkin, a twenty-eight-year-old who had recently moved to Broad Arrow Court from Hartshorn Court – where she had lived opposite the privy. 'If you come along with me, I'll give you a penny,' Culkin was overheard saying to the child at around six o'clock in the evening. Culkin had often played with the child and was said to have always shown her kindness.

When Mary Duffey's older daughter asked Culkin, just before nine o'clock, what she had done with little Margaret, Culkin openly stated that she had left her in Hartshorn Court; Culkin then became aggressive and refused to give a good reason for abandoning the child. She was arrested half an hour before the body was discovered.

At her Old Bailey trial for murder Culkin was proved to have supplied two false alibis for the hours between six and nine o'clock of the 3rd, and several witnesses – people who knew Culkin by sight – told the court that they had seen her that night, leading a crying, shoeless child up Whitecross Street and into Hartshorn Court.

What had looked even worse for Culkin was that she was the lover of one Robert Tighe (or Tye), who also went by the name of James Kettle (or Cattle), a known resurrectionist who worked with a gang that usually included John and Thomas Shearing, William ('Boney') Dunkley and George Long. The landlord and landlady of the Fortune of War went to the authorities to denounce Bridget Culkin as an associate of snatchers; even more damningly, they claimed that she had often been seen in the pub with Bishop, Williams and May and had been observed receiving money from them.[6] (Interestingly, Hartshorn Court backed on to Nag's Head Court, address of Rosina Carpenter, lover of James May.) It is quite possible that Culkin knew May and Bishop and other resurrectionists, and perhaps the payments were for information about where a body was likely to be found; Ellen O'Brien, one of Culkin's friends, who failed to alibi her, was a nurse at St Bartholomew's.

The publican of the Fortune of War appears to have been poacher turned gamekeeper (as with the assembling of snatchers for the 1828 Anatomy Select Committee), and it is quite possible that he was being retained as a police informer, as a way of keeping an eye on the resurrection trade. The New Police were not supposed to behave in this way; but in trying to keep such a covert community as the snatchers under surveillance, doubtless they felt they had little choice but to cultivate certain publicans.

Culkin was found not guilty at her trial – though people were often hanged by far less compelling circumstantial evidence of involvement in murder – and no one else was ever tried for Margaret Duffey's killing.

There is a curious feeling for the modern reader looking over the Culkin case that what we may be reading about is a sex crime. (Though couched in euphemism, sexual assaults on children were reported in the newspapers of the day, even when these happened within the family.)[7] The point of a burking was to obtain a body, not to abandon it when interrupted, and the public nature of the scene of the killing – a privy in an overpopulated court – seems strange. If Margaret Duffey had been murdered to supply the surgeons, this was a foolhardy choice of venue.

Meanwhile, imaginations were running away with themselves in Bethnal Green. Superintendent Thomas recounted to the Bow Street magistrates tales of local women who had gone missing, of one John Bishop trying to tempt girls back to his house for a nip to drink. A police handbill had been circulated detailing the female clothing found in the privy of 2 Nova Scotia Gardens, and a number of people had come forward but failed to recognise the items, when, on Saturday 26 November, the identity of the owner was decided: Fanny Pighorn, or Pickbourne, or Pigburn – the latter being the choice eventually settled on by most reporters. The name was just one of many discrepancies in the various published reports of the identification. Here follows *The Times*'s account of proceedings at Bow Street with regard to Fanny, along with, bracketed and in italics, the *Morning Advertiser*'s version; in underscore, the *Globe and Traveller*; in bold, the *Sun*; and in double-underscore, the *Observer*.

Mr Thomas stated that the female dress found in the privy of No 2 Nova Scotia Gardens, next door to the residence of Bishop, had been identified by two females, Mrs Hitchcock and Mrs Low (*Anne Hitchcock, residing at No 10 Holywell Lane, Shoreditch, came to the station-house in Covent*

Garden, accompanied by a girl named Mayhew, the niece of the missing woman), who had called upon him in consequence of having seen an advertisement stating that such clothes had been found. [After much trouble, Serjeant Taylor discovered the sister of Elizabeth Pigburn, lately resident at Hoxton.] It appeared that a poor woman called Fanny Pighorn, who used to obtain her living by washing, left the house of her sister, Mrs Low, one of the applicants, who resided in Chart Street East, City Road (*Charles Street, Curtain Road*) about six (*five*) weeks ago, at eight o'clock in the evening, and had never since been either seen or heard of. When she left her sister's, she said she should not be long, as she was going as far only as (her brother-in-law) Mr Campion's {**Mr Chaplin's**} (Mrs Champion's) in Church Street, Bethnal Green. (*After remaining within for a short while she put on her cloak and said that she had to go on some business, which would not detain her—long. She went out and was never afterwards seen.*) It appeared that she had called there on the evening in question, and left the house at about nine o'clock {**half-past nine**} (9 o'clock) for the purpose, it is supposed, of returning to her sister's. Mrs Hitchcock, who had known the missing woman for 35 years, described the dress which she used to wear, which exactly corresponded with the clothes found in the privy. She spoke particularly to the shawl, which she said she herself had worn and afterwards gave it to Fanny Pighorn; and she also identified the blue cloth pocket found with the other articles, and the fellow of which she produced (*a blue cloth pocket of a very peculiar make, and having a small secret pocket within it*), saying that they had both belonged to a Mrs Bell, who on her death had bequeathed one of them to her, Mrs Hitchcock, and the other to Fanny Pighorn. (*The two women, Hitchcock and Mayhew, not only recognised this, but one of them produced the fellow pocket.*) [Mrs Pigburn at length said, 'If my sister is dead I should know her clothes, particularly her pocket, for I have by me the pattern from which it is made', at the same time she produced the paper pattern, which agrees with the pocket in every particular.] The moment that the clothes were produced, they were identified by both women, and Mrs Low positively declared that they were the same which her unfortunate sister had on when she left her house to go to Church Street.

Thomas then asked the women to swear the truth of this before the magistrates, which they did, Mrs Low weeping. \

Mrs Low said that her sister [sister-in-law] was about 45 years of age (*35*) [45], that she was of a cheerful disposition, in the enjoyment of good health and of particularly sober habits. (*The women informed Mr*

Thomas that Fanny Pighorn was unmarried, but that she had a child about ten years old, who is now in Shoreditch workhouse.) Mr Thomas said that the shawl which Mrs Hitchcock had so fully identified was not found with the rest of the clothes, but in a deep well in Bishop's garden, where it had been sunk by means of a large stone, and he had ascertained that about the time spoken to by the applicants, Bishop had disposed of the body of a woman at one of the hospitals. He had also been informed that cries of 'murder' were heard to proceed from the direction of Bishop's cottage, late one night about six weeks ago. [Mr Thomas says on the evening she went missing she was met by two men in the Hackney Road who pretended they wanted her to go on an errand for them and prevailed on her to drink porter with them.] {**She was seen to go into a public house in the Hackney Road in company with two men, one of whom exactly answers the description of Bishop, and there she took a pint of porter with them and was sent by them on a message to Birdcage Walk. The men left the house without waiting for her return, and did not come back. It is supposed that the sending her on a message was a mere pretence, and that she was followed by the two men and inveigled to Bishop's house, and there murdered.**}

At a subsequent period of the day, the two women were brought by Mr Thomas before Mr Minshull in the private room, when the clothes were produced and again fully identified by them, except the petticoat and shift, which could not be distinctly sworn to, as the clothes of Fanny Pighorn. (*Mrs Low also identified a straw bonnet, which had once been white but was dyed black, which had been found near Bishop's house. Mrs Low had dyed it herself, and sewn in a lining, because Fanny had said that a white bonnet was too smart for her to wear.*) Mr Harmer was present and submitted that a warrant should be lodged at Newgate against Bishop and Williams, charging them on suspicion with the wilful murder of Fanny Pighorn. Mr Thomas said he should use every exertion for the purpose of ascertaining the hospital at which Bishop disposed of the body of a female about the period stated, with a view to obtain further evidence tending to identify it with that of Fanny Pighorn.[8]

Many questions were begged by these early reports – and many were never to be satisfactorily answered. Why was there no attempt to elicit a more exact date – or even day of the week – for the last sighting of Fanny than 'five or six weeks ago'? Did Mrs Low (usually Fanny's sister; occasionally relegated to sister-in-law) live in Great Chart Street East (a street of Georgian terraced homes that still runs between East Road and Pitfield

Street to the north of Old Street); or Charles Street, Curtain Road (which is also still there – just – as the eastern end of Luke Street); or in another nearby Charles Street, which used to run just north of Leonard Street? Whichever of the three streets it was, the distance to Church Street and the mysterious Mr Campion/Chaplin/Champion/Mrs Champion – who was never to be summoned to tell his/her story – was at most a twelve-minute walk (Church Street is today's Redchurch Street, just south of St Leonard's church and opposite Hollywell Lane). These accounts contradict themselves from paragraph to paragraph, as, for example, with the *Morning Advertiser* of 28 November describing the pocket as blue, and a few lines later as black. (It is little wonder that Charles Dickens was able, before the age of twenty, to gain a formidable reputation as a shorthand reporter – the competition was so poor. In Chapter 33 of *Bleak House*, Dickens refers to court/inquest reporters as 'gentlemen not very neat about the cuffs and buttons', who are paid by the word and therefore produce repetitious and occasionally nonsensical reports.) The garbled reporting that dogged the London Burkers case reached new depths with the Fanny Pighorn/Pigburn episode.

The district in which Fanny's relatives, or friends, lived was notoriously poor, and getting poorer. Paintings and sketches from the start of the nineteenth century show that the area to the west of Shoreditch High Street largely comprised meadows, ponds, copses and tenter grounds, but by the 1820s, noxious industries, warehouses, tenement housing, the inevitable pubs (and, by extension, the inevitable chapels and tabernacles) had obliterated these, and dispelled the rich romance of its past. Holywell, Shoreditch, had been the site of an Augustinian priory, founded in 1128. With the dissolution of the monasteries, the quarter was commandeered by actors who, in the 1570s, founded London's first two theatres – the Theatre and the Curtain – in the little enclave that centres on New Inn Yard.[9] In the 1780s the grassy hillock immediately to the west of this spot, Holywell Mount, was levelled and became a private burial ground run by two elderly women who lived on the site. Here, a notorious feud between local resurrectionists had contributed to the bad repute of a desperately poor neighbourhood. In the years between 1810 and 1820 a two-man team of bodysnatchers was said to be emptying the Holywell Mount burial ground. One of the men was known only as Murphy, the other was tentatively identified as Patrick Connolly; both were among surgeon Sir Astley Cooper's elite of lifters and were helped in their work by the ground's corrupt sexton/gravedigger, a man called Whackett.[10] Two envious rivals, Hollis and Vaughan, went to the local magistrates' office and shouted this information out in open court, whereupon the crowd who had been in the court room rushed to the Holywell Mount ground, dug up some of the most recent graves and found the coffins to be empty. Whackett, his wife and children, and the old women (who had, apparently, been unaware of any body-trafficking from their ground) were assaulted and their homes attacked. Now here was Shoreditch/Holywell once again linked to one of the most reviled crimes.

Corrupt gravedigger and snatchers' assistant Michael Shields read one of the accounts of the identification of Fanny Pigburn, and on the night of Monday 28 November paid a visit to Superintendent Thomas. Having decided that Shields's word on any matter was worthless, Thomas and Minshull nevertheless listened to the tale he told them.

Shields recalled that he had been woken at five o'clock in the morning on Sunday 9 October by John Bishop and Thomas Williams banging on his door in Eagle Street. They wanted him to carry a trunk to St Thomas's Hospital. Shields walked at dawn the two miles to Nova Scotia Gardens with Bishop and Williams. There, Bishop placed a large but fairly light trunk on Shields's head and told the porter that he was to walk to St Thomas's on one side of the roadway, accompanied by Williams's wife; Rhoda would be carrying a small box tied up in a handkerchief, and the two of them were to give the impression that Rhoda was a servant going to a new post, with Shields employed as a porter to carry her possessions for her. Bishop and Williams would walk on the other side of the street and would pretend, if anyone stopped them, to have no connection with Shields and Rhoda.

In this formation they walked from Nova Scotia Gardens to St Thomas's in the Borough – a distance of nearly two miles – crossing new London Bridge on opposite sides of the roadway. On arriving, Rhoda waited outside as the three men entered the hospital dissecting-rooms and failed to make a sale. Bishop had asked the footman of Dr John Flint South, demonstrator of anatomy,[11] if he was in need of a body, and his footman said that South was in need but did not have time to come down and look at the corpse – could Bishop come back tomorrow? They decided to leave the trunk at St Thomas's and go to a nearby pub to ponder the offer. Rhoda was then left at the pub as a pledge, since there was no money to pay for the beers they had just drunk.

They walked to Grainger's school in Webb Street, and Bishop spoke alone with John Appleton, porter to the dissecting-room, a conversation that lasted a few minutes. The three then went back to St Thomas's for the trunk, and at Grainger's Bishop pulled from it a corpse for Appleton to inspect. It was the body of a thin, middle-aged female, extremely fresh and with no grave-dirt upon it, thought Shields. The Subject's hair was dark and short. Appleton and Bishop spent quite a time striking a bargain, and when the sum had been agreed – £10 – Appleton paid Bishop half of the money and promised to pay him the remainder on the following day. Gin was then sent for, and all four men had a genial drink together.

Bishop, Williams and Shields went back to the pub to collect Rhoda and found her weeping. The landlord wanted his payment and had been unpleasant to her. Bishop flew into a rage and, as he paid up, shouted that he would never drink there again, and would tell his friends not to drink there either. They all left together and walked over London Bridge and up Bishopsgate Street, where Bishop bought them all some gin at the Flowerpot inn.[12] Bishop paid Shields his ten shillings for the job, and even offered to pay him a little more when he got hold of the rest of his earnings the next day. At this point, Shields went home.

Shields told Superintendent Thomas that the reason he had mentioned none of this at the various hearings was that he had been too frightened of implicating himself. He now wished to atone, he said. Thomas was quite satisfied, since Shields's story seemed roughly to tally with the time that Fanny Pigburn was last seen, and the corpse that Shields described appeared to match Fanny Pigburn in age and stature. The information also confirmed the superintendent in his suspicion that the women of Number 3 Nova Scotia Gardens were implicated in murder. He gave orders for Rhoda to be rearrested, which she was the following afternoon, as she sat at the porter's lodge at Newgate waiting to visit her husband.

She was brought before Minshull at Bow Street and charged with being an accessory after the fact in the wilful murder of Frances Pigburn. Thomas declared that on a future day he expected to be able to produce further evidence against her. Rhoda wept. Minshull asked her if she had anything to say, warning her that whatever she did say would be taken down in writing and might be used as evidence against her, and she said, 'I thank you, sir, but I want to say what I know. I wish to speak the truth.'

She told of how her 'father' had awoken her at six o'clock on a Sunday morning 'about six or seven weeks ago'. He asked her if she would carry a small box for him to the Borough. She agreed and walked with Bishop, her husband and Shields over London Bridge. Just over the bridge they came to a pub and Bishop told her to go in and wait until they returned. They came back again in about half an hour, and then they all went together to another pub and had a pot of 'half-and-half' (half-ale, half-porter) and smoked pipes. There was no money to pay for the drinks, and Bishop told her to wait there. When he came back he paid the barman, and then all four of them went to Bishopsgate and drank gin in a pub. Shields then left, and later Rhoda, her father and husband went home. 'That is all I wish to say, I have nothing more to add.'

Minshull remanded her for a fortnight, though Thomas said he would be able to find more evidence against her within a week. As Rhoda rose to be taken down, Thomas said he believed she had not eaten all day and said he hoped she would be given some food, since she was now passing out of his jurisdiction. Minshull replied, 'Most certainly – the gaoler shall provide her with what is necessary. No prisoner shall want food while I sit here as a magistrate.'

It was all shaping up very nicely now – which was just as well, because the Old Bailey trial, at which Bishop and Williams would now be charged with three counts of murder, May with one, was set for three days' time, Friday 2 December; and while the identities of Carlo Ferrari and Fanny Pigburn seemed reasonably well fixed – certain enough, probably – no name had yet been suggested for the missing-presumed-burked owner of one of the sets of clothes unearthed in the garden of the House of Murder.

On Wednesday 30th Minshull received his first visit from an anatomist. George Pilcher was lecturer in anatomy – and keeper of the Anatomical Theatre of Medical Specimens – at Grainger's school.[13] He had read Shields's statement in the newspapers and came to give Grainger's side of the story as far as Fanny Pigburn was concerned. Pilcher also wanted to

point out to Thomas that he had in fact come forward to the superintendent as soon as the discovery of the Italian Boy's body had been made
and had explained how Grainger's had refused to buy it. Had the
policeman not remembered his visit?

With regard to Fanny, Minshull asked: 'When did you first see the body?'

Pilcher: 'The body, I understand, was brought to the theatre on the
morning of Sunday 9th October, but I did not see it until the following day.'

Minshull: 'In what state did the body appear to you then?'

Pilcher answered that the body had seemed far fresher than most Subjects
brought in for dissection. He thought that it looked as though it had never
been buried, or prepared for burial, and he had assumed that Bishop, as a
resurrectionist, had probably stolen it from a bone-house or an undertaker's
premises. Pilcher said that Appleton, the dissecting-room porter, had thought
the same thing; and both men took Bishop's willingness to accept only part
of his payment on the Sunday as further proof that there was nothing unusual
about the way in which the corpse had been obtained. (The inference being
that a man guilty of murder would want all his money at once.) 'Of course,
had there been any suspicion that the woman had been unfairly dealt by,
the body would not have been purchased at all,' said Pilcher.

Minshull: 'Did you perceive any marks of violence on the body when
you saw it on the Monday?'

Pilcher: 'I was not aware of any, but Mr Dunn, the pupil by whom the
body was dissected, is now present and ready to be examined.'

Minshull said that he 'did not think it proper to put any questions to
Dunn then', a move that did nothing to assist the case, but was likely to
have been an example of Minshull's characteristic, if sometimes mis-
directed, courtesy. The young man risked implicating himself, his tutors
and his school since his statements would be printed in the press.

Pilcher then took it upon himself to speak on behalf of the London
medical profession. He told the magistrate, with the court reporters sitting
nearby, that he regretted 'as much as any man, the horrible disclosures that
had taken place; and he was truly sorry that the profession was driven to the
necessity of dealing with men such as Bishop, Williams and May. He, however,
begged to repeat that no suspicion existed in his mind of anything wrong,
until he heard that Bishop and Williams were charged with the murder of
the Italian Boy; and then he immediately came forward to state that the body
of a woman had been sold at Webb Street by Bishop early in October.'
Thomas said, yes, that was right, Mr Pilcher had indeed come forward straight
away to tell of that particular purchase, he remembered now.

Minshull had had his curiosity about dissecting-room etiquette stimu-
lated, and in a reply to a question from the magistrate, Pilcher said that

the normal practice was for the porters to wash and prepare for dissection any Subjects that were brought in. Appleton had washed the middle-aged thin woman before the student Dunn had wielded the scalpel.

Minshull: 'Do you remember whether or not the face of the woman was marked with the small-pox?'

Pilcher: 'Mr Dunn told me that the face was slightly marked with the small-pox. But I did not perceive any such marks myself. Generally speaking, they are not easily discoverable after death.'

Thomas, still dwelling on an earlier point, said that it was utterly out of the question that the woman's body could have been stolen from a mortuary because he had obtained additional evidence which left him in no doubt that this woman had been murdered. *The Times*, the *Morning Advertiser* (in italic) and the *Sunday Times* (in bold) pick up the tale:

Superintendent Thomas said that Fanny

> was proved to have left the house of Mr Campion in Church Street, Bethnal Green, at half-past nine o'clock on the night of Saturday 8th October, and at half-past eleven o'clock on the same night he had ascertained that Bishop and Williams were seen dragging a woman, who appeared to be intoxicated, in the direction of their own house. In about an hour after, cries of murder were heard proceeding from Nova Scotia Gardens. At seven o'clock the following morning, Shields was hired by Bishop and Williams to carry the body of a woman to St Thomas's Hospital, where it was conveyed at eleven o'clock on that day, but refused to be purchased, and between twelve and one o'clock it was ultimately disposed of at the establishment in Webb Street. (*Mr Thomas would be able to prove . . . that the deceased was seen on the same night, and that within half an hour of the time that she left her brother-in-law's house, taking porter with two men in a public house* (**The London Apprentice**)*; that some persons who watched them, and thought from conversation which they overheard that all was not right, followed them and saw them take her to another public house* (**The Feathers**)*, where they gave her some mixed spirits and beer called 'hot' – that after the deceased was very much overcome with what she had drunk, the same two men conducted her, leading her between them, arm-in-arm, towards Nova Scotia Gardens, and were lost sight of within a very short distance of Bishop's house.*)

But strange friends these, to follow so assiduously and then abandon Fanny at the very last.

Furthermore, quite a coup this, Thomas announced that he had reason to believe that Fanny had died by drowning: he had found her shawl at the bottom of the well in Bishop's garden; this well consisted of a wooden barrel sunk into a hole in the ground, and he wondered whether the victims were told to bend down and drink from the well and were then pushed in head-first. He had learned that the vessels of Fanny Pigburn's heart had been engorged, which, as he understood it, was generally the result of drowning – the medical gentlemen present would correct him if he was wrong.

TEN

A Horrid System

'By Jove! The boy died a nathral death!' lisped Herbert Mayo, professor of anatomy at King's College, gazing at the dead child delivered by Bishop, Williams, May and Shields. As the sunlight streamed through the windows of the watch-house of St Paul's, Covent Garden, Professor Mayo had held his characteristic stance – bolt upright with hands thrust deep into his breeches pockets – and given his verdict. George Beaman, surgeon to the parish of St Paul's, and Richard Partridge, junior colleague of Mayo, both politely suggested carrying out further investigation, and, a few hours later, at the end of the post-mortem, Mayo concluded, 'By Jove! This boy was murthered!'

Had Mayo been a more stubborn or imperious man and overruled the other surgeons, it is likely the London Burkers case would never have been discovered. At thirty-six, he had established a formidable reputation as an anatomist, having been made house surgeon at the Middlesex Hospital at the age of twenty-two, in the same year that he published his *Anatomical and Physiological Commentaries*, in which he revealed his discovery of the functions of individual facial nerves. A bitter row followed publication, with his former teacher, Sir Charles Bell, claiming that Mayo had made these discoveries only as a result of unattributed groundwork carried out by Bell. Mayo replied that the opposite was true – that Bell's work had been based on research by Mayo. This dispute became one of the most famous medical wrangles of the day, and those who mulled it over later in the century tended to concur that most of the glory should have been Mayo's. (Had the junior man won his argument, a temporary paralysis of the face might today be referred to as Mayo's Palsy.) But, like most of his peers, Mayo was not quite so acute in the new field of forensic medicine, and it was just as well for his latest employers that his *volte-face* in St Paul's watch-house was not reported at the time.[1]

Mayo had been chosen as King's College's first professor of anatomy – properly, Professor of Morbid Anatomy and Physiology – just as Mayo's own school and anatomical theatre in Great Windmill Street, Soho, was going into decline.[2] King's (which had been officially opened just one month before Bishop, Williams, May and Shields made their troubling delivery to its dissecting-rooms) was founded as a response to the new University College – 'the godless institution of Gower Street', as its critics called it. University College had been refused a royal charter since no religious instruction was given there and Catholics, Jews and Dissenters were allowed to take courses. King's, by contrast, was built on Crown land just to the east of Somerset House and reeked of Anglican religiosity. Its founder, Reverend George D'Oyly, was a future chaplain to the Archbishop of Canterbury; its first principal, Reverend William Otter, would soon be made Bishop of Chichester. Present at the inaugural meeting of the council of King's College in June 1828 were George IV (patron), the Duke of Wellington (governor), three archbishops and seven bishops, while the governors of the medical school included two baronets. The Bishop of London's address at King's opening ceremony was entitled 'The Duty of Combining Religious Instruction with Intellectual Culture'. The lower orders were not overlooked in this regard: a (never-observed) rule in King's constitution stated that 'post-mortems must not be performed at such times

2. Robert Smirke's King's College building was brand new in 1831.

as would interfere with the presence of the hospital porters at divine service in the chapel'.[3]

The medical journal the *Lancet* missed no chance to pillory the place. Refusing to defer to King's royal links, the journal nicknamed it Strand Lane College, and the Church and Tory College in the Strand, while the cap and gown that King's students were required to wear were, it said, 'disgusting mummeries'. Mayo himself was impaled on the *Lancet*: he was dubbed the Owl because he lectured with his eyes half-closed; he was castigated for his 'Cockney' accent, in a strangely snobbish attack (for a Radical publication) on his non-gentry background (Mayo was born and brought up just north of Oxford Street); and a contributor pondered on how very un-King's College it was that Mayo had taken out advertisements in the newspapers to publicise his book *Observations on Injuries and Diseases of the Rectum*.[4] Mayo was taken to task for being a poor lecturer, with bad diction; a student complained to the *Lancet* about the Owl who 'does not whoop with a clear voice'.[5]

That Mayo's lectures were hard to follow would have been of significance to *Lancet* founder Thomas Wakely and his editorial team. The *Lancet*

53. Herbert Mayo.

had been set up, in October 1823, to prod the medical establishment into reforming itself, and medical education was the field in which change was most urgently needed, Wakely believed. Students paid fees directly to the teaching surgeon/anatomist; the more pupil revenues, the wealthier the institution. But Wakely revealed that pupils rarely got their money's worth. Teachers who did not turn up to lectures; who were too busy or too lazy to field questions; who refused even to acknowledge complaints; whose information was out of date or simply wrong; who would peremptorily shun or have excluded any student – these were the men Wakely was out to shame, the 'selfish oligarchy' who comprised the 'junta' that was the Royal College of Surgeons of England.[6]

An editorial reply to an anonymous complaint about Mayo made to the *Lancet* read:

No wonder. Owls feed upon bats – a species of prey which is not to be found so abundantly in the neighbourhood of Somerset House as about the walls of the West End hospitals. Nothing less could be expected than that the ill-constructed nest should suffer some severe damage in its removal from Windmill Street to the Strand. Besides, what a stupid owl was it, which could suppose that a new 'College' was better suited to its beckings and whoopings than the whistling crevices of an old, rotten establishment.[7]

This referred to the fact that, upon joining King's, Mayo had asked for (and received) the enormous sum of £900 for his jars and bottles of interesting specimens (human parts showing rare pathological conditions; unusual animals; 'monster' stillborn babies) that had been stored in the anatomical museum of the Great Windmill Street School.[8] The £900 included a £300 payment for 'assistance' – which may or may not have been money to pay resurrectionists. 'Bats' was Wakely's name for the men who ran the London medical Establishment – mediocre, highly resistant to change and, in certain cases, driven less by interest in science than by petty rivalries, indulging in rancorous feuds that could last for years. Bats were creatures that thrived in the dark, in the gloom of an aristocratic system of patronage that exhibited all the perceived corruption and skullduggery of the Hanoverian age. And now, many influential people believed, it was time for this age to end.

Wakely's views were not unusual within medical circles. Comparatively few autobiographies and reminiscences from these years are free from at least implicit criticism of senior surgeons and how they ran the medical profession. Joseph Carpue – founder of the Dean Street School of

Anatomy, where John Bishop had tried to sell the fresh adolescent on 4 November – told the parliamentary Select Committee on Medical Education that he was 'disgusted' by the Council of the Royal College of Surgeons: 'I considered the Council a select vestry, which did not like to let in any but the friends, allies and connections of their own body.'[9] Its exclusivity expressed itself in the College building: the Council entered through the main entrance fronting Lincoln's Inn Fields; mere Members came and went by the back door, which opened on to filthy, tumbledown Portugal Street – the haunt of James May and site of the noxious, much-pillaged St Clement Danes graveyard.

The Royal College of Surgeons had been granted its charter in 1800, changing its name from the Company of Surgeons – the organisation formed in 1745 when the surgeons broke from the medieval Barbers and Surgeons Company, thereby throwing off any connection with tonsure, shaving and teeth-pulling. The Royal College was the only body that granted qualifications in surgery in England; whoever wanted to qualify as a surgeon – and thereby become a Member of the College – had to fulfil its requirements. And from 1823 these requirements underwent a controversial change. All summer courses in anatomy – and these were only taught at private schools – were derecognised, and certificates of attendance at lectures in surgery and anatomy were only to be accepted from London's teaching hospitals: St Thomas's and Guy's (known until 1826 as the United Hospitals); St Bartholomew's; and the London Hospital in Whitechapel. Before undergoing examination at the College the candidate now had to produce certificates of attendance from a hospital school (and then stump up fees for the examiner). So no matter how good the anatomy teaching at London's various private schools – and much of it was reputed to be excellent, with Joshua Brookes, Edward Grainger, Joseph Carpue and Edward Tuson said to have superior learning and technical skill – any courses undertaken with independent tutors would not count towards qualification.

Quite apart from alleged poor teaching and social/familial exclusivity, hospital schools had two major drawbacks for the medical student: their courses were expensive; and tuition stopped in April for five months. A pupil who wanted to study under England's most famous surgeon – Sir Astley Cooper at Guy's – would pay the baronet £10 10s for his course of lectures, and a further £10 10s for his dissection course.[10] But for ten guineas all-in a pupil could, for instance, attend lectures and perform dissections at Joshua Brookes's school in Blenheim Steps, just off Oxford Street.[11] Brookes was an outstanding anatomist and had founded his school in 1787, closing it down in 1826 because of ill-health – he was by then sixty-seven years old and had worked for nearly forty years in typically appalling conditions. His school stank of rank meat because of his unique method of preserving Subjects by injecting them with potassium nitrate – which was more usually the method of extending the shelf-life of ham and sausages – and filth was present on every floor of the school. (Such an environment was the norm in these pre-Florence Nightingale, pre-Joseph Lister days. Joseph Carpue was remembered as having dirt-encrusted hands and nostrils exuding snuff, no doubt placed there to keep out the stench; Edward Tuson's Little Windmill Street school was said to be rat-ridden.)[12] The Brookesian Comparative Osteological Museum filled the two upper storeys of the tall, narrow house in Blenheim Steps and, with around 6,000 specimens – including three elephants and a number of whales – it was said to rank second only to the impressive collection amassed by the famous eighteenth-century anatomist John Hunter; many of Brookes's exhibits had been donated by his brother, who kept a small indoor zoo in a crumbling house in Exeter 'Change in the Strand.[13] While it was debatable whether much of use could be learnt from pickled oddi-ties in jars, the Royal College used as one of its weapons against private schools the argument that since private schools did not have access to museums, their teaching was likely to be defective. In fact, the existence of the Brookesian and the collections owned by Sir Charles Bell and Herbert Mayo proved that private anatomists often had very good museums in the 1820s; but the Royal College and the hospital schools bought up the private museums (starting with the Hunterian as soon as the Royal College was formed), thereby making their original accusation become true in time.[14]

Upon qualification, the next step for the surgeon-to-be was to become apprenticed to a surgeon – the more illustrious the better – by becoming his 'dresser'. These posts earned the surgeon around fifty guineas a year per dresser; and as each surgeon had between four and six dressers, this ensured an annual income of at least £200. Only students who could afford such fees were likely to make it into the top echelons of medicine; and those with blood ties, or who enjoyed other forms of favouritism, were first in the queue for dresserships. As 'A Student of 1815' commented in the *Lancet*: 'Tell me the name of the successful individual and I will tell you who his uncle was.'[15] The consequent waste of talent was lamented by those campaigning for reform. Sir Astley Cooper played straight into the hands of those who were demanding change when he expressed his pride that of the surgeons at the United Hospitals of St Thomas's and Guy's, Joseph Green was his godson, while Charles Aston Key, Bransby Cooper and Frederick Tyrrell were his nephews.[16] Bransby Cooper was a

54.–56. Anatomist Joshua Brookes taught in his private school, the Brookesian, in Blenheim Steps, Great Marlborough Street; its top floors housed a museum of 6,000 specimens. His garden contained his Vivarium – a chunk of Gibraltar Rock to which were chained unusual animals and birds, many of which were on loan from his brother's private zoo in the Strand.

poor surgeon, as Thomas Wakely pointed out in the *Lancet* and was sued for his pains. To accusations that the wrong man had reached the wrong position for the wrong reasons, Sir Astley said: 'I do not say that he is a perfectly good surgeon, but give him time, gentlemen, give him time. Do not crush him in the outset of his career.'[7] At this point, Bransby Cooper had been operating for three years. It was a reply that would be extremely funny if it could be forgotten how many lives Bransby brought to a painful, premature end.

Wakely persistently depicted the iniquities and inequities of the London medical establishment as stemming from an as-yet unrevoked age of aristocratic misrule. Unfair systems, networks and behaviours were, he and others believed, poisoning all of Great Britain's institutions. Wakely had written: 'We hope the age of Mental Delusion has passed and that mystery and concealment will no longer be encouraged.' And of Bats, Wakely wrote:

> In youth they are always, by the instinctive precautions of their parents, kept from contact with the ground; and before these disgusting creatures are allowed to take their flight in the air, they are invariably either forced upon some eminence by parental exertion, or they succeed in crawling to some elevated point, through, possibly, the most filthy channels of rottenness and corruption.[18]

However, many (perhaps most) Bats were in fact 'self-made' men of comparatively humble beginnings;[19] but it is true that their careers had flourished only when they managed to get patronage to work in their favour; it was vital that they accepted and manipulated the networks, and never challenged them. And once they attained their elevated station, the Bats took upon themselves the privilege of behaving in an elitist way, ensuring that their own offspring or relatives were favoured over 'outsiders'. George Guthrie would not resign his post at the Westminster Hospital until his son was ready to take it over, in 1843.

Wakely was to feel badly let down when two of his medical-reform allies went over to 'the other side' as soon as they were able to achieve good positions within hospitals. However, the more usual fate of the bright and able but not-well-connected was either to become a surgeon in the army or navy, or to set up practice in the provinces. Sir Astley Cooper told the talented and assiduous Edward Grainger to try his luck in Birmingham when refusing him the post of demonstrator of anatomy at Guy's. He appointed instead his own unremarkable nephew, Charles Aston Key. But Grainger decided to join the ranks of London's independent anatomy teachers and in June 1819, at the age of twenty-two, he rented an attic in a tailor's shop on the edge of the graveyard of St Saviour's church – today's Southwark Cathedral – and began to teach a summer course in anatomy, just across Borough High Street from Guy's. A few months later he moved the school to a former Catholic chapel in Webb Street, where he was able to offer year-round classes at around half the price of those at the United Hospitals of Guy's and St Thomas's. It is not known whether Grainger availed himself of the slumberers in St Saviour's graveyard; but what is certain is that, like all private teachers, he relied on the resurrectionists for Subjects, since he had no hospital morgue to supply (albeit illicitly) any teaching material. What seems to have happened between 1819 and 1824 – the year of Edward Grainger's death from consumption – is that a turf war broke out, not among the resurrectionists, but between London's anatomy teachers – a battle between the buyers, not the sellers. The story goes that Sir Astley, furious at the success of what he called 'the cheap school of anatomy', sought to pay resurrectionists *not* to supply Grainger, with the aim of driving him out of business. The resurrectionists, however, seeking to capitalise on this schism, chose to supply Grainger almost exclusively, in order to bolster his school and maintain another outlet for their goods. The hospital schools had therefore to offer higher prices to the resurrectionists – forcing the hospital surgeons to break their own club-cum-cartel, the Anatomical Society (set up some time in the first decade of the century to keep fees to resurrectionists as low as possible). Prices, as a result, were said to have hit a high of twenty guineas per corpse. Grainger, in reply, offered even higher prices, thereby securing for himself a good supply of corpses and – as a result – a greater number of pupils.[20] According to Grainger's friend and competitor Joseph Carpue, an estimated 250 to 300 pupils a year were enrolling at the Webb Street school in the early 1820s, a very impressive figure, particularly since there was an ongoing decline in the number of medical students in London. Pupils were increasingly heading for Paris to study surgery, since the French state supplied a steady – and free – flow of corpses for dissection from centralised public morgues. Fewer students meant lower revenues for the hospital surgeons of London.[21]

Edward Grainger had managed to upset the medical hierarchy in a way that Joshua Brookes, Joseph Carpue, Edward Tuson and other note-worthy private teachers in London had not. Perhaps it had seemed like a personal affront to Sir Astley that a man who was not related to him had defied his patronising advice and set up in direct opposition, geographically and commercially, to Guy's, and prospered, all the while disturbing the uneasy but workable relationship between the Bats and the body-snatchers. Sir Astley had in the past praised Joshua Brookes's academy, saying that his summer courses could be a useful adjunct to hospital teaching; and he would, in the future, support Richard Dugard Grainger, who would take over the running of the Webb Street school on his brother's death. But Edward Grainger's refusal to accept the *status quo* would not be forgiven.

In *Death, Dissection and the Destitute*, an analysis of the 1832 Anatomy Act (which would make legally available to surgeons the bodies of paupers unclaimed by family or friends), historian Ruth Richardson has written that Edward Grainger's action, and the Anatomical Society's reaction, was one of the triggers of the events that would lead to the passing of the Act. She writes:

> In 1823, probably as a result of the failure of the Anatomical Society to control corpse prices, Astley Cooper solicited from several fellow anatomists ideas about what could be done to break the power of the bodysnatchers. . . . It is remarkable that most of the replies seem to favour covert official connivance at existing supply routes.[22]

As Richardson points out, 'official connivance' had been vital to the nation's surgeons if they were to avoid the implications of the Rex *v.* Lynn case of 1788, which made taking a body from a churchyard a misdemeanour. For thirty years, only resurrectionists had gone to prison or been fined for obtaining or possessing corpses for dissection. The price paid by the surgeons was comparatively low, consisting of stumping up bail fees and legal defence costs, providing gaol 'comforts' and helping to support the family of the imprisoned man. (The 'humble petition' found on Sarah Bishop when she was arrested at the Fortune of War was just such a calling-in of the debt.) But in February 1828, a Liverpool anatomy teacher was convicted of causing a body to be disinterred; and one month later, a Lancaster court convicted three of a gang of five – which included a surgeon and a medical student – of possession of a body that had been obtained illegally. The Edinburgh Horrors provided another spur to legislation, and the first Anatomy Bill was introduced to parliament by Henry Warburton in March 1829, just six weeks after William Burke had been hanged for the sixteen murders he had committed with William Hare in order to supply Dr Knox with fresh Subjects to dissect. The Bill's supporters declared that burking would end as soon as a legal supply – the unclaimed poor from workhouses and hospitals – was made available to the surgeons. But while Warburton's Bill was passed by the Commons, it failed in the Lords; and not until 1832 would its heir start its progress through parliament.

So, in 1831, London's anatomy teachers – at hospitals and in private schools – were continuing to rely on the authorities turning a blind eye to the trafficking of corpses; on policemen not making arrests, or, if arresting, leaving the buyer out of the charge; and on magistrates and the higher courts ensuring that a surgeon or school was not implicated when a resurrectionist was in the dock. Discretion was paramount if doctors, schools and hospitals were to avoid being the target of the angry crowds that seemed to materialise as though from nowhere whenever resurrection was suspected – just as they did when a beggar was being arrested. Reliable reports of attacks and threats by the London public upon individual doctors or medical institutions are not easy to come by; whether this indicates that there was less interest in the issue in London than elsewhere in the country, or whether it reflects the under-reporting of popular dissent in the metropolis, cannot now be known. There were violent attacks on provincial medical schools before and after the passing of the Anatomy Act,[23] and the Burke and Hare case caused city-wide civil disturbances in Edinburgh in 1828–9, but in London no medical school was burnt down, no doctor hanged in effigy. The extent of opposition to London anatomists, and the risks that doctors ran of exposure and attack, can only be guessed at by the ripples – memories, anecdotes, hearsay – caused by individual events. It was an old, oft-repeated story, but it worked to underline the perils of treating dead flesh irreverently: in 1810, a medical student at the Great Windmill Street school climbed on to the roof of the building carrying a human leg and posted it down the chimney of the house next door. It fell into a pot of stew cooking over the fire below, and a hue and cry was raised; angry citizens gathered and only dispersed when the surgeons of the school paid them to go away.[24] Nearly twenty years later, after Burke and Hare, the misdeeds of medical students were rather more likely to lead to a hearing before the magistrates, even if it were quite cursory. In October 1829, a year to the month after Burke and Hare killed their final victim, London's chief magistrate, Sir Richard Birnie, found before him at Bow Street a 'very elegantly dressed young man' who was charged with attempting to burke a seventy-year-old woman in St Martin's Court, off St Martin's Lane. The young man was a medical student and along with three other students had been drinking in the Shades tavern on Leicester Square; by seven o'clock in the evening the four were very drunk. The student in the dock had seized the old woman by the throat and she had passed out; when passers-by rushed to help her, the students assaulted them. Birnie made light of the matter, chortling that it looked to him as though they were carrying out some sort of experiment on the woman but that 'the burking system, thank God, was not prevalent in the metropolis'. However, he remanded the student for a further hearing, perhaps fearing public reaction if he did anything less.[25]

Joshua Brookes, an unlucky man in so many ways, comes down to us as the London anatomist most closely connected with public fury. Perhaps he did not have the guile to be as circumspect as other medical men; perhaps he was too proud to care about discretion. One night, date unknown, disgruntled resurrectionists, angry that Brookes would not pay them a retainer, dumped two badly decomposed bodies near his school – one at the corner of Great Marlborough Street and Poland Street, the other at the corner with Argyle Street. Two 'well-dressed ladies' stumbled over them in the dark, and their screams caused a mob to assemble outside Brookes's school.[26] The anatomist sought refuge in Great Marlborough Street police station/magistrates' court, not for the first time. (When Brookes turned up to give evidence at the Select Committee on Anatomy in 1828 he was alarmed to see that one of the men waiting outside the Committee room was part of a resurrection gang who had once broken into his school and slashed into pieces a body lying on his dissection table because Brookes had refused to agree to their financial terms. This could have been Select Committee witness 'AB' – and so perhaps John Bishop.) In addition to Brookes having to flee to the magistrates' court to avoid a lynching, it was reported that Brookes's school was frequently raided by constables from the same police station. He is likely to have been the victim of informing, by both snatchers and Bats – having managed to arouse the dislike of both.

Brookes is the nearest London has to a Dr Knox figure. When Knox was discovered to have been the buyer of Burke and Hare's victims, and suspected of having known how the corpses had been obtained, he was besieged in his Edinburgh home by crowds, and his windows were smashed, while his effigy was hanged, then torn apart; in another part of the city his image was burned. But the greater damage was done to Knox by his peers; gradually, colleagues and acquaintances began to withdraw support, and Edinburgh's most brilliant surgeon found himself unable to obtain the humblest post. The social shunning saw him leave Edinburgh for London, where he was also ostracised, and dwindled into poverty and a lonely death, in 1862. Brookes died poor and alone, in 1833, but without the ignominy endured by Knox.[27]

There are other, smaller, ripples. Here is poet Thomas Hood's 1826 response to the anxieties about a Londoner's possible afterlife:

'Twas in the middle of the night
To sleep young William tried;
When Mary's ghost came stealing in
And stood at his bedside.

Oh, William, dear! Oh, William, dear!
My rest eternal ceases;
Alas! my everlasting peace
Is broken into pieces.

I thought the last of all my cares
Would end with my last minute,
But when I went to my last home
I didn't stay long in it.

The body-snatchers, they have come
And made a snatch at me.
It's very hard them kind of men
Won't let a body be.

You thought that I was buried deep
Quite decent like and chary;
But from her grave in Mary-bone
They've come and bon'd your Mary!

The arm that us'd to take your arm
Is took to Dr Vyse,
And both my legs are gone to walk
The Hospital at Guy's.

I vowed that you should have my hand,
But Fate gave no denial;
You'll find it there at Dr Bell's
In spirits and a phial.

As for my feet – my little feet
You used to call so pretty –
There's one, I know, in Bedford Row,
The other's in the City.

I can't tell where my head is gone,
But Dr Carpue can;
As for my trunk, it's all packed up
To go by Pickford's van.

I wish you'd go to Mr P.
And save me such a ride;
I don't half like the outside place
They've took for my inside.

The cock it crows – I must be gone;
My William, we must part;
But I'll be yours in death, altho'
Sir Astley has my heart.

Don't go to weep upon my grave
And think that there I'll be;
They haven't left an atom there
Of my anatomie.[28]

'If you go to stay at the Cooks, they'll cook you!' Anne Buton told her grandmother on 19 August 1831. The impoverished eighty-four-year-old, Caroline Walsh, was unhappy at her digs and had decided to take up the offer made to her by Edward Cook and his common-law wife Eliza Ross of a bed in their rooms at Goodman's Yard, Minories, East London. Buton told Walsh that the pair were bodysnatchers, warning, 'They're sure to put a black plaster on you and then sell you to the doctors.' (Once more, the Burke and Hare pitch-plaster myth.)

Buton never saw her grandmother alive again, and when Eliza Ross eventually told Buton that Walsh had left Goodman's Yard after just one day, Buton mounted her own search of East London streets, workhouses and hospitals. By late October, the newspapers had begun to take Buton's worries seriously and under the heading 'Mysterious Disappearance' the *Globe and Traveller* newspaper of 28 October reported that the old woman may have been 'burked for the base object of selling the body for anatomical purposes'. Nine days before the Italian Boy arrests, Ross was taken into custody on suspicion of murder; her twelve-year-old son had told the police that Ross – acting alone – had suffocated Walsh on the evening of the 19th, had put her body in a sack and lugged her off to be sold at the London Hospital, three-quarters of a mile away in Whitechapel Road. On 6 January 1832 at the Old Bailey Eliza Ross was found guilty of murder and was executed three days later.[29] Surgeons at the London Hospital vigorously denied that they had bought any cadavers in August (which, in any case, was the medical school's summer recess), and there is evidence to suggest that Cook and Ross's neighbours were intent on blackening their name. One of the lodgers called to give evidence claimed that he had often seen coffins in their parlour – an obvious concoction, since no resurrectionist ever went to the trouble of lugging a coffin up out of the grave or stealing one from an undertaker.

As with the dead boy in the watch-house of St Paul's, Covent Garden, identity proved problematic in the Walsh case. An old woman who had died on 3 September after being taken to the London Hospital with a broken hip was twice exhumed for Anne Buton to identify. But this old lady proved to be Catherine Welch, sixty-one, originally from Waterford in Ireland; she was tall but stooping and feeble, with no front teeth, feet in very poor condition, and with filthy skin and matted hair. She had been wearing a blue gown and a black silk bonnet, all her clothing being verminous. Welch had made her living selling matches in the streets but had broken her hip in a fall in Whitechapel on 20 August. Caroline Walsh, Anne Buton's grandmother, hailed from Kilkenny, was energetic, did not stoop, had a full set of teeth and looked clean. She was a pedlar of laces, tapes and ribbons. Her clothing consisted of a black gown, a black bonnet, a blue shawl (stained) and she wore men's shoes. (In a telling detail of the case, Buton had also searched for her grandmother at the houses of those 'who were very kind to her [Walsh] for many years by giving her victuals &c'.)

But where had Anne Buton got her notion that burkers cooked or boiled their victims? Poet John Clare, on his first visit to London from his native Northamptonshire in March 1820, learned some 'fearful disclosures' from his city-dwelling friend, artist Edward Rippingille, who described to Clare 'the pathways on the street as full of trap doors which dropped down as soon as pressed with the feet, and sprung in their places after the unfortunate countryman had fallen into the deep hole . . . where he would be robbed and murdered and thrown into boiling cauldrons kept continually boiling for that purpose and his bones sold to the doctors'.[30] Perhaps Rippingille was simply having fun frightening a naive countryman; but as with Anne Buton's warning to her grandmother, the notion of boiling, cooking and consuming had become intermingled with the notion of dissection and anatomy. It crops up again in the Nattomy Soup incident of May 1829,[31] in which an inmate at Shadwell workhouse in East London claimed that the institution's broth included human remains; a local magistrate sentenced the man to twenty-one days in gaol for making such an allegation.

*

Dr James Craig Somerville, who was teaching at the Great Windmill Street school in the late 1820s, told the Select Committee on Anatomy – months before the Burke and Hare case was discovered – that he had only started to be 'annoyed' by locals since the occasion on which he took in a murderer's corpse to dissect.[32] The dissection of a felon was an event that the public could – and did, in great numbers – pay to witness. Many surgeons believed this to be a good thing, since it helped to dispel ignorance about the nature of dissection; others worried that it would have exactly the opposite result. (Dr Knox himself believed that 'the disclosures of the most innocent proceedings even of the best-conducted dissecting rooms must always shock the public and be hurtful to science'.)[33] Somerville said that he was now plagued by members of the public wanting to see each body 'whom they believed may be a victim'. A victim of what? Of being resurrected? Of dying accidentally and ending up as a Subject? Or a victim of something more sinister? This tantalising throwaway remark is the best evidence we have that even before Burke and Hare there may have been widespread suspicion that individuals were being killed in order to supply the surgeons.

The ground floor of Sir Astley Cooper's private house in St Mary Axe, just east of Bishopsgate, contained a dissecting-room, with windows painted so that his neighbours would not be offended or passers-by alarmed. Upstairs, in his attic, up to thirty dogs at a time were kept, stolen from the street by Sir Astley's butler, Charles, who would also inveigle youngsters, Fagin-style, into stealing stray dogs or luring them from their owners, paying the boys half a crown a beast. (And Sir Astley had once called bodysnatchers 'the lowest dregs of degradation'.[34]) According to his biographer – and nephew – Bransby Cooper, Sir Astley killed the dogs in order to discover whether a catgut ligature tied around the carotid artery would dissolve (it wouldn't).[35] In a gorgeous example of the hypocrisy and arrogance to which the clan Cooper seem to have been so prone, Bransby makes the perpetrator the injured party: 'These circumstances, to which surgeons were unavoidably rendered victims, perhaps may be considered as some of the principal causes which have prevented the members of the medical profession maintaining that rank in society of which the usefulness of their purpose rendered them justly worthy.' The worst thing about dog-napping, corpse theft and inciting children to steal was that it could prevent a doctor considering himself a gentleman.

Mysterious attics, rooms with opaque windows, creatures pickled in bottles, body parts in cooking pots, disappearances, strange goings-on after dark:

it was the stuff of gothic fiction and fairy tales. A physician, Dr James Johnson, used another gothic trope when he wrote (one month before the arrest of Bishop, May and Williams) that in comparison to London hospitals 'the cells of the Spanish Inquisition were not sealed up from public observation with a much stricter secrecy'.[36] But surgeon George Guthrie was having none of this, and in an open letter to the Home Secretary he claimed that dissection and the teaching of anatomy involved no secrecy or need for circumspection whatsoever:

> The doors of every dissecting-room in London are always open, there is nobody to watch them, they swing backwards and forwards on a pulley weight, they may shut of themselves, in case anybody leaves them open; every man may walk in and walk out wherever he pleases; many persons do, but no one gives himself any concern about what is going on. The neighbours care nothing about it, and unless, from some accident, the place becomes offensive, no one interferes; although the resurrection men, for their own purposes, sometimes endeavour to excite a little commotion. . . . In London . . . no one knows or cares what is going on, unless he is interested in it.[37]

Guthrie's diagnosis of metropolitan apathy was in keeping with the growing view that Londoners were self-absorbed and unobservant, though it clashed with the simultaneously increasing wariness of 'the mob' – a fear that dictated a great deal of establishment behaviour. But London street protest in these years is notable for the fact that it never truly did evolve into systematic revolt. Insulting or striking a constable who was arresting a beggar was a familiar enough rumpus; setting up a hue and cry when a graveyard was discovered to have been plundered by resurrectionists was not unusual. But the Reform Bill and opposition to its collapse – what had that amounted to in London? One abandoned mass meeting at the second loss of the Bill; early closing for the shops of the West End; a few Tory windows put out; smaller meetings and marches here and there. Five hundred Metropolitan Police officers lined Whitehall and Old Palace Yard when parliament reconvened after the Bill had been rejected by the Lords in October 1831: a huge crowd jeered the carriages of the anti-Reform members, and cheered the supporters of the Bill. The 'mob' laughed when they realised they should have been jeering not cheering Lord Ellenborough. A piece of orange was thrown at the anti-Reform Duke of Wellington.[38] No soldiers were needed, no firearms. Six months earlier demonstrators marched through town and smashed windows where no light was showing on the night of the General Illumination; when they reached Apsley House – Wellington's London home, at the southern end of Park Lane – and had commenced stoning, they were informed that the Duchess of Wellington had died and was lying in state within. The mob withdrew immediately as a mark of respect.[39] There was nothing here to compare to London's last mass civil action, the Gordon Riots of 1780. Only No-Popery seemed to galvanise Londoners, who had shown atypical vigour in the Puritan/Parliamentarian cause during the English Civil War. In the Reform era, the capital's citizens failed to match the organised, planned mass protests in other British cities and the countryside.

'No one knows or cares what is going on,' said Guthrie, who in his letter went on to state his belief that there was far less popular opposition to becoming a Subject than was generally supposed. 'Few individuals really care much what becomes of their bodies after they are dead,' he claimed, adding that he had heard the poor in hospital wards laughing and joking about the idea of their bodies being lectured over, or being preserved in bottles. But his assertion that there was nothing secretive about hospital dissecting-rooms is hard to fathom. That the doors were not closed is not proof that anyone other than medical men ever passed through them. And against Guthrie must be set the rest of London's anatomy teachers, who certainly acted as though there were very good reason to be cautious. The more secret, the better; the less the public knew, the quicker science could advance.

The mysteries of the dissecting-room were having an uncomfortably bright light shone upon them by the Italian Boy hearings. If anyone could, as Guthrie stated, easily penetrate London's anatomical theatres, it was quite clear that George Rowland Minshull and other justices had never taken advantage of that freedom. A number of procedural niceties from London's dissecting-rooms were revealed as the evidence against Bishop, Williams and May piled up: the hampers left by hospital railings for resurrectionists to use; the convivial relationships that existed between the porters and Bishop, May and Shields; the small-change tips given to porters by resurrectionists; the fact that there was, in October and November of 1831, a body glut in London; the preference of anatomists for male corpses rather than female, and the acceptability of children in the absence of either.

To Bow Street came solicitor James Isaacs, who had formerly brought forward the Jewish clothes-dealer of Field Lane who claimed to have sold clothing to Bishop, May and two other men on Friday 4 November. This time Isaacs's client was a tailor named West who said he had seen strange goings-on in his neighbourhood. West lived close by an anatomical theatre 'near to Golden Square'. (It was not named, and could have been one of several in the Soho area.)[40] The tailor told Isaacs that three or four days before the arrests at King's College he had seen Bishop and Williams bring to the theatre the body of a boy 'supposed to be about ten'. Since so many children were missing, said Isaacs, Minshull should interview his client. It seems curious that Bishop and Williams would allow themselves to be spotted carrying about a corpse so badly wrapped that an onlooker could describe its gender and age. However, the next day Superintendent Thomas called on the theatre in question and was told that Bishop had sold to the surgeon there a child of three and a woman of fifty.

This was not a revelation likely to inspire the confidence of the public in the medical profession. Nor was the evidence of King's College porter William Hill with regard to the events of Saturday 5th November.

Hill: 'The prisoners then asked me for the money.'

Minshull: 'Do you mean the price of the body?'

Hill: 'Yes.'

Minshull: 'Did you not inquire of the men how they got possession of a body so fresh as they described?'

Hill: 'No. We never ask that question. We are not in the habit of doing so.'

Hill had given a similar answer to the Covent Garden coroner: 'I did not ask them how they got the body because I never ask such a question. It is not likely they would have answered me truly if I did.'

So far, so good: only the porters had besmirched themselves, and the only anatomist placed in an awkward position had been the unnamed Golden Square private tutor. But an error in the proceedings now forced a hospital surgeon to break cover. John Hilton (nicknamed 'Anatomical John' since he was rarely out of the dissecting-room and would always do 'an inch or so' of dissecting before starting work in the morning)[41] was demonstrator of anatomy at Guy's. He wrote to *The Times* on 30 November:

Through the medium of your journal and some others, a most unfounded report prevails respecting the teachers of anatomy of Guy's Hospital having sanctioned an easy disposal of any subject which might have been offered to them for dissection by the prisoner Bishop. It was stated at Bow Street that a female had been recently purchased by us from him. As you have participated in this mistake by giving circulation to it, I trust, in justice to the school, you will insert the following remarks in reply not only to this point, but as a general refutation to several most unmerited errors, at any rate as regards the dissecting-room to which I am attached. Allow me to assure you not one subject of any kind has been purchased of Bishop since October 19th 1829. The last boy dissected was in March 1831, and no bodies were obtained during the past summer of any person, from April 15 to October. Lastly . . . detached portions of the body have never been purchased for our dissecting-rooms, although it may be the practice at other schools.

This was disingenuous. Guy's dissecting-room porter, James Davis, had admitted at Bow Street that he had bought two corpses from James May on 2 or 3 November, and at the Old Bailey he would repeat this evidence. So while no Subject had been bought between April and October – which was, in any case, the summer recess – purchasing had resumed by early November. Even more compromising was the reported exchange between Davis and May when the bodysnatcher turned up on the evening of Friday 4 November with Bishop and Williams – a friendly, chatty conversation that made it clear how cordial such relationships could be.

But Anatomical John was correct about the error. The source of the mistake was Superintendent Thomas, who had told Minshull in open court that he had ascertained that the bodies of two women had been sold to Guy's Hospital. What Thomas had meant to say was 'Grainger's', not 'Guy's'. Guy's and missing women were now linked in the minds of newspaper readers, and Hilton's efforts to disengage them looked like trying just a little too hard.

Richard Grainger of the Webb Street school was also tying himself in knots. With a city-wide panic aroused, the condition of Subjects being brought into dissecting-rooms by resurrectionists was under scrutiny, and one of Grainger's own pupils had gone to the magistrates when the corpse of a forty-year-old man with a head injury turned up at Webb Street. Grainger came forward to explain that this was a disinterred convict who had died on the Woolwich Marshes. The body had been caked in mud and the injury had, Grainger believed, occurred when the body was pulled from the grave. The *Morning Advertiser* reported:

> that in consequence of the mis-statements which had appeared in some of the public journals, respecting the connection of the Webb Street school with Bishop and his gang, he was extremely anxious to remove an unfavourable impression which had been in the minds of many on the subject. In the first place, the body of the unfortunate Italian boy was not brought to Webb Street, nor was it ever seen by Appleton, the porter. Bishop merely called to inquire if a Subject would be purchased, and was answered that none was wanted. Secondly, that with the exception of one body, bought in October, no Subjects had been received

from Bishop and Williams in two years. [Strange, Appleton was very friendly with Bishop; Williams wouldn't have been in a position to sell any corpses – having spent most of the previous two years in Millbank Penitentiary.] Thirdly, that on its being known that Bishop and his vile associates were apprehended on the charge of having murdered the Italian boy, information was given by Mr Pilcher, one of the lecturers, to Mr Thomas, the superintendent of police, of the fact that those men had brought the body of a female to Webb Street early in October. The circumstance of Mr Thomas having omitted to mention this fact, when he communicated Shields's confession, although he acknowledged it at Bow Street on Thursday last, has led the public to suppose that the lecturers in Webb Street had concealed this important circumstance, when, in point of fact, they had done everything in their power to assist the cause of justice. . . . The circumstance of bodies being occasionally stolen from dead houses before interment, and disposed of for dissection, no suspicion was excited in Appleton's mind by the state of the body brought early in October.[42]

This denial only served to underline Webb Street's involvement in flesh-trading, and suggests that the public had in some way been making known its disapproval of the school's anatomists.

One person was covering himself with glory in this affair. Richard Partridge would distinguish himself in little else during the rest of his career (one epitaph would claim 'he was best operating on a body that was already a corpse');[43] but he would be credited with uncovering the case of the London Burkers. He had arrived in London from Birmingham four years earlier, and had studied under John Abernethy at St Bartholomew's. He was just twenty-seven when he was appointed King's first demonstrator of anatomy. He dressed in a dandyish fashion – highly polished boots, beautifully tailored trousers – and drove a very smart coach and horses. He was no Bat, but – like so many self-made men of the nineteenth century – he quickly adopted the condescension and waggishness of the gentleman-born. He told his class one morning that his carriage had just run over 'a little street urchin' but that the child had jumped straight up and made a rude gesture to Partridge. 'Really, you cannot break the bones of these street arabs – they're so elastic!' he told his students.[44] Confidential details about colleagues and off-colour jokes about the corpses in front of him punctuated his lectures. (Partridge was not alone in this facetiousness: Joseph Carpue claimed in classes to have known some of the Subjects that ended up on his dissecting table. 'That

Richard Partridge

57. Richard Partridge as a young man.

skeleton is one of the prettiest girls I ever saw,' he once told his students.)

King's medical department had been open just four weeks when William Hill came up to the theatre from the dissecting-room to tell Partridge and his pupils about Bishop's fresh Subject with a still-weeping wound. The medical school had been founded for those whose ambition for their sons was 'to fix in their minds the true principles of morality', according to its charter. Perhaps these young men genuinely did want to see change; perhaps it was their earnestness that urged Partridge to look further into the matter of the too-fresh corpse and so make King's stand apart from other, conniving, medical schools. Or perhaps the new school was receiving so steady a supply of bodies from St Clement Danes workhouse just across the Strand in Portugal Street that it felt secure enough to raise the alarm when a suspect Subject turned up. Whichever way it was, porter William Hill was to have no credit:

Minshull: 'Was it by direction of the persons in the College, under whom you act, that the prisoners were taken into custody?'

Hill: 'Certainly. Mr Partridge and the gentlemen who belong to his class agreed that the appearance of the body was so suspicious that information should be given to the police.'

Minshull: 'In doing so, they acted very properly.'

*

58. The lecture theatre at King's College.

With King's College in receipt of so much praise, certain sections of the press now felt able to criticise the rest of the medical profession for its inability, or unwillingness, to differentiate between a burking victim and an honestly-dishonestly obtained Subject. *The Times* of 2 December editorialised thus:

In the case of Frances Pighorn, who was seen alive on the evening of 8th October, and whose body was disposed of early on the morning of the 9th at Mr Grainger's, there must have been appearances to excite suspicion, had attention been properly directed to them. Though no marks of violence on the surface betrayed the hand of the murderer, yet the freshness of the body, which could scarcely be cold, the absence of all signs of interment, and the certain evidence supplied by the corpse of the unfortunate woman, that she must have died suddenly, and in the enjoyment of perfect health, ought to have suggested to the purveyors for the dissecting knife in Grainger's establishment, or to the lecturer himself, the necessity of putting some questions to such customers as Bishop and Williams about the history of their prize. We should be sorry to accuse the purchasers of the body in this case of being accessories to murder after the fact, or to excite any vulgar clamour against a most useful and honourable profession, whose necessary means of instruction the law has rendered unattainable, except by the commission of an offence; but we cannot help stating that in our opinion a culpable negligence appears on the face of this transaction. . . . If the deposition of Shields be true, it will require a good deal of explanation to remove the charge of blameable carelessness from the parties which it implicates.

It is curious to note that in showing concern at the moral inertia of surgeons in general, it was the most successful of the private schools that was singled out for criticism. Guy's willingness to buy May's corpses, and to store Bishop and Williams's dead boy overnight, did not bring Sir Astley Cooper's former hospital into disrepute.

Many alarmed individuals wrote to urge all surgeons and their porters never to accept corpses that looked suspiciously fresh – to be always alert to the signs of murder. But this assumed a level of skill in forensic medicine that had not yet been achieved. Hope and expectation were running ahead of scientific advance. Of the medical men who had examined the dead boy brought to King's College, and the three who had seen Fanny Pigburn's body, not one had come close to identifying the cause of death. Three people knew it, and none was a doctor.

ELEVEN

At the Bailey

The indictment was all one sentence, weaving its way past many points of interest before coming to rest; the Jurors were the Grand Jury, who decided ahead of a trial whether there really was a case – a True Bill – for the accused to answer.

The Jurors for our Lord the King upon their oath present that John Bishop, late of the parish of St Matthew, Bethnal Green in the county of Middlesex, Labourer, Thomas Williams, late of the same, Labourer, and James May, late of the same, Labourer, being evil disposed persons and not having the fear of God before their eyes and being moved and seduced by the instigation of the Devil on the fourth day of November in the second year of the Reign of our Sovereign Lord William the Fourth by the Grace of God of the United Kingdom of Great Britain and Ireland King Defender of the Faith with force and arms at the parish aforesaid in the County aforesaid in and upon Carlo Feriere otherwise called Charles Ferrier in the peace of God and our said Lord the King then and there being feloniously, wilfully and of their Malice aforethought did make an assault – And that the said John Bishop, Thomas Williams and James May with a certain Wooden Staff of no value the said Carlo Feriere otherwise called Charles Ferrier then and there feloniously, wilfully and of their Malice aforethought did strike and beat – And that the said John Bishop, Thomas Williams and James May by such striking and beating the said Carlo Feriere otherwise called Charles Ferrier in and upon the back part of the neck of him the said Carlo Feriere otherwise called Charles Ferrier as aforesaid then and there feloniously, wilfully and of their Malice aforethought did give unto the said Carlo Feriere otherwise called Charles Ferrier divers mortal bruises and contusions in and upon the back part of the neck of him the said Carlo Feriere otherwise called Charles Ferrier of which said mortal bruises and contusions the said Carlo Feriere otherwise called Charles Ferrier did then and there instantly Die – And so the Jurors aforesaid upon their Oath aforesaid do say that the said John Bishop, Thomas Williams and James May the said Carlo Feriere otherwise called Charles Ferrier in manner and form aforesaid feloniously, wilfully and of their Malice aforethought did Kill and Murder against the peace of our said Lord the King his Crown and Dignity – And the Jurors aforesaid upon their Oath aforesaid do further present that the said John Bishop, Thomas Williams and James May not having the fear of God before their eyes but being moved and seduced by the instigation of the Devil afterwards to wit on the same day and in the year aforesaid with force and Arms at the parish aforesaid in the County aforesaid in the peace of God and our own said Lord the King then and there being feloniously, wilfully and of their Malice aforethought did make an assault and that the said John Bishop, Thomas Williams and James May with a certain Wooden Staff of no value the said Male person whose name is unknown as aforesaid in and upon the back part of the neck of the said Male person whose name is unknown to the Jurors aforesaid in the peace of God and our sovereign Lord the King then and there did strike and beat – And that the said John Bishop, Thomas Williams and James May by such striking and beating the said Male person whose name is unknown as aforesaid then and there feloniously, wilfully and of their Malice aforethought did give unto the Male person whose name is unknown as aforesaid divers mortal bruises and contusions in and upon the back part of the neck of him the said Male person whose name is unknown as aforesaid of which said mortal bruises and contusions the said Male person whose name is unknown as aforesaid did then and there instantly Die – And so the Jurors aforesaid upon their Oath aforesaid do say that the said John Bishop, Thomas Williams and James May the said Male person whose name is unknown as aforesaid in manner and form aforesaid feloniously, wilfully and of their Malice aforethought did Kill and Murder against the peace of our said Lord and King his Crown and Dignity.

Well, at least it wasn't Latin or Norman French: from 1730, indictments had to be written in English, albeit of an archaic kind. The strange, meandering nature of the prose derived from the need for at least some mud to stick: the accused could be acquitted if a charge were not accurate; and in a case as serious as murder, as many variations on a theme as possible were included in the indictment.[1] The victim would have to be proved to have been Carlo Feriere/Charles Ferrier in order for a conviction to be secured. So a second boy, 'Male person whose name is unknown', appeared in the text, to cover the possibility that prosecution witnesses might be unable to convince the jury of the identity of the King's College body. However, it didn't matter that 'Thomas Williams' was an alias; this was the name that Thomas Head had let himself be known by, and would therefore be the name by which he faced conviction and execution.

The killing of Fanny Pigburn was not in the indictment. Despite Shields's testimony, Rhoda's statement, the clothes found at Number 2 Nova Scotia Gardens, and the admission by the Webb Street porter John Appleton and the medical student Dunn that a woman resembling Fanny had been delivered to the school at about the right time, there was no body and thus no forensic evidence to substantiate such a charge. What's more, Fanny's case would have brought a surgeon in the role of receiver into the witness box. No hint of any connivance in murder by doctors would be heard in so public an arena as the Old Bailey. A similar judicial sleight of hand had ensured that Dr Knox and his colleagues had not been compelled to give evidence at the trial of William Burke. Burke was charged with three counts of murder, of a possible sixteen, and the Lord Advocate, after legal argument, decided to hear each of the three cases separately, starting with the one count in which Knox and his assistants had not seen the body; the other two charges (the killings of vagrant 'idiot' Daft Jamie and young prostitute Mary Paterson) would never be heard, since Burke was found guilty on the first charge – the murder of an old woman named Mary Docherty, whose corpse had been seen only by David Paterson, Knox's dissecting-room porter. This happy turn of events for Knox was bitterly noted by the Edinburgh press, though no direct accusations of chicanery were made against the Lord Advocate.

William Burke had come surprisingly close to being found not guilty; members of the jury later admitted that two of their number had been in favour of acquitting him. Burke's co-defendant for the Docherty murder, his common-law wife Helen M'Dougal, had been found 'not proven', and was released, since she was not implicated in the other two counts. ('Nelly, you are out of the scrape,' Burke had murmured to her when her verdict was read out.) Before the trial, the Lord Advocate had felt that there was insufficient evidence to mount a prosecution against either Burke or Hare unless one of them were to become a prosecution witness; it was only because William Hare turned King's Evidence that allegations against Burke and M'Dougal could be substantiated. In London, none of the four who were originally arrested had taken the role of Hare. By the time Michael Shields had co-operated on the disappearance of Fanny Pigburn, he had proved himself to be such an unreliable witness that the prosecution could have no use for him. Neither Bishop nor Williams had chosen to betray each other; and May, for reasons the prosecution could not fathom, had refused to grab immunity for himself by revealing when, where and how the child in the trunk had met his death. This was unforgivable: he was going to be made to pay.

The average Old Bailey trial lasted eight and a half minutes, from opening address to sentencing, though some 'capitals' – cases that could end in the donning of the black cap – might take hours.[2] Today was going to be different: everyone knew there was little chance of a verdict coming in before nightfall. Charles Phillips, barrister at law, knew it, and only the night before had withdrawn from acting as the prisoners' defence attorney since he felt unable to commit himself to a trial that was likely to last the whole day.[3] It is probable he had a number of more lucrative cases lined up in the second court-house, adjacent to the Old Sessions House; he would earn a great deal more money from several eight-and-a-half-minute jobs than from an all-day capital case, and there was nothing to stop him simply abandoning his clients at no notice – plenty of attorneys did it every day.

Prisoners were obliged to seek out legal representation (and to corral witnesses) from their prison cell – no easy task – and Bishop and Williams had asked for the trial to be delayed because of the problem they had had in finding a barrister. Phillips had only been acquired with difficulty. Their request had been rejected, however, even though both Minshull and Superintendent Thomas had publicly stated that the case should only go to court when it seemed 'perfect'. Both had been hoping for a postponement, and even the Recorder of London, the city's most senior judge, had given his opinion that it would be wisest to wait until January. Whichever mysterious power ordered these matters, though, had decided that the swifter the better with this trial. At the last minute John Curwood and J.T. Barry, a barrister who campaigned against the death penalty, had volunteered to act as defence counsel. To modern eyes reading the trial, it looks as though Curwood and Barry barely acted at all; but there were reasons for their seeming passivity. An attorney hired by a defendant did not mount a defence case as we understand it; he was restricted to cross-examining prosecution witnesses and could read out to the court any statements that the prisoner wanted to submit, but he could not address the jury. Since he had no right to know what evidence was going to be given against the prisoner, the prisoner's statement, prepared before the trial began, had limited effectiveness. Not until 1836 would a barrister in a criminal case be able to make a narrative defence on a client's behalf; and not until 1898 would the accused be able to take the stand in an English court of law, the idea having earlier been held that defendants should not be allowed to incriminate themselves. But with the defence attorney's actions so restricted, this right to silence acted against the prisoner, since he or she had no chance to put forward an alternative version of events, or to impress a jury with an appearance of honesty through speech or gesture. Silence had a tendency to look like guilt.

It was a growing criticism in legal circles that cases often had to be abandoned and prisoners discharged because witnesses for the prosecution failed to show. For, unless subpoenaed, a witness (both for the defence and the prosecution) was not obliged to come to court; and, given the possibility of reprisals on behalf of the accused, plus the loss of earnings as a result of attending court, many people did choose to absent themselves from the witness box. Subpoenas proved hard to enforce, and there was even a name for evading a summons: 'running up and down' was street slang for making sure you were not at home, and not to be found anywhere around town, when an official came to deliver a subpoena. Many witnesses who did come forward were often found to be drunk by the time they came to testify; the order of trials at the Old Bailey was only very loosely fixed, and those waiting to be called would often repair to the King of Denmark, the George, the Bell, the Plough, or any of the many pubs and inns around the Sessions House. (It was not just the sobriety of witnesses that gave cause for concern; evening sittings, which would be abolished in 1845, were notable for the inebriation of lawyers after lunch and dinner – at which wine was plentiful – and one judge was regularly seen clutching the bannisters as he lurched back to the Old Bailey bench after meals.)[4]

Forty individuals had turned up to assist the prosecution of Bishop, Williams and May; six had come forward for the defence. Sarah, Rhoda and the three little Bishops were not among them, since spouses and offspring were deemed 'incompetent witnesses'. Surgeon Edward Tuson of the Little Windmill Street school had been subpoenaed by the defence but was protesting that he had no idea what the prisoners expected him to be able to say in their favour. Perhaps they were prepared to make embarrassing disclosures about his practice if he would not speak for them; perhaps he had accepted too many 'smalls' and 'large smalls' than was compatible with respectability; perhaps he had made off-colour jokes about the produce, or even made comments that could be construed as instructions to murder. As it was, the public gallery was crowded by eight o'clock in the morning of Friday 2 December, and surgeons comprised a sizeable proportion of the onlookers. Offers of over a guinea were being made for a seat (the sheriffs normally pocketed a shilling a head but put prices up for the more interesting cases), and some people had tried to pass themselves off as court officials, newspaper reporters and even jurors in an attempt to get into the room. One man hired a barrister's wig and gown at a theatrical costumer in Clare Market for 3s 6d and sat unchallenged in the well of the court.

The customary aromatic herbs had been strewn about the court-room – an attempt to block out the infamous Newgate Stink. (Not just Newgate: to legal noses, those they defended and prosecuted typically had the aroma of last night's gin, cheese and onions on their breath, clothes and skin.)[5] At nine o'clock, the assistant judge, Serjeant Arabin, deputy Recorder of London, entered the court to open the proceedings by reading over the indictment and to hear the pleas from the prisoners. William St Julien Arabin was a notorious figure of fun on the circuit, so much so that one young lawyer, Henry Blencowe Churchill, had started to scribble down verbatim his bizarre sayings, non-sequiturs and eccentric decisions; these were privately published and circulated among cognoscenti in 1843 as *Arabiniana: or The Remains of Mr Serjeant Arabin*. It included such oddities as: 'A man with a cold is not fit to try on a ladies shoe'; 'Woman, how can you be so stupid? You are tall enough to be wise enough'; 'She goes into a shop and looks at several things, and purchases nothing. That always indicates some guilt'; and 'No man is fit to be a cheesemonger who cannot guess the length of a street'. On the notorious draughtiness of the Old Bailey Sessions House: 'When I sit here, I fancy myself on the top of Mount Breeze, and the first thing I do every morning of the Session is to go to the glass and see if my eyes have not been blown out of my head.' One of those who would one day own a copy of *Arabiniana* was William Henry Bodkin, co-founder of the London Society for the Suppression of Mendicity, chairman of the Houseless Poor Association, member of the 1828 Select Committee on Policing London, Tory member of parliament to be (from 1841) and one of the three prosecution barristers at the trial of Bishop, Williams and May.[6] Bodkin's colleagues that day were John Adolphus, who had also interested himself in the administration of the poor laws, publishing in 1824 a pamphlet, *Observations on the Vagrant Act*; and William Clarkson, of whom a contemporary recalled a loud, swaggering demeanour in court and a habit of bullying junior members in chambers.[7] In their wigs, the assembled lawyers looked, according to one of the more astute reporters in court that day, like nothing so much as 'a row of cauliflowers'.[8]

The dock of the Old Sessions House had a notable feature – a mirror that was fixed above the heads of the accused, tilted in such a way that the bench and most of the court-room could have a view of the back of the prisoners, from the crown of the head down to their boots. Three

59.–60. Two unconvincing Old Bailey court-room sketches of Bishop, Williams and May.

heads now appeared in the mirror: the thick, dark, wavy hair of John Bishop; the dark-blond mop of James May; and the nondescript mousiness of Thomas Williams. Still in his smock frock, which was by now filthy, Bishop looked like a rustic, according to the *Morning Advertiser*, but 'tinged with metropolitan cunning'; he stood at one side of the dock, and gazed at the floor. Alongside him, and seeming to hang back slightly, was Williams in a fustian jacket with a brown neckerchief at his throat; he looked, wrote one reporter, 'extremely inoffensive' and 'shorter than average' – though at 5 foot 4 inches he was by no means short for a working man of the time. May, also in fustian, and with a yellow silk cravat carefully tied at his neck, appeared to be brimming with life, athletic and alert, with lips pressed tight together and a stern, determined expression on his face. 'Their appearance rather indicated low cunning than hardened ferocity,' declared *The Times*'s man of the trio.

Serjeant Arabin asked how they pleaded, and each said 'not guilty'. Then the jury was sworn in – twelve good men and true, between twenty-one and sixty years of age and inhabiting a property of £10 per annum freehold or £20 per annum leasehold. No one else might sit in judgement on their fellow Londoner. At ten o'clock the three judges took their place on the bench: Sir Nicholas Conyngham Tindal, Lord Chief Justice of the Common Pleas and Tory member for Cambridge University; Sir John (Baron) Vaughan; and Sir Joseph Littledale. Each man had around thirty-five years' legal experience. Sitting alongside them were the Lord Mayor of London, John Key; two sons of the prime minister, Earl Grey; and the Duke of Sussex, younger brother of the king, uncle to the future Queen Victoria (he would give her away at her marriage to Albert of Saxe-Coburg-Gotha) and England's highest ranking freemason. Augustus Frederick Hannover was an enthusiastic amateur follower of many matters scientific, literary and political. (He had been keen to leave his body to medical science but in the event ended up in a sealed vault at the brand-new Kensal Green cemetery, in 1843.) The duke had requested and been granted a place on the bench for the Bishop, Williams and May trial in order to see for himself the workings of England's judicial system. But it is possible that as Grand Master, he was concerned at how this trial would affect London's surgeons, many of whom were masons. (The Anatomical Society met at the Freemasons Arms in Great Queen Street, Covent Garden.) The Duke of Sussex clamped a pocket telescope to his eye and took particular interest in the appearance of Williams, who was seen to return the royal gaze with a glare.

Bodkin opened for the prosecution, and said that he wished to place particular emphasis on the conversation overheard by porter Thomas

Wigley at the Fortune of War on Friday 4 November; the exchanges between Bishop and May that evening had excited suspicion in all who had heard them. (All of Thomas Wigley, Bodkin must have meant; no one else had claimed to have heard the conversation.) Next, John Adolphus rose to instruct the jury not to allow the 'interest' that the case had 'excited out of doors' to affect their judgement in this 'painful and extraordinary inquiry'. It was a revolting crime, he said, precisely because it had not stemmed from any strong feeling or passion: 'Nothing but the sordid and base desire to possess themselves of a dead body in order to sell it for dissection had induced the prisoners at the bar to commit the crime for which they were now about to answer.' Bodkin acknowledged that the case relied on circumstantial evidence, 'but he contended that a large and well-connected body of circumstantial evidence was in many cases superior to the positive testimony of an eye witness.' He concluded that he relied utterly on the good sense and integrity of a British jury, 'which a long life of practice had left him no room to doubt'.

William Hill, dissecting-room porter at King's, was the first witness called by the prosecution. He repeated his former evidence of the events of the afternoon of Saturday 5 November, though this time there was a little more local colour, and the role that May, though 'tipsy', had taken in the negotiations was foregrounded. (Williams, Hill admitted, had been party to none of the bargaining; like Shields, he had been a silent partner on that day.) It came out that with regard to resurrectionists, even so modern a building as King's anatomical department had 'a place appropriated for them'. Hill recalled asking Bishop and May, 'What have you got?'; 'What size?'; and, on hearing that it was a boy of around fourteen, Hill had merely asked the price. Hill said that the freshness, the strangeness of the boy's bent left arm with clenched fingers, together with the absence of any sawdust in the hair (which would indicate that the corpse had been in a coffin) had triggered his suspicion. Hill's testimony also revealed Richard Partridge haggling in person with May over the price of the child, no doubt to the discomfort of the anatomist, who was next into the witness box. But Partridge told the Old Bailey, 'I do not recollect whether I saw the prisoners before I went to the police', in response to Hill's clearly remembered, 'He was talking with May in the room.' Partridge then explained his findings during the post-mortem on Sunday night in the Covent Garden watch-house:

'There was a wound on the temple, which did not injure the bone. That was the only appearance of external injury. Beneath the scalp on the top of the skull, there was some blood effused . . . the skull was taken off and the brain examined. That was perfectly healthy, as well as the spinal part. In cutting down to remove the bone which conceals the spinal part at the back of the neck, we found a quantity of coagulated blood within the muscles, and on removing the back part of the bony canal, some coagulated blood was found laying in the cavity opposite the blood found in the muscles of the neck. There was blood uncoagulated within the rest of the spinal canal. The spinal marrow appeared perfectly healthy. I think these internal marks of violence were sufficient to produce death. I think a blow from a stick on the back of the neck would have caused those appearances and I think it would produce a rapid death, but perhaps not an instantaneous one.'

He had noticed that the face was flushed and swollen and the heart empty of blood.

'What do you infer from the heart being empty?' asked Bodkin.

'I do not infer anything from it, except that, accompanied with blood-shot eyes, it has been found in persons who have died suddenly and evidently from no violence.'

Curwood, cross-examining on the nature of the injury to the spinal canal, asked, 'Mightn't this have been caused by other means as well as by a blow – by pressure otherwise applied?' Perhaps Curwood was recalling a forensic detail from Burke and Hare: in Edinburgh, surgeon Robert Christison had stated that in his view, extravasated blood – that is, blood that had escaped from blood vessels into surrounding tissue – would have the same appearance regardless of whether the injury had happened before or after death. Christison had pointed this out when Burke and Hare had claimed that the injuries found on Mary Docherty had been caused when her body had been doubled up to be packed into a tea-chest for delivery to Knox; she had died of drink and old age, not from violence, Burke and Hare had said. In Burke's confessions, the Edinburgh killers' *modus operandi* was revealed – suffocation with bare hands; no blows had been struck, in order to keep the corpses looking as though they had died from natural causes. Partridge had evidently never read this aspect of the famous case; or, if he had, he had rejected Christison's (and Burke's) findings, for he answered Curwood: 'I think not. I cannot conceive any thing but a blow would produce those appearances.'

Surgeon George Beaman knew a thing or two about spinal injuries, having killed many animals with a blow to the back of the neck in order to observe the results upon dissection. But he too thought spinal injury had been the cause of death:

'On the top of the skull we detected a patch of blood about the size of a crown. This appearance must have been produced by a blow given during life. . . . On removing the skin at the back part of the neck, I should think from three to four ounces of coagulated blood were found among the muscles. That blood must have been effused while the subject was alive. On removing a portion of the spine to examine the spinal marrow, a quantity of coagulated blood was laying in the canal, which, by pressure on the spinal marrow, must cause death. There was no injury to the bone of the spine, nor any displacement. All these appearances would follow from a blow with a staff, stick or heavy instrument.'

Cross-examined by Barry, Beaman admitted that there was no injury to the skin at the back of the neck; he saw nothing odd in that, claiming that the boy had died too quickly to have developed a bruise or weal.

The body had been in 'very good health', Beaman added, and had been generally clean, apart from some obviously smeared-on mud or clay. All the other organs had been in good condition, though Beaman had never before seen a heart empty of blood; along with Partridge, he took this to indicate a very quick death – probably within two or three minutes of the fatal blow.

Beaman estimated that the body had been dead for thirty-six hours by the evening of Saturday 5th, when he had first opened it; though, as he pointed out to the court, the coldness of the weather at that time 'was very favourable to the preservation of dead flesh'. He believed that the teeth had been removed two to three hours after death, and that the boy had eaten a meal around three hours before being killed. (Thirty-six hours before the 'evening' of Saturday 5th was between 5 a.m. and 10 a.m. on Friday 4 November, if 'evening' can be interpreted as any time between 5 p.m. and 10 p.m.) Cross-examined, Beaman would not swear to the time of the teeth being removed but said that he was certain twelve hours had not passed between death and extraction. James May claimed to have removed them at around half-past six on the Friday evening.

In order to give some weight to the findings of the unillustrious Beaman (he was just a parish surgeon) and the young Partridge, Frederick Tyrrell, nephew of Sir Astley Cooper, was called, and backed up Partridge and Beaman, stressing that the child had certainly not died from a stroke; the injuries could have been caused 'only by violence'.

That ended the medical evidence. Next, PC John Wilson of F Division told of the violent struggle that May had put up in Catherine Street as he was being taken into custody: 'He struck me because I would not let Bishop and him talk together.' Superintendent Thomas took up the story, saying, 'I should observe that the prisoners were under the effects of liquor, in my judgement – May and Bishop more particularly so. May was carried in on all fours and his frock over his face. He was scuffling.' The noose was tightening.

Two of the more foggy, fluid parts of the story were next recounted by Henry Lock, barman at the Fortune of War, and Thomas Wigley, beer-drinker at the same – with new emphases on May and the three prisoners acting in concert. It had been May and Bishop's claim that their meeting at the Fortune of War that Friday morning had been a chance encounter, that they had arrived separately, though neither had been able to give specific times. May had remembered being there already, some time after eleven or twelve, when Bishop and Williams walked in and asked him if he would 'stand' anything to drink. Lock now pinned the time to 'about eleven o'clock . . . I remember seeing them all three at the Fortune of War, they had some drink there and stayed till about twelve.' Lock claimed that Bishop, May and Williams were accompanied by another man, 'a stranger to me'. (Shields would not meet them at the Fortune of War for another whole day; even Superintendent Thomas had given up the goose-chase of trying to place the four original prisoners together in the pub on the Friday morning.) Lock told the Old Bailey that Bishop, Williams, May and the stranger all left the Fortune of War 'together' – 'together' now being the motif of his evidence. He said that Bishop, Williams and May returned at around three o'clock, left at dusk, returning at about eight o'clock with a different fourth man, 'who appeared to be a coachman'. After a drink, the coachman left, and 'one of them said in the tap-room that "he had had a ride".' The three prisoners were in the tap-room for quite a while, said Lock, and then a little before nine, May came to the bar, rubbing a set of teeth with his handkerchief. Lock remarked to May that these looked like the teeth of a young person, and would no doubt be worth some-thing, and May said he would be looking to get £2 for them. 'They all left together, some short time after this,' said Lock. At around eight o'clock the next morning, Lock saw Bishop and Williams with Michael Shields at the Fortune of War; the latter was heard to refuse to go across the road and take a hamper from just inside the railings of St Bartholomew's Hospital, so Bishop went and collected it himself.

Thomas Wigley gave the gist of his former evidence, though timings still seemed a little wobbly: 'About half-past six o'clock I was at the Fortune of War, and between half-past seven and eight I saw Bishop come in; May followed in five or six minutes afterwards. Bishop sat down on a bench, and May sat down on a bench opposite him. Bishop said to May, "What do you think of our new one, didn't he go up to him well and collar him

– was he not a game one?" May said, "I don't know what you mean."
Bishop said, "That's all right then."'

'Did May see you in the room?' asked the prosecution, keen to interpret this interchange as May attempting to put on a show of being unfa-
miliar with Bishop, with Bishop's resurrection slang and with Williams –
the object of the praise. It was being inferred that May's 'I don't know
what you mean' was for Wigley to overhear. 'Yes,' Wigley answered. 'I sat
in the corner, having a pint of beer and he saw me. May got up and went
out. He came back in a few minutes with a handkerchief in his hand and
sat down rubbing it. Williams came in. Bishop said, "There he is. I knew
he would come – I knew he was a game one." Bishop seemed as if he
had been drinking. He got up and said, "I am going home." May said,
"I am not going away yet." Bishop and Williams went out together. May
sat down but went out presently, and I saw no more of him. Bishop said
to May, "You stick by me and I will stick by you" – that was just before
he went out for the handkerchief.'

Curwood asked: 'It was Bishop who said, "Isn't our new one a game
one?"'; to which Wigley replied, 'Yes. I do not know what he meant.'

Next, May's role in procuring a cab was highlighted by the drivers he
and Bishop had approached in and around Old Bailey. Then the eyewitness accounts were heard from the neighbours who had seen Bishop,
Williams and May arrive at Nova Scotia Gardens in a yellow chariot then
carry something away in a sack, though twelve-year-old George Gissing
inconveniently said that 'the strange man' in the smock frock he had seen
that evening with Bishop and Williams was not the third man in the dock,
and neighbour Ann Cannell – who had failed to pick out Bishop at Bow
Street when taken there to do so – now maintained that she hadn't seen
enough of any of the three to recognise them at the time or on any subsequent occasion.

When Robert Mortimer, the elderly tailor who lived near the Bishops, and
who had cut Williams a coat for his wedding day just ten weeks earlier,
was not found to be among the prosecution witnesses at the Old Bailey,
two sheriff's officers were dispatched to Nova Scotia Gardens to collect
him. Mortimer welcomed the men into his cottage, apologised for having
forgotten the day of the trial, and asked them to excuse him while he got
shaved. He picked up his razor and, in front of the officers, drew the blade
across his throat.

Guy's Hospital porter, James Davis, and his assistant, James Weeks,
repeated that they had bought two bodies from May earlier in the week

of the arrests; that they knew both Bishop and May well; that the two had delivered a sack from which protruded the foot of what they took to be a woman or a child; that Guy's had stored it overnight and delivered it up safely to the resurrectionists on Saturday morning. Like William Hill, Davis said that Williams had taken no part in the brokering of the body on the Friday night – it had all been done by Bishop and May; Davis hadn't even seen Williams until the latter's appearance at Bow Street. Nor had John Appleton of Grainger's school seen Williams – only Bishop and May. And May's apparently detailed knowledge of the boy's corpse was reiterated by dentist Thomas Mills. May, said Mills, had called between nine and ten o'clock on the Saturday morning, and when challenged about whether the teeth were in fact a set, said 'upon his soul to God, they all belonged to one head, and not long since, and that the body had never been buried. He said, "The fact is, they belong to a boy between fourteen and fifteen years old."' In Mills's opinion, great violence must have been used to get the teeth out of the head, since part of the jaw socket was still attached; he said that the brad awl found in May's room in Dorset Street, and produced in court, was exactly the sort of implement that would have been used to extract the teeth.

Augustine Brun, the Birmingham *padrone*, was interpreted to the court by Joseph Paragalli. According to *The Times*, this was not a satisfactory arrangement, and the judge reprimanded Paragalli for appearing to alter the questions and Brun's answers, and for 'impertinence and frivolity not at all in character with the solemn investigation which was then pending'. There was laughter when Brun said that he had not seen the boy alive since July 1830, and, presumably in reply to a clumsily worded question, said that he couldn't have seen the boy alive after he was dead. That aside, it is difficult to make out, in the official transcript of the trial and the various newspaper reports, why Paragalli would have been criticised for levity; and how much of the following testimony represents what Brun really meant to say cannot be known:

'I knew an Italian boy named Carlo Ferrier. I brought him over from Italy about two years ago, he was then about fourteen years old. He lived with me for about six weeks. I saw him alive on 28th July 1830. The last place I knew him to lodge at was Mr Elliott's, No 2 Charles Street, Drury Lane. On 19th November I saw the body of a boy at the burial ground near Covent Garden. I can only say that I suppose it to be the boy of whom I have spoken, by his size and hair, but the face I cannot give an opinion upon, from the state it was in, and the teeth were taken out. The size and the hair were exactly the same as Ferrier's. I have not seen that boy alive since.'

Brun said that he could perceive no trace of resemblance to Carlo Ferrari in the corpse's face, which, in any case, he had not had the heart to look at for very long.

Curwood asked him: 'Supposing you had heard nothing about Carlo Ferrier, and had looked at that body. Should you at all have known it?'

'Yes, I should, from the hair and size. If I had known nothing about this occurrence and had seen the body, I should be of the opinion that he was "my own".'

Curwood wanted Brun to confirm that he was completely sure of this, and Brun said: 'At first sight, if anybody had asked me who the body was, the face was so disfigured, I could not tell.'

'Have you seen him since July twelve months?'

'No. He might grow a little in fifteen months, but not much.'

It is difficult to guess how much a poor boy, aged around fourteen, would have grown in fifteen months; malnourishment meant that in the early part of the nineteenth century, the poorest London fourteen-year-olds were between four and six inches shorter than the fourteen-year-old sons of the gentry.[9] But George Beaman had found this child to be healthy, even slightly 'stout'.

Giving his own testimony, Joseph Paragalli said:

'I play an organ and pandean pipes about the streets, with my wife and three children. I knew Carlo Ferrier. I saw him every morning at Mr Elliott's. I knew he was once in Brun's service. I have known the boy from 22nd May 1830. I saw him alive in the Quadrant, Regent Street, at half-past two o'clock on a Saturday afternoon, four weeks before I saw him at the station house. He was then dead. When I saw him in the Quadrant he had a little cage round his neck, and two white mice in it. He was the same boy as I saw dead at the station house, undoubtedly.'

Paragalli also revealed that Carlo had been brought to England with his sister, who had died in Scotland. Extraordinarily, he offered the information that Carlo was the only Italian boy who made money exhibiting animals in the streets of London. The boy he had seen in the Quadrant could only have been Carlo.

He was now handed the brown furry cap, which had been sitting in court all morning alongside the sack, hamper, trunk, set of teeth, and all the articles of clothing exhumed at 3 Nova Scotia Gardens; the garments had been described in great detail in every national newspaper the day after Superintendent Thomas had brought them back in triumph to Bow Street. 'I cannot swear to this cap,' said Paragalli. 'He always wore a cap. I cannot say whether I ever saw him in one like this. He had one on in the Quadrant, but I cannot say whether it was cloth, leather or skin. I am sure the shade [visor] of this cap is of foreign manufacture.'

Barry asked: 'Is it not eleven weeks since you saw him?'

'It was four weeks before I saw him a corpse. He lodged close to me. The rest of the Italian boys live by Saffron Hill. I have seen many about town. I do not keep company with my countrymen here.'

Paragalli's wife Mary said:

'I knew a boy who carried two white mice about. I do not know his name. I saw that boy on Tuesday 1st November in Oxford Street, near Hanover Square, exactly at a quarter past twelve o'clock. He had a little cage, like a squirrel's cage, which turns round, with two little white mice in it. I did not speak to him. I do not recollect how he was dressed. He had a little cap on but it is impossible for me to say what colour, or what it was made of. On Sunday morning, 6th November, about nine o'clock, I saw the dead body of the very same boy at the station house, Covent Garden. I had known him all the summer. I know Brun, but did not know him till the boy had left him. I do not know what name the boy went by. I never spoke to him much. I was with my husband when we saw him in the Quadrant. That was the same boy that I saw dead. I have a son eight years old, who knew the boy well. He went with me to the station house and knew him. He is not here.'

Hearsay had not been allowed in an English court of law since the seventeenth century; Mary Paragalli should have been allowed to mention her son's views only if he were there himself to be questioned on them. She was not challenged.

A new Italian witness had come forward. Andrew Colla lived at 4 Saffron Hill and was a peripatetic seller of birdcages, which he constructed in his home. He said, without an interpreter:

'I knew Carlo Ferrier by seeing him about the street. On Tuesday 1st November, I saw him in Oxford Street and spoke to him. I saw a dead body at the station house in Covent Garden on the following Monday – it was the body of the same person as I had seen in Oxford Street. He had a cage with white mice in it, and a tortoise. [The tortoise had absented itself from the story quite some time ago; now here was Colla resurrecting it.] He had a cap on his head, something like the one produced. [Someone had evidently handed Colla the cap.] It was torn on one side. I believe this to be the same cap. He had on a blue coat and grey trousers. [Colla would now have been looking at the disinterred outfit.] I observed a large patch on the left knee and from the patch on the left knee of these trousers I believe them to be the same he had on. They are the same kind. I did not so particularly notice the colour or patch as I did the stitches, being so great a distance from each other as these are. I do believe these to be the trousers. I have not seen them since I saw them on the boy in Oxford Street.'

Colla had taken in a great deal of detail that day in Oxford Street; Superintendent Thomas must have been extremely pleased. As he must have been with little John King. Children of any age could give evidence at the Old Bailey, provided the judge was satisfied that the child knew good from evil and understood the nature of an oath. John King was nine, quite old enough in their honours' view to give testimony at a capital trial:

'I live with my mother, who is now confined. I remember one day when my mother was washing seeing a foreign boy near Nova Scotia Gardens. I believe it was on the Thursday before Guy Fawkes day, and between one and two o'clock. I was looking down upon him from the loft window and could not see whether he had a cage or a box as my mother would not let me go down to him. I believe it was a cage for I saw some wire on the top of it. He was standing still, with the cage hanging around his neck by a string. He had a brown hairy cap on his head, the peak of it was lined with green. The cap produced looks exactly like it. I do not know how long he remained there. I was looking at him for a few minutes.'

Barry asked: 'Were you in the first or second floor?'

'In the first, not very high from the ground. I was looking out at the loft door and could see the green of the peak.' The child must have realised the import of the question: how could he have seen the colour of the cap's visor but not the cage?

Martha King, aged eleven, said:

'I remember seeing an Italian boy near the Birdcage public house. I was at the front part of the house. It was on the Wednesday or Thursday before Guy Fawkes day, and about twelve o'clock. I am sure it was either Wednesday or Thursday. He was standing still opposite the Birdcage with his box slung round his neck and a cap on his head. The cap was just like this. Bishop's house is about a minute's walk from our house. I have never seen the boy since.'

Rebecca Baylis was a new witness; she also lived opposite the Birdcage, at Number 1 Virginia Row (today's Virginia Street), which approached the pub from the south-west.

'On Thursday 3rd November, about a quarter before twelve o'clock, I saw an Italian boy. He was very near my own window, standing sideways. I could see the side of his face and one end of the box, which he had in front of him. I think it was slung round his neck. He had a brown fur or seal-skin cap on, a small one, rather shabby. I could see the peak was lined with green and cut off very sharp. [Here, she looked down at the cap in her hands.] It was this colour . . . but the front appeared to me to come more pointed. It was a cap much like this. I cannot swear whether this is it. He had on a dark blue or a dirty green jacket and grey trousers, apparently a dark mixture, but very shabby. About a quarter of an hour after, I had occasion to go to the Virginia Planter [a pub in Virginia Row] to see if it was time to put on my husband's potatoes. I went a little way down Nova Scotia Gardens to look for my little boy. I saw the Italian boy standing within two doors of Number 3. There are three houses together and he stood by Number 1. I do not think the jacket produced is the one he had on . . . I thought it was darker. These have the appearance of the trousers he had on.'

Curwood questioned her about the jacket. 'No,' said Baylis, 'it appeared darker at the distance I was, which was about six yards. I will not say it is the same.'

Another new witness: John Randall, labourer, lived in Orange Street (which ran south from the Birdcage and no longer exists). He told the court:

'On Thursday morning 3rd November, between nine and ten o'clock, I saw an Italian boy standing under the window of the Birdcage public house, near Nova Scotia Gardens. He had a box or cage with two white mice – the cage part of the box went round. I turned round to the boy. I saw he looked very cold and I gave him a halfpenny and told him he had better go on. He had on a blue coarse jacket or coat, apparently very coarse, and a brown cap with a bit of leather in front. I did not notice whether it was fur or not. It was similar to this in colour, and the jacket was this colour. I did not notice his trousers.'

For a peripatetic beggar, this Italian boy wasn't very mobile. Allowing the smallest margin of error in the sightings, the boy was stationary in a not very well-off neighbourhood for two hours; if John Randall's earliest estimate – nine o'clock – is accepted, and John King's latest – two o'clock – the boy is placed close to Nova Scotia Gardens for five hours.

Sarah Trueby described the topography of Nova Scotia Gardens. Her husband, she said, owned Numbers 1, 2 and 3 and rented them out. The well in the Bishops' garden was easily accessible – and gates in the palings between Numbers 1 and 2, and 2 and 3 showed that this well was meant to be used by all three sets of residents. Many others could easily reach it too. Trueby said that the Bishops had lived at Number 3 since July 1830, and that Williams had rented Number 2, in the name of Head, a year to the month later. Head/Williams had stayed just six or seven weeks. Number 2 was subsequently empty 'for a few weeks' and then the Woodcocks had moved in, on 17 October. Trueby said she had often seen Head/Williams at Number 3 after he left Number 2.

All the Woodcocks took the stand – twelve-year-old William to repeat his belief that Williams was living with the Bishops, and that he had from time to time seen Rhoda doing her washing at Number 3; his mother Hannah to say the same; and William Woodcock senior to repeat his evidence about the noises that had awoken him in the early hours of Friday 4 November, after what he guessed had been four, or four-and-a-half, hours of sleep. He claimed that without any doubt one of the three voices he had heard during the scuffle belonged to Williams. Woodcock had chatted to him for around two hours on the afternoon of Sunday 23 October, when Williams had come up to the palings and dissuaded Woodcock from digging at the bottom of the garden of Number 2, suggesting instead the area close to the cottage where, to Williams's knowledge, some lily bulbs could be found.

Abraham Keymer kept the Feathers public house in Castle Street (the south-western continuation of Virginia Row). He said that 'about a quarter before twelve o'clock on Thursday night, 3rd November, Bishop came to my house with another person, who I think was Williams, but I am not quite certain of him. My house is one or two hundred yards from Bishop's. I think they had a quartern of rum and half a gallon of beer – they took the beer away with them in a half-gallon can. This is the can.' Superintendent Thomas had seized it at Number 3, and proffered it as evidence. Keymer added that he could not be positive that Williams had come that night 'as I had never seen him before'. This contradicted eyewitness evidence that Bishop and Williams had made the Feathers their last port of call as they made Fanny Pigburn drunk on the night of 8 October.

PC Joseph Higgins told of the digging-up of Bishop's garden and detailed the state of the clothing he had found one foot down, below a spot that had been scattered with cinders and ashes 'which would prevent my noticing its having been turned up'. He told of the implements found in Bishop's house and at May's lodgings. The blood had been fresh on the brad awl and breeches found at May's. The dug-up clothing was passed around the jury. The prosecution asked Higgins whether such clothes would have been 'useful' to Bishop's own children. 'The coat would be very useful and has not got a rent in it. It would be very useful for a working boy.' So why would a family bury clothing that still had plenty of life in it? was the unvoiced question. Superintendent Thomas told the court that he had been requested by May to point out that the blood on the breeches had been so fresh that it must have been shed after his arrest; Thomas felt it only right to make that point clear on behalf of the prisoner.

Edward Ward of Nova Scotia Gardens came into the witness box. He told the court that he knew that it was a very bad thing to tell a lie, that it was a great sin. He said he knew that people who lied went to hell and were burned in brimstone and sulphur. Then he took the oath. He was six and a half. 'I remember Guy Fawkes day – my mother gave me a half-holiday before Guy Fawkes day. I do not recollect what day of the week it was. I went to Bishop's house on the day I had the half-holiday. He lives in Nova Scotia Gardens at a corner house. I have seen three of his children – he has one big boy, another about my age, and a little girl. I saw them that day in a room, next to the little room, and the little room is next to the garden. I played with the children there. I had often seen them before.'

'Did the children show you anything that day?' the prosecution asked their witness.

'Yes. Two white mice – one little one and one big one. They were in a cage, which moved round and round. I never saw them with white mice before, nor with a cage. I often played with them before. I saw my brother John when I got home and told him what I had seen.'[10] Brother John confirmed that Edward had told him about the mice and the cage, and said that the half-holiday from school had been on Friday 4 November.

PC John Kirkman of F Division then stated that he had been watching over the prisoners in the Covent Garden watch-house late on Saturday 5th:

'I saw all three prisoners in the front room. There was a printed bill stuck up there, referring to this supposed murder. It was behind where they sat. Bishop looked at the bill and then sat down. Williams was between him and May. Bishop leaned his head over Williams to speak to May and observed, in a low tone of voice, "It was the blood that sold us." I heard no answer made to that. He then got up, looked at the bill, read it over a second time and sat down with a sort of forced laugh, and said, "This states 'the marks of violence'. The 'marks of violence' were only breakings-out on the skin." Nothing was said in answer to that.'

This was the case for the prosecution. Curwood announced that he felt it was his duty to ask that the murder charge against Thomas Williams be dropped; his client was clearly not a principal in the crime, though Curwood conceded that he may have acted as an accessory after the fact. He wanted the indictment changed with regard to Williams.

It was true that very little of what had been presented in court connected Williams with the bartering of the body. By Bishop's own admission, his stepson-in-law/half-brother-in-law was very new to the trade and none of the resurrection community had appeared even to recognise Williams. But Lord Chief Justice Tindal was having none of it. He told Curwood that it would be up to the jury to decide the guilt or innocence of Williams, as charged.

James Davis was recalled by the prosecution, who wanted to be absolutely sure – he had bought two bodies from James May at the very start of November, hadn't he? Davis confirmed that this was correct.

So now the defence did what the defence was restricted to doing: putting forward the written statements of the accused and bringing forth the defence witnesses. An officer of the court read the statements out. Bishop admitted that he had been a bodysnatcher for twelve years, though, probably on the advice of his attorney, he described his work as 'procuring bodies for surgical and anatomical purposes'. Then he stated:

'I declare that I never sold any body but what had died a natural death. I have had bodies from the various workhouses, together with the clothes which were on the bodies. I occupied the house in Nova Scotia Gardens fifteen months. It consisted of three rooms and a wash-house, a garden, about twenty yards long, by about eight yards broad, three gardens adjoin, and are separated by a dwarf railing. I could have communication to either cottage, or the occupiers of them to mine. The well in my garden was for the joint use of all the tenants. There was also a privy to each house. The fact is, there are twenty cottages and gardens which are only separated by the paling already described, and I could get easy access to any of them. I declare I know nothing at all about the various articles of wearing apparel that have been found in the garden, but as regards the cap that was found in the house and supposed to have belonged to the deceased Italian boy, I can prove that it was bought by my wife of a Mrs Dodswell, of Hoxton Old Town, clothes-dealer, for my own son, Frederick. The front I sewed on myself after it was purchased. The front was bought with the cap but not sewed to it. They were sold to my wife along with other articles. Mr Dodswell is a pastry cook, and has nothing to do with the business of the clothes shop – the calling of Mrs Dodswell, therefore, as evidence to prove the truth of my statement, will put it beyond a doubt that the cap never did belong to the deceased boy, and Mrs Dodswell should also prove how long she had the cap in her possession, and how she came by it. As much stress has been laid upon the finding of several articles of wearing apparel, and also the peculiar manner in which they appear to have been taken off the persons of those supposed to have come in an improper way into my hands, I most solemnly declare I know nothing whatever of them. The length of the examinations and the repetition of them have been so diligently promulgated and impressed on the public mind, that it cannot but be supposed that a portion of the circumstances connected with this unfortunate case (if not all) have reached and attracted the attention of the jury. But I entreat them, as they value the solemn obligation of the oath they have this day taken, that they will at once divest themselves of all prejudice and give me the whole benefit of a cool, dispassionate and impartial hearing of the case, and record such a verdict as they, on their conscience, their honour, and their oath, can return. May and Williams know nothing as to how I became possessed of the body.'

Towards the end of the statement lawyer language is clearly detectable. Williams's brief statement bore the mark of a legal hand to a far greater extent:

'I am a bricklayer by trade, and latterly worked at the glass-blowing business. I never was engaged in any instance as a procurer of dead bodies or Subjects. Into the present melancholy business I was invited by Bishop. I know nothing whatever about the manner in which he became possessed of the dead body. Bishop asked me to join him on the Friday. I made no inquiry about the nature of the business. I shall, therefore, leave my case entirely to the intelligence and discrimination of the jury and the learned and merciful judge, but I trust I may be allowed once more to state that I am entirely innocent of any offence against the laws of my country.'

May's statement said that he had had a 'moderate' education and

'first became engaged in the traffic of anatomical Subjects six years since, and from that period up to the time of my apprehension have continued so, with occasionally looking after horses. I accidentally met Bishop at the Fortune of War, a house that persons of our calling generally frequent and are known there as such. Bishop wanted to speak to me, called me outside the door, and asked me where the best price could be procured for Things. I told him where I had sold two for ten guineas each, at Mr Davis's, and I had no doubt I could get rid of that Thing for him at the same price. He said if I did, I should keep all I got above nine guineas to myself. There was no questions asked as to the manner in which the body had been procured, and I knew nothing about it. As to what has been said in the public papers, or the prejudice that exists against me, and the other prisoners, it is of no moment. I here declare that during all the years that I have been in this business, I never came into possession of a living person, nor used any means for converting them into Subjects for the purposes of dissection. I admit that I have traded largely in dead bodies but I solemnly declare that I never took undue advantage of any person alive, whether man, woman, or child, however poor or unprotected. I have not been accustomed to make application for bodies at the different workhouses and I now solemnly declare that I know nothing at all of the circumstances connected with the procuring of the body, which is suspected to be that of the one named in the indictment, nor did I ever hear, nor understand, how Bishop became possessed thereof. I shall, therefore, leave my fate entirely to the intelligence and discernment of the jury and the learned judge.'

May's cavalry had arrived: Rosina Carpenter was the woman with whom May said he had spent the night of Thursday 3 November – the suspected, though not named, murder night, if George Beaman's time-of-death estimate and William Woodcock's disturbed-sleep testimony were accepted. Rosina said:

'I have known May fourteen or fifteen years but have not seen him for four or five years till within the last four months. On Thursday 3rd November he came to my house in Nag's Head Court, Golden Lane, between four and five o'clock in the evening. I am sure it was Thursday.

He stopped with me till between eleven and twelve o'clock the next morning, which was Friday. I am sure he never left me.'

But as a single woman seeing a married man on a casual, adulterous basis, Rosina's word was not considered enough.

'Nobody is present in court who saw him at my residence, although there were several persons at my house drinking with us at the time May was there. I cannot particularly name the persons who drank with us. He had passed several nights with me before this. I didn't know he was married.'

Next, Mary Ann Hall said:

'I am single and live at Number 4 Dorset Street, New Kent Road. On Sunday morning, 30th October, May left me and said he was going into the country. I saw no more of him till the Wednesday night following, when I met him at the corner of William Street and we went home and May went to bed. I sat up till three o'clock in the morning to air his jacket, which was very wet indeed, and also his under jacket. He got up on Thursday morning, put on a clean shirt, clean waistcoat and breeches and went away. I saw no more of him till Friday night when I met him by the Alfred's Head, facing Elephant and Castle, at half-past eleven o'clock. He went home with me, got up about eight o'clock and went out. I asked if he could give me a little money. He said he should be back by the time I wanted any. My landlady kept a jackdaw. She is Mrs Carroll – she is not here. I and May live upstairs. We do not live together exactly, but I think he is more with me than with anybody else. He did not come home at all on Thursday night – he left me at half-past seven o'clock on Thursday morning, and I saw no more of him till half-past eleven on Friday."'

Charlotte Berry, who had the room along the landing at 4 Dorset Street, and Jane Lewis, another lodger, told the jackdaw story – helping to explain the bloodied breeches, though the prosecution had given up on that item long before. Charlotte and Jane both admitted that they were 'in the habit of seeing gentlemen', while Mary Ann Hall, when asked by Adolphus how she made a living, had offered the fact that she had been in custody twice at Bow Street on charges of prostitution and for the past two years had made her living walking the streets. Prostitutes defending a bodysnatcher: it was not likely to look good to the jury.

It was Bishop's turn: he had lined up Sarah Trueby, Mary Dodswell and Edward Tuson. They were to prove catastrophic choices. Tuson got out of the witness box very quickly, saying of the prisoners 'I know them by seeing them. I believe I have seen Bishop once or twice, but I do not know what I am to prove.' He was asked no questions, and *The Times* report chivalrously omitted even to mention that he had appeared.

Sarah Trueby was recalled and Bishop, abandoning Curwood and Barry and interviewing his witnesses himself, asked his landlady to recall the time she had seen white mice at Number 3, in an effort to undermine six-year-old Edward Ward's testimony. Trueby said: 'I never saw any white mice in the possession of you or your family.'

'Do you not recollect any mice running out of my garden and into yours?'

'No, Mr Bishop. Never.'

'Not about six months ago? Don't you recollect your cat having killed some in my garden?'

'Never.'

Mary Dodswell was supposed to explain away the furry cap. It is possible that as a second-hand clothes-dealer, Dodswell received and sold on the garments that clothed the bodies stolen or obtained fraudulently from workhouses by snatchers; perhaps Bishop had threatened to expose her trade; and perhaps Superintendent Thomas had then told her not to worry about any threats from Bishop. 'I am the wife of George Henry Dodswell, we live at 56 Hoxton Old Town and sell second-hand clothes – my husband is employed as a pastry cook. I know Bishop's wife perfectly well. I sold her a cap about two years ago – it was a cloth cap with a leather peak at the front. I am perfectly sure it was cloth – the front was attached to the cap when I sold it. It had a black front but I am not sure how it was lined.'

'My wife bought two caps of you.'

'She only bought one. I am quite confident.'

'Mrs Dodswell, recollect, you sold two caps to my wife – one for each of my boys. My wife gave you three pence for the peak, which you sold separately.'

'I never sold but one cap to her. I never sold a peak.'

She told the court, 'I never saw Bishop or any of the family but his wife,' though she added, 'His daughter [Rhoda] lived servant with me twelve months ago.'

It was half-past five in the afternoon, and Lord Chief Justice Tindal began his summing up. He reminded the jury that they were to base their decision only on what they had heard that day – to disregard anything they might have read or heard about the prisoners. They had first to consider whether the child had died of natural causes or not; and if not, whether each of the three prisoners was involved in the murder, and to what degree they were implicated. With regard to the first point, his lordship said that he felt the jury would have little trouble 'after the explicit evidence of the medical gentlemen who had been that day examined and whose conduct it was but justice to say was an honourable rebuke to any calumnious imputations on the medical profession to which the present case may have given birth.' (The Duke of Sussex here whispered into his lordship's ear.) He said that in order to convict the men of murder, the jury must be satisfied that all three were present aiding, assisting and abetting the actual commission of the crime. If a constructive assistance were proved – though that man were not actually on the spot of the killing, but nearby, ready to lend his assistance, or was watching a door in order to prevent the detection of the parties within the house – the law considered him as much a principal offender as if his hand actually committed the deed.

He continued that the jury had heard evidence that placed the Italian boy close to Bishop's home at noon on Thursday 3 November, which was the night on which the murder was most likely to have taken place. That was the night a scuffle was heard, and Williams's voice was discerned. But it was by no means certain that May was present at that time, and it was for the jury to decide whether he was a principal or an accessory. If they had any reasonable doubts, they must acquit May. There was not convincing evidence that May had access to, or was connected with, the other two prisoners previous to the death of the deceased. But he asked the jury to bear in mind the 'loose and obscure' conversation overheard in the Fortune of War by Thomas Wigley, which could be taken to indicate that Bishop and May were a well-established team, with Williams the novice to be welcomed into the trade; and then there was Bishop's comment to May 'It was the blood that sold us', overheard by PC Kirkman. And May had claimed part-ownership of the body, both at Guy's Hospital and to Mills the dentist. Would they then feel justified in considering May a principal? The jury might perhaps decide that only Bishop and Williams had committed the deed; or perhaps Bishop alone. Or they might decide that all three were equally guilty; or that all three were guilty but not to an equal degree. The jury must accept the fact that there were no eyewitness accounts of the killing; that they would be relying on circumstantial evidence. He then went over the day's evidence with what *The Times* called 'the most painstaking minuteness'. Alas, no full transcript of the summing up has come down, so we cannot know how Tindal chose to interpret the witnesses' statements. But his speech must have been painstaking indeed, because it did not end until eight o'clock, at which time the jury went out and the prisoners were removed from the dock.

Half an hour later, the jury came back. The talk around the courtroom had been that Bishop and Williams were likely to be convicted, but that May was probably in the clear. Over to our reporter, whose account appears in *The Times* and was syndicated in various other national newspapers and broadsheets:

The most deathlike silence now prevailed throughout the court, interrupted only by a slight buzz on the reintroduction of the prisoners. Every eye was now fixed upon them; but though their appearance and manner had undergone a considerable change from what they exhibited on being first placed at the bar and during the greater part of the trial, they did not seem conscious of the additional interest which their presence at this moment excited. They scarcely raised their eyes as they entered, beyond a glance or two at the jury box.

Bishop advanced to the bar with a heavy step, and with rather a slight bend of the body, his arms hung closely down, and it seemed a kind of relief to him, when he took his place, to rest his hand on the board before him. His appearance was that of a man labouring for some time under the most intense mental agony, which had brought on a kind of lethargic stupor. His eye was sunk and glassy; his nose drawn and pinched; the jaw fallen, and, of course, the mouth open; but occasionally the mouth closed, the lips became compressed, and the shoulders and chest raised, as if he was struggling to repress some violent emotion. After a few efforts of this kind, he became apparently calm, and frequently glanced his eye towards the bench and jury box; but this was done without once raising his head. His face had that pallid, blueish appearance which so often accompanies and betokens great mental suffering.

Williams came forward with a short, quick step, and his whole manner was, we should say, the reverse of that of his companion in guilt. His face had undergone very little change, but in his eye and manner there was a feverish anxiety we did not observe during the trial. When he came and laid his hand on the bar, the rapid movement of his fingers on the board shewed the perturbed state of his feelings. Once or twice he gave a glance round the bench and bar, but after that, he seldom took his eye from the jury box.

May came forward with a more firm step than either of his fellow prisoners, but his look was that of a man who thought that all chance of life was lost. He seemed desponding, but there appeared that in his despondency which gave an air of – we could not call it daring, or even confidence – we should rather say, a physical power of endurance, which imparted to his whole manner a more firm bearing than that of the other prisoners. He was very pale, but his eye had not relaxed from that firmness which was observable in his glance throughout the whole of the trial.

Ordinary physiognomists, who, without having seen the prisoners, had read the accounts of their examinations at the police office, of their habits and mode of living, and of the horrible atrocities with which there is now no doubt they are familiar, would have been greatly disappointed in the appearance of all of them as they stood at the bar yesterday. . . . There was something of heaviness in the aspect of Bishop, but altogether his countenance was mild. Williams had that kind of aspect with which men associate the idea of sharpness and cunning, and something of mischief, but nothing of the villain. May, who was the best looking of the three, had a countenance which most persons would consider open and manly. There was an air of firmness and determination about him, but neither in him nor his companions was there the slightest physiognomical trait of a murderer, according to the common notions on the subject. They were all those kinds of common vulgar men in appearance of which one sees hundreds every day, without being struck with any indication in them of good or evil disposition.[12]

There was silence. The Duke of Sussex raised his telescope to observe the accused. The jury was asked if they had reached their verdict on each man, and the foreman said yes. John Bishop, Guilty of murder. Thomas Williams, alias Head, Guilty of murder. James May, Guilty of murder. In court, more silence; but as soon as the vast crowd outside heard the outcome, a tremendous roar of cheering and applause began, so loud that court officials had to shut every window so that the sentence could be heard. The judge first praised the jury and recalled that he had often had occasion to note of Old Bailey juries that nothing but the most satisfactory evidence and a conviction of the solemn obligation they owed to their Maker and to their country could induce them to pronounce a verdict which was to condemn their fellow man to a disgraceful death. He heartily agreed with their verdict, which was supported by the most conclusive evidence. 'By false evidence, my Lord,' said John Bishop. The judge now turned to the dock and said he would not take up any more moments than was necessary of the short time they had left before appearing before their Creator. He hoped that in the month since their arrest they had taken time to reflect on 'the horrible agony which they had inflicted on the feelings of so many of their fellow men'. He expected they would spend every instant remaining to them in fervent prayers to the Almighty for pardon through the merits of their Redeemer. They would find plenty of help in this regard at Newgate, he said. He concluded by saying that each of them would be hanged on Monday morning and their bodies handed over to the anatomists for dissection.

TWELVE

A Newgate Stink

They said nothing, initially; they just stood there, as though they expected something more to be said. After a few moments a court official indicated that it was time for them to leave the dock, and James May, in a firm voice, told the bench, 'I am a murdered man, gentlemen – and *that* man knows it,' and he pointed to Bishop. Bishop made no reply, still appearing to be deeply self-absorbed, but Williams responded, 'We are all murdered men.' He had turned a ghastly pale colour on hearing the verdict, but soon a scornful smile appeared on his face. He leaned over the edge of the dock and shook his fist at Andrew Colla, saying, 'I hope you and that other Italian will be somewhere else as well as us on Monday morning,' and shouted to the Italian witnesses that within three months they would pay for the lies they had told about him. Then he looked up to the public gallery, and spotting somebody among the huddle, raised his hand and called out, 'Goodbye, goodbye.'

They left the dock, and were escorted back down the winding stone tunnels that led between the Sessions House and the prison, and up and across the Press Yard to Newgate's condemned cells. Walking with them was Reverend Dr Theodore Williams, vicar of Hendon, magistrate and prison visitor, who had called on Bishop every day while he was on remand; Bishop had been the recipient – willing or unwilling, it is not known – of the vicar's visits during previous incarcerations. As they walked, Bishop told Dr Williams that he wanted to confess to him at once; but the vicar said no, wait a while, and urged him to speak when he was feeling calmer; the reverend would be happy to hear Bishop's tale first thing the next morning.

Sir Nicholas Conyngham Tindal, his fellow judges, the Lord Mayor and the Duke of Sussex had repaired to the private apartments above the Sessions House. Here, over dinner, the Duke told the Lord Mayor that trials such as these made him proud of England, which had 'the most perfect, intelligent and humane system'.[1] Evidently overheard by someone who was transcribing his words, the Duke continued: 'The judges of our land, the learned in our law, nobility, magistrates, merchants, medical professors and individuals of every rank in society, anxiously devoting themselves and co-operating in the one common object of redressing an injury inflicted upon a pauper child, wandering friendless and unknown in a foreign land. Seeing this, I am indeed proud of being an Englishman, and prouder still to be a prince in such a country and of such a people.'

In the condemned block, the three were searched to ensure they had no means of cheating the hangman, and were then locked into their separate cells – each with two guards. The fifteen condemned cells (built in 1728 and retained when the prison was reconstructed in the 1770s) stood at the northern end of the Newgate/Old Bailey complex, three storeys of five rooms, each 9 feet by 6, and 9 feet high. A dark staircase led between the floors, which, Charles Dickens would later note, was luridly lit by a charcoal stove.[2] The condemned block was built of stone that was 3 feet thick, and each cell was panelled with planks of wood. In summer, these were chilly rooms; in winter, bitterly cold. The cell door was 4 inches thick with a small, grated hole; the cell window was one foot square, double-grated and barred. At best, the cells were in semi-darkness, and after sundown each was lit by a single candle. On the floor was a hemp mat, which acted as a mattress and was tarred to keep out damp and vermin; and one or two horse-rugs, which served as blankets.[3]

Separating the condemned cells from the rest of Newgate was the Press Yard, at the southern end of which were two 'Press Rooms' – wards where the condemned were allowed to spend their daytime, and containing tables, benches and a fire. In the Press Yard remand prisoners used to be pressed to death by iron weights placed on a board if they refused to enter a plea of 'guilty' or 'not guilty', which meant that their trial could not begin – an act that was viewed as treasonable. This *peine forte et dure* had squashed its last victim in 1726, but the memory of the ancient cruelty was retained in the name of the yard. It was just 10 feet wide but 70 feet long, running down from the Newgate Street wall to the garden of the Royal College of Physicians (the College once backed on to the prison/Sessions House complex) and to the site of another reminder of the medical profession, Surgeons Hall, where, between 1752 and 1796, members of the Company of Surgeons had taken apart the bodies of the executed. (This had been the site of Sir Astley Cooper's earliest triumphs, by his own admission: 'The lectures were received with great *éclat*, and I became very popular as a lecturer. The theatre was constantly crowded, and the applause excessive.')[4]

Dare it be said, Newgate was not so bad. Not so bad as it had been.

61.–62. Newgate Prison, and Debtors Door, photographed shortly before the building's demolition in 1902.

WARD FOR CONDEMNED MALE PRISONERS.

63. A sketch of the Newgate Press Room, where the condemned passed their remaining daytimes.

John Wontner had been in charge since 1822 and his governorship was regarded by many at the time as something of a golden age, though over-crowding continued to be a problem.[5] George Dance the Younger's building was supposed to hold 350 prisoners, but in 1826 the population was 643, down from over 900 in 1815. (If two men were kept in the same cell, the warders had noted that 'crimes have been committed of a nature not to be more particularly described'.)[6] Newgate housed both men and women (the ratio was four to one), though they were segregated; while children between the ages of eight and fourteen were kept in the 'School' area. One of the most serious criticisms was that those awaiting trial mixed with the already convicted, the innocent and the novice being 'contaminated' by the older felon, and the same old faces would come back into the gaol time and time again. No strenuous efforts were made here to 'redeem' the criminal – unlike at Millbank Penitentiary. However, compared to many other London gaols, Newgate's death rate was low, at three a year; and suicide was uncommon.

There were no limitations on visitor numbers, and family and friends could bring in food and drink to augment the prison ration, which was in itself not ungenerous. Every day, breakfast consisted of half a pint of gruel; each prisoner had a pound of bread a day; and dinner alternated between half a pound of beef on one night and soup on the next, with vegetables and barley. The Newgate diet was a source of criticism, since the meals in

64. Dead Man's Walk – the subterranean passage that led from the prison to the scaffold at Debtors Door.

the gaol were said by many to have been more plentiful and of better quality than those eaten by the non-offending poor outside the prison walls. There was no restriction on the amount of porter that could be drunk (it was safer than the water), and visitors noticed high levels of drunkenness among the inmates. The tradition of 'garnish', or 'chummage', had each new arrival buy a round of drinks for those who shared his cell or ward – under threat of humiliation, though, such as the removal of trousers. It is impossible to gauge the extent to which psychological bullying went on, though an idea of the mores of Newgate thieves in the late 1820s is found in the tale of one prisoner who found himself being shunned when it became known that during the robbery at the London Docks for which he was imprisoned, he had knocked unconscious his victim, an aged sea captain.[7]

Physical violence among inmates was said to be rare, and rioting even rarer, with the only dissent tending to occur after lock-up on the nights

when the 'transports' were announced – those who the next day would
be taken, in 'drafts' of twenty-five, to the hulks, either to finish their gaol
term there, or to set sail for the other end of the earth. These announce-
ments seemed to trigger anger and despair across the gaol.

John Bishop slept soundly in his cell and woke at around six on Saturday
morning. The Reverend Dr Theodore Williams, true to his word, turned
up at ten. The vicar took Bishop into the room of Brown, the turnkey of
the condemned block, and here, as the two men sat on either side of
Brown's table, Bishop began to reveal a number of most interesting matters
– one of which was that James May had had no knowledge of how the
boy's body had been obtained, that he was entirely innocent and must
have his death sentence overturned. Bishop continued, and the vicar's pen
flew over his notebook as he tried to capture the killer's account. Suddenly
there erupted into the room a party of furious men: Dr Horace Cotton,
the chaplain (or 'Ordinary') of Newgate; governor John Wontner; and
Alderman Wood, City sheriff. 'Come, come, Mr Williams,' said Dr Cotton,
'what is all this about? I suppose you want to extract confessions with a
view to publishing them.' The extraction and publication – for money, via
the newspapers – of condemned men's confessions was one of the perks
of the ordinary's job; it was one of Newgate's many interesting ancient
traditions. Dr Cotton demanded that this confession stop immediately, and
Bishop was ordered from the room and told to walk a while with Brown
in the Press Yard. Dr Cotton told Dr Williams that he had no right even
to be in the prison, since these were condemned men and therefore came
under the jurisdiction of the Ordinary of Newgate. Alderman Wood told
Dr Williams that any written account of Bishop's story would not be
allowed out of the prison – it would have to be surrendered at the sheriff's
office. If Bishop were to go giving his account of events, it was highly
likely that he would implicate others – hadn't Dr Williams remembered
that Rhoda Head was still in custody on suspicion of being an accessory
after the fact of murder?

The vicar of Hendon was astonished but not daunted, and when the
party had swept out of Brown's room, and Bishop was brought back in,
he asked the killer to pick up the tale – Bishop had just reached the most
extraordinary part of it when the interruption had occurred. But Bishop
would not go on. He had become dejected again, and said, 'It is now of
no use to implicate others.'[8] He was returned to his cell by Brown, and
the vicar of Hendon went off to see if Thomas Williams had anything
to say for himself. He did.

*

65. Theodore Williams,
the controversial vicar
of Hendon, photo-
graphed in old age.

At around noon, solicitor James Harmer was informed by Dr Cotton that Bishop and Williams were in the process of making confessions, and that anything they might say could compromise Rhoda. So on Saturday afternoon Harmer went along to Bow Street and asked Minshull to set Rhoda free, on the grounds that she could not be held accountable for any crimes that her husband may have compelled her to commit. Besides, with Rhoda out of danger, the men would feel able to tell everything. Minshull saw the wisdom of this, and so it was that late on Saturday afternoon Rhoda found herself in a coach with James Harmer travelling to Newgate. There, in one of the Press Rooms, 'a most affecting scene' (according to the *Morning Advertiser*) took place, as Rhoda was reunited with Bishop and Williams. All three wept, and she told them that they must feel free to make the fullest confession possible, and not to worry about her and Sarah.

James May, the former legal clerk with beautiful handwriting, had expressed himself in verse.

James May is doomed to die,
And is condemned most innocently.
The Lord above, he knows the same,
And will send a mitigation for his pain.

He had written these lines on some sheets of paper on which he was revealing the secrets of the London resurrection world.[9] When the vicar of Hendon came calling at May's cell and urged him to unburden his soul, May told him, 'I've been guilty of many offences, but I never committed murder.' Even as he faced execution, May was proving unable to supply information on any part of the story before the encounter at the Fortune of War on the morning of Friday 4 November. He told Dr Williams everything he had ever known about both Bishop and Williams, but none of it was new or remarkable. And it was not as if May considered himself above snitching: Superintendent Thomas had been among the Newgate visitors on that busy Saturday morning. The superintendent and others had compiled a list of all the London resurrectionists they had ever come across, or heard talk of; it numbered fifty men. Thomas placed the list in front of May and asked him to make a pen mark against the name of any whom he considered to be capable of burking. When he handed the list back, May had marked six names.

Bishop had some surprise visitors too. Magistrates from the Lambeth Street police court applied to him to see if he could help in the case of Caroline Walsh – the supposed victim of Eliza Ross, who was being held on suspicion of murder. No hospital dissecting-room porter had been able to assist with this case, though John Appleton of Grainger's school had been keen to impress the magistrates by coming forward with a dissecting-room book, detailing all bodies that had passed through his theatre (the book must have been a new phenomenon; it never put in an appearance during the Fanny Pigburn inquiry). The magistrates also wondered if Bishop knew anything about Eliza Ross and Edward Cook, who were suspected of burking Caroline Walsh. The result of the interview is not known.

A Mr Evans, the owner of a toyshop in Newgate Street, called to ask governor John Wontner to ask Bishop if he knew anything about the disappearance of his nephew. The boy had gone for a walk in Hampstead in July and had not been seen again. Bishop told Wontner it was nothing to do with him.

At nine o'clock on Saturday evening, the statements of all three prisoners, and May's list and poem, were taken to the London home of Sir Nicholas

Conyngham Tindal by Wontner, Cotton, Dr Williams (whose presence was now being tolerated), James Corder of St Paul's, Covent Garden, and two City of London under-sheriffs. The meeting was to establish whether May had a good case to present to the Home Secretary, Lord Melbourne, for a pardon, or at least a 'mitigation' while the possibility of a new trial was considered, with the charge reduced to being an accessory after the fact of murder, not a principal. The other two trial judges, Sir John Vaughan and Sir Joseph Littledale, were summoned too, to give their opinion.

There was no Court of Appeal (that was seventy-six years away) and pardons were obtained by personal intervention to the Home Secretary's department in Downing Street, one reason why the judges' support would have been so helpful. The more prestigious the pleader, the more likely a reprieve.[10] 'All their proceedings are conducted in the dark,' wrote one law reformer of the Home Office and the Privy Council. '[They] now affect to take every pains in coming to a right decision; but what they do is of an occult nature, and unsatisfactory.'[11] Historian Albany Fontblanque thought so too: 'In this mysterious supreme court no parties appear for or against the prisoner; no witnesses are called; the convicts have no opportunity of protecting themselves against malicious or erroneous representations.'[12]

There were four hours of discussion about May's case, none of which will ever be known since it was 'in the dark'. But while Sir Nicholas and Sir John were in favour of reprieving May, Sir Joseph was not so minded. The warrants for three executions on Monday morning were written out in Downing Street.

Sunday arrived. May was still protesting his innocence; and Bishop and Williams told Dr Williams, Dr Cotton, John Wontner and anyone else who asked them that May had had nothing to do with any killings – that they were not a gang, that Thomas Williams had barely known May, and that when May had come on Friday 4 November to extract the dead boy's teeth, this was the first time he had ever been to Nova Scotia Gardens.

Reverend Theodore Williams convened a meeting in the private apartments above the Old Bailey Sessions House, of Tindal, Vaughan and Littledale, with Wontner, Cotton and their sheriffs and under-sheriffs present too. Though Littledale would still not budge, a new request, with copies of the various further statements that had been made by Bishop and Williams, was forwarded to Lord Melbourne at his private residence. At half-past four in the afternoon the Home Secretary returned his final decision.

Cotton and Wontner went without delay to the Press Room, where all three prisoners were found with their warders. Cotton opened the dispatches from the Home Secretary and read first to Bishop, then to Williams, the official decision that they would be hanged by the neck on Monday morning. He addressed May 'that the execution of the sentence upon James May shall be respited during His Majesty's most gracious pleasure'. May dropped to the floor as though he had been shot; then his body began to twist and jerk, his arms flailing. Four officers attempted to sit him up and bring him to his senses (Bishop and Williams looked on unconcerned, as though the room were empty), but it took a quarter of an hour before May was able to speak. At first it was just meaningless syllables, then he laughed, then he cried, then he tried to pray but he was shaking too much. Wontner and Cotton had never seen anything like it in all their Newgate years; they told him not to get upset, they knew what he meant to say, it was all right. Everything would be all right. May gibbered out his thanks to God, thanks to Wontner, to Cotton, to Dr Williams. When he calmed down further he said that when Cotton had turned to him to read out his warrant, he had been so earnestly expecting to hear the same words that had been delivered to Bishop and Williams that on hearing the word 'respite', despair had suddenly changed to elation – so suddenly that he lost consciousness. He described it as feeling like his heart had burst in his chest. He never had killed anyone, he said; he knew he had not been a good man, but he had never killed anyone.

At some point after the final pronouncements had been made, Bishop and Williams were allowed to say farewell to Sarah and Rhoda. No report of the meeting has emerged; but the newspapers pointed out that none of Bishop's children had been permitted to visit Newgate.

Later that night another squabble erupted in the gaol. While Dr Williams appears to have been allowed to stay on at the prison to be with Bishop, Thomas Williams had requested the presence of one of his former confidants, the Reverend Dr Whitworth Russell, chaplain of Millbank Penitentiary. Whitworth Russell had already established a reputation as a dogmatic campaigner for prison reform, and an intense, one-to-one relationship with his charges – in which he urged rehabilitation through repentance and religiosity – was one of his radical measures. He would soon become Britain's joint first inspector of prisons and would seek to create a uniform, systematic approach to penal care. Yet Thomas Williams had gone in to Millbank a petty thief and emerged a killer.

Thomas Williams had several private conversations with Whitworth

Russell in his cell. But Dr Cotton was supposed to be the only shepherd of Church of England souls at the gaol. Catholics, Jews and Dissenters could do as they pleased and import their own holy men into Newgate; but Anglicans were to be given succour only by the Ordinary. Cotton thought Whitworth Russell's and Theodore Williams's approaches to religion were unorthodox and not 'useful' to condemned men (though Cotton himself had been criticised for his 'condemned' sermons, preached with a coffin placed at the centre of Newgate's chapel, which were said to frighten unduly those who were to be executed). Yet it seemed that only Whitworth Russell had any rapport with Thomas Williams; he had the killer praying fervently at times. Bishop, by contrast, had sunk back into his unresponsive stupor: in Cotton's words, 'He seems to be of a reserved and sullen temper. It was difficult to lead him into conversation, so as to learn anything of his state of mind.'[13] One of the guards asked him if he wanted to be read to from the tracts that Cotton had left in the cell, and Bishop said, 'Don't bother me – I was teazed quite enough by the parsons with religious talk during the day and I'll have none of it tonight. I can say no more than I have said.'

'I shall now go to bed for the last time,' said Thomas Williams to his warders at half-past midnight on Sunday. He knelt and prayed aloud, then undressed, and took to his mat and horse-rugs. Nevertheless, he stayed up talking with the guards for a further hour, and wrote the following note for the governor of Millbank:

> Mr Russell, If you will be kind enough to let my brother prisoners know the awful death which I shall have suffered when you read this, it will, through your expostulations, prevent them from increasing their crimes when they may be liberated; and tell them bad company and drinking and blasphemy is the foundation of all evil. Give my brotherly love to them, and tell them never to deviate from the paths of religion, and have a firm belief in the blessed Saviour. Give my love to John Edwards, John Justin and John Dingle, and receive the prayers of the unfortunate and guilty
>   Thomas Head.

THIRTEEN

'I, John Bishop . . .

. . . do hereby declare and confess that the boy supposed to be the Italian boy was a Lincolnshire boy. I and Williams took him to my house about half-past ten o'clock on the Thursday night, the 3rd of November, from the Bell, in Smithfield. He walked home with us. Williams promised to give him some work. Williams went with him from the Bell to the Old Bailey watering-house, whilst I went to the Fortune of War. Williams came from the Old Bailey watering-house to the Fortune of War for me, leaving the boy standing at the corner of the court by the watering-house in the Old Bailey. I went directly with Williams to the boy, and we walked then all three to Nova Scotia Gardens, taking a pint of stout at a public house near Holywell Lane, Shoreditch, on our way, of which we gave the boy a part; we only stayed just to drink it, and walked on to my house, where we arrived at about eleven o'clock. My wife and children and Mrs Williams were not gone to bed, so we put him in the privy, and told him to wait there for us. Williams went in and told them to go to bed, and I stayed in the garden. Williams came out directly, and we both walked out of the garden a little way to give time for the family getting to bed; we returned in about ten minutes or a quarter of an hour, and listened outside at the window to ascertain whether the family were gone to bed. All was quiet, and we then went to the boy in the privy, and took him into the house; we lighted a candle, and gave the boy some bread and cheese, and after he had eaten, we gave him a cup full of rum, with about half a small phial of laudanum in it. I had bought the rum the same evening at the Three Tuns, in Smithfield, and the laudanum also in small quantities at different shops. There was no water or other liquid put in the cup with the rum and laudanum. The boy drank the contents of the cup directly in two draughts, and afterwards a little beer. In about ten minutes he fell asleep on the chair on which he sat, and I removed him from the chair to the floor, and laid him on his side. We then went out and left him there. We had a quartern of gin and a pint of beer at the Feathers, near Shoreditch Church, and then went home again, having been away from the boy about twenty minutes. We found him asleep as we had left him. We took him directly, asleep and insensible, into the garden, and tied a cord to his feet to enable us to pull him up by, and I then took him in my arms, and let him slide from them headlong into the well in the garden, whilst Williams held the cord to prevent the body going altogether too low in the well. He was nearly wholly in the water of the well – his feet just above the surface. Williams fastened the other end of the cord round the paling, to prevent the body getting beyond our reach. The boy struggled a little with his arms and legs in the water, and the water bubbled for a minute. We waited till these symptoms were past, and then went in doors, and afterwards I think we went out, and walked down Shoreditch to occupy the time, and in about three-quarters of an hour we returned and took him out of the well by pulling him by the cord attached to his feet; we undressed him in the paved yard, rolled his clothes up, and buried them where they were found by the witness who produced them. We carried the boy into the wash-house, laid him on the floor, and covered him over with a bag. We left him there, and went and had some coffee in Old Street Road, and then (a little before two in the morning of Friday) went back to my house. We immediately doubled the body up, and put it into a box, which we corded, so that nobody might open it to see what was in it, and then went again, and had some more coffee in the same place in Old Street Road, where we stayed a little while, and then went home to bed – both in the same house, and to our own beds, as usual.

I declare that this statement is all true, and contains all the facts as far as I can recollect. May knew nothing of the murder, and I do not believe he suspected that I had got the body except in the usual way, and after the death of it. I always told him that I got it from the ground, and he never knew to the contrary until I confessed since the trial. I have known May as a body-snatcher four or five years, but I do not believe he ever obtained a body except in the common course of men in that calling, by stealing from the graves.

I also confess that I and Williams were concerned in the murder of a female, whom I believe to have been since discovered to be Fanny Pigburn, on or about the 9th of October last. I and Williams saw her sitting, about eleven or twelve o'clock at night, on the step of a door in Shoreditch, near the church. She had a child, four or five years old, with her, on her lap. I asked why she was sitting there. She said she had no home to go to, for her landlord had turned her out into the street.

I told her that she might go home with us, and she walked with us to my house, in Nova Scotia Gardens, carrying her child with her. When we got there, we found the family abed, and we took the woman in and lighted a fire, by which we all sat down together. I went out for beer, and we all partook of beer and rum (I had brought the rum from Smithfield in my pocket); the woman and her child lay down on some dirty linen on the floor, and I and Williams went to bed; about six o'clock next morning I and Williams told her to go away, and to meet us at the London Apprentice, in Old Street Road, at one o'clock; this was before our families were up; she met us again at one o'clock at the London Apprentice, without her child; we gave her some halfpence and beer, and desired her to meet us again at ten o'clock at night at the same place; after this we bought rum and laudanum at different places, and at ten o'clock we met the woman again at the London Apprentice; she had no child with her; we drank three pints of beer between us there, and stayed there about an hour. We should have stayed there longer, but an old man came in, whom the woman said she knew, and she said she did not like him to see her there with anybody; we therefore all went out; it rained hard, and we took shelter under a door-way in the Hackney Road for about half an hour. We then walked to Nova Scotia Gardens, and Williams and I led her into No. 2, an empty house, adjoining my house. We had no light. Williams stepped out into the garden with the rum and laudanum, which I had handed to him; he there mixed them together in a half-pint bottle, and came into the house to me and the woman, and gave her the bottle to drink; she drank the whole at two or three draughts; there was a quartern of rum, and about half a phial of laudanum; she sat down on the step between two rooms in the house, and went off to sleep in about ten minutes. She was falling back; I caught her to save her fall, and she lay back on the floor. Then Williams and I went to a public-house, got something to drink, and in about half an hour came back to the woman; we took her cloak off, tied a cord to her feet, carried her to the well in the garden and thrust her into it headlong; she struggled very little afterwards, and the water bubbled a little at the top; we fastened the cord to the palings to prevent her going down beyond our reach, and left her and took a walk to Shoreditch and back in about half an hour; we left the woman in the well for this length of time that the rum and laudanum might run out of the body at the mouth; on our return we took her out of the well, cut her clothes off, put them down the privy of the empty house, carried the body into the wash-house of my own house, where we doubled it up and put it in to a hair-box, which we corded, and left it there.

We did not go to bed, but went to Shields' house in Eagle Street, Red Lion Square, and called him up; this was between four and five o'clock in the morning; we then went with Shields to a public-house near the Sessions House, Clerkenwell, and had some gin, and from thence to my house, where we went in and stayed a little while to wait the change of the police. I told Shields he was to carry that trunk to St Thomas's Hospital. He asked if there was a woman in the house who could walk alongside of him, so that people might not take any notice. Williams called his wife up, and asked her to walk with Shields, and to carry the hat-box, which he gave her to carry. There was nothing in it, but it was tied up as if there were. We then put the box with the body on Shields' head, and went to the hospital, Shields and Mrs Williams walking on one side of the street, and I and Williams on the other. At St Thomas's Hospital I saw Mr South's footman, and sent him upstairs to Mr South to ask if he wanted a subject. The footman brought me word that his master wanted one, but could not give an answer till the next day, as he had not time to look at it. During the interview, Shields, Williams, and his wife were waiting at a public-house. I then went alone to Mr Appleton, at Mr Grainger's, and agreed to sell it to him for eight guineas, and afterwards I fetched it from St Thomas's Hospital and took it to Mr Appleton, who paid me five pounds then, and the rest on the following Monday. After receiving the five pounds I went to Shields and Williams and his wife at the public-house where I paid Shields ten shillings for his trouble, and we then all went to the Flower Pot in Bishopsgate, where we had something to drink and went home.

I never saw the woman's child after the first time before mentioned. She said she had left the child with the person she had taken some of her things to, before her landlord took her goods. The woman murdered did not tell us her name; she said her age was 35, I think, and that her husband, before he died, was a cabinet-maker. She was thin, rather tall, and very much marked with the small-pox.

I also confess the murder of a boy who told us his name was Cunningham. It was a fortnight after the murder of the woman. I and Williams found him sleeping about eleven or twelve o'clock at night, on Friday 21st October, as I think, under the pig-boards in the pig-market at Smithfield. Williams woke him, and asked him to come along with him (Williams), and the boy walked with Williams and me to my house in Nova Scotia Gardens. We took him into my house, and gave him some warm beer, sweetened with sugar, with rum and laudanum in it. He drank two or three cups full and then fell asleep in a little chair belonging to one of my children. We laid him on the floor, and went out for a little while and got something to drink, and then returned, carried the boy to the well, and threw him into it, in the same way as we had served the other boy and the woman. He died instantly in the well and we left him there a little while, to give time for the mixtures we had given him to run out of the body. We then took the body from the well, took off the clothes in the garden, and buried them there. The body we carried into the wash-house, and put it into the same box, and left it there until the next evening, when we got a porter to carry it with us to St Bartholomew's Hospital, where I sold it to Mr Smith for eight guineas. This boy was about ten or eleven years old, said his mother lived in Kent Street, and that he had not been home for a twelve-month and better.

I solemnly declare that these are all the murders in which I have been concerned, or that I know any thing of; that I and Williams were alone concerned in these, and that no other person whatever knew any thing about either of them; and that I do not know whether there are others who practise the same mode of obtaining bodies for sale. I know nothing of any Italian boy, and was never concerned in, or knew of, the murder of such a boy. There have been no white mice about my house for the last six months. My son, about eight months ago, bought two mice, and I made a cage for them. It was flat, with wires at the top. They lived about two months, and were killed, I think, by a cat in the garden, where they got out of the cage. They were frequently seen running in the garden, and used to hide in a hole under the privy. I and my wife and children saw one of them killed by a cat in the garden whilst we were at tea.

Until the transactions before set forth I never was concerned in obtaining a subject by destruction of the living. I have followed the course of obtaining a livelihood as a body-snatcher for 12 years, and have obtained and sold, I think, from 500 to 1,000 bodies; but I declare, before God, that they were all obtained after death, and that, with the above exceptions, I am ignorant of any murder for that or any other purpose.'

John Bishop
Witness: Robert Ellis, Under-sheriff
Newgate, December 4th, 1831

'I, Thomas Head, alias Williams, now under sentence of death in Newgate, do solemnly confess and declare the foregoing statement and confession of John Bishop, which has been made in my presence, and since read over to me distinctly, is altogether true, so far as the same relates to me. I declare that I was never concerned in or privy to any other transaction of the like nature – that I never knew any thing of the murder of any other person whatever – that I was never a body-snatcher or concerned in the sale of any other body than the three murdered by Bishop and myself – that May was a stranger to me, and I had never seen him more than once or twice before Friday, the 4th of November last – and that May was wholly innocent and ignorant of any of those murders in which I was concerned, and for one of which I am about to suffer death.'

Thomas Head

Witness: R. Ellis

Newgate, December 4th, 1831.

'The above confessions taken literally, from the prisoners, in our presence,' T. Wood, R. Ellis, Under-sheriffs.

FOURTEEN

Day of Dissolution

John Bishop and Thomas Williams wake before dawn on Monday 5 December. Williams says, 'Now for it,' and seems to become more afraid by the minute. He is attempting to pray when Reverend Whitworth Russell enters his cell; Russell watches as Williams mutters the start of various prayers but proves too agitated to finish any, and breaks off, appearing to be in despair.

In his cell, Bishop is listless and appears not to notice anything around him. He has slept soundly, but woke in the night with a start on seeing someone in the room with him; when asked by his warder if he wanted anything, he replied 'No' and fell back to sleep. At half-past five he stands up, scratches his head and says, 'The time is coming very fast.' He is offered and accepts some toast and coffee. He tells his warder, 'I deserve what is to come.'

While they have been sleeping, a crowd of between 30,000 and 40,000 has amassed in Old Bailey and Giltspur Street. The scaffold has been in place outside Newgate's Debtors Door since half-past midnight, and workmen have completed the final adjustments by torchlight. Large wooden barriers are installed at all entrances to Old Bailey, in order to prevent a surge when the men are brought out; it is to protect the spectators, and it is to protect the condemned – no one can recall such a desperate, anxious crowd at an execution, and it is believed the people will want to take their own revenge. Their pain and anger seem personal. By five in the morning the entire Old Bailey is packed. Sill-side seats are being sold for upwards of ten guineas; a guinea buys you a spot further back from the window. 'Will you take a window to see the execution, sir?' is chirruped to every well-dressed man in the vicinity. The publican of the King of Denmark watering house – right opposite Debtors Door – has made a small fortune by cramming spectators in. A nearby shop-owner has removed his entire frontage to accommodate as many seats as possible. Many people have climbed up lamp-posts or found their way on to rooftops;

every window is crammed with sightseers. It is a very foggy day, and the scaffold cannot be seen from Ludgate Hill, just 200 yards to the south.[1] At ground level people are starting to faint, clothes become torn in the jostling; those who pass out are relayed over the heads of the throng to a less crowded spot. The pickpockets are hard at work, scarcely seeming to care if they are seen. Some eager male spectators are attempting to pass themselves off as constables in order to get right up to the gallows, from which hang three ropes. At around seven o'clock the error is noticed, and the rope that would have dispatched James May is removed. The Last Dying Speech Man has had a good morning, and many in the crowd have purchased one of a number of hastily cobbled together broadsheets purporting to feature 'the dying words of Bishop and Williams', some featuring woodcuts that show May dangling alongside them. Nevertheless, the crowd doesn't seem very surprised by the removal of the third rope; some cheering is even heard at the news that May is not to hang.

It is half-past seven and time for the prisoners to be formally handed over to the sheriffs and under-sheriffs of the City of London for execution. It is an ancient tradition. The men are escorted downstairs to the Press Room, where many reporters and around thirty paying visitors (including the two sons of Earl Grey who so enjoyed the trial; and John Philips Bean, assistant master at St Paul's School, who felt 'a very urgent desire to watch the workings of such atrocious minds towards the last')[2] are waiting to view Bishop and Williams and the ceremony through which they are about to pass. The guests are told that if they speak, they must do so only in whispers.

Bishop enters the room gazing at the ground, though he appears to be in such a stupor he may not even be seeing it. He gives no indication that he realises where he is or what is happening to him. But halfway across the room, he looks up, sees all the eyes upon him and groans and gasps. Then he sinks back into his trancelike state, continues to move slowly, almost mechanically, across the room, and, approaching a prison officer, holds out his arms, wrists together, for them to be bound. When this is done, and his collar folded back and his black neckerchief removed, he sits down on a bench and stares at the floor. His demeanour impresses the visitors, who see it as a sign of firmness and resolve. An under-sheriff sits down next to him and asks him softly if there is any further confession he would like to make. 'No, sir,' says Bishop. 'I have told all.'

Now Williams enters the room, and moves with a nervous, jerky walk – he is shaking so badly that he needs to be supported as he walks the length of the room. As his arms are pinioned, one officer must hold them steady as another ties the cord. His face is flushed, there are tears in his eyes, and he is muttering, 'I deserve all this. I deserve all this and more. I deserve what I'm about to suffer.' He looks younger than ever. He is sat down on the bench alongside Bishop, and the under-sheriff asks him if he has anything more to say, and Williams says, 'Oh no, sir, I have told all – I hope I am now at peace with God – What I have told is the truth.' He is also heard to say, 'Remember me to . . .', but the final word is not clearly audible because he is crying.

Dr Cotton says that he understands the men wish to receive the sacraments, but Dr Williams tells him that this won't be necessary – the prisoners have changed their minds. Dr Cotton says that he hopes that they have spent the night asking for God's mercy. 'Now gentlemen,' says Cotton to the interloping churchmen, 'you'd better take your man and retire to different parts of the room, where you can talk without interrupting each other.' Dr Whitworth Russell takes Thomas Williams to the furthest end of the room where they are seen speaking earnestly; Dr Theodore Williams sits with Bishop close to the blazing fire. Cotton doesn't like the version of Anglicanism he is hearing and approaches each of the two-man huddles and says, 'Now gentlemen, time is hastening. Suppose you let them go and pray to God. You go there,' he says to Bishop, pointing to a bench near the window of the Press Room, 'and you kneel down there,' he tells Thomas Williams, indicating a spot near the sink where crockery can be rinsed, 'and pray heartily to God to forgive you your sins and have mercy on your souls through your Redeemer.' They do as they are told, and as they are praying Cotton is heard to remark, 'Now this is a blessed sight.'

When they return to the bench near the fireside, Cotton asks them if they would like a little wine. They say yes, and Bishop downs one teacupful, but Williams is shaking and crying so much he is given a little more. Drs Williams and Whitworth Russell have rejoined them, and have started to discuss the crimes once again, and then they begin to advise them on how they should approach their imminent deaths, at which point Cotton says, 'I will give those directions, if you please. All matters of that kind had better be left to me.'

St Paul's Cathedral can be heard striking eight. Bishop stands and says 'I am ready' and Cotton starts reciting the funeral service as Bishop and Williams, the sheriffs, under-sheriffs, clergymen and visitors rise and begin the walk to the scaffold. They descend into the subterranean walkway as Cotton reads, passing along the Dead Man's Walk that connects Newgate to the Old Bailey, with the remains of the executed lying under the slabs they walk on, and then up into the small entrance hall behind Debtors Door, up a flight of stairs and through the prison's Bread Room and the Soup Room, from which lead the stairs that lead directly out to the gallows.

They are opposite the King of Denmark. Bishop walks steadily, slowly, to the foot of the steps leading out to the scaffold, but Williams becomes even more frenzied in appearance and begs to see Reverend Whitworth Russell once again. As Bishop moves out on to the platform, the chaplain of Millbank Penitentiary comes alongside Williams, sitting on a bench in the Soup Room, and their conversation is at first inaudible, but now, with Williams clasping Whitworth Russell's hand as he moves on to the stairs to the scaffold, the condemned man is heard saying, 'I hope God will have mercy upon me.' Whitworth Russell says that since Williams seems genuinely penitent, God is likely to be merciful. 'Then I am ready to die. I know I deserve it, for other crimes I have done.' Whitworth Russell says, 'You have just another moment between this and death, and as a dying man I implore you, in God's name, to tell the truth. Have you told me the whole truth?'

'All I have told you is true.' He won't let go of the chaplain's hands.

'But have you told me all?'

Williams hesitates, then says, 'All I have told you is quite true.'

The crowd has spotted the executioner, William Calcraft, and his assistant on the scaffold and a cry of 'Hats off!' is shouted around the thousands there: you get a better view with hats off. Silence falls. But the moment Bishop appears, there is a roar. He does not seem to notice the shouting, yelling, hooting, screaming, cursing, and he moves obediently as Calcraft places him beneath the beam, which faces south to Ludgate Hill; his last glimpse will be of thick fog, as Calcraft pulls a cloth sack over his head and puts the noose around his neck. The crowd is pleased with the preparation and begins to cheer. It is likely that Bishop knows of Calcraft's reputation for ineptitude, choosing too short a drop and having to hang on the back of the condemned to ensure the neck breaks (he has strangled three men in this way in 1829), and that he often stinks of brandy at his public appearances. Williams's conversation with Whitworth Russell at the foot of the stairs has delayed him by two minutes, so Bishop stands alone, not moving a muscle or making a sound.

Williams appears, totters to the edge of the scaffold and bows to the crowd. Why is he doing this? Why? Does he think he's a performer on a stage? Is it a gesture he has seen the condemned make at executions? Is he trying to show remorse to the mob he preyed on? The crowd screams and jeers and curses him. Shaking violently, he is led to the beam, hooded and noosed. Cotton encourages both men to pray, and Williams does this eagerly, calling out the words along with the churchman, who, mid-sentence, gives Calcraft the signal for the drop, and both men fall.

Bishop dies instantly. But Williams is seen drawing his legs upwards several times, with immense effort, while his neck and chest muscles throb; it is five minutes until his legs stop twitching. He has been slowly strangled. By which time, Cotton, the sheriff, the under-sheriffs and the paying visitors are on their way back through the prison to enjoy the breakfast that ancient tradition specifies on the occasion of executions at Newgate.

The excitement of the burkers being 'turned off' has led to a catastrophe at the southern end of Giltspur Street. The wooden barrier there has collapsed and many people are crushed in the panic. By a quarter to nine, an entire ward at St Bartholomew's is filled with injured spectators. Ribs are crushed, limbs are broken, flesh torn, but surprisingly no one has been killed. Robert Mortimer, the Nova Scotia Gardens tailor who cut his throat rather than give evidence, is in Bart's too, sitting up chatting and wondering why he'd been so silly.

It is nine o'clock, and time for the bodies to be cut down, although this is scarcely the right term, since modern executions involve the rope being connected to a chain, which is attached to the beam by a hook kept in place by a screw and bolt. It is seen as a great advance. Calcraft simply turns the bolt and Bishop and Williams fall into the cart waiting below the scaffold. The crowd loves this. The bodies are covered by two sacks and then the cart is driven by the City Marshal, wearing full ceremonial regalia, to 33 Hosier Lane, the house rented by the Royal College of Surgeons for the official reception of the bodies of executed murderers. It is only a short distance – really just behind the Fortune of War. The cart moves in a slow, stately manner, and the crowd appears to enjoy the ritual and the costume of this traditional journey. They would love to get their hands on the corpses, and the police have their job cut out to keep people back as Bishop and Williams are carried into Number 33.

They get quite a reception: Sir William Blizard himself, eighty-eight-year-old president of the Royal College of Surgeons, has come to Hosier Lane in his college robes. He is there, along with the entire court of the college, to officiate as William Clift, conservator of the college library and museum, draws his knife – ceremonially – across the chests and stomachs of Bishop and Williams, creating large cruciform wounds on each man.[3] Then they are – ceremonially – stitched back up again before presentation to the anatomists. Having witnessed the opening and closing of the bodies, the City Marshall leaves. Calcraft, having been given the men's clothes and their nooses, beats a retreat too – these are his perks, and he will make money exhibiting the trophies. (Calcraft isn't particularly interested in his job, preferring gardening, breeding prize rabbits and caring

66.–67. The true likenesses of John Bishop and Thomas Head, sketched by William Clift of the Royal College of Surgeons.

for his pet pony; he is also said to be good with children.)[4] William Clift sketches the dead men, and will later work these up into likenesses that, many will say, are undoubtedly the faces of monsters.

Now Bishop and Williams take their leave of each other for the last time (though to be fair, they have known each other for only five months). Bishop is heading for King's College, as a reward for Richard Partridge and Herbert Mayo, while Williams is off to the Great Windmill Street school, where George Guthrie and Edward Tuson are waiting for him.

FIFTEEN

The Use of the Dead to the Living

And once the scalpels are set to work, it becomes clear what manner of men these were, and how and why these murders came to be committed. At King's College, Bishop had a lecture on medical jurisprudence read over him as he lay on the slab before once again being sliced from throat to abdomen and across the chest – this time by Richard Partridge as Herbert Mayo stood by. Bishop, it was discovered, had an extraordinarily good physique, proving far more useful as a specimen than the produce he used to deliver. 'A more healthy or muscular Subject has not been seen in any of the schools of anatomy for a long time,' cooed the *Morning Advertiser*. 'The body presented a remarkably fine appearance across the chest. The deltoides were splendidly developed, and the pectorals, major and minor, were particularly displayed." Bishop was 5 feet 7 inches tall, and had an inordinate amount of body hair; at some point in his life he had broken both his legs, and he had two scars on his chin – perhaps an inexpertly scaled graveyard wall had left its imprint. It was also discovered that Calcraft had made yet another hash of his job: Bishop's spinal cord was intact. The rope had bitten deep into the flesh on the left side of his neck. With the top of the skull carved off, Bishop's brain was reported to look as though it was in an 'unhealthy' state; the observers deduced that this was visual evidence of the mental anguish he had been suffering in the days before his death.

Later, but before he began to smell, Bishop was set up as an exhibit in a room next to the Anatomical Theatre at King's College; a huge crowd came to see the London Burker, who had been disembowelled and had had all his various cuts sewn up with thick twine. Later still, when he ceased to be a money-spinning concern, Bishop was gradually stripped down to the bone by the students and lecturers of King's.

The clothes that Bishop had died in, alongside Williams's, were exhibited in a private house in Sun Street, Shoreditch, for 'only a penny', according to the advertisements.

68. The Great Windmill Street School, where Thomas Head caused a riot.

The exhibition of Williams's body caused a minor riot. For a fee, the curious were allowed into the dissecting-room where Edward Tuson and George Guthrie were at work. (Guthrie had put his request in early, writing to the secretary of the Royal College of Surgeons on 4 December: 'If May is not executed, pray do me the favour to beg Mr Clift to send to Windmill Street the best of the two remaining, for a natural skeleton.' But he was short-changed, since King's College was given 'the best'.)[2] A large crowd gathered outside the school to wait for admittance, and a number of medical students took it upon themselves to police them – although there were Metropolitan officers on the spot – arming themselves with staves and chair legs, with which they threatened people in the queue. Inside, students helped themselves to locks of Williams's hair. Two students were seen brawling close by the corpse (which had its eyes wide open); they had become drunk on pots of beer hauled up on ropes over the heads of the crowd and in through the school windows. The police wrote to Tuson to warn him that the 'exhibition' must end immediately since the noise from inside and around the school was disturbing residents.[3] Those who did gain admittance will have seen Williams's tattooed forearms – which should have settled the issue of his true identity once and for ever. But it just led to more confusion; his left forearm now featured a number of crudely drawn flower-pots, an anchor and a scroll (which had not been there in 1827, when his 'distinguishing marks' had been so carefully sketched into a prison ledger) surrounding the four initials. In 1827, the prison authorities had transcribed these as THNA, the NA probably relating to the hearts and arrows on his right forearm. But William Clift, conservator of the Royal College of Surgeons museum, sketched them into his diary as 'JOHN HEAD'; while a newspaper reporter transcribed them as 'J. HEAD'. Pierce Egan also saw 'JOHN HEAD' when he viewed the body, written above the letters 'CE', and Egan wrote to *The Times* expressing his view that the truth of the killer's confession was perhaps to be doubted, since he had signed the document 'Thomas Head', not 'John'.[4] But Head had consistently described himself as 'Thomas' in all the documentation that mattered: his wedding certificate, his Old Bailey trial for theft, his entries in prison ledgers. Did Thomas decide to inscribe himself 'John' at some point in Millbank, or upon his release? Or were Clift and Egan mistaken in what they saw on the forearm?

It was with some confidence that phrenologist Dr John Elliotson stated, on examining plaster casts taken of Bishop and Williams's skulls, that 'Bishop had got ideality, and no reflection', while with Williams 'the portion devoted to the animal propensities – the lower posterior and the lower lateral parts, especially destructiveness, acquisitiveness, secretiveness – is immense.' Williams's head was 'by far the worse', claimed Elliotson: it was clear that Williams's combativeness was very large and his veneration very small, while his self-esteem was full and his love of approbation large. No wonder his life had been low and villainous, since he had been deficient in the 'sense of what is refined and exquisite in nature and art'.[5]

The early 1830s were the high noon of phrenology, and celebrated murderers such as Bishop and Williams were the most sought-after theory-proving material there was. What relation did the shape and size of the skull have to the mind that it contained? Were morality and intellect revealed in human tissue? What functions could be deduced from the way an organ looked? Sadism knew no social class, according to Dr Joseph Gall (1757–1828), one of phrenology's pioneers; Gall took pains to demonstrate – anecdotally – that the propensity for murder was as likely to be found in the wealthy lover of the arts as in the poorest peasant. He cited Nero, Henry VIII, a senior member of the Dutch clergy and a count at the court of Louis XV as particularly depraved (though he never did see their heads).[6] It would be interesting to know what phrenologists would have made of the plaster casts of Bishop and Williams's heads if these had turned up with no history attached; as it was, the craniometrists knew in great detail the deeds of the men whose skulls they were measuring. Elliotson's report interweaves his analysis of Williams's head shape with regurgitated background details about Williams's life that were taken straight from the newspapers. Alas, Elliotson's favoured plaster-cast-maker, a Cockney called Deville, had omitted to shave the entire scalps, which rather compromised Elliotson's assessment of Bishop's moral faculties, since matted hair had rendered this particular bump bigger than it really was.

Bishop's head was smaller than Williams's, which, deduced Elliotson, 'agrees with the fact' that it was Williams who had first suggested the burkings (that was what had been reported, at least); and Bishop's enlarged organ of acquisitiveness tallied with his history as a paid informer and perjurer – more details gleaned from the papers. What we were to learn from these casts, said Elliotson, was gratitude that we did not ourselves possess such terrible 'organisation' of faculties, and that it was our duty to encourage virtue and to ensure a steady supply of legally obtained corpses to anatomists, thereby removing the motive for Bishop and Williams's crimes. These two men might even, he said, have made decent, if disagreeable, Christians, if murder had not come so easily into their lives.

Elliotson tabulated his findings, just to make matters entirely clear:

	WILLIAMS	BISHOP
Amativeness (what we would call sex drive)	Very large	Large
Philoprogenitiveness (fertility; will to reproduce)	Moderate	Large
Inhabitiveness (urge to settle in one place)	Moderate	Moderate
Adhesiveness (tenacity)	Large	Moderate
Combativeness	Very large	Small
Constructiveness	Small	Moderate
Acquisitiveness	Very large	Very large
Destructiveness	Very large	Large
Secretiveness	Very large	Large
Self-esteem	Full	Large
Love of approbation	Large	Full
Cautiousness	Very large	Moderate

Benevolence	Very small	Small
Veneration	Very small	Moderate
Hope	Very small	Small
Conscientiousness	Very small	Very small
Ideality	Small	Small
Firmness	Small	Small
Knowing faculties	Large	Large
Intellectual faculties	Small	Very small

The opponents of 'bumpology', as they called it, claimed that there was no relation between cranium and brain – that the brain was a single organ able to perform various functions, with mis-shaped skulls being the result of a number of perfectly mundane factors, such as a blow to the head, or tight-fitting headwear for children. Much muck was raked in the battle of phrenology, with one often-repeated anecdote (never sourced) about a trainee of Gall who had once disinterred his own mother in order to prove a point.[7] Phrenology, though, was not a phenomenon that could be proved or disproved by advances in anatomy. Looking at dead matter, however brilliantly dissected, would not reveal how a brain, or brain faculties, worked. The soul, or spirit, could not be located; nor did there seem to be a way of demonstrating that it was merely the product of the nervous system. Discovering the essence of humankind – of life – was eluding those who wielded the scalpel.

While phrenology would decline into a parlour game by the 1860s, physiognomy – the observation and categorisation of facial, rather than cranial, features – emerged into greater respectability as the nineteenth century wore on. It appeared to gain validity from the pioneering work of physiologists such as Herbert Mayo, Charles Bell and vivisectionist François Magendie, who all helped to reveal the mysteries of facial muscle movement. Physiognomy – the reading of 'character' and future prospects from the human face – had formerly been an illegal practice undertaken by itinerant showmen, who might also offer palmistry and the divination of omens, similarly outlawed by puritans in the sixteenth century, and still illegal under the 1824 Vagrancy Act; but it was proving irresistible to the new society that was busy segregating itself into mutually exclusive groups. Anxiety about social flux could be allayed by typologising and categorising; and the need to feel certain about the 'types' one was living among is likely to have been the driving force that made physiognomy increasingly prescriptive rather than merely descriptive – nowhere more so than in the analysis of criminality. Thieves and street prostitutes were said to know how to wear a 'mask of decorum'[8] by the late 1820s, where less than twenty years before they had made little attempt to disguise who they were, what they did. Beggars could be adept as Drury Lane actors in striking poses, adopting airs, drumming up pathos. The city-dweller was becoming his or her own work of art; self-consciousness and self-presentation were becoming key.

But like phrenology, physiognomy was not innocent of eye; visual data was used to prove points already decided by other types of evidence. So Thomas Williams was described, after his death, as having a 'coarse and vulgar physiognomy . . . a low, designing brow, a harsh severity of features'.[9] A week after the executions, having viewed the sketches published by printer Charles Tilt of the Bow Street and Old Bailey hearings, *The Times*, on 12 December, decided:

> May looks more stupid, perhaps, than vicious, and yet his countenance is extremely revolting. The face of Williams exhibits the same attempt at disguise as is apparent in his costume, and an equal failure attends both: the metropolitan blackguard is not concealed by the countryman's smock frock, and the brutality of his nature breaks through the affected sheepishness which he put on for the occasion. Bishop is rather more like a hog than a human being, and there is no attempt on his part to soften the harsh character with which Nature has branded him.

(Except that it was Bishop who wore the smock frock, not Williams – the picture had been wrongly labelled by Tilt.) But before the guilty verdict, it was the very ordinariness of the prisoners' appearance that had been commented upon. At that point, the worst that had been said of any of the three was that Williams looked 'cunning' (*The Times*), though the same newspaper had also claimed that he looked 'inoffensive – simple even', while Bishop had never appeared worse than 'sullen'.

Nevertheless, as late as 1883, plaster casts of Bishop and Williams's heads were being advertised 'suitable for public or private museums, literary or scientific institutions', along with the heads of Oliver Cromwell, 'the Idiot of Amsterdam', Coleridge, Sir Isaac Newton, William Palmer the Poisoner, and the five idiot progeny of one Mrs Hillings;[10] they cost a mere five shillings each, or forty shillings for a dozen.

No death portrait had ever been circulated of the child corpse of King's College, and so the publishers of broadsheets and ballads were free to make up their own minds about how the victim of the Bethnal Green Tragedy might have looked. London was in love with its Poor Italian Boy, and he was memorialised in many catchpenny prints – often as a

9.–71. Inexpensive broadsheets, plagiarising the official accounts, meant that the poor could enjoy reading about trials and executions. Some printers were so keen not to spend money, they re-used the wood-block artwork that had accompanied Burke and Hare broadsheets three years earlier ('An Italian Boy', *overleaf*), while others used very dated stock scenes from past murders ('The Bethnal-Green Tragedy', *above*).

BISHOP, WILLIAMS, and MAY, Fully Committed to Newgate, charged with BURKING and MURDERING

AN ITALIAN BOY:

The interest which this dreadful tragedy excites seems to increase hourly. Such was the crowd assembled round Bow Street Police Office on Tuesday, that it was deemed necessary to have an additional force to prevent the multitude from obtaining forcible admission; and in order to avoid the indignation of the multitude against the prisoners, such as was expressed on the Friday previous, they were brought to the office at an early hour and placed in one of the lock-up cells.

Bishop, May, Williams, and *Shields,* were brought in about half-past twelve o'clock, and placed at the bar on the charge of having murdered Carlo Ferrier, an Italian boy.

Samuel Atkinson deposed that he was porter at St. Bartholomew's Hospital. He left a hamper inside of the hospital gate, on the 4th November, a hamper like that produced. He believed it to be the same which he so left.

Edward Chandler, waiter at the King of Denmark, Old Bailey, said he remembered on the 4th inst. the prisoners Bishop and May coming in about five o'clock, and he served them with tea. They had also half a pint of gin, and after drinking a glass each May chucked the rest into Bishop's tea, upon which he said, ' Do you want to *Burke,* or *hocus* me?' He had known the prisoners before.

Henry Mann, a hackney coachman, stated that his coach was on the stand in Bridge Street Blackfriars on the same day, between five and six, when May applied to him to take up a fare to Bethnal Green; but he refused, as he knew that May was.

Margaret King, who had seen the Italian boy near Bishop's house, on the Thursday before the prisoners were taken, said that the boy she saw had a short blue jacket, and his dress was shabby.

Joseph Higgins, the police constable stated that he and another officer had instructions to search Bishop's house and garden. He accordingly went there, and tried first with an iron rod, and having felt something soft, like clothes, and then dug up a small blue jacket, a pair of trowsers, and a little shirt. On trying further with the rod he found a blue jacket, a short coat, a pair of grey trowsers, a striped waistcoat, and a small piece of a fine tooth comb. There were a pair of braces attached to the trowsers. The shirt was torn, and there were stains of blood on the neck of the waistcoat.

James Wady corroborated the witness's statement.

Mr. Thomas deposed that upon a further search in Bishop's house, he had found some old clothes, and a boy's fur cap among them, which he then produced.

Mrs. King was then shown the blue coat found, who said it appeared exactly like the one worn by the Italian boy, but could not speak positively.

The cap was shown to the boy, King, who said the Italian boy's cap was exactly like it.

Augustus Brun, an Italian, knew a boy named Carlo Ferrier; he took him from his parents in Piedmont, and brought him to this country about two years ago. Witness saw the body of the deceased, and had no doubt it was the Italian boy's. The witness described his having wens on his hand, which was the case. He could not speak more positively to the body, because it was so disfigured.

Joseph Paragalli swore positively to the body, and said the cap produced was like that worn by the boy, but the shade was longer.

The shade appeared to be cut, but that is left for the jury to decide.

Mr. Corder then said he should go no further with the evidence, and they were remanded until Friday.

After the prisoners had been removed from the public office to the lock-up room, for some time the attention of Dodd, the gaoler, was called to the cell in which Bishop and May were placed, he found them engaged in a desperate quarrel, and in such a state of excitation, that if they had not been well secured, it is probable that personal contest, perhaps ending in the death of one or the other of the parties would have ensued. In the course of the quarrel they called each other murderers, and other reproachful names, such as men of their infamous calling might be expected to make use of; at last they were separated until the arrival of the police van, in which they were conveyed to prison.

During the whole of the afternoon the outside of the office presented a scene that will not be forgotten by those who witnessed it. The mob had increased, at four o'clock, the time at which the vans came for the prisoners, to such intense numbers, that the greatest apprehensions were entertained of an attack on the van, and the officers were obliged to have recourse to stratagem, to deceive the multitude, and convey the prisoners to their destination.

Friday, Nov. 25.

At an early hour this morning the office was literally besieged by the populace, such was the extraordinary degree of excitement that prevailed in the minds of the public. Shortly after 10 o'clock the ruffians were placed at the bar.—W. Woodcock, stated that he lived next door to Bishop, on the morning of the 3d inst. he was awoke about three o'clock in the morning, and distinctly heard three voices in Bishop's house, and heard a tremendous struggling. The moment after the struggling ceased he heard two men go out of the house & heard them return again, & then all was si-

TRIAL and SENTENCE
Of Bishop, May, & Williams,
For the Murder of
Charles Fariere, an Italian Boy

Print. by J. V. QUICK, 42, Bowling Green Lane, Clerkenwell; and Sold by J. PITTS, Great St. Andrew Street, 7 Dials.

A CORRECT LIKENESS OF

Charles Fariere,

The Old Bailey, and neighbourhood of the same, during the day has been crowded to excess anxious to Trial and Sentence of the Murderers of the Italian Boy.

The court opened at an early hour, the prisoners were accordingly placed at the bar.

The council for the Crown after making the charge against the prisoners, called the following witnesses to substantiate the same.

Mr. Bodkin opened the case.

Robt. Mortimer, deposed that he is a tailor, lived in Nova Scotia-gardens, Williams, employed him to turn a coat, he left it for him at Bishops house, and frequently called there for payment, as he told me he lived there.

Wm. Woodcock, I am a brass-founder, live at 2, Nova Scotia-gardens, next door to Bishop, went there 7 of October. Since then he had frequently seen Williams and his wife in Bishops house and garden, they appeared to live there. He recollected the 3rd of Novbr. that night he went to bed about half past 9 and was awoke about one, by a noise in Bishops house, he heard a scuffle as if between 3 men. He listened & heard 2 go through the garden gate, they were absent a short time, & during their absence I heard the heavy tread of themen who was left behind: during the scuffle I also heard the voices of two men, one of whom was Williams, but on their return all was quiet.

The prisoner Williams, here observed that on the 3 of November referred to by the witness Bishop kicked up a row and broke his things.

Witness. That row was on Sunday night.

Williams. It was not so sunday but on thursday I fetched a Policeman, but he refused to come in.

Thomas Wigley deposed that he was a porter at the Cross Keys in Wood Street, on the night of fri-

day 4th November, was in the Fortune of Wales [...]

[text illegible]

A Copy of Verses

All you that has a feeling heart come listen
unto me,
While I unfold this horrid tale, this woeful
tragedy,
Committed by some wretched men, as plain-
ly may be seen,
In Nova-Scotia Gardens, not far from
Bethnal Green.

Those wretched men into a den of late they
did decoy
A little harmless, friendless, & poor Italian
Boy,
To sell his body all for gain, these villains
did prepare,
And by the same of very late suspicious has
arose.

The Officers has been implored in digging
up the ground,
And several suits of children's clothes therein
has late been found,
Many people are lamenting, they have lost
their children dear,
And to distraction many run when they this
case did hear.

These villains are to Newgate sent, their
trial for to take,
And justice sure will punish them here, for
the people's sake;
Of such a horrid deed as this no mortal
heard before,
And they in Newgate cells now lie, and
wretchedly deplore.

God that orders this horrid deed should soon
be brought to light,
But in consequence thereof there are many
people in a fright;
And justice will then overtake for this most
cruel deed,
Which does cause the hardest heart to ache
this circumstance to read.

JOHN MORGAN.

corpulent little chap with an insipid grin beneath a hugely exaggerated furry cap – while doggerel poured from hack poets' pens. 'The Italian Savoyard Boy', for example, by one F.W.N. Bayly, appeared in the *Weekly Dispatch*:

> Poor child of Venice! He had left
> A land of love and sun for this;
> In one brief day of tears bereft,
> Of father's care and mother's kiss!
> The valleys of his native home,
> The mountain paths of light and flow'rs;
> The Savoyard forsook, to roam
> For wealth and happiness in ours.
>
> And pitying thousands saw the boy,
> Feeding the tortoise on his knee;
> And beauty bright, and childhood coy,
> Oft flung their mite of charity.
> And as he rested on the stone,
> His organ tun'd to some old air!
> Men paus'd at its familiar tone,
> And left their little tokens there.
> Et cetera

In a similar way, *The Trial and Execution of the Burkers for Murdering A Poor Italian Boy*, a broadsheet produced by the most successful of cheap publishers, James Catnach (and so shoddily cobbled together that it reports James May being executed), contains the verse:

> 'Tis of a poor Italian Boy, whose fate we now deplore,
> Who wandered from his native land unto old England's shore;
> White mice within his box confin'd he slung across his breast,
> And friendless, for his daily bread, through London streets he prest.

From the cheapest broadsheet to *The Times* and the Houses of Parliament, it was decided that the Italian Boy case had revealed London, the world's wealthiest city, failing in the duties of care that its superiority forced upon it. That a nation as great as Britain had let down a young stranger from another land provoked much striking of attitudes. A *Times* leader on 10 November fulminated against the 'wretches' who had 'picked up from our streets an unprotected foreign child, and prepared him for

72. After the trial, artist John Hayes painted this representation of Carlo.

the dissecting knife by assassination.' For the anonymous writer of *The History of the London Burkers*, a sense of national disgrace was invoked: 'Can this be England – the most enlightened, the most civilised country of the globe? Alas! that England should now stand indelibly stained by guilt of so foul, so unnatural a blackness.'

Poor houseless Fanny – kicked out by her landlord; afraid to return to her relations (for reasons unknown); unwilling to inflict herself on any other friend or family member, and so lacking in self-worth that she had dyed a new white bonnet black because she felt a white one was too smart for her to wear – was never sentimentalised. Carlo had been given the role of Daft Jamie (James Wilson), the eighteen-year-old murdered by Burke and Hare, whose sixteen known victims also included Mary Paterson, eighteen, who was so fine-looking that her corpse was sketched and painted at Dr Knox's school and preserved in spirits.[11] But Fanny – poxed, skinny, fond of a drink, unmarried mother of two children she could not afford to care for – was not considered worthy of commemoration. Similarly,

73. Fleet Street printer Tillotson sold many copies of his impression of Carlo, with tortoise.

Cunningham of Kent Street – today's Tabard Street, and in 1831 an almost continuous line of pubs and flash-houses – was dully British; a London street boy, a runaway quite possibly surviving on the fringes of Smithfield's criminal culture, having none of the Latin glamour of Carlo or the pathos of Daft Jamie. In five years' time, Charles Dickens would give a character and voice to boys like Cunningham, bringing them into focus with the creation of the Artful Dodger and Charley Bates; but until then, London urchins appear in writing as a disreputable composite – dirty, dishonest and barely human. 'Your true London boy of the streets [has a] mingled look of cunning and insolence,' wrote journalist Charles Knight; while the author of *Old Bailey Experience* decided 'they have a peculiar look of the eye ... and the development of their features is strongly marked with the animal propensities. . . . They may be known almost by their very gait in the streets from other persons. Some of the boys have an approximation to the face of a monkey, so strikingly are they distinguished by this peculiarity. They form a distinct class of men by themselves.'[12]

Meanwhile, trade was as brisk as ever in Nova Scotia Gardens. Broadsheet sellers were crying out their titles and opening lines, and various religious tract societies were cashing in with fire-and-brimstone pamphlets on the wages of sin, with particular reference to the Late Murders. Even during a long downpour of rain, the atmosphere was that of a village fair. The tours of Number 3 were still attracting hundreds of people. An elegantly dressed woman was seen to stoop down and scoop up water from the fatal well in order to taste it, while outside the front of the cottage, a lollypop-pedlar had set up a stall to sell sugar figurines of three burkers dangling from a miniature sugar gallows (a passer-by was seen pointing out May's respite and suggesting the confectionery be adapted accordingly). Local women were overheard agreeing with each other that Bishop and Williams's punishment should have been longer and more painful. Inside the house, a self-appointed master of ceremonies was pointing out to visitors the relevant parts of Number 3, using a large stick: 'This here was the wery bed wot he and his woman slept on,' he announced in the Bishops' bedroom,[13] though it is surprising that the bed had survived the first waves of visitors – perhaps a replacement had been installed in order not to disappoint.

A contemporary account reveals the more typical entertainment available for high days and holidays in the vicinity during those years, and puts the House of Murder hubbub into perspective. The anonymous essayist who contributed the article 'Four Views of London' to the *New Monthly Magazine* described a Whitsuntide Holiday trip he had made to Spitalfields – his first visit to the area in thirty years and his chance to note its shocking decline since the collapse of the silk trade. For the poor, a holiday treat was tea in a tea garden, where two pennies was the price of hot water and crockery, but the tea leaves were not supplied. The writer watched as families sat on a blackened lawn, where the entertainment was one improvised swing for the children, a tiny, covered skittle ground and a soaped pole to climb. For spectacle, the publican compelled an ill-looking boy to pick up 100 pebbles within a set time. The eyewitness noted 'an entire absence of all mirth and enjoyment'.[14]

In Radical circles, Bishop and Williams were providing material for satirical entertainment. *Figaro in London* was a scurrilous, anti-establishment weekly newspaper (price one penny), edited by Henry Mayhew, that took its name from the famous French daily, and throughout its short life campaigned vigorously for electoral reform. In its Christmas Eve edition, 1831, the details of the Italian Boy case were used to lampoon the Duke of Wellington and the Bishop of London, Charles Blomfield, who had been prominent among the Lords who had killed off the Second Reform Bill in October 1831:

> I, Bishop, of London, do hereby declare and confess, that I took a prominent part in the Burking of the Bill which has caused so great a sensation in the country. My principal accomplice, was the person known as the Head of the Tories who endeavoured to cover his notoriously bad character, by boasting of being of William's family. We both got the Bill into our power in a house in the neighbourhood of Westminster, and commenced our operations by plying it with a quantity of half and half, and in a very moderate measure, with which we had intended to stupify it at once, but it did not take sufficient effect . . .[15]

But thrills, pathos and laughter were not Bishop and Williams's biggest legacy. Twelve days after their execution Henry Warburton MP introduced his second Anatomy Bill to the Commons; by 20 December it was having its second reading. In 1829 Warburton's original Bill – to make the unclaimed bodies of paupers who died in workhouses and hospitals available to teachers of anatomy for dissection – had been passed by the Commons but thrown out by the Lords. As with the Reform Bill, the upper house rejected attempts to tinker with God's natural order – the aristocracy had ordained rights and privileges but also had a duty of care towards its inferiors. No upstart doctors should be allowed to interrupt this beautiful, natural, sacred design.

As with the original bill, the opponents of Warburton's second attempt at legislation comprised a broad coalition of a number of Tories who believed the traditional social order was under attack and foresaw the potential for further civil unrest if such a socially divisive act were to be passed; and Radicals, who believed the poor should never become fodder for middle-class self-betterment.

74. This Radical, pro-Reform journal used the Italian Boy trial to lampoon the anti-Reform Bishop of London and Duke of Wellington.

Sir Frederick Trench, Tory member for Cambridge, told the Commons that in his view, Warburton's measure should be renamed 'a Bill to Encourage Burking', claiming that legalising the supply in no way removed the premium for hastening a relative's death. All that was needed to prevent another Bishop and Williams was for surgeons to examine far more carefully the Subjects that were offered to them, said Trench.[16]

Similarly, Cresset Pelham, the member for Shropshire, recognised that

Warburton's Bill treated the human body as an item of trade, while merely bringing down the price of such a commodity. 'The bill would give a legal encouragement to the traffic in human blood,' said Pelham, who suggested that the best way to put an end to burking would be to inflict stronger punishment on the 'receivers'. Alexander Perceval, Tory member for Sligo, also wanted the onus to be placed on the surgeons, and said that in his view, possession of a Subject should be upgraded from a misdemeanour to a felony.

The Bill's most vociferous opponent, Henry ('Orator') Hunt, capitalised on the mysteriously unsavoury nature of anatomy schools, and spoke of the lack of respect that was shown to corpses by teachers and students, claiming that 'the cutting up and mangling of the bodies of human beings was done with as little concern in those human shambles as the bodies of beasts were cut up in Newgate, Smithfield or any other market'. Hunt claimed that he had it on the best authority that 'the conduct of the young students in the dissecting-room was too often perfectly disgusting – too disgusting to be described even in an assembly like that, composed as it was entirely of men.'[17] (Surgeon George Guthrie had rather blown the gaff when he wrote, in 1829, an open letter in which he urged anatomists to end the pretence that dissected corpses had a decent burial once they were finished with. Since the flesh was removed at a slow rate, he wrote, it could not be stored up until the skeleton had been revealed; the flesh simply ended up with all the other refuse produced by the schools.)[18]

Three weeks later, Orator Hunt told the Commons that in the schools of Paris and Dublin wax models of the human anatomy had proved quite adequate for teaching purposes, while London 'required human carcasses to be sold like pigs or sheep'. Henry Warburton's withering reply was that only 'the ingenious foreigner' who made and marketed wax anatomical figures would claim that they were good enough to use to teach medical students.[19]

No matter how trenchant and perceptive the arguments put by opponents of the Bill, references to Bishop and Williams were reiterated by its supporters to induce a sense of panic, along with the likelihood that these imitators of Burke and Hare would spawn imitators.[20] The supporters of the Bill were also able to argue convincingly, if insincerely in many instances, that it was the poor who had most to benefit from the Act: no longer would the impoverished need to fear the bodysnatcher or the burker. Whig member for Calne in Wiltshire (and future historian) Thomas Babington Macaulay told the Commons on 27 February 1832,

That a man has property, that he has connections, that he is likely to be missed and sought for, are circumstances which secure him against the burker. It is curious to observe the difference between murders of this kind and other murders. An ordinary murderer hides the body and disposes of the property. Bishop and Williams dig holes and bury the property, and expose the body to sale. The more wretched, the more lonely the human being may be, the more desirable prey he is to these wretches. It is the man, the mere naked man, that they pursue.

The Bill was passed by forty-three votes to five in the Commons on 11 May 1832, and two months later the Lords passed the measure, with the Bill's sponsor in the Lords, the Whig-leaning Earl of Minto, still harping upon one particular rumour concerning Bishop and Williams that had failed to be dispelled, despite months of official denials.

SIXTEEN

How Many?

Orator Hunt had addressed the House of Commons on Monday 12 December to ask a question 'calculated greatly to relieve the mind of the country'. The honourable members laughed. Hunt said that according to a statement in the newspapers, the men recently executed for burking, instead of confessing to three or four murders, had, on the day before their execution, confessed to sixty, but were stopped in the middle of their confessions by Dr Cotton, the Ordinary of Newgate. Hunt realised that the House might consider this a laughable subject ('Hear, hear,' they roared) but 'it had greatly agitated the public mind, and was, he believed, at present the source of much excitement'. Did the government know whether the tale of the interrupted confession were true or not?

George Lamb, the right honourable secretary for the Home Department (and Lord Melbourne's youngest brother), said he did not know on what authority the statement in the newspapers had been put forth, but he was not aware of any other confession than that officially published.

Alderman Waithman, member for the City of London, replied to Hunt that he himself had spoken to the sheriffs and under-sheriffs at Newgate, and the latter had declared that Bishop and Williams had told everything they knew in the 'official' confession. Waithman claimed to have been astonished to read the allegations that there had been sixty victims.[1]

The official confessions – the 'I, John Bishop' and 'I, Thomas Head' statements – had been taken down by under-sheriffs Robert Ellis and Thomas Wood and authenticated and approved for publication by Dr Cotton. Since the start of the eighteenth century, one of the perks of the Ordinary's job was to publish, within twenty-four hours of an execution, the confession of the dead felon; it was a practice sanctioned by the Lord Mayor of London and his Court of Aldermen. But with Bishop and Williams, strange, unsourced additions to the official confessions had been appearing in the national newspapers. The *Observer*, then as now a Sunday paper, had been among the first to publish an unauthorised alternative account (it was reprinted in full by *The Times*, with acknowledgement, on Monday 5 December). Twenty-four hours before the executions took place, the *Observer* reported:

> Yesterday morning, the Rev. Mr Theodore Williams, vicar of Hendon, according to a promise he made to Bishop, visited him in his cell. . . . After some hesitation, Bishop admitted that he had been concerned in the commission of three murders, viz., that of the Italian boy, the murder of Frances Pigburn, and of a drover – a boy who had come to London with cattle from Lincolnshire, which boy the witnesses on his trial had sworn was the Italian boy, to the best of their belief, though he had disposed of that body before. Bishop entered into a minute description, most horrible in its details, of the mode by which he had perpetrated the inhuman murders. He did not deny that Williams was an actor in the murder of the Italian boy, which had been committed in the cottage in Nova Scotia Gardens. Williams also made a confession which was consistent with the facts stated in that of Bishop; but he declared that he had been involved in the horrid transactions by Bishop's persuasion, whose daughter he had married only three months ago. He also exonerated May from all participation in the murder.

Cunningham of Kent Street does not appear in this report. Instead, there is the confession of killing an Italian boy. Was this admission to a (backdated) murder of an Italian boy a change of heart by Bishop; or sloppy journalism; or wishful thinking by the reporter? And who was the reporter? Who had smuggled out an advance confession – an exclusive – presumably for a good sum of money?

The *Observer* continued:

> On further interrogation, both Bishop and Williams declared that the corpse offered for sale at the King's College, and sworn to as the Italian boy, Carlo Ferrari, was not the body of that ill-fated lad, but they again asserted that it was the corpse of a boy who had come from Lincolnshire to Smithfield with a drove of cattle. They, however, did not deny that the Italian boy was murdered by Bishop.

But nor did they state it; which was odd, in light of the comment Bishop is reported to have made that 'he had disposed of that body before'.[2]

The *Observer* report concluded:

> A veil of secrecy has been thrown over the circumstances which have transpired in Newgate, and if there be any inaccuracies, they are attributable to the want of unreserved communication on the part of those who are possessed of the 'secrets of the prison house,' than to the want of zeal on our part to gratify the curiosity of our readers.

This seems to be an attack on Cotton and the sheriffs, and it is tempting to conclude that Dr Theodore Williams had not surrendered his version of the confession at the sheriffs' office, as he had been requested to do, but had smuggled it out and delivered it to the *Observer* on Saturday evening. (The *Observer* offices were at 169 Strand – around fifteen to twenty minutes' walk from the gaol.)

There are other suspects, though. It is quite possible that reformist prison chaplain Dr Whitworth Russell, pamphleteering solicitor James Harmer (a personal friend of Cotton's), any of the sheriffs, under-sheriffs or warders (Bishop and Williams each had two guards) were rushing out different versions of confessions, or the gist of conversations overheard, in order to raise a guinea or two. In addition to the hunger for newspaper reports about murderers, the 'last dying speeches' produced by broadsheet-manufacturers could realise a small fortune if prepared in advance to be sold at a 'popular' execution. Even Pierce Egan, famous for his *Life in London* books of the mid-1820s, had got in on this act, quite probably using his friendship with Cotton to publish his slightly dearer version of events, *The Murder of the Italian Boy* ('price only 1s and 6d').[3]

The author of *Old Bailey Experience* would, the following year, complain bitterly about rival confessions being sent to newspaper offices by 'interlopers' in the gaol, and noted the time that a 'Dr R' was caught out when he went home and penned the final moments of a condemned man who was respited at the last minute on the following morning. (It is possible that 'Dr R' was Dr Whitworth Russell.)[4] *Old Bailey Experience* also made the claim that there were politically inspired factions at work within Newgate, and that each 'side' enjoyed the complicity of various aldermen in gaining access to noteworthy criminals. Rival factions within the Church of England wanted to be seen to be offering the best form of religious instruction and spiritual comfort to those about to die. Those of an evangelical tendency placed importance on a thrusting, practical, personalised Christianity; the state of mind of the condemned was paramount. Evangelicals were aghast at the seemingly supine approach of High Anglicans, who appeared content to rely on ritual and liturgy, without tailoring pastoral care to the individual receiving it.

But a vigorous, reformist approach to religion had its pitfalls. Words that certain of his parishioners used to describe Hendon's Reverend Theodore Williams included 'overbearing', 'dictatorial', 'hasty' and 'irritable'. While many considered him a fine preacher (attendance figures at his sermons were high), the local Methodists dubbed him 'the cock-fighting parson' because he refused to support a ban on that sport in his parish, and they accused him of inciting local youths to pelt the Methodist minister in Hendon with eggs and old vegetables.[5] In 1823, following a dispute over burial fees, Reverend Williams had wrecked the new tomb of one Mrs Warren with his bare hands, scattering debris across the road outside the church. He had served time in a debtors' prison, and would do so again in his old age. In 1836 he would be involved in an infamous brawl in the vestry of St Mary's, Hendon, and three years after that would clash with Thomas Wakely when Williams refused to sanction the disinterment of a body for a coroner's hearing. (A seventy-nine-year-old pauper, Thomas Austin, had fallen into a copper of boiling water at the Hendon workhouse.)[6] His family had made their money from plantations in the West Indies, worked by slaves, and Williams spoke out in opposition to the anti-slavery movement. His own personal expenditure was compared unfavourably by some of his parishioners to his parsimony in his role in administering the New Poor Law in Hendon, from 1834. It would be quite in keeping with what is known of the vicar of Hendon that he should have had some hand in making money from newspapers and, in doing so, stirring up controversy.

The *Sunday Times* and the *Atlas* newspapers had run an additional Newgate confession too, which was also printed in full by *The Times* and the *Globe and Traveller* on Monday 5th. Someone had smuggled out the story that on Saturday night, alone in his cell except for his warder, Thomas Williams had become 'anxious and uneasy towards midnight. His agitation increased, and the vigilance of his keeper became more marked. Williams observed it and said, "Don't be frightened, sir, I am not going to do anything wrong, but I wish to ease my mind. Let me see the governor." Mr Wontner was then called from his bed and the Reverend Mr Cotton, the Ordinary, was also in attendance in a few minutes. When these gentlemen came into the cell, Williams, looking at them steadfastly for a moment or two, burst into tears and said, "Gentlemen, I wish to unburden my mind. I know I am guilty, and ought to suffer the utmost punishment of the law. I am a murderer, I confess it; but the witnesses were all mistaken as to its being the Italian boy."'

The report went on:

On Thursday 3rd November, he [Williams] was in the neighbourhood of Smithfield when he saw a boy, whom he had often observed before, assisting in driving cattle to the market. This boy was about fourteen or fifteen years of age, and exactly corresponded with the description given of the Italian boy. He enticed him from the cattle, and took him to the Fortune of War public house, and sent for Bishop, who was waiting at another pub in the neighbourhood for the purpose of receiving communications from Williams. Bishop came, and they took the boy home to Nova Scotia Gardens, giving him some soup and potatoes by the way. When they got him there, they set him to play with Bishop's children until near dusk, when they gave him some rum and he became stupefied. Bishop and Williams then took him into the garden, and on the way threw him down, and, pushing his head into the water barrel sunk into the ground, held him until he was suffocated. They then conveyed the body back to the house, kept it snug until the next day, when May was applied to, to assist in disposing of it. 'May had nothing to do with the murder of that boy.'

There were only three people in the room who could have taken this story out of the prison and on to the presses: the warder; Cotton; and Wontner. Perhaps Cotton was anxious to pre-empt any publication that Theodore Williams was planning. Perhaps the warder passed the story on to a sheriff/under-sheriff who dashed around to the newspaper offices of Fleet Street/the Strand. (In a similar way, there were very few people – none of them journalists – who could have written up the eyewitness account of James May's seizure when he heard that he had been reprieved.)

The *Observer*, however, reported that during the night, Williams had revealed to his warder that it was Bishop who had picked up the drover's boy in the pig-pens, had promised him work, and had taken him to the Fortune of War to meet Williams and to drink some beer; this boy had been the first victim, according to Williams in the *Observer*, and Cunningham of Kent Street had been the second boy to die. Williams also admitted, here, to attempting to burke two aged workhouse paupers, whom he and Bishop had tempted back to Nova Scotia Gardens with promises of drink but who did not succumb fully to the laudanum. Bishop reportedly said to Williams that 'it was no go – they were old drinkers and were not to be so easily done. . . . We shall be grabbed for poisoning them.'

The *Atlas* newspaper claimed that on another occasion, Reverend Theodore Williams had been told by both Bishop and Williams that they had killed three people, the Lincolnshire drover boy, Fanny Pigburn and – quite a while before – *an* Italian boy; and that all the clothes found in the garden and privy had indeed belonged to the three victims. In this version, rather more violence was used in the killings, with the victims having their mouths held shut as they were marched to the well. However, the *Morning Advertiser* stated that both men on the Sunday had been vehemently denying that any Italian boy had ever been killed.

In the *Sun*, an evening newspaper, it was claimed that

> Bishop several times endeavoured to inveigle to his residence the sister of the young woman who was some time ago missed from the neighbourhood of Bethnal Green; and whose scalp and hair, it is believed, were those found in the privy, but fortunately the young woman resisted his importunity. He also prevailed on a young woman to leave her place, under a promise to take her into keeping; but she felt compunctious, and declined his overtures just in sufficient time to save her life.[7]

Yet the ownership of the scalp and hair had never been established.

The Times of Tuesday 6 December stated that Williams had told his warder that he had never, until his marriage, been a resurrection man, and had not even known that this was how Bishop made his living. Rhoda had told him of this on his wedding night and asked him to promise not to join the 'snatchers'. But when Williams had had his glass-making apparatus seized, Bishop had asked his neighbour to become a partner, and Williams had agreed. However (Williams is said to have told the warder), after just three graveyard forays, Williams had found it a difficult and dangerous job, so, thinking of the Edinburgh Horrors, he had proposed murder.

Williams was highly likely to have been aware of how his neighbour made a living before his wedding night of 26 September; in any case, Customs and Excise had made their raid on 6 August – seven weeks before Rhoda supposedly told Williams of Bishop's profession. If this account of a conversation between Williams and his warder has been reported accurately, the most probable explanation for its contents is that Williams was attempting to depict Rhoda as a voice of innocence and reason, in order to try to save her from public hatred. By getting this version of events into the newspapers, Williams could die knowing that he had at least tried to redeem Rhoda in the eyes of her fellow citizens.

The Times report continues with Williams telling the warder that the day after the murder of 'the woman Pigburn', he and Bishop had tried to burke a man whom they had lured to Nova Scotia Gardens. This time the laudanum failed and the man was not completely unconscious, just dozing, and (in the manner of Lady Macbeth), Bishop froze as he was poised to attack because the sleeping man so resembled his father; the next morning, the man awoke and let himself out of Number 3. On the following Tuesday (presumably 11 October), claimed Williams, the laudanum failed again, and this intended victim also left the cottage none the wiser. These may or may not have been the two old workhouse paupers mentioned by Williams to his warder.

The *Globe and Traveller* and the *Morning Advertiser* added into their reports of 5 December the story of Cotton's interruption of the confessions, stating that it had happened just as Bishop was talking about a fourth murder, of a black vagrant, and appeared to be implicating other people in this crime. The *Globe and Traveller* and the *Observer* had put a name to the Lincolnshire drover's boy – White – and reported a claim by Thomas Williams that William Woodcock could not possibly have heard anything in the early hours of Friday 4 November, since the killers had taken their shoes off; and besides, by that time, the drover's boy was 'as dead as a log'. The *Globe and Traveller* also included the information that Cunningham of Kent Street used to help out around Smithfield, and had put up a fight on the night of his killing, surprising Bishop and Williams with his strength. The former had uttered 'a horrible oath' as he held the boy's legs upright in the well as Williams pushed his head below the surface of the water, waiting until he finally stopped struggling.

The *Sun* of 5 December claimed,

Among the murders which they have confessed to, we understand, is one of a little child, whom they found in a destitute condition in the street and covered with filth and vermin. This poor child they inveigled to Bishop's house and destroyed in a similar manner to that of the other unfortunate victims.

Was this an inaccurate description of White or Cunningham (hardly 'little' children)? Or was this the 'large small' bought from Bishop by the anatomical school 'near Golden Square' in the first week of November? Or was this the fate of Fanny Pigburn's child, who had been sitting on her lap when they found Fanny crying on a doorstep in Church Street, Shoreditch, but who disappears from the story soon afterwards?

Many of the unofficial accounts of confessions contain internal evidence that they are not accurate eyewitness reports; in some instances, words are quite plainly being put into the killers' mouths. The 'I, John Bishop' confession, which runs to 2,500 words, is a lucid, linear tale, told in plain but vivid language. Certain touches give it a compelling, phantasmagoric feel; all-too-real, mundane phenomena interweave with the nightmarish narrative of relentless, pitiless slaughter. It is a tale of coffee-stalls, child-sized chairs, gin, privies, pouring rain, mean-minded landlords, piles of dirty clothes. There are points at which a bizarre tenderness pokes its way into the act of killing: 'I then took him in my arms, and let him slide from them headlong into the well'; 'She went off to sleep in about ten minutes. She was falling back; I caught her to save her fall'; 'We gave him some warm beer, sweetened with sugar . . . [he] then fell asleep in a little chair belonging to one of my children.' The insistent voice of Bishop, the cadence of his unreflective, phlegmatic outlook, is dissimilar to the add-on accounts in the newspapers, where a melodramatic note often appears. We have Bishop saying to Reverend Theodore Williams: 'Surely, sir, there is a hope of mercy for a repentant sinner. Was not the thief on the cross pardoned?'[8] There are clearly other hands writing their way into these final scenes. The authorship of the *Globe and Traveller* report of 5 December becomes clear when we read Theodore Williams's reply to Bishop's enquiry about the thief on the cross:

> Yes, but he had no knowledge of our blessed Redeemer till that moment, but you have from your earliest days been taught to know Christ and have rejected his precepts. Besides, yours cannot be called a true repentance, it is incomplete. Yours is more the fear of human punishment, in consequence of your offence having been discovered, than the repentance of a true Christian. The first step towards a true repentance is a full and open confession of your crimes. Still, I exhort you to pray with all the sincerity and fervour you are capable of. And as the mercy of God is unbounded, your prayers may obtain favour in his sight.

(In this way, not only would Theodore Williams save a soul, he would get the full confession to publish too.) And we learn that 'after having partaken of the Sacrament, Thomas Williams complained of thirst, and said his mouth was so parched that he was quite sure it was a foretaste of hell.' (The version of this incident that appears in the *Sun* is even more florid: '"I thirst, I thirst – I feel the burning drought of hell in my breast and I know it is ready for me".')[9]

The *Weekly Dispatch* of 11 December reported that on the morning of the execution, when the Sacrament of the Lord's supper was offered to them, Bishop said derisively that he had no understanding of it, but Thomas Williams is reported as clamouring to be taught to understand it and asking Dr Whitworth Russell to explain the meaning of the ritual to him. And Cotton would write in his journal that Thomas Williams had cried out to him that he hoped God 'would hear his prayers and forgive him, notwithstanding he had been one of the greatest sinners in his time'.[10]

Bishop was an intelligent man; Williams's attainments are harder to discern. Both were literate, at least. Bishop's straightforward, fluent account, and the fragments of his speech that have survived, indicate some level of education. He may well have brought up the subject of the thief on the cross, and Williams may have mentioned the fires of hell; but the phrasing here is altogether too purple. Similarly, the letter addressed to Dr Whitworth Russell by Thomas Williams on his final night sounds like the gist of an honestly felt response on to which has been grafted a sermon:

If you will be kind enough to let my brother prisoners know the awful death which I shall have suffered when you read this, it will, *through your expostulations, prevent them from increasing their crimes when they may be liberated*; and tell them bad company and drinking and blasphemy *is the foundation of all evil. Give my brotherly love to them, and tell them never to deviate from the paths of religion, and have a firm belief in the blessed Saviour.* Give my love to John Edwards, John Justin and John Dingle, and receive the prayers of the unfortunate and guilty, Thomas Head.

On 10 December the most controversial of the discrepancies came to light. In that day's edition of *The Times*, a letter was published from Sir John Sewell, a magistrate at Marylebone police office. Sewell claimed that 'one of his brother magistrates' had told him of a confession made by Bishop on the Sunday 'which comprehended a catalogue of about 60 murders' until Dr Cotton had intervened to put a stop to it. Now, the interruption of the conversation between Bishop and Reverend Theodore Williams in the chamber of Brown the turnkey had happened on the Saturday morning – all parties agreed to that. So had Sewell got his dates wrong; or had Cotton made other interruptions? And who had told Sewell of this in any case?

Two days later *The Times* published a letter from 'James Stone' (the inverted commas indicated a pseudonym, and no address was given):

Sir, Can you inform me by what authority the Rev. Mr Cotton interposed to suppress the confessions of the two murderers? Were they in consequence better qualified to receive from him that spiritual instruction which he professes to give, or had he any other motive by which his conduct was actuated?

This looks like another attack on a High Anglican churchman in a position of civic authority. Sewell was in fact a member of the non-Conformist

Society for Promoting Christian Knowledge and may have held an ethical grudge against Cotton for his approach to condemned men. Sewell's letter provoked the following response from under-sheriff Thomas Wood, friend and supporter of Cotton and co-transcriber of the official confessions:

> I have in vain endeavoured to ascertain from Sir John Sewell what authority he had for his assertions, and am favoured with no other answer than that of an after-dinner conversation with some magistrate, whose name he withholds. From the inquiries made in other quarters, as well as from the circumstances of having been with the prisoners, on the Sunday alluded to, from 10 o'clock in the morning till about 4 o'clock in the afternoon, I believe the assertions contained in Sir John Sewell's letter to be totally destitute of foundation. The confession was taken in detail from the prisoners, written down as they gave it, and published in the newspapers from the original documents, signed by them and authenticated by my colleague and myself, and I do not believe that during their imprisonment they ever gave a catalogue of 60 murders or of any other number committed by them than those contained in the statement before the public. I am also bound in justice to the Rev. the Ordinary, whom I attended on some of his visits to the culprits, to say, that so far from his having interfered to prevent or even to check a confession, he used every means in his power to induce them to make a full statement of their crimes, with an earnestness befitting his sacred office.[11]

Sewell had replied to Wood in a private letter of 13 December, refusing to name his source but saying that he heard the 'sixty' story at a magistrates' dinner on 8 December from 'a Middlesex justice of the peace', and that the allegation was heard by at least four other magistrates present. Reverend Theodore Williams was a Middlesex justice of the peace and in January 1832 he owned up to being Sewell's source, during the official inquiry held into Cotton's conduct on the weekend of 3–4 December. However, the vicar of Hendon claimed during the inquiry that what he had said to Sewell at the magistrates' dinner was 'six', not 'sixty'.[12] Six 'cases' is how Reverend Theodore Williams puts it, which is not six murders, and could include the two failed hocussings along with the actual killings of Fanny Pigburn, the black vagrant, Cunningham of Kent Street and White-the-drover's-boy/Carlo Ferrari. Or it could have meant the killings of Cunningham, White, Pigburn, the black vagrant, the small verminous child and an Italian Boy.

Whatever the case, the damage had been done by Sewell's letter and the ensuing furore: the notion that Bishop had been a mass-burker had easily gained a foothold in the popular imagination and was probably accepted as fact within poor communities, which were the most vulnerable to burkers. It was certainly accepted in the House of Lords. As late as 28 June the following year the Earl of Minto, speaking to promote the Second Anatomy Bill, would still be hammering home the notion that Bishop was a mass-killer, claiming that Bishop had been on the point of augmenting his official confession 'when he was interrupted in his recital'.[13] Radical journalist and reformer William Cobbett, meanwhile, made use of the higher estimate to attack surgeons (he called them the 'cutters-up') and to show that the poor were merely considered fodder for their scalpels, much as they were fodder for the capitalist and the industrialist. Cobbett claimed that sixty was probably a conservative estimate, and that the true total of poor London citizens killed had been 'probably hundreds'.[14]

No matter how many people really had been slaughtered at Nova Scotia Gardens, no peace of mind would be obtainable on the issue, because many of the newspapers had published a claim allegedly made by Bishop in Newgate that the majority of London resurrectionists committed murder when graveyard or bone-house security tightened, or when demand simply exceeded supply (though James May had put the figure of potential killers at six). A full-blown panic had arrived.

A private letter from James Corder, vestry clerk of St Paul's, Covent Garden, to Home Secretary Lord Melbourne, dated 5 December 1831, stated that the crimes 'engage to a considerable degree the public mind and I have reason to believe from the many communications which Mr Thomas and myself daily receive on the subject that the public do look for some answer to, or notice of, the Confessions, which have appeared in all the public journals.'[15] The alarm and confusion was not being helped by the floundering of the authorities on the issue of the identity of the dead child delivered to King's College. Richard Partridge, James Corder and Superintendent Thomas would tie themselves into knots in print in their attempts to prove that the body had been Carlo Ferrari's. First off the mark was Richard Partridge, who wrote to *The Times* on Sunday 4 December:

I received an anonymous note yesterday evening which contained some pertinent queries respecting the identity of Carlo Ferrari and the body taken to King's College by Bishop and his companions. They were to the following effect: 1. Was Paragalli or Augustus Brin [*sic*] asked whether the ears of Carlo Ferrari were bored [pierced], and if so, what was their reply? 2. Were the ears bored of the body which was offered for sale at the King's College? In reply to these inquiries, I beg to state that when the body was opened at the police station in Covent Garden, I particularly remarked that the ears were not bored. The circumstance struck me at the time as worthy of notice, and as Paragalli, who had recognised the body as that of an Italian boy, was standing at the other end of the room, in a situation where he could not see the head of the corpse, I asked him whether the boy he had known wore ear-rings – he replied, 'No.' I next inquired if his ears were bored, to which he replied in the negative.

This morning I have put the questions separately to Brin and to Mrs Paragalli and their answers agree with those of Paragalli himself. Moreover, their description of the colour of Carlo Ferrari's eyes and hair and of his general complexion corresponds in every particular with those of the body which was examined at the police station.

I regret that it did not occur to my mind at the Old Bailey to mention this fact, touching the ears, and I shall, therefore, feel much obliged if you will insert this statement of it now in the columns of *The Times*.

It seems strange that an anatomist at a post-mortem should take so much notice of whether the corpse had once been a wearer of earrings; as strange as it was to have a civilian – Paragalli – in the room while a dissection was taking place. And why had Paragalli not been able immediately to come up with the name of the boy, if, as he later claimed, he had been present when Carlo was signed over to a new master by Augustine Brun in the summer of 1830? Why was Paragalli's son – whom Mary Paragalli claimed had named the boy on viewing the corpse – not brought forward at any stage? And why had Partridge forgotten to bring the pierced-ears matter up at the Old Bailey, or at the coroner's inquest, or at the magistrates' hearings, or at any point during the month-long inquiry?

'A Lincolnshire boy! Where are his friends or relations?' an indignant James Corder wrote in *The Times* on 16 December. 'It is now nearly six weeks since the murder, and no inquiries are made for him. On the contrary, where is Charles Ferrier? Why does he not appear?' The Paragallis and Andrew Colla had gone as a deputation to Bow Street on 8 December to refute before the magistrates Bishop and Williams's claim that the body had not been Carlo's; and Corder had promised them that he would put the record straight in the newspapers. As he pointed out, the doubt about the victim's identity reflected badly on his parish and on the prosecution it had mounted. Corder's letter stated that 'several witnesses of unimpeachable character and integrity' had sworn that the body had been Carlo's, having seen the corpse within three days of death.

Corder claimed that one of them, Andrew Colla, had in fact made the cage in which Carlo carried about his white mice. Two of the Italians had seen him alive and well in the week of his death, and one had accurately described the trousers worn by the deceased without having seen the pair dug up in Bishop's garden. In addition to this, wrote Corder,

> we have it in evidence that an Italian boy with a cage and white mice was seen close to Bishop's house on the day of the murder, wearing a cap similar to the one found on the premises, and which Bishop endeavoured in vain to account for. We then find the white mice and cage at Bishop's house, in the possession of his children on Friday the 4th instant, the day after the murder, as proved by the very young witness, but who gave his evidence with all the simplicity characteristic of truth. And lastly, we find the clothes of the deceased in Bishop's garden; the lower buttons being cut off the jacket apparently to admit the revolution of his cage; the tapes also stitched to the lower part of the same garment for the passage of the strap or riband by which the cage was confined to his body. And against this body of evidence, what is set up? The unsupported assertion of the wretched culprits, who to the latest hour of existence evinced no penitent or religious feeling. Were there any appearances to indicate that the deceased was a Lincolnshire drover boy? None; his hands were smooth and soft, and no horny substance upon them as though he had been used to manual labour.

As with Partridge, Corder here brings up matters that should have come to light during the coroner's inquest, or the trial, or the weeks between. (It is possible that these matters did arise, but it seems highly unlikely that they would so completely have escaped the attention of all the newspaper reporters and the official Old Bailey account.) So this is the first we have heard of Carlo's apparently specially adapted clothing, and that the jacket was damaged in this particular way; it is the first time anyone has mentioned the skin quality of the corpse (apart from the matter of Carlo's warts – never resolved); and Colla had never before been referred to as the maker of the boy's cage, nor was it ever reported that Colla had seen the body. There had never been any accurate description given of the boy's clothing until *after* the garments were unearthed in Bishop's garden, at which point many people began to recall with great clarity how the Italian Boy had been dressed. And no reports indicate that Colla had described the boy's clothing before the items were placed in front of him in the Old Bailey court-room. Similarly, no cap was mentioned until one was found at Number 3; then suddenly many people could recall it in detail. Colla had told Minshull and Corder at Bow Street that Carlo Ferrier had always had a smiling face – he always looked as though he were about to burst into laughter – and the corpse had looked serene and happy, said Colla; yet Paragalli had noted how miserable the boy he took to be Carlo had looked in the rain in Regent Street. Even Minshull himself could now fondly remember many a time seeing a smiling Italian Boy around Oxford Street;[16] the magistrate had always wanted to give him a few halfpence but never did, since he worried about encouraging vagrancy, he said. Why had Minshull never mentioned this before?

But the oddest matter of all was that the Italian witnesses, who had known the boy 'intimately' (Corder's word), did not come up with a likely name for him until days after the arrests. In fact, Paragalli, *after* seeing the body, but before the coroner's hearing, had gone in person to the Alien Office to try to put a name to the corpse – an unnecessary trip if it really had been clear to him that this was Carlo.

It was a feature of the case noted by the *Sun*, in its edition of 8 November, that no Italian of the many who had viewed the body had been able to put a name, or even a nickname, to the boy. In his letter, James Corder was either forgetting, or wilfully confusing, the sequence of events in the case.

Corder also challenged Bishop's statement on the cause of death. Where the killer claimed that the victims had been drowned, Corder noted peevishly that 'it is for professional and other scientific men to judge whether the appearances described are compatible with the supposition of death having been produced by drowning, hanging, strangulation or any other mode of suffocation.' Corder had assembled from Partridge and George Beaman lengthy reiterations, printed in full by *The Times*, of their findings at the coroner's inquest and again at the trial. But new matters had crept into these post-mortem reports, with Partridge claiming to have noted down 'general appearance that of a foreigner' and 'palms of the hands quite soft' (though the warts that Superintendent Thomas had noted on the corpse's left hand, and which Brun had failed to corroborate as being a feature of Carlo's, do not appear at all in Partridge's new statement).

The icing on Corder's cake came with the verdict of Frederick Tyrrell, lecturer in physiology at St Thomas's, to whom Corder had sent these post-post-mortem reports: 'It is my opinion,' wrote Tyrrell, 'that the death of the boy could not have been caused by any mode of suffocation, as drowning, smothering, &c. I have no doubt that injury to the upper part of the spine, which created the effusion of blood into the spinal canal, was the immediate cause of death.' But Bishop and Williams had both stated that the injury to the back of the neck had happened when they had put the body into the trunk in the wash-house, and that this always happened when a corpse was 'doubled up while it is warm'.[7] As practising murderers, they had been in a position to observe phenomena the surgeons never saw.

The leader-writers quashed their own sense of unease about the mystery of the dead boy by plumping heavily and clumsily in favour of the view that Bishop and Williams had lied in their official confessions. Their reasoning was that, as criminals, they had gone to their graves attempting to unsettle society; trying to undermine trust in lawyers, policemen, doctors, vicars. Such rogues knew no other way of behaving. But that credited Bishop and Williams with having an organised political purpose, rather than being psychopathic opportunists with a drink problem and uncertain employment prospects.

The Times's editorial of 16 December 1831 stated that

the last words with which Bishop and Williams went out of the world were false. There has nothing ever been heard of any Lincolnshire boy missing – it is most likely none such was murdered; but at all events it is certain, beyond doubt, that the murder for which the wretches suffered was that charged upon them at the trial, namely, the murder of the poor Italian boy.

The *Globe and Traveller* claimed Bishop and Williams had merely been seeking a respite on the grounds of a legal quibble over the identity of the dead child. That was the sort of thing criminals did all the time, the newspaper claimed.[18] However, the wording of the indictment had made provision for them to be found guilty and hanged for the killing of Boy Unknown. Bishop and Williams simply had nothing to gain for themselves by lying in their official confessions about the identity of the people they killed.

And in any case, the *Globe and Traveller* was overlooking a short report that had already appeared in its own pages: on 3 December the newspaper had reported that Carlo Ferrari was alive, residing in 'a distant part of England'.

Time has never revealed the extent of the killings at Nova Scotia Gardens, nor the identity of the dead boy delivered to King's College. The tale was a puzzle of sometimes garbled, often contradictory, statements. But whoever really had been drowned in the well, this was the Italian Boy Murder – an easy-to-recount tale, full of pathos, which sought a strange kind of comfort from giving a name and persona to its victim. The official version is that Carlo Ferrari, the Italian Boy, was killed by Bishop and Williams on Thursday 3 November 1831, and that it was eventually discovered that at least two more destitute people, another boy and Fanny Pigburn, had also died at their hands. Within weeks of the Old Bailey trial, the series of killings had been contracted into one, with a stage version, *The Italian Boy*, playing at the Shakespeare – an unlicensed theatre in Curtain Road, just behind Shoreditch High Street.

The constituent fragments of the London Burkers' story can be arranged and rearranged to create a variety of plausible narratives; but factors that were not explored at the time (not, at least, by anyone capable of committing them to print) can help suggest the more likely solutions to the puzzle.

In 1826, Robert Peel, then Home Secretary, attempted to modernise the traditional 'blood-money' common-informer system by giving the courts the power to remunerate, at their own discretion, those who had 'been active in the apprehension of certain offenders', including murderers. These 'conviction moneys' were paid by the prosecutor, who in turn claimed the money from the Treasury. The archives of the vestry of St Paul's, Covent Garden, reveal the sums changing hands in the Bishop and Williams case. First off the mark was dentist Thomas Mills, who was impatient for his share of the conviction money. James Corder wrote to him on 5 December:

> I beg to acquaint you that none of the witnesses in the late prosecution
> have yet been paid, nor was it thought so well to take any steps towards
> obtaining some allowance from the county for that purpose until after
> the day on which the solemn sentence of the law was carried into effect.
> I will mention your request relative to the teeth to Mr Thomas.[19]

(Mills was seeking the return of the set of teeth sold to him by May. The dentist did indeed get the grinders back, and they went on display in his shop window, with a label attached, reading 'The teeth of Carlo Ferrier – the murdered Italian Boy'.)[20] For his part, Joseph Paragalli wrote directly to the Home Office to ask for his share of the reward money, on 6 January, and was directed to apply instead to the solicitor to the Treasury.[21]

Although the original £200 reward offered by the Home Secretary went unpaid, since no individual was able to deliver the crucial proof of guilt, the forty-two witnesses for the prosecution were paid a total of £45 12s 6d. 'They have severally received at the Treasurer's Office the amounts respectively awarded them by the order of the court,' wrote Corder to the Home Office on 9 February 1832, though the account book does not specify how much money individual witnesses received. Corder continued:

> The sundry incidental expenses incurred in the course of the prosecution were innumerable – an exact account of which it was impossible to keep. These expenses, many of which were incurred in the course of inquiries made in the neighbourhood of the murder with a view to compleat and duftail the evidence, could only have been avoided by risking the attainment of Justice in the case. . . . There was no moral doubt of the guilt of the parties charged and the great object to be accomplished was to establish that guilt by legal evidence – and that evidence too of a circumstantial nature. Under these circumstances, more than ordinary exertion was necessary to be made – no fair or allowable exertion towards preventing a failure of justice was unmade – and I think it will not be said that one shilling in the enclosed account was improperly incurred.[22]

Is this an admission that money had been spent in making circumstantial evidence appear less circumstantial? Could sums have been offered to the Kings, Rebecca Baylis and John Randall to change by a day, or by a week, or by a month, their sighting of an Italian Boy close by Bishop's cottage? The frustration of knowing that the right killers were in custody, but for a killing with an unidentified victim and no timetable to it, could have led to bribery. S.M. Phillips at the Home Office wrote to Corder on 20 February to say that the Home Secretary and G. Maule, Treasury Solicitor, had approved the accounts and the reimbursement to St Paul's, which totalled £112 10s (a sum that included the payments to witnesses). Melbourne considered the payments 'fair and reasonable'. Could that latter sum have included even more money paid to witnesses, on top of the £45 12s 6d already specified for that purpose?

And could payment have been behind the mystery of the mice? In his confession, Bishop – in what appears to be a non-sequitur – claimed:

> There have been no white mice about my house for the last six months. My son, about eight months ago, bought two mice, and I made a cage for them. It was flat, with wires at the top. They lived about two months, and were killed, I think, by a cat in the garden, where they got out of the cage. They were frequently seen running in the garden, and used to hide in a hole under the privy. I and my wife and children saw one of them killed by a cat in the garden whilst we were at tea.

At the Old Bailey, Bishop had summoned Sarah Trueby, his landlady, specifically to tell the court that she had seen white mice at Number 3 some months before – that it was her cat that had killed one of them. This she refused to do – perhaps she had been persuaded by Superintendent Thomas and the open purse of St Paul's, Covent Garden.

The superintendent had claimed that Bishop's five-year-old son had told a young neighbour – Edward Ward – that he had some white mice at home, and that his father had used the cage for firewood. Ward at first had claimed to have seen the mice at Number 3 'a few days before Guy Fawkes Day'. It took his elder brother, John, to fix the date more accurately – Friday 4 November. Edward Ward told the Old Bailey: 'I had often played with Bishop's children before, but I never saw them with a cage or white mice before that.'

If an Italian Boy had been killed at Nova Scotia Gardens on late Thursday night/early hours of Friday morning, then Friday is the only day on which this sighting of white mice can have happened; but this means that the only time at which Bishop could have broken up the box/cage for firewood was Friday evening, and he did not get home that night until after ten o'clock: (hostile) eyewitnesses at the Fortune of War agree that he, Williams and May did not leave the pub until after nine o'clock. There is something very convenient about this explanation for why the cage seen on the Friday afternoon could not be found anywhere in the cottage during subsequent police searches. If Bishop did break up the cage, in the two or three hours between getting home from the Fortune of War on Friday night and going to bed, he must have been prompt about telling his little son about it the next morning, for he had left the house by half-past eight (at the latest) on Saturday morning, never to return.

Joseph and Mary Paragalli may have had something more than simply cash to gain from co-operating with the police and magistrates. While they may not have had any direct involvement in child-trafficking, it is clear that they mixed with *padroni*, socialising with Elliott, at whose house they claimed to have seen Carlo Ferrari bound over to his new *padrone*. As it was, the Paragallis were now firmly in favour with Superintendent Thomas – very handy for a family that made its living from street activities that were on the cusp of legality under the Vagrancy Act. Their prevarication about supplying Carlo's name, and Joseph's claim that he knew of no other Italian boys who made their living by exhibiting animals in the street, are both highly suspect.

Payment and favours aside, a solution to the enigma of the official confessions may be found by entertaining the notion that a monster can be capable of kindness, loyalty and love – that a killer's final act could be altruistic. Certain commentators were wrong to assume that Bishop and Williams had anything to gain for themselves by misleading the authorities after their conviction; no privy council in the world would have mitigated their death sentences – even if they were to be hanged for the wrong killing. And, as mentioned before, these were not the sort of men to care about stirring up working-class distrust of policemen, magistrates, courts and the government. Rather, it seems that what John Bishop was doing in his confession was adapting an essentially true story in order to present a strong impression that his wife and family had no knowledge of the murders committed within their own small home. Bishop well knew that anyone tainted by association with the resurrection trade – let alone burking – could be subject to physical attack. So Sarah, Rhoda and his children simply disappear from the narrative, forced off stage by often highly artificial means. Bishop states that having walked all the way from Smithfield on the night of Thursday 3 November, Bishop and Williams told the boy to hide in the privy in the garden, since Sarah and Rhoda had not yet gone to bed:

> Williams went in and told them to go to bed, and I stayed in the garden. Williams came out directly, and we both walked out of the garden a little way to give time for the family getting to bed ... and listened outside at the window to ascertain whether the family were gone to bed.

All this time, we are to believe, the boy would be compliantly waiting in a cold, damp, reeking privy, even though in such a dark district – and with trees, shrubbery and outhouses to hide behind – there would have been no need for him to have been so elaborately kept from view. (And just before bedtime is surely the hour that a family privy would be in greatest use.)

The silence of the killing is also emphasised by Bishop ('We found him asleep as we had left him. We took him directly, asleep and insensible, into the garden'), as is the hiding of the corpse ('we immediately doubled the body up, and put it into a box, which we corded, so that nobody might open it to see what was in it').

With the killing of Fanny Pigburn, again 'we found the family abed'; 'this was before our families were up', with the unlikely scenario of Bishop getting up at six in the morning to hustle Fanny out of the house before the family awoke and discovered her asleep on the pile of dirty clothes in the parlour of Number 3 (when all along she could have slept in the empty Number 2).

The message from Bishop is clear: the wives and family saw and heard nothing. They had nothing to atone for.

Williams's official confession is merely a short, uninformative corroboration of Bishop's statement. The only other time Williams expressed himself at any length was in the story given to Wontner and Cotton on Saturday night in his cell and reprinted in four newspapers (see pages 255–6). Here, Williams appears to be telling the same story as Bishop about the events of Thursday 3 November – the luring of a fourteen- or fifteen-year-old boy from Smithfield. But there is one crucial deviation from the script: 'They took the boy home to Nova Scotia Gardens, giving him some soup and potatoes by the way. When they got him there, they set him to play with Bishop's children until near dusk.' (Potatoes, along with rum, were found in the boy's stomach at the post-mortem.) Bishop, though, claimed that they had arrived home with this boy 'at about eleven o'clock' at night; similarly, Fanny and Cunningham were described as late-night/early-hours killings.

A possible time-scale for Williams's daytime narrative could be: the killers starting their working day in Smithfield at around 10 a.m.; luring the boy and starting him on his journey east at around noon; reaching Nova Scotia Gardens around one to two o'clock in the afternoon; and the boy and Bishop's children playing together until around five o'clock (dusk set in at around a quarter past five). The boy would have been further put off his guard by this apparently friendly inclusion in the family, and after bedtime, the killing could have happened just as Bishop described it.

Margaret King and her children variously placed seeing their Italian Boy between ten o'clock in the morning and one o'clock in the afternoon of Thursday 3rd; Rebecca Baylis saw him a quarter of an hour before midday, then again slightly after twelve noon; labourer John Randall, however, saw the boy 'between nine and ten o'clock' in the morning. It is possible, though very unlikely, that Bishop and Williams got up, walked to Smithfield, executed the abduction and walked back to Shoreditch (stopping on the way to eat) before ten in the morning. If these sightings of an Italian Boy by the neighbours were truthful and accurate, the more likely explanation is that there was indeed an itinerant Italian beggar doing the rounds of Nova Scotia Gardens/Crabtree Row over a three- to four-hour period on Thursday 3 November, but that this was not the boy lured from Smithfield. Margaret King told the magistrates that 'she had often seen the same boy in the environs of Nova Scotia Gardens'. Her son John said: 'He used to carry a doll with two heads in a glass case. I saw him about a month ago. He looked like the same boy.' Which raises the possibility that the neighbours could have become confused about the date on which they saw the beggar boy. Or they could have been asked to become confused.

Alternatively, the neighbours' tales could all have been true – and Bishop's confession a complete fabrication. Perhaps there was no trip to Smithfield on Thursday 3rd; perhaps an Italian Boy, Carlo Ferrari, had lingered too long near the Gardens, had been invited in by Bishop and Williams – with the wives and children present in or around the cottage – and been murdered late that night, just as the prosecution claimed. And Bishop had simply been distancing his family from the crime by claiming that the inveigling had happened in Smithfield. Interestingly, the only other discrepancy between Bishop's official confession and Williams's confession to Wontner and Cotton on the night of Saturday, 3 December is the order of the Smithfield/Old Bailey pubs visited. According to Bishop, Williams picked the boy up in the Bell – an old coaching tavern which stood just to the east of where today Grand Avenue runs through the present Smithfield market building – and brought him to the King of Denmark; Bishop, meanwhile, was drinking in the Fortune of War, to where Williams came to collect Bishop and bring him to meet the boy, whom he had left standing outside the King of Denmark. But Williams presents a different sequence of pub visits, which is perhaps understandable if this abduction was one of two, or even one of many; and is even more understandable if the killers had been drinking all day. Williams says he 'enticed' the boy from his cattle at Smithfield, and took him to the Fortune of War, and sent for Bishop, who was waiting at another pub – presumably the King of Denmark. This confusion may be of little note, or it could indicate that the two men had failed to agree the minor details in a jointly narrated fallacious story.

Perhaps in this way resurrection honour had been preserved. Bishop and Williams never chose to turn King's Evidence and betray one another; and the figures who hover in the background of this story (the stranger who accompanied Bishop and May to buy second-hand clothing in Field Lane on 4 November; the person who waved goodbye from the gallery of the Old Bailey; the six men on James May's list of potential killers) may have had their necks saved by Bishop and Williams twisting the narrative of their crimes.

EPILOGUE

On Sunday 18 December 1831, a man and a woman stood sobbing at the dockside in Woolwich. The estranged wife of James May had come, with their young daughter, to say goodbye – May was about to board the hulk *Justitia*, bound for Botany Bay, where he was to spend the rest of his life.

But May never made it to Australia; he was destined for a different New World. Despite being described as 'Healthy' (his behaviour was judged 'Good') by the compiler of the hulk registers,[1] he died aboard the prison hospital ship the *Grampus*, moored off Greenwich, to which he was transferred from the *Justitia* on 20 January 1832 when his health on the outbound ship declined dramatically. No cause of death was given, but his fit at Newgate on hearing of his reprieve must surely have been a contributing factor, and the newspapers claimed that he had been roughly treated by other inmates on the *Justitia*, who were outraged at having to share a ship with a snatcher.

In the same week as the Mays' farewell, Michael Shields turned up at Covent Garden market at ten o'clock one morning, hoping that one of the salesmen who had formerly employed him as a porter would hire him again. The salesman loudly, indignantly, refused to have anything to do with Shields. A crowd gathered and began to jostle Shields, pushing him from one to another, chanting, 'I don't want him', 'I won't have him'. Shields made a run for it, grabbing a wrench and brandishing it at those who came close. He fled up Bow Street, screaming for the police officers to help him, as the pursuing crowd yelled, 'That's Shields the Burker,' 'There he goes, knock his brains out.' The officers hauled him into the police office and used their batons on any of the crowd who tried to reach the front door. 'Turn him out!' they screamed. 'Let us have him – we'll dispose of him.' Inside, the officers who had known Shields could scarcely recognise him: he had lost so much weight he looked like an animated skeleton. Five hours later, believing it was safe, officers smuggled Shields out of the office, disguised in a voluminous great-coat; they took him across the road to the Grapes public house and stayed with him until darkness fell, when they felt it was safe for him to leave the pub alone. Within yards he was spotted and a mob assembled. He ran down into the Strand, then into a small courtyard on the north side, opposite King's College, and into the warren of alleys beyond, where we lose sight of him for good.

On the evening of Saturday 17 December, Andrew Colla was walking home on Great Saffron Hill when three men surrounded him. One was masked, but Colla nevertheless recognised him as the person to whom Thomas Williams had waved goodbye at the Old Bailey. Though Colla did not know it, all three men had been on James May's list of resurrectionists capable of burking: John Shearing, the masked man; his brother, Thomas; and Robert Tighe/Tye, also called James Kettle/Cattle, resurrection man and lover of Bridget Culkin. Just two weeks earlier Tighe had been released from custody on suspicion of having been Culkin's accomplice in the supposed burking of five-year-old Margaret Duffy in Golden Lane. 'This is the bloody bastard!' shouted John Shearing. 'Let's serve him out!' and all three set about Colla, kicking him to the ground. Passers-by rushed to help and, outnumbered, the Shearings and Tighe fled. But when a police officer arrived he refused to go after them, even though some in the crowd knew that the Shearings lived in nearby Rosoman Street; nor

75. The *Grampus* hospital hulk, moored off Greenwich.

would the officer raise the alarm, claiming that as he himself had not witnessed the assault, there was nothing he could do to help.

A month later, John Shearing, 'a very powerful-looking young man', according to the *Morning Advertiser*, was arrested and taken before the magistrates at Bow Street, accused of sending a threatening letter to Colla. Shearing admitted to the JPs, 'I deal in the stiff line, but I'm no burker,' and denied having written the note, which read,

> You bloody murdering bugger, do you expect you'll be suffered to live, after the evidence you gave at the Old Bailey? No, you bloody thief, you and Hill shall share the fate of those you have assisted in sending to the other world. Prepare yourself, for in a very short time you will be a dead one.

A former associate of Shearing's, a snatcher called Stringall, claimed that this note was in Shearing's handwriting. Shearing was remanded.

On Boxing Day a letter had been received, by two-penny post, by William Hill, dissecting-room porter at King's College. It read:

> You bloody murdering bugger, you think you are all right to get tip, but only loke out, for you will have your bloody guts out before many days his over, for blow my eyes if there shan't be another tucked up for you, you gallus life-selling warmint. You think you've done the trick up, master Billy, but I will put a spoke in your weal, damn my eyes if I don't, you noing kovy,
>
> Yours affectionately,
> The Gost of Bishop and Williams.

Doubtless another Shearing effort.

Hill took the letter to George Rowland Minshull, telling the magistrate that Mrs Hill was sick with worry about the family's safety, and asking if he could be licensed to carry a small pistol for protection. Best not, said Minshull, who told Hill that the threats were probably nothing to worry about – Superintendent Thomas and Minshull himself would see that no harm came to Hill.

Within a year, Hill was sacked by King's College, without character references. The rumour reported (or was it started?) by the *Lancet* was that the college anatomy department's entire supply of corpses had ceased because the London resurrectionists refused to do business with the porter who had alerted the authorities to Bishop and Williams's boy-cadaver. The point that the *Lancet* writer was making was that despite the passing of the

Anatomy Act in the summer of 1832, the resurrection trade continued to thrive, since the machinery of the Act was yet to bring about a large enough supply of friendless, unclaimed paupers, and arguments about unfair distribution between the medical schools rumbled on, with resurrectionists helping to make up the corpse shortfalls at many schools. Thus it was stated in the *Lancet* of 17 November 1832 that 'practices which would disgrace a nation of cannibals' remained common in the capital a year after the Italian Boy case. (In fact, snatching was being referred to in official documents as late as 1838; in that year the Poor Law Commissioners reported that two resurrectionists had died from fever caught from a putrid corpse disinterred in a Somers Town graveyard.)[2] However, an anonymous letter that appeared in the following week's *Lancet* denied there was a paucity of corpses at King's, stating that the college had used 'secret and undue' influence to obtain a higher number of workhouse corpses than other London medical schools. The correspondent claimed that King's now had access to so many bodies, it was burying them without bothering to dissect them first. (Another rumour was that King's was using its fine Portland-stone water-gates to dispose of its unwanted corpses and body parts by flushing them into the Thames.)

Whatever the truth about events at King's, the dismissal of Hill appeared unfair and unjustifiable to a number of medical people. A whip-round was carried out for him by a previous employer, private anatomy teacher George Dermott, and his pupils, raising £1 1s, and Dermott raised a subscription for Hill through the pages of the *Lancet*, claiming that he had been the best servant/porter that Dermott had ever had.

Late one night in December, dentist Thomas Mills was awoken by someone hammering at his door. When he looked from his window, a man below claimed to have bad toothache – would Mills treat him? Despite the darkness, Mills could make out two other men lurking behind the first, and saw that all three were in smock frocks and carried bludgeons. Mills refused to open up, and the three walked off, shouting threats of future violence.

Before Christmas Sarah Bishop took lodgings in Paradise Row, Battle Bridge, and Rhoda in nearby Edmund Street. Paradise Row was laughed at at the time for being distinctly unheavenly: lying behind the Smallpox Hospital (the site of today's Great Northern Hotel, just west of King's Cross station), it was a half-built, half-tumble-down, undrained, unlit street, whose piles of manure (human, horse, donkey and dog) left it reeking and dangerous to health. But the living condition that most worried the residents was the presence among them of the kin of burkers. Newspaper reports stated that local women were refusing to let their children play outside so long as Sarah and Rhoda were known to be living in the area.

Nothing more appears in the newspapers about Bishop and Williams's widows and children, though four young Bishops, Thomas William, twelve, Frederick Henry, ten, Thomas, seven, and Emma, two, were admitted together to the Shoreditch workhouse on 5 March 1832, staying for three weeks. These seem likely to be the killer's children, along with one older boy; confusingly, Frederick – John Bishop's eldest – was in fact twelve, not ten. Perhaps Thomas William was a cousin, since, when the three boys – without Emma – turned up at the workhouse again two and a half years later for a one-night stay, they were discharged to Thomas William's father, described in the workhouse register as living in Norwood, south London. Frederick and Thomas Bishop were admitted once again, for two days, in April 1835.[3] After that, the children's whereabouts and fates – how they felt about their parentage, whether they were shunned or were shown sympathy – are unknown.

Joseph Sadler Thomas was never able to capitalise on the recognition he gained from his role in the Bishop and Williams investigation. Despite the eulogies that appeared in all the newspapers on the New Police as a body, and Thomas as an individual officer, for securing the conviction of the London Burkers, his enemies never ceased to pillory him, and he was singled out for criticism for 'high-handedness' during the Coldbath Fields Riot of 13 May 1833. This meeting of 300 members of the National Union of the Working Class and their supporters took place on a large stretch of open ground just behind Coldbath Fields Prison and was broken up by an equal number of badly organised and belligerent Metropolitan Police officers, who managed to turn a good-humoured gathering into a general brawl, with one fatality – a police officer.

But it was a more petty row that sealed Thomas's fate. Just after the Coldbath Fields Riot, he was accused of victimising a publican called Williams who had applied for a pub licence in Seven Dials. Thomas opposed the licence, saying that there were already thirty pubs within 150 yards of Williams's proposed venue, and he was one of fifty local residents who signed a petition for a limit to be put on the number of pubs in the area. Two magistrates (one of whom, Rotch, loathed the New Police, and Thomas in particular) complained to the Home Office about Thomas's antipathy to Williams's licence application, and Thomas was, at the justices' behest, suspended from the Metropolitan Police for five weeks until the Commissioners themselves intervened and apologised to Thomas for this over-reaction.

Thomas felt that he had been humiliated once too often 'in a neighbourhood where I had been for 20 years with an unpolluted character';[4] he would, he said, 'as well have met my death' than endure the disgrace of suspension. On 22 July 1833 he resigned from the Metropolitan Police, and with his wife and three children moved north, becoming deputy constable of Manchester's 'old police', and being among the first of Manchester's 'new' Borough Police Force, when this Met-style organisation was created in 1839. His salary – £600 *per annum* – was three times his Covent Garden rate of pay.

He did not stay long with the new force, however. His health deteriorated, and for the last two years of his life he was unable to work and was supported by a public subscription – a vote of thanks from many in Manchester who had appreciated his work as a constable. He died in October 1841.

On Christmas Eve 1831 an article by John Gordon Smith, professor of medical jurisprudence, appeared in the *Lancet*, attacking the official postmortem findings in the Bishop and Williams case and backing up the killers' claim that the injury to the back of the boy's neck had happened when the still-warm corpse was doubled up and placed in the trunk. Smith found Beaman's, Mayo's and Partridge's claim that all four chambers of the boy's heart had been 'empty', indicating a sudden death, 'inconceivable . . . I am fearless in calling upon every medical jurist in the world to corroborate the assertion that emptiness – even total emptiness of the heart – is a sign of a lingering death from disease, rather than indicative of sudden death from violence in the healthy state.'

Herbert Mayo was sacked by King's College in 1836 for his poor teaching skills, though he went on to be co-founder of the successful Middlesex Hospital anatomy school. By 1842 he was crippled by osteo-arthritis and moved to the German spa town of Bad Weilbach, where he became increasingly mystic, publishing such works as *On the Truths Contained in Popular Superstitions* (1849). He was also intrigued by phrenology and physiognomy, and his medical writing now appeared to have more in common with the Tudor theory of the humours than with the brave new world of anatomy and physiology, in which latter field he had once been such a brilliant pioneer. Typical observations from Mayo's later years were that Sanguine people tend to have red hair and respond well to being bled; Italians are bilious or melancholic and have olive complexions; cards, angling and chess are excellent defences against insanity (from *The Philosophy of Living*, 1837). He died in a German hydropathic hotel in 1852.

Richard Partridge failed to fulfil his potential. Though he succeeded

76. Richard Partridge's disastrous examination of Garibaldi in 1862; the anatomist's career did not recover.

Mayo as King's College's Professor of Anatomy in 1836, he never ceased to be nervous as a surgeon, and maintained a stolid, unremarkable role as teacher and anatomical draughtsman. In 1862 he had the honour to inspect, before a number of onlookers, the injured foot of Italian patriot and freedom-fighter Giuseppe Garibaldi. He failed to spot that a bullet was lodged in Garibaldi's ankle; another surgeon approached, and located and removed the bullet straight away. Partridge's reputation never recovered, and he died in poverty eleven years later.

While lecturing at King's College, Partridge would tell his students the Bishop and Williams story, embellishing it with the fiction that the convictions had been secured when the New Police had placed cheese on the floor of Number 3 Nova Scotia Gardens, and a number of little white mice had crept out of hiding to nibble it, thereby proving that the Italian Boy had been killed in the house.

Thomas Williams was pledged to St Bartholomew's Hospital museum, though he does not appear in the nineteenth-century catalogues of that institution, and his whereabouts are unknown at the time of writing. The remains of John Bishop maintained a moderate profile for much of the century: his skeleton and the skin of his arms had pride of place in King's College's pathological museum for decades. However, in 1871 he was spotted in a private, money-making concern, Dr Kahn's Anatomical Museum, in Tichbourne Street (today, the north side of Piccadilly Circus).

Either King's had decided to sell on their once-famous villain, or Dr Kahn was practising on the public with an imitation John Bishop among his display of Siamese twin foetuses, hare lips, haemorrhoids, hernias, 'the dreadful effects of lacing stays too tightly', plus plenty of oddly formed genitals, displayed 'for medical gentlemen only'.[5]

But the London Burker has not taken up his rightful place in a glass cabinet alongside John Thurtell, William Corder and other long-forgotten villains in the Hunterian Museum in the Royal College of Surgeons, though it is possible that he was once there and that his remains perished in the same Luftwaffe direct hit that destroyed many items in the museum in May 1941, including the skeleton of Chunee the berserk elephant killed by troops in the Strand, and the (alleged) intestine of Napoleon Bonaparte.

So much for the actors. As for the location, Nova Scotia Gardens acquired a new soubriquet, Burkers Hole, by which it would be known for the next twenty-five years, and a myth arose that the cottages communicated with each other via a warren of cellars and subterranean passages – a vivid image of how London's criminal fraternity were felt to be able to move around unseen along secret pathways of their own making. In the 1840s Nova Scotia Gardens was one of the slums traversed by such sanitary reformers as George Godwin, Henry Austin (Charles Dickens's brother-in-law) and Dr Hector Gavin. Godwin, in 1859, decided that

> an artistic traveller, looking at the huge mountain of refuse which had been collected, might have fancied that Arthur's Seat at Edinburgh, or some other monster picturesque crag, had suddenly come into view, and the dense smell which hung over the 'gardens' would have aided in bringing 'auld reekie' strongly to the memory. At the time of our visit, the summit of the mount was thronged with various figures, which were seen in strong relief against the sky; and boys and girls were amusing themselves by running down and toiling up the least precipitous side of it. Near the base, a number of women were arranged in a row, sifting and sorting the various materials placed before them. The tenements were in a miserable condition. Typhus fever, we learnt from a medical officer, was a frequent visitor all round the spot.

77. Architectural/sanitary campaigner George Godwin discovered a mountain of rubbish and sewage when he visited Nova Scotia Gardens in 1859; this sketch appeared in his campaigning book *Town Swamps and Social Bridges*.

'Refuse' was Godwin's euphemism for human faeces; Dr Hector Gavin described the same scene as 'a table mountain of manure', which towered over 'a lake of more liquid dung'.[6] A refuse collector was using Nova Scotia Gardens as his official tip, accumulating this vast mound from which the still-destitute residents of that part of Bethnal Green came to salvage some sort of living. So much for the New Poor Law: people chose to live from, and play on, noxious rubbish tips rather than enter the workhouse.

Half a century later a nostalgia column, 'Chapters of Old Shoreditch', in the local newspaper, the *Hackney Express & Shoreditch Observer*, featured an aged local resident's eyewitness memory of 'the fearful hovels . . . once so famous in the days of Burking . . . a row of dilapidated old houses standing back from the line of frontage and in a hollow, with a strip of waste land in front, on which was laid out for sale flowers, greengrocery and old rubbish of all kinds'; the following week another contributor also recalled 'the antiquated property known as The Hackney Road Hollow'.[7]

Royalty came to gawp at the natives too, and discovered that nature always finds a way: Princess Mary Adelaide, Duchess of Teck – grand-daughter of George III and mother-in-law to the future George V –

recalled of the Gardens: 'There was a large piece of waste ground covered in places with foul, slimy-looking pools, amid which crowds of half-naked, barefooted, ragged children chased one another. From the centre arose a great black mound . . . the stench continually issuing from the enormous mass of decaying matter was unendurable.'[8] But the most important visitor to these foetid regions was Angela Burdett-Coutts (1814–1906), million-airess, philanthropist, baroness (from 1871) and, for two decades, close friend of Charles Dickens. Together, the baroness and the novelist would take long night-walks to some of the 'vilest dens of London' during the 1840s and 1850s; and from time to time Nova Scotia Gardens, 'the resort of murderers, thieves, the disreputable and abandoned' featured on their East End itinerary, according to Mary Spencer-Warren, author of the only press interview that Burdett-Coutts ever gave.[9]

No documentary evidence survives to reveal whether it was Dickens or Burdett-Coutts who first suggested Nova Scotia Gardens as a destination. As the extended footnote in Chapter 11 suggests, Dickens may have had personal knowledge of the Bishop and Williams case; at any rate, he is almost certain to have followed it in the newspapers of 1831. But what is less well-known is that there was a link between Burdett-Coutts and Burkers Hole. Angela Burdett-Coutts was the daughter of Radical MP Francis Burdett and Susan Coutts, whose father, Thomas Coutts, had founded the bank Coutts & Co. Thomas died in 1822, leaving his £900,000 fortune to his second wife, actress Harriot Mellon, who, in 1827, married the Duke of St Albans and became even richer.

Her mother dead, and with no close female relative, Angela spent weeks, even months, with her adored step-grandmother in Harriot's Highgate villa, Holly Lodge. Harriot, who was spoken of fondly by, among others, William Wordsworth, Sir Walter Scott and poet laureate Robert Southey, had a quick wit, a deep purse and a very kind heart; perhaps too kind. 'Her charities were abused and misapplied by too many of the thankless wretches who had partaken of her bounty,' according to one who knew her.[10] One of the many local people whom Harriot tried to help out, in 1816, was the pregnant young Highgate widow Sarah Bishop. It is known that at the time of the Bishop and Williams case, Angela, then seventeen, was living with Harriot; had she perhaps heard plenty of background detail on the case from her sprightly hostess? Did she and Dickens share a common interest in the killings when they became friends in 1839?

Harriot died in August 1837 and left her fortune to twenty-three-year-old Angela. (She had intended to leave it to Lord Dudley Stuart, who, in 1834, had been so indignant when four Italian Boys were arrested outside his home; but Harriot had cut him out of her will when he went against

8.–79. Millionairess philanthropist Angela Burdett-Coutts built Columbia Market (*above*) and Columbia Square on the site of Nova Scotia Gardens in the 1860s.

her advice and married the niece of Napoleon Bonaparte.) Possibly inspired by Harriot's kindness, but determined to be more discriminating in her giving, Angela set out upon a lifetime of philanthropy, which she conducted according to both her religious principles and the dominant social ideals of the mid-century. Dickens, while their friendship endured, from 1839 to 1859, was to be one of her mentors as she struggled to transcend the narrow limits of her outlook and experience.

In 1852 Angela bought Nova Scotia Gardens for £8,700. She intended to raze the cottages and in their place build salubrious homes that would lead to the moral, spiritual and physical improvement of the dwellers of Burkers Hole. But she had not been informed that the refuse collector was legally entitled to stay on the land – no matter who owned it – and to use it as he saw fit until 1859. It was only in that year that she was able to set about her grand project. She employed architect Henry Darbishire to create Columbia Square, a magnificent five-storey block of one-, two- and three-room apartments, housing 180 families who paid between 2s 6d and 5s a week in rent; there were shared washing facilities and WCs on each floor, and a library, club room and play areas. Before long, there was a waiting list of families keen to move into the apartments.

Columbia Square was an odd amalgam of industrial-dwellings-style tenements on to which were grafted the pinnacles and pointed arches of Gothic; plain yellow stock bricks were dressed with Portland stone and terracotta mouldings. What followed next was even more exotic: Columbia Market, built just to the west of the Square between 1863 and 1869, was a Castle Perilous extravaganza that included 36 shops and 400 market stalls for local traders and costermongers. It looked like a miniaturised cathedral and came complete with pieties painted on the walls, such as 'Speak everyman truth unto his neighbour', and orders forbidding swearing, drunkenness and Sunday trading. It went bust within six months.

The baroness's housing continued to be popular for nearly 100 years, but Columbia Square was finally condemned as unfit for human habitation in the 1950s; the Market died alongside it (Britain's heritage bodies having not yet realised their lobbying skills), and Henry Darbishire's masterpieces fell to the demolition ball in 1960. A local authority housing estate, still in use, was built on the site. The Birdcage pub opposite has watched all this, unscathed.

The Bishop and Williams case itself began a slow decline into obscurity, a number of factors combining to push the London Burkers into the shadows. The 'Asiatic Cholera' had entered the country at Sunderland in August 1831; it reached London in February 1832 and by the summer had killed an estimated 32,000 people in Britain, 5,500 of them Londoners. The fear of urban miasma – the exhalations of graveyards and the stinking, sluggish air in courts, alleys and warrens that were (mistakenly) blamed for the outbreak – quickly pushed Burkiphoby from its top billing. The bacillus *cholera vibrio* could kill within hours of being ingested in food or, more frequently, in drinking water, where it could live for up to a fort-night – all of which would remain unknown until the 1850s, and not fully accepted by the medical community until the 1880s. A typhus epidemic struck London in 1837–8, while cholera revisited London in 1848–9 (killing 15,000), 1853–4 and 1866–7. It was the air of London – its smells, mists, fogs, smoke – rather than its criminal element that held a mysterious terror for the city's inhabitants and visitors in the 1830s.

Besides, Burke and Hare were continuing to do perfectly good duty as archetypal murderers-for-dissection. The story of the Edinburgh Horrors had charming, voluble Burke; hideous, cretinous Hare; sinister, proud Dr Knox; pathetic Daft Jamie and alluring Mary Paterson. And from the mid-1830s a new era of complex and exciting murders was ushered in, reported by an increasingly sophisticated newspaper and periodical press that could now reproduce high-quality illustrations of scenes of crime and *dramatis personae*. An ever-more-literate population wanted to read about people of quality (professionals, many of them) murdering each other in drawing-rooms, boudoirs, hotel rooms. They preferred their killers and victims to be able to express themselves at great length in letters. They wanted – and got – swindlers and fraudsters; adulterers and adulteresses; bigamists, usurped heirs, jealous spouses, all pursued, from August 1842, by the specialist Detective Branch of Scotland Yard, the first permanent plain-clothes squad.[11]

But before they disappeared from the murder map, Bishop and Williams provided a source of inspiration for one of the mid-century's biggest-selling works of fiction. In 1844 journalist George William MacArthur Reynolds (1814–79), Radical, bankrupt and teetotal, read an English trans-lation of the French popular literary sensation *Les Mystères de Paris* (1842), written by Eugène Sue, and immediately struck upon producing a British imitation. Reynolds's *The Mysteries of London* was published between October 1844 and 1856 in weekly issues, at the low price of 1d to attract the working-class reader.[12] It is said to have outsold every other rival serial and novel, with 30,000 to 40,000 copies a week being printed at the height of its popularity. In 1846 three different stage adaptations of the book could be seen in London. Those who were unable to afford a penny a week for fiction, or who were illiterate, could nevertheless enjoy the stories since literate members of the community would read aloud to groups of twelve or so, in a tavern or some other public space.

80.–82. In 1844, sightseers queued to visit the soon-to-be-demolished Old Red Lion Tavern in Smithfield (*above*) and its warren of passages and hidden chambers. It had been built on the banks of the filthy Fleet, from which people scavenged a living (*opposite*) and above which were cheap lodging houses for the poor (*overleaf*).

The Mysteries of London is a vast, rambling series of interconnecting episodes in which the misdeeds of a corrupt, enervated aristocratic elite are juxtaposed with the depredations of London's underworld characters. The most important of the latter – occupying the dark heart of the book – is the Resurrection Man.

The Resurrection Man lives in Bethnal Green, in a squalid, damp house that has an eight-room dungeon beneath it, accessed by the pull of a lever near the hearth. A small alley runs alongside the house, and late one night, the Resurrection Man is observed with another man in the alley – they are dragging between them a blindfolded woman, who never emerges alive from the Resurrection Man's cellar. His favourite drinking places are the Dark House at the northern end of Brick Lane (not far from Nova Scotia Gardens) and the Boozing Ken on Saffron Hill; he serves time in Coldbath Fields; he disinters a girl's body from beneath the flagstones of Shoreditch Church. In the series' opening scene, a youth becomes lost in the maze of alleys near the Fleet Ditch and then trapped in the Old House in Smithfield and is flung by two men through a trap-door into a well that empties into the Fleet. *The Mysteries* opens in July 1831 – a very specific time, though its significance is not explained to the reader; perhaps it is coincidence, but this is the month in which Bishop and Williams first met.

Though the Anatomy Act had killed off the trade by 1844, resurrection, it seems, remained a potent folk memory – a fact that Reynolds was keen to play on in his choice of bogey-man, who in the course of *The Mysteries* is stabbed, blown up, imprisoned and left for dead on a plague ship, but who nevertheless returns to stalk the heroes of the book.

Reynolds's story also cleverly capitalised on the deeper physical strata of London that were being unearthed in the mid-1840s, with the so-called Metropolitan Improvements – new roads, railway lines, bridges, tunnels, and the laying of drains. The discoveries made during these works revealed some uncanny facts about the old fabric of the city, and fed into a particularly urban paranoia about subterranean spaces – the sort of anxiety that created the legend that Nova Scotia Gardens was sitting atop a warren of passages connecting up the cottages. In 1837 a parliamentary select committee that had been convened to examine the feasibility of bricking over the Fleet River and converting it into a sewer revealed that the neighbourhood of Saffron Hill featured a great many man-holes leading to 20- to 30-foot-deep shafts into which a person could descend below the level of the street. These had never been properly mapped or charted before, and, along with the Fleet and its foetid tributaries, were being investigated as possible miasmatic sources of the cholera and typhus outbreaks.[13] In 1844, as part of these same belated 'Clerkenwell Improvements', Farringdon Road was driven through the slums around the Fleet, and to the thrilling horror of non-locals, the Old Red Lion Tavern at Number 3 West Street was discovered to have been a warren-like house, hollowed out and customised to hide booty and prisoners on the run; it featured secret passages, trap-doors, subterranean rooms, sliding panels and escape routes into other houses or on to the slimy banks of the Fleet. (The site is now approximately under Farringdon Road near its north-western corner with Charterhouse Street.) The building dated back to 1683 and was also known locally as the Old House in West Street and Jonathan Wild's House – after the notorious magistrate-cum-thief hanged in 1725. Sightseers paid to be taken on tours of the house and the remains of the semi-demolished streets around Saffron Hill, Field Lane/West Street, Turnmill Street, Cow Cross. A similarly uncanny honeycomb of rotting old houses and convoluted streets was discovered in the same year when St Giles was razed for the building of New Oxford Street, and in the following year, when Victoria Street was constructed through the Devil's Acre slums in Westminster.

The Metropolitan Improvements revealed that some of the worst imaginings by 'respectable' Londoners about criminal enclaves and how the topography of these might assist wrongdoers to evade justice had been accurate in substance as well as in spirit. But by then, the moves to sweep away the rottenness of previous ages had gathered unstoppable momentum, and the recent past was feeling as ancient as Biblical times.

NOTES

A Note on Sources

I have based the narrative of the case on *The Times*'s reports of the inquest, committal proceedings and trial of Bishop, May and Williams, supplemented by reports from the other main national newspapers whenever these give additional information or direct quotations; the printed Old Bailey Sessions Papers of 1831 filled in gaps in the newspapers' reports of the murder trial.

Few original records exist of proceedings at London's magistrates' courts in the late 1820s/early 1830s, and I have had to rely heavily on newspaper accounts of summary justice.

The reports of Parliamentary Select Committees have proved a rich source of evidence about street life in London in the 1820s and 1830s, though doubtless these are somewhat bowdlerised accounts, and they do not, generally, encompass the views of the poor themselves; nevertheless, fascinating snippets creep into the witnesses' testimony.

1 Suspiciously Fresh

1 *The Times*, 9 November 1831.

2 The *Morning Advertiser* reports the boy's name as Giacomo Montrato; but their cloth-eared reporter also calls Michael Shields Sheen until quite late in the case – Shiel is a variant the *Globe and Traveller* and the *Morning Herald* used. The name Paragalli went through many transcriptions, as did all the Italian names mentioned in the case; even *The Times* and the Old Bailey Sessions Papers contain wild variations of the Italian witnesses' names.

Liquorpond Street now lies under the line of Clerkenwell Road, running east from Gray's Inn Road.

3 West Street was also called Chick Lane and led into Smithfield. Torn down in 1844, it followed roughly the line that Charterhouse Street traces today.

4 This phrase puzzled lawyers and reporters covering the case, and was also widely transcribed as 'to locus or burke me'. To 'burke' is the method of killing used by William Burke. 'Hocus' was contemporary slang for alcohol to which a drug – usually opium in its liquid form, laudanum –

had been added, and to hocus was to stupefy someone with such a concoction before robbing them. To 'locus' was slang for spiriting away someone after getting them drunk. 'Locust', meanwhile, was a slang term for laudanum; and 'locus-ale', beer containing laudanum, is referred to as early as 1693, according to *A Dictionary of Slang and Unconventional English* by Eric Partridge (1937).

5 A 'topper' was boxing slang for a violent blow. For example, 'to topper his smellers' meant to land a punch on an opponent's nose. From Partridge's *Dictionary of Slang*.

6 Rum-hot was a variant of 'egg-hot' – strong ale brought to the boil with sugar, cinnamon and a little lemon juice, to which was added a glass of cold ale; this mixture was then poured over beaten egg yolks, with nutmeg and more sugar added to taste. Some preferred to heat it by thrusting a hot poker into the mixture and making it bubble. Source: *The Curiosities of Ale and Beer* by John Bickerdyke (1886).

7 The *Globe and Traveller* of Saturday 26 November reported this conversation as: 'What do you think of our new one now? Isn't he a staunch one? Didn't he go up to him well? You stick to me old fellow and I'll be true to you. I know the other one is all right – he is a good 'un. I told you he was a staunch one.'

8 The *Globe and Traveller* reported May's reply to Bishop as 'I don't know what you mean by "It's all right."'

9 In the *Morning Advertiser* of 9 November 1831, May's reply to Hill is reported as: 'That is nothing to you or us. Here it is, and that's all about it.'

10 St Giles-in-the-Fields is Henry Flitcroft's 1731 church in St Giles High Street, beneath today's Centrepoint. St Mary's Moorfields stood on the north corner of Blomfield Street and Finsbury Circus between 1820 and 1899; it had a small cemetery as well as burial vaults beneath the church, and it is possible Shields was stealing more than the silverware.

11 Public Record Office, Petitions and Pardons 1830–1831, HO 64/2.

2 Persons Unknown

1 The Bishop of London's figures as given in the pamphlet *Evidence of the Reverend William Stone, Rector of Christ Church Spitalfields, & Others as to the Operation of Voluntary Charities* (1833).

2 This is the number given for 1832 by historian M.J. Durey in the essay 'Bodysnatchers and Benthamites' in the *London Journal*, Volume 2, Number 2 (1976). However, this figure is unlikely to include many far smaller enterprises, such as those private courses given by hospital surgeons from their

own homes; Dr C. Walker, for example, gave classes in midwifery at his lodgings at 93 Bartholomew Close, and a Dr Ryan gave lectures on medical jurisprudence at his rooms in Hatton Garden. Source: advertisements in the *Lancet* in the late 1820s.

3 The *Morning Advertiser*, 16 October 1827.

4 A variety of views on the number of corpses required for teaching purposes was given by surgeons in their evidence to the Select Committee on Anatomy in 1828, and three per student is the average that was settled upon by the Select Committee Report's authors; *Report*, p.4.

5 Over 200 offences were punishable by death in 1800; by 1837, the figure had dropped to eight. Still capital in 1831 were treason, murder, attempted murder causing injury, rape, sodomy, forgery, several forms of counterfeiting, horse-stealing, house-breaking with larceny, returning from transportation, sacrilege, stealing letters, stealing goods to the value of 5*s* and over from a shop and of £5 and over from a private house.

6 Source: *The Report and Evidence of the Select Committee into the State of the Police of the Metropolis*, 1828, pp.284–5; and the same committee's report of 1833.

7 Report in *The Times*, 9 April 1830.

8 The *Globe and Traveller*, 19 October 1831; he gave his name as William Jones – which was the name of a noted East London snatcher (see note 11 below).

9 The *Morning Advertiser*, 30 December 1828.

10 Evidence of retired parish constable James Glennon given to the 1828 Select Committee on Anatomy; *Report*, p.105.

11 In January 1830 at Lambeth Street police office in Whitechapel, Cornelius Fitzgerald, George Gibson, George and William Kent were discharged when they appeared upon a charge of attempting to rob the burial ground at Globe Lane, Bethnal Green, since they had been arrested on suspicion only and no other evidence was offered.

In April 1830 at Union Hall police office, Southwark, resurrectionists complained of increased police vigilance at graveyards during the hearing of a pair named Williams and Edwards, who were arrested at St John's, West Lane, Walworth; it is possible they were members of the gang so determined to get their hands on Miss Christy.

In August 1830 George Robins and William Jones, two well-known bodysnatchers, were charged at Lambeth Street with attempting to steal the body of Mrs Brown from the rear of a chapel in Cannon Street Road, off Ratcliffe Highway, in the East End. A Metropolitan Police officer had spotted them near to midnight, and saw that Mrs Brown's grave was half open, with tools lying around it. Robins and Jones were sentenced to three months in gaol.

In March 1831 James Bailey, John Chapman and Daniel Baker were charged at Union Hall with stealing two dead bodies, which had been found when police officers had stopped their cart in Brixton Road. The magistrate granted them bail.

M.J. Durey's 'Bodysnatchers and Benthamites' essay alerted me to these references in *The Times*, editions of 25 January, 9 April and 24 August 1830, and 21 March 1831 respectively.

12 *Report*, pp.93–101.

13 Partridge's £50 allowance minuted in King's College Archives, file KA/C/M2; Bell quotation from *Sir Charles Bell: His Life and Times* by Sir Gordon Gordon-Taylor (1958), p.30.

14 According to Ruth Richardson, in her 1988 book *Death, Dissection and the Destitute* (reissued in 2001), 'CD' was likely to have been Joshua Naples (p.115). Naples is also strongly believed to be the author of the other major contemporary source of knowledge about resurrection in London: *The Diary of a Resurrectionist*, a diary cum logbook, dated 1811, is housed in the library of the Royal College of Surgeons of England in Lincoln's Inn Fields. 'CD' told the Committee that although he was virtually the sole supplier of corpses to the London schools between 1809 and 1811, he gave up the trade in 1820 because it had become too dangerous, with guards at graveyards increasingly likely to be armed and ready to fire; *Report*, p.118.

15 This was how anatomist Joshua Brookes (1761–1833) described them to the Select Committee; *Report*, p.82.

16 *All the Year Round*, 16 March 1867.

17 Source: *Quaint Signs of Olde Inns* by G.J. Monson-Fitzjohn (1926). But William West in his *Tavern Anecdotes* (1825) – a compendium of London inns and pubs – guesses that the Fortune of War was named after a prize fighter who retired with his winnings to open a pub.

The *Lancet* points out that there was a small theatre of anatomy – a private medical school – at Number 18 Giltspur Street, though, perhaps surprisingly, this does not feature in our story. Nor does the Giltspur Street Compter – a small gaol at the southern end of the street, opposite Newgate, that held many convicted under the Vagrancy Act.

18 The *Weekly Dispatch*, 27 November 1831.

19 The Bishops lived near the Red Lion inn, which was at 90 North Hill (demolished in 1900), and the Wrestlers inn, which dates back to 1547 and today still holds the medieval Swearing on the Horns of Highgate drinking ritual. John Bishop the younger's pub of choice, the Green Dragon (which dated back to at least 1730), was at 10 North Road, the southern end of North Hill; it was demolished in 1898 and Highgate School is on the site.

20 Their marriage licence is in the St Leonard's, Shoreditch, marriage

registers at Guildhall Library and it reveals that Sarah was illiterate, signing with an X.

St Leonard's, by architect George Dance the Elder (1695–1768), was completed in 1740, and still stands, at the busy junction of Shoreditch High Street, Old Street, Kingsland Road and Hackney Road.

21 The *Morning Advertiser*, 25 November 1831.

22 London Metropolitan Archives, Clerkenwell New Prison Committals Lists, MJ/CC/V/003.

23 George Laval Chesterton, *Revelations of Prison Life* (1856), pp.28–30.

24 Old Bailey Sessions Papers, First Session, 1827, p.31.

25 Report in *The Times* of 2 April 1831 and the *Morning Herald* of the same date.

26 The *Globe and Traveller*, 5 December 1831.

27 *The Victoria History of the Counties of England: A History of the County of Middlesex*, Volume 11, *Early Stepney with Bethnal Green* (1998), p.114.

28 Figures given in the pamphlet *Evidence of the Reverend William Stone* etc.

29 'Four Views of London', an anonymous essay in the June 1833 issue of the *New Monthly Magazine*.

30 Editions of 7 November 1831 and 12 November 1831 respectively.

31 The Heads' baptisms and burials took place at St Leonard's Church, Bridgnorth; the registers are held in the Shropshire Records and Research Centre in Shrewsbury, at P40/68 to P40/71 (1803–8).

In a number of accounts, including those published by the Crown and by *The Times*, his names are used interchangeably, and James Williams and James Head are also thrown into the mix.

32 *Old Bailey Experience: Criminal Jurisprudence and the Actual Working of our Penal Code of Laws*, anon (James Harmer?), 1833, p.112.

33 Old Bailey Sessions Papers, Fourth Session, 1827, p.323. Pontifex's had been in business since 1780 and by 1831 stretched almost halfway down Shoe Lane on the east side; its main building survived until 1894. Source: *The Parish of St Andrew Holborn* by Caroline M. Barron (1979), pp.107–8.

34 Public Record Office, The Newgate List, 1826–8, PCOM 2/199.

35 The riots are referred to in Michael Ignatieff's *A Just Measure of Pain: The Penitentiary in the Industrial Revolution, 1750–1850* (1978), p.172.

36 The *Weekly Dispatch*, 11 December 1831. If found guilty, Williams would have faced a fine of £100.

37 St Leonard's, Shoreditch, marriage registers, Guildhall Library; Rhoda was illiterate, signing with an X. Thomas Head, 'bachelor of this parish', could read and write.

The records of St Leonard's, Shoreditch, also show that one Mary Ann Bishop died aged five months in the workhouse on 2 March 1828; it is possible this was a daughter of John and Sarah.

38 Dorset Street was a short road running east–west just north of Rockingham Street. Today, the Rockingham Estate, post-war London County Council flats, covers the site, approximately where Rennie House stands.

39 Clare Market opened in 1657. Until 1900 it stood where the north-eastern section of Aldwych is today. Both New Inn and Clare Market disappeared during the construction of Aldwych and Kingsway, though a small section of street bearing the name Clare Market remains.

40 Figures given by journalist Charles Knight writing in 1841 in his book *London*, Volume 1, p.164 – a compendium of essays on the capital previously published as newspaper columns.

3 The Thickest Part

1 *Oliver Twist*, Chapter 54.
2 Public Record Office, Bow Street Magistrates' Outgoing Correspondence, MEPO 1/49 and 1/50.
3 Public Record Office, Home Office Letters, HO 59/2.
4 Report of the hearing in *The Times*, 22 November 1831.
5 Public Record Office, Petitions and Pardons 1830–1, HO 64/2.
6 Public Record Office, Home Office Domestic Letter Book, Volume 67, letter dated 15 November 1831, HO 43/41.
7 Middle Row stood at the bottom of Gray's Inn Road in front of Staple Inn and comprised a small cluster of Tudor buildings forming an island in the middle of High Holborn. It was pulled down in 1866 to widen the road.
8 *The Times*, 19 November 1831.
9 The *Globe and Traveller*, 12 November 1831.

Nag's Head Court is still there; timber merchants Travis Perkins use most of it as a private yard. All the buildings from Carpenter and May's day are long gone.

10 The outer walls and basement cells of the Clerkenwell New Prison (also called the Clerkenwell House of Detention) still stand, at Clerkenwell Close.
11 Exchange reported in the *Sun*, 14 November 1831.
12 'A Detective Police Party', in *Household Words*, 27 July 1850, reprinted in *Dickens' Journalism: The Amusements of the People and Other Papers*, edited by Michael Slater (1996), Volume 2 of the *Dent Uniform Edition of Dickens' Journalism*.

In *Oliver Twist*, Dickens had shown his contempt for their acumen by naming the two Runners called upon to investigate a burglary Blathers and Duff.

13 In a stimulating essay, historian Ruth Paley has disputed the stereotype of the Charley, claiming that he was no older, more decrepit or badly paid than the majority of New Police officers in the early years of the Metropolitan Police; 'An Imperfect, Inadequate and Wretched System?': Policing London Before Peel', in *Criminal Justice History*, Volume 10 (1989), pp.95–130. Certainly, a look through papers in the Public Record Office (at MEPO 1/44) shows a high turnover of recruits in the early years of the Met, with dismissals given largely on grounds of lack of physical fitness, absenteeism and drunkenness. The first Metropolitan Police officer to be sworn in, PC William Atkinson, was sacked within an hour for drunkenness, as was the second, PC William Alcock. Some 1,790 of the first 2,800 men enlisted were sacked for being drunk on duty.

14 The *Morning Chronicle*, 26 September 1828.

15 Papers at the Public Record Office (at MEPO 1/44) include what amounts to an apology from Commissioner Rowan to the editor of *The Times* for the number of reprimands and dismissals of Metropolitan Police officers, dated 11 November 1830; while on 16 December 1830 the chief clerk of Bow Street wrote to the editors of *The Times*, the *Morning Chronicle* and the *Morning Herald* to deny reports that there were plans to enlarge the force.

16 *Memoirs of a Bow Street Runner* by Henry Goddard; written in 1856 but not published until 1956.

17 The most recent literary sensation before Vidocq's *Mémoires* – similarly reaching all classes of Londoner – had been Pierce Egan's *Life in London* books, published (and much plagiarised) between 1821 and 1828. The appeal of Egan's comic series lay in its evocation of high life and low life, with its heroes crossing social boundaries in a way that real Londoners could not.

18 *Report*, p.73.

19 *The Report from the Select Committee into the State of the Police of the Metropolis*, 1828, hereafter referred to as *Report of the 1828 Police Select Committee*, p.76.

20 *Ibid*, p.80. The Marquis of Anglesey is still there; the Brown Bear is no more.

21 *Report from the Select Committee on Allegations Relative to the Conduct of Certain Magistrates in the Holborn Division of Middlesex in Granting Licences for Victualling Houses*, 1833, p.261.

22 Public Record Office, Letter from Richard Mayne dated 19 May 1830, MEPO 1/44 3.

23 Among Minshull's judgements to cause merriment and alarm in equal

measure was his decision in December 1831 to commit to gaol four boys – itinerant pedlars of broadsheets – for selling prints of a picture of a child playing with a kitten that was dressed in a petticoat; Minshull took it into his head that this picture was somehow indecent, and, according to the *Sun* of 26 December 1831, his aim 'was to stop the circulation of such an infamous publication'. The article goes on to sneer that if Minshull is right, the reporter would never let his grandmother visit the British Museum again, in case any of the antiquities should inflame her passions.

24 *The First Detectives* by Belton Cobb (1957).
25 *British Police and the Democratic Ideal* by Charles Reith (1943), pp.90–3.
26 The Place Papers, British Museum Add Mss 27,789, Volume 1, ff184–6.
27 *Report of the 1828 Police Select Committee*, p.81.

4 *Houseless Wretches*

1 *Lord Melbourne* by L.G. Mitchell (1997), p.152.
   William Lamb, second Viscount Melbourne (1779–1848), became Home Secretary in November 1830 in the Whig government led by Earl Grey; his under-secretary was his brother, George.
2 Public Record Office, Petitions and Pardons 1830–1, HO 64/2.
3 The *Morning Advertiser*, 9 November 1831.
4 He worked at Warren's blacking factory at 30 Hungerford Stairs, just off the Strand, near to where Charing Cross station stands today, and then in Chandos Street when the factory moved premises. The work involved pasting labels on to pots of blacking – used to keep fire-grates, stoves, boots and metalwork freshly black. In Camden his landlady was Mrs Roylance, 'a reduced old lady', as he later described her, whose house was in Little College Street. Source: *The Life of Charles Dickens* by John Forster (1872), Volume 1, pp.31–8.
5 John Wontner's evidence in the *Report from the Select Committee appointed to Inquire into the Cause of the Increase in the Number of Commitments and Convictions in London and Middlesex*, 1828, p.54.
6 *The Times*, 21 March 1826.
7 *The Sixth Report of the London Society for the Suppression of Mendicity* (1824).
8 The *Morning Chronicle* of 27 September 1829 reported 120 vagrants being repeatedly cleared from a brick-field in Ratcliffe, East London, where they were accustomed to spending the night; they included children as young as eleven years old.
9 The *Morning Post*, 29 September 1828.
10 *Report*, Appendix D, p.317. An attempt to assess each child's educational

level is made in this table; Elizabeth Butler could make out a few words but was unable to write; her only schooling had been at a Sunday school in Whitechapel. The majority of children who passed through London's judicial and penal systems in the 1820s seemed to have acquired at least a small degree of literacy.

The Tothill Fields bridewell that held Elizabeth Butler occupied the site of today's Westminster Cathedral. The main Bridewell prison stood just west of New Bridge Street, Blackfriars.

11 The Corn Laws, introduced in 1804, set high import tariffs to prevent foreign corn coming into the country until British corn had attained a certain price, whereupon the tariff dropped. This protectionism kept bread prices high until the repeal of the Corn Laws in 1846. By contrast, 'free trade' had ensured the collapse of the English silk industry.

12 From Brenton's open letter to the Bishop of London, published in 1832 in pamphlet form as part of a series of addresses to the great and good entitled *On Population, Agriculture, Poor Laws and Juvenile Vagrancy.*

On retiring from the navy, Brenton (1774–1839) founded the Society for the Relief of Shipwrecked Mariners and the Children's Friend Society and set up the Brenton Juvenile Asylum at East Ham. He was also on the board of management of the Society for the Suppression of Juvenile Vagrancy.

13 London would not get a unitary authority until 1888 (decades after Britain's other cities) with the creation of the London County Council. Until then, London's local government was administered by its parish vestries – of medieval origin – and, in the last two-thirds of the century, a series of separate boards for lighting, paving and 'works' (construction) and so on.

14 For example, of 3,035 convictions for vagrancy between February 1827 and April 1828, only 73 were properly documented by London magistrates, which meant that almost 3,000 people were being detained in prison with no written proof of their guilt, or of the evidence that had been used to convict them. Source: the evidence of Serjeant Pell, a Middlesex magistrate, given to the 1828 Police Select Committee; *Report*, p.236.

15 The edition of 24 November 1831. Similarly, police officers are on record for showing kindness to vagrants. In 1831 officers took a sick and homeless man to St Giles workhouse in order to find him a meal and a bed for the night but were told by the doorkeeper that since it was after nine o'clock at night there could be no new admission, and that they could take the man 'to hell'. Instead, the officers formally arrested the beggar to give him shelter in a tiny cell in Covent Garden's Dyott Street station.

In the morning they found him dead. Source: The *Lancet*, 13 August 1831.

16 The hall is long gone, though its name remains, in White Conduit Street.

17 A total of nineteen men were executed for taking part in Swing disturbances.

18 Conway lived at 52 North Road, close to the Bishop family home. Source: *Report from the Select Committee on the Existing Laws Relating to Vagrants*, 1821, p.39.

19 *The Twelfth Report of the London Society for the Suppression of Mendicity* (1830). One of the Dicity's founders was William Henry Bodkin, who crops up later in our story as a prosecuting counsel at the Old Bailey. Bodkin had also been chairman of the Houseless Poor Association charity and had a place on the 1828 Police Select Committee.

20 *The Eleventh Report of the London Society for the Suppression of Mendicity* (1829).

21 The *Morning Chronicle*, 22 September 1829. Laing would be satirised by Charles Dickens as the arrogant and vicious magistrate Fang in *Oliver Twist* (Chapter 11), while the satirical newspaper *Figaro in London* claimed of Laing, 'his inhumanity is as proverbial as his ignorance'; issue dated 24 December 1831.

22 *The Twelfth Report of the London Society for the Suppression of Mendicity* (1830). The year before, the following people had arrived at Red Lion Square:

> 'MS', 17, a female pilferer, keeps running from home;
>
> 'EB', 21, a Bristol girl, persistently begs in London;
>
> 'AG', 30, deserted by husband and has a child, no legal settlement given since she is Irish, though has spent 19 years in London;
>
> 'CF', 12, a girl sent out to beg by her mother;
>
> 'JR', 14, a Scot, his father's vessel sailed and he was abandoned in London, taken in by a woman, sent to the Society and thence to Scotland;
>
> 'TL', and 'WL', two strong, lazy, idle fellows arrested for infesting the Kent Road and given three months in Guildford jail;
>
> 'RG', borrowed a wife and three children to beg at the office;
>
> 'PC', 16, 'Swiss', an impostor with a wealthy brother;
>
> 'WM', queued at the dock gates for fourteen days applying to get shifts;
>
> 'MC', 29, Irish with four children, found in a doorway in Chancery Lane with three women standing by looking worried, all were fakes, even the children – whatever money is procured by the deception is equally divided, and the night spent most jovially in the purlieus of St Giles.

Source: *The Eleventh Report of the London Society for the Suppression of Mendicity* (1829).

23   *The Twelfth Report of the London Society for the Suppression of Mendicity* (1830).

24   *The Times*, 2 April 1834.

25   Young Charles Dickens amused himself by looking at the pineapples during his lunch hour. Source: *The Life of Charles Dickens* by John Forster, Volume I, p.36.

26   *The Cries of London* by J.T. Smith (1839).

27   *Eighth Report* (1826).

28   The *Globe and Traveller*, 12 November 1831.

29   Two books contain fascinating background to the trade in Italian children: *The Little Slaves of the Harp* by John E. Zucchi (1992); and *Italian Immigrants in 19th-Century Britain: Realities and Images* by Lucio Sponza (1988).

30   Giuseppe Leonardi, fifteen, died of lung disease – thought to have been brought on by neglect – in St Giles workhouse in 1845; his *padrone*, Rabbiotti, was charged with manslaughter but acquitted. In 1861, five-year-old Carminello Ada died in St Pancras workhouse after having been found suspended by his arms and legs from a ceiling and covered in bite marks. Source: *The Little Slaves of the Harp*.

31   *The Times*, 2 April 1834. Stuart failed to free the boys, and he left the court declaring his intention to petition Lord Melbourne for their release, though I have been unable to find any such petition in the surviving Home Office records in the Public Record Office.

Stuart (1803–54) was the grandson of Thomas Coutts, banking tycoon. His cousin was the philanthropist Angela Burdett-Coutts, who in 1837 would inherit the Coutts fortune.

32   Charles MacFarlane, *Popular Customs, Sports and Recollections of the South of Italy* (1846), p.135. Charles Knight, *London*, Volume I (1841), p.423.

5 *Systematic Slaughter*

1   *The Registers of St Paul's Church, Covent Garden*, edited by the Reverend William H. Hunt. Volume 5, *Burials, 1752–1853* (published in 1909). The entry says 'supposed to be about 14'.

Although the graveyard in Cleveland Street has been cleared, the workhouse building, dating from 1778, remains as the outpatients' department of the Middlesex Hospital.

2   14 November 1831.

3   Method described in *The Sack 'Em Up Men* by Richard L. Hewer (1928), p.152.

4   *The Life of Sir Astley Cooper* by Bransby Cooper (1843), p.395.
5   The *Weekly Dispatch*, 20 November 1831; and the *Observer* of the same date.
6   21 November 1831.
7   The *Morning Advertiser*, 12 November 1831.

6 Houseless Wretches Again

1   Horsey, Johnson, Dancing Doll Man and Blind Charles Wood feature in J.T. Smith's *Vagabondiana* (1817).

   In journalist Charles Knight's book *London*, Volume 1, Samuel Horsey is also fondly remembered as 'half a Hercules' (p.424), though it is claimed that Horsey had lost his limbs in London's anti-Catholic Gordon Riots of 1780, and not as a result of injuries sustained in the Napoleonic Wars, as Smith believed.

2   Tim Buc Too was also known as Brutus Billy and he lived in White Horse Yard, off Stanhope Street, Drury Lane, dying in 1854 at the age of eighty-seven. Source: *Some Account of the Parish of Saint Clement Danes Past and Present* by John Diprose (1868), p.164.

   'TL' is mentioned in *The Thirteenth Report of the Society for the Suppression of Mendicity* (1831). Work on Marc Isambard Brunel's tunnel from Wapping to Rotherhithe started in 1825 but was not to be completed until 1840, by which time ten men had died during construction and the project was over budget. *The Times* dubbed it the Great Bore.

3   Knight, *London*, Volume I, p.424.

4   *Report of the 1828 Police Select Committee*, p.83.

5   *Suggestions for the Architectural Improvement of the Western Part of London* by Sydney Smirke (1834).

6   De Quincey, 'The Nation of London', an essay of 1834, republished in *The Selected Writings of Thomas De Quincey*, edited by Philip Van Doren Stern (1939), p.173; Poe, 'The Man of the Crowd' (1840), reprinted in *Selected Tales*, edited by Julian Symons (1980); and Dr John Hogg, *London As It Is* (1837).

   Hogg claimed that even the upper-class London male was haggard, glassy-eyed and emaciated: 'Everything is getting later and later, due to the pressure of commerce and business,' he diagnosed, p.342.

7   To what extent the police took advantage of these powers has been discussed by Steven Inwood in his essay 'Policing London's Morals: the Metropolitan Police and Popular Culture, 1829–1850', in the *London Journal*, Volume 15, Number 2, 1990, pp.129–46. Inwood points out that although the following activities were banned from 1839, accounts from

the 1840s and later show that they nevertheless proliferated: causing public obstruction or danger with animals or vehicles; rolling tubs, hoops and wheels unnecessarily; sticking bills; writing on walls; using threatening or abusive words or behaviour; using noisy instruments in the process of begging, selling or entertaining in the street; throwing stones; lighting fires/fireworks; ringing or knocking at doors; putting out lamps; soliciting/loitering; selling indecent pictures; singing indecent songs; using profane language; flying kites and using a dog-cart.

8 George Boulton Mainwaring, a JP at Worship Street magistrates' court – one of the offices that dealt with the East End of London. *Report from the Select Committee on the Existing Laws Relating to Vagrants*, 1821, p.61.

9 Williams Burke and Hare and their wives spent a large portion of the proceed of murder on ostentatious clothing; their new glamour was noted by neighbours, who did not suspect how they had come into the money.

10 *Report of the 1828 Police Select Committee*, p.128.

11 John Wade, *A Treatise on the Police and Crimes of the Metropolis* (1829), p.135.

12 There were many others engaged in the trade of London typologising: Francis Grose, for instance, published his *Lexicon Balatronicum: A Dictionary of Buckish Slang, University Wit, and Pickpocket Eloquence* in 1823; and *The Stranger's Guide, or Frauds of London Detected* was published in 1808 by George Smeeton, who later published *Doings in London*, in 1828.

13 Ann Taylor story from the *Morning Chronicle*, 29 September 1829; Taylor was sentenced by magistrates to three months in the Bridewell for attempting to obtain charity under false pretences. Jane Weston case reported in the *Hue and Cry*, 27 January 1826. James Prior case in the *Hue and Cry*, 7 February 1827.

14 J.T. Smith, *The Cries of London*.

15 *Report of the 1828 Police Select Committee*, p.128.

16 The alderman's comment was reported in the *Morning Chronicle*, 6 October 1829; the attraction of the Temple Bar shenanigans is mentioned in *British Police and the Democratic Ideal* by Charles Reith, p.73.

17 31 March 1832.

18 *Report*, p.81.

19 5 Geo IV c 83.

20 The 1662 Act was modified over the course of the eighteenth century and places of settlement could be changed in a number of other ways: paying £10 per annum or more in rent in a new parish automatically granted re-settlement, as did the payment of local taxes for a specified period, the completion of a year's service in a parish office or the fulfilment of an indentured apprenticeship – all of which factors tended to favour those who were either reasonably wealthy or educated or in a fairly

secure trade. However, some parishes were 'closed', forbidding any kind of settlement to newcomers in order to keep the poor rates down.

James Stephen Taylor's excellent book *Poverty, Migration and Settlement in the Industrial Revolution* (1989) gives many examples of settlement disputes within the City of London's St Martin Vintry ward.

21 A Select Committee of 1828 claimed that parish poor relief was un-coordinated across the country, and that while some people received help without having to perform any parochial tasks, others had to do a great deal of work; the level of financial support given was supposed to reflect the number of people the head of the family maintained. Some parishes refused to give any outdoor relief, insisting that the work-house was the only option, even for the sick or elderly; the Committee estimated that nine out of ten impoverished people were refusing to go into the workhouse – even if that were the only source of aid. Source: *Report from the Select Committee on that Part of the Poor Laws relating to the Employment or Relief of Able-Bodied Persons from the Poor Rate*, 1828, p.169.

22 Richard Burn's five-volume *Justice of the Peace and Parish Officer* – a manual of legal rules and precedents for JPs, published in various editions from 1818 onwards – dedicated one whole volume, Volume 4, at 1,286 pages, to the 'relief and ordering of the poor', with advice on settlements and removal orders.

23 *A Treatise on the Police and Crimes of the Metropolis*, pp.137–40. Wade's life's work was to expose in print the idiocies and inequities of a nation ruled by a backward-looking aristocracy. A working man made good (he had been a wool-sorter), he was a Benthamite Radical, whose *Extraordinary Black Book* (1831) was colloquially known as 'the Reformer's Bible' as it listed the abuses of the undemocratic, unaccountable bodies that controlled British public life.

24 The *Morning Chronicle*, 9 October 1829.

25 Wade's *Treatise*, p.6; *The Selected Writings of Thomas De Quincey*, pp.173–4; Grant, *The Great Metropolis*, Volume 1 (1837), p.6.

26 J.T. Smith, *Vagabondiana*.

The Select Committee that investigated vagrancy in 1821 heard evidence from Yorkshire that no member of the working class ever refused money to a blind beggar, and would even borrow in order to be able to give alms; those in receipt of parish relief had also been spotted helping beggars. *Report from the Select Committee on the Existing Laws Relating to Vagrants*, 1821.

27 Quoted by Edward Gibbon Wakefield in *Facts Relating to the Punishment of Death in the Metropolis* (1831), p.210.

28 *Lord Melbourne* by L.G. Mitchell, p.127.
29 The *Weekly Dispatch*, 20 November 1831.

7 Neighbours

1 Edwin Chadwick, 'Preventive Police', an essay in *The London Review* (1829); Grant, *The Great Metropolis*, Volume 1, p.10; Wade's *Treatise*, p.6.
2 Dodd was appointed to his position in June 1831 at a wage of 25 shillings a week; his predecessor had been sacked for sexually assaulting a woman in custody. Source: Public Record Office, Bow Street Magistrates' Outgoing Correspondence, MEPO 1/49 and 1/50.

8 Meat – an Interlude

1 Evidence given to the second Select Committee on the State of Smithfield Market, 1828, p.72: hereafter referred to as *The 1828 Report on Smithfield Market*.
2 An anonymous pamphlet of 1847 entitled *Smithfield and the Slaughterhouses*.
3 *Report of the 1828 Police Select Committee*, p.292.
4 Evidence of John Bumpas, local bookseller, *The 1828 Report on Smithfield Market*, p.72.
5 *Ibid.*, p.16. Later in the century, Charles Dickens recounted the tale of another victim of Smithfield's droving practices, whom he discovered while visiting the vast St Luke's insane asylum, which stood in Old Street from 1782 to 1966, to the north-west of the present underground station, '. . . a woman of great strength and energy, who had been driven mad by an infuriated ox in the streets – an inconvenience not in itself worth mentioning, for which the inhabitants of London are frequently indebted to their inestimable Corporation. She seized the creature literally by the horns, and so, as long as life and limb were in peril, vigorously held him; but the danger over, she lost her sense.' 'A Curious Dance Round a Curious Tree' in *Household Words*, 17 January 1852.
6 *The 1828 Report on Smithfield Market*, pp.144–5.
7 Public Record Office, Daily Police Reports, HO 62/8.
8 It is likely that the publication of this pamphlet was timed to coincide with the attempt, in 1823, to pass a parliamentary act banning animal fights and baiting (the measure was defeated in the Commons by twenty-nine votes to eighteen); and with parliamentary debate on the forthcoming Vagrancy Bill.

9 *The 1828 Report on Smithfield Market*, p.15; evidence of William Hickson, shoe warehouse owner.

10 Issue dated Saturday 1 October 1825.

11 *The 1828 Report on Smithfield Market*, p.148; evidence of William Collins, salesman.

12 *The Times*, 25 February 1832. *Wives for Sale* by S.P. Menefee (1981) explores the British phenomenon of wife-selling in detail.

13 Chapter 21: The Expedition; *Oliver Twist* (1837–8). *Great Expectations* Chapter 20; though written in 1860–1, *Great Expectations* is set in the 1820s/early 1830s.

14 *The 1828 Report on Smithfield Market* contains horrifying eyewitness accounts of slaughter, though many of these are comments on the (even more appalling) conditions in the slaughterhouses of Whitechapel and Shoreditch. Though it is true that many of the accusations were made by reformers keen to provoke change, the substance of their reports was not challenged by any of the slaughtermen/butchers who also gave evidence to the Committee.

15 John Hogg, *London As It Is*; Hogg estimated that around 10,000 cows were kept for milk in London yards and cellars.

16 Evidence on horse slaughter in Smithfield was given to the 1828 Police Select Committee (*Report*, p.186) by one Charles Starbuck, the stockbroker who mistakenly identified an Italian boy to the coroner's court of St Paul's, Covent Garden. Starbuck was a Quaker and involved in a number of reform campaigns – the 'Friends' were renowned for their political lobbying skills. Although he claimed not to be a member of an anti-cruelty league, Starbuck was most keen to tell the 1828 Police Select Committee that he had himself inspected knackers' yards in Cow Cross, Smithfield, and found half-starved horses awaiting slaughter – many of them stolen, in his opinion.

It is puzzling that Starbuck was co-opted on to the list of witnesses, since he had no obvious expertise or involvement in the trade; it may be that he enjoyed some kind of personal rapport with whoever convened the witnesses – perhaps using whatever networks Quakers had at their disposal – and thus a channel for his views was opened up.

17 The hospital treated, and learned from, market injuries. *Histories of Specimens in the Museum*, a logbook compiled by surgeons Edward Stanley and James Paget between 1832 and 1845, describes a typical case of 'a drover, 25, brought into the hospital for a wound in the back part of the right leg which had bled profusely. His boot was full of arterial blood and his steps could be traced for some way across the square of the hospital and in Smithfield in large spots of blood. The wound had been inflicted

by a large pointed instrument and had passed about two inches deep.'
Three days after admission, 'delirium tremens' set in, and the drover died
not long after. Source: manuscript volume MU3 in St Bartholomew's
Hospital Archives, p.139.

18 The phrase belongs to 1828 Smithfield Select Committee witness Michael
Scales; *Report*, p.129.

19 Quoted in *Old and New London*, edited by Walter Thornbury, Volume 2,
p.350 (in six volumes, published 1879–85). 'Aleph's' original column had
appeared in the newspaper the *City Press*.

The city fog of these years – the True London Particular – had a taste
and smell too, according to the writer of *The Mirror of the Months* in 1831:
'There is something tangible in a London fog . . . you can feel what you
breathe and see it too . . . the taste of it, when dashed with a due seasoning
of sea-coal smoke, is far from insipid. It is also meat and drink at the
same time, something between an egg flip and omelette soufflé, but much
more digestible than either.' Reprinted in the *Weekly Dispatch*, 13 November
1831.

20 After the Act of Union of 1801, Irish MPs sat in Westminster.

Main sources of information on Richard Martin: *Humanity Dick* by
Shevawn Lynam (1975); *Richard Martin* by Wellesley Pain (1925); *Valiant
Crusade* by A.W. Moss (1961); *A Century of Work for Animals* by E. Fairholme
and Wellesley Pain (1924).

21 After losing all his spare change at cock-fighting at Hockley-in-the-Hole,
Saffron Hill, George IV turned up at the Castle inn – on the corner of
Cowcross Street and Turnmill Street – and pledged his watch and chain
to pay off his gaming debts. As a favour to the obliging landlord, the pub
was granted a licence to receive pledges as well as sell alcohol – a unique
honour. Today, the Castle still has its pawnbroker status, plus a highly flat-
tering portrait of George IV standing at the bar, to commemorate his visit.

22 Today, Portcullis House is near the spot. Dickens reveals the gloomy
decrepitude of Manchester Buildings in *Nicholas Nickleby*, Chapter 16.

23 *Richard Martin* by Wellesley Pain, p.91.

24 Reported in *François Magendie* by J.M.D. Olmsted (1944), p.140.

25 Bell and Magendie quotes, *ibid.*, p.93 and pp.117–18.

26 From the *Lancet*, quoted in Isobel Rae's biography *Knox the Anatomist* (1964),
p.17.

27 *A Century of Work for Animals*, pp.35–6.

28 The name has nothing to do with killing; the inn's first landlord, in 1692,
was Thomas Slaughter. Slaughter's stood on the south-west corner of the
junction with Cranbourn Street – today a coffee/sandwich chain has the
site.

29 *The 1828 Report on Smithfield Market*, p.48.

30 *Cursory Remarks on the Evil Tendency of Unrestrained Cruelty, Particularly on That Practised at Smithfield Market* (1823), pp.7–12.

31 Recalled by Percy Fitzgerald in his *Chronicles of a Bow Street Police Officer* (1888).

32 The phrase is from the anonymous pamphlet *Smithfield and the Slaughter-houses*, p.6.

33 The wiping out of slums was not to be the main thrust of nineteenth-century metropolitan improvements, but it was viewed as a highly desirable side-effect. Run-down districts were almost always the location for new roads and railway lines, since low-grade housing stock was the cheapest to buy up for demolition.

34 George Godwin, *Town Swamps and Social Bridges* (1859), p.13. Frying Pan Alley got in the way of Clerkenwell Road in 1878.

35 Old Bailey Sessions Papers, Fourth Session, 1827, p.323; evidence of James Spoor.

36 But impossible now: it lies approximately where the Underground runs alongside Farringdon Road, on a latitude with Benjamin Street.

9 *Whatever Has Happened to Fanny?*

1 'The Diseased Appetite for Horrors' in the *Examiner*, 11 December 1831, p.787; reprinted in Fontblanque's book *England Under Seven Administrations* (1837).

2 Harmer (1777–1853) was the orphan of a Spitalfields weaver and rose to become a wealthy attorney. He would be elected alderman of the City ward of Farringdon Without in 1833 and became a sheriff of London and Middlesex and proprietor of the campaigning newspaper the *Weekly Dispatch*. He was a prolific pamphleteer on the subject of criminal law reform, and is the most likely candidate for author of the anonymous 1832 account of the Bishop and Williams case, *The History of the London Burkers*, which relied heavily on *The Times*'s account of the investigation. Harmer had already published a number of reformist pamphlets arising from his intimate knowledge of some of London's most notable trials, including those of John Holloway and Owen Haggerty, hanged for murder in 1807, though they may have been innocent. Harmer knew personally the Reverend Dr Cotton, the vicar – or 'Ordinary' – of Newgate, and this may have given him greater access to the accused and the condemned.

I also believe Harmer to be the author of the anonymous book *Old Bailey Experience: Criminal Jurisprudence and the Actual Working of our Penal Code of Laws* (1833), which has variously been attributed to John Wontner (governor of Newgate Prison) and Edward Gibbon Wakefield (who was once a schoolmaster in Newgate during his three-year sentence for eloping with an heiress, and who wrote the influential *Facts Relating to the Punishment of Death in the Metropolis*, published in 1831). Close reading shows that both Wontner and Wakefield were robustly criticised for their views on penal matters in *Old Bailey Experience*. The author of *Old Bailey Experience* also mentions that he met James May at Newgate, which suggests a shared authorship with *The History of the London Burkers*.

3 Two days later, James Gardener, a cart-driver, of Caroline Place, Lambeth, was charged with assaulting White, and of attacking another boy, fourteen-year-old Thomas Hammond, in Webber Street, Waterloo, at eleven o'clock at night. Gardener denied the pitch-plaster attack on White but admitted grabbing Hammond by the wrists, saying he had been so drunk, he could remember nothing about the incident. Source: the *Globe and Traveller*, 25 November 1831.

4 Henry Edward case, the *Morning Advertiser*, 22 November 1831; Martha Allenby and Henry Fore cases, *ibid.*, 2 December 1831; Elizabeth Turner case, the *Globe and Traveller*, 15 November 1831.

5 The *Globe and Traveller*, 1 December 1831.

6 Report in the *Weekly Dispatch*, 11 December 1831. Details of the Culkin case are taken from the Old Bailey Sessions Papers, Second Session, 1832, pp.178–84.

Hartshorn Court is no more; Broad Arrow Court is today's Milton Court.

7 The *Morning Advertiser* of 12 December 1831 carried a news story that is fairly typical of the style in which such cases were reported: 'J. Moore, an old and deformed pauper, who walks on crutches, and who has been frequently before the magistrates for various outrages and assaults, was charged with committing a series of the most indecent attacks on several little girls in Shadwell workhouse. The evidence against the prisoner was wholly unfit for publication.' An 'outrage' was one of the contemporary euphemisms for rape.

Sexual assaults within the family were openly reported too. The *Morning Chronicle* of 11 October 1829 published the case of Alexander Barry, in his fifties, who was taken to court by his nineteen-year-old daughter Elizabeth on a charge of attempted rape; she said that he had been 'repeatedly taking liberties with [her] person' since she was six years old. Joseph Woodhouse, meanwhile, 'a fiend in human shape', was executed at Chester for raping his eleven-year-old daughter. Source: the *Morning Chronicle*, 29 September 1829.

8   *The Times*, 28 November 1831; the *Morning Advertiser* and the *Sun* of the
    same day; the *Globe and Traveller*, 26 and 29 November 1831; the *Observer*
    4 December 1831.

9   These tiny streets are largely given over to the motor trade now, with
    lock-ups, repair-shops and a large NCP car-park.

10 According to Bransby Cooper in *The Life of Sir Astley Cooper*, pp.374–6.

11 John Flint South (1797–1882) had succeeded Sir Astley Cooper as demon-
    strator of anatomy on the baronet's retirement in 1825. Apparently 'deeply
    religious' (according to his entry in *Plarr's Lives of the Fellows of the Royal
    College of Physicians of England*), South retired early, in 1841, 'due to neurosis'.
    South's professional reminiscences, *Memorials of the Craft of Surgery in England*
    (1886), contain little on his dealings with resurrectionists.

12 This large coaching inn stood on the northern corner with Camomile
    Street and was demolished in 1863 for architect John Gibson's stunning
    National Provincial Bank, which still stands today, as Gibson Hall.

13 Pilcher (1801–55) was a surgeon and an ear specialist.

10 A Horrid System

1   J.F. Clarke was one of the young doctors present in the watch-house, and
    he gives an account of the Italian Boy autopsy in his memoirs,
    Autobiographical Recollections of the Medical Profession (1874), pp.101–2; Clarke
    was on the editorial team of the *Lancet*, and his autobiography has all the
    gossipy scurrility of Thomas Wakely's journal.

    The early eighteenth-century watch-house ('a miserable hole',
    according to Clarke), which was used as a makeshift police station/gaol,
    with underground cells, was demolished in 1833, having been made obso-
    lete by the completion in 1832 of a police station at numbers 33 and 34
    Bow Street, on the east side; the public toilets alongside St Paul's church
    no doubt fill the space that the watch-house cells once occupied.

    The Unicorn tavern next door, which doubled as a coroner's court in
    the 1820s and 1830s, was demolished in 1888 to make way for the Norman
    Shaw office block that still stands.

2   The Great Windmill Street school was founded in 1737 and closed in
    1835; in 1878 the building was reconstructed as part of the Lyric Theatre,
    Shaftesbury Avenue.

    Interestingly, the rear of Joseph Carpue's anatomy school at 72 Dean
    Street, Soho, was also incorporated into a theatre, when, in 1840, a Miss
    Kelly built the Royalty next door. (Carpue had vacated his school in 1833.)
    In 1845, Charles Dickens performed at Miss Kelly's theatre in Ben Jonson's

Every Man in his Humour. It is likely that Dickens knew of the building's history, since as a child he had been a regular visitor to the house, at 10 Gerrard Street, Soho, of his maternal uncle, Thomas Culliford Barrow, when Barrow was laid up with a broken thigh during the winter of 1822–3. Eventually, the leg had to be amputated, and it was taken off by Carpue in the Dean Street school. Barrow fainted during the operation, and Dickens's family lore had it that when he came round, he asked, 'Where's my leg?' and was told by Carpue, 'Under the table.' Source: 'The Barber of Dean Street' by William J. Carlton in the *Dickensian*, Volume 48, Part 1, Number 301 (1952), p.8.

3   *King's and Some King's Men* by H. Willoughby Lyle (1935), p.7.

4   The *Lancet*, 14 September 1833.

5   *Ibid.*, 16 October 1831.

6   *Ibid.*, 29 September 1832.

7   *Ibid.*, 3 December 1831.

8   *The Centenary History of King's College London* by F.J.C. Hearnshaw (1928), p.22.

9   *Report from the Select Committee on Medical Education*, Part 2 (1834), Q6714/ p.203.

10 This had been Sir Astley's price list according to the *Lancet*, 3 November 1832.

11 The Brookesian building survived until the early 1920s, having served as offices to a publisher and then an architectural practice. Blenheim Steps is today Ramillies Street, and the school was near the eastern corner with Great Marlborough Street.

   In his back garden, Brookes had constructed his Vivarium – a grotto-like folly built of rock to which were chained live birds and animals, including an eagle, a hawk, an owl, pheasants, foxes, raccoons and a tortoise. The site of the garden is now 1 and 2 Ramillies Street. Source: 'Joshua Brookes's Vivarium' by Tim Knox, an essay in *The London Gardener, or The Gardener's Intelligencer*, Volume 3 (1997–8).

12 Joseph Constantin Carpue (1764–1846) was of Spanish descent, born in Brook Green, Hammersmith, and had been a priest, bookseller, barrister and actor before entering the medical profession; later he became a Liberal member of parliament. A tall, ungainly, grey-haired man, he always dressed in black with a huge white neckerchief. He was said to be one of the best anatomical draughtsmen in London but nevertheless was one of a number of anatomists/surgeons ostracised by the medical establishment. A pioneer of plastic surgery, his *Account of Two Successful Operations for Restoring a Lost Nose from the Integuments of the Forehead* was published in 1816. Carpue's other specialism was galvanism and he was present at the attempt, on 18

January 1803, to pass an electrical current through the body of executed wife-murderer George Foster, hanged at Newgate. Foster opened one eye, wiggled his legs and clenched his right hand but failed to be revived. Source: *The Newgate Calendar*, George Theodore Wilkinson's abridged edition (1962); Volume 2, pp.80–2.

In 1800, painters Benjamin West, Richard Costway and Thomas Banks asked Carpue to nail up a just-executed criminal (a murderer called Legg), who was still warm, so that they could take a plaster cast of how the body hung, in order to produce more realistic Crucifixion scenes; a cast of the crucified Legg is in the Royal Academy, London.

Edward William Tuson (1802–65) trained at Carpue's school, and at the age of twenty-two became a surgeon at the Middlesex Hospital – close to the Little Windmill Street school where he gave private lectures in anatomy. (Little Windmill Street is plain Windmill Street today, running between Tottenham Court Road and Charlotte Street; Tuson's school was at numbers 8–10, now demolished.) While still in his twenties, Tuson published his celebrated work *Myology* (1825), which revealed the various layers of muscles; he was said to have got through a great many Subjects in his research for *Myology*.

13 Exeter 'Change – built in Tudor times – was pulled down in 1829; Exeter Street is near the spot today.

Joshua Brookes was involved in the notorious Chunee incident in 1826, when an enraged elephant of that name burst out of another menagerie, owned by one Edward Cross, close to that of Brookes's brother. After Chunee had finally been destroyed by armed troops, and when his corpse had lain stinking in the Strand for days, Brookes publicly dissected the beast, and later angrily denied newspaper reports that he had grilled and eaten a slice of Chunee as part of his investigations. Source: *Memoirs of a Bow Street Runner* by Henry Goddard (1856; published 1956).

Chunee had been brought from India in the ship the *Lady Astell*, and had worked at Astley's Theatre in Lambeth; Astley's sold him to menagerie owner Stephen Polito (sale negotiated by Mr Norman, the clown); on Polito's death, Chunee passed to Edward Cross, who succeeded Polito at the menagerie. Source: the manuscript diaries of William Clift, housed in the Library of the Royal College of Surgeons.

14 Sir Astley Cooper himself was the proud owner of a chunk of intestine, featuring a fungal growth, which he claimed was a section of Napoleon's gut. Its authenticity was uncertain at the time and will always remain so since it was destroyed when the Royal College of Surgeons was hit during an air-raid in May 1941, in which Chunee's skeleton also perished.

15 24 November 1832.

16 Reported in *Memoirs of John Abernethy* by George MacIlwain (1853), p.305.

17 *The Lancet*, 23 July 1833.

18 *Ibid.*, 1 October 1831.

19 Sir Benjamin Brodie – Royal College Council-member, and, later, RCS president – was the son of a rural clergyman and became a baronet on the strength of his being made surgeon to William IV; Sir William Blizard, president of the Royal College in 1831, was the son of an auctioneer and had had no formal education until his late adolescence; Sir Charles Bell had been excluded from the Edinburgh medical elite, and subsequently suffered seven years of being overlooked in London before gaining respect for his work on nerve function; George Guthrie had been a child prodigy, becoming an RCS member at the age of fifteen before going off to the Napoleonic Wars as a surgeon, his skills coming to the notice of the Duke of Wellington (Guthrie turned down a knighthood).

20 The *Lancet* gives a slightly different version of the story, claiming that the Anatomical Society put the price of bodies up in order to destroy Grainger, and that when the resurrectionists heard this, they decided to supply Grainger for free in order to make Webb Street flourish, and so force the prices paid by hospital schools even higher. The *Lancet*, 24 November 1831.

21 *Report from the Select Committee on Medical Education*, Part 2, Q6602/p.192. The 1828 Select Committee on Anatomy put the number of medical students in London at 1,000 in 1823 and 800 in 1828; *Report*, p.4.

22 *Death, Dissection and the Destitute* (1988; reissued 2001), p.163.

23 Ruth Richardson discusses attacks on medical schools in Paisley, Sheffield, Inveresk (near Edinburgh) and – most dramatically – in Aberdeen, where the school of anatomy was burnt to the ground upon the discovery of discarded dissected human remains.

24 This anecdote is told in *Westminster Hospital, 1716–1966* by J.G. Humble and Peter Hansell (1966); and by Hubert Cole in *Things for the Surgeon* (1964).

25 The *Morning Chronicle*, 2 October 1829; I have been unable to find any further reports of this case.

In October 1831, Superintendent Joseph Sadler Thomas told George Rowland Minshull that 'young medical students had repeatedly annoyed the neighbourhood'. Minshull had just remanded a student for assaulting Thomas in Brydges Street, Covent Garden; the *Globe and Traveller*, 20 October 1831.

26 *Report and Evidence of the Select Committee on Anatomy*, 1828, p.81.

27 Isobel Rae's biography *Knox the Anatomist* is a moving account of his life; while Owen Dudley Edwards, in *Burke & Hare* (1980), presents an equally compelling, though more hostile, portrait of Knox.

28 'Mary's Ghost' published in *Hood's Whims and Oddities* (1826), a volume of verse on the topics of the day.

29 The *Globe and Traveller*, 28 October 1831.

    Edward Cook was named as 'a known resurrectionist' by 'a publican who 12 years ago kept a house in West Smithfield', according to the *Sun*, 14 November 1831; this house may well have been the Fortune of War.

    Eliza Ross ostensibly made her money from selling old clothes, reputedly stripped from bodies snatched by Cook; and the dealers she sold to, at Rag Fair, near the Tower of London, were able to name a number of articles that tallied with Walsh's belongings which had been sold to them by Ross at the end of August. Ross's neighbours in Goodman's Yard also alleged that she was a notorious cat-skinner – stealing and killing local cats and selling the furs at Rag Fair.

    Sources: reports in the *Sun*, the *Globe and Traveller* and *The Times*, November and December 1831; and January 1832.

30 *John Clare's Autobiographical Writings*, edited by Eric Robinson (1983), p.132. It is ironic that when Clare died, insane, in 1864, his friends in the Northamptonshire village of Helpston held a wake for his body, as it had been rumoured that a London anatomist intended to get hold of Clare's brain in order to dissect it and discover how it was that a madman had been able to write poetry. Source: *A Right to Song: the Life of John Clare* by Edward Storey (1982), p.297.

31 Ruth Richardson tells this story in *Death, Dissection and the Destitute*, p.221.

32 *Report*, p.47.

33 Knox's letter to the *Caledonian Mercury*, written two months after William Burke's execution, and Knox's only public pronouncement on the affair; quoted in Isobel Rae's *Knox the Anatomist*, pp.98–9.

34 *Report and Evidence of the Select Committee on Anatomy*, 1828, p.18.

35 *The Life of Sir Astley Cooper* by Bransby Cooper, p.334. An example of one of these experiments is on show in the Gordon Museum at Guy's Hospital.

    According to R.C. Brock in *The Life and Work of Astley Cooper* (1952), Cooper kept human corpses in his attic from time to time and had obtained permission to do so from the Lord Mayor of London, who assured Cooper that he would not be troubled by constables and magistrates about this matter.

36 The *Lancet*, 16 October 1831.

37 *A Letter to the Right Honourable the Secretary of State for the Home Department containing Remarks on the Report of the Select Committee of the House of Commons on Anatomy* (1829).

38 The *Morning Advertiser*, 11 October 1831.

39 *British Police and the Democratic Ideal* by Charles Reith, p.94.

40 George Douchez, who had been present at the 6 November post-mortem in St Paul's watch-house, lived – and may have had a theatre of sorts – in Golden Square itself; Thomas Copland, surgeon, lived at 4 Golden Square, on its east side; while John Joberns, surgeon, lived at 9 Upper John Street, which led into the square. Joseph Carpue's school in Dean Street, the Brookesian, and the Great Windmill Street school could have been described as near to Golden Square. But the most likely candidate is George Darby Dermott's practice; Dermott was working from a theatre actually on the square before taking his anatomy academy to Gerrard Street in 1833. Douchez was actor Edmund Kean's personal surgeon. A dapper, shrewd, convivial little man, Douchez was said to spend his evenings at the Harp pub in Little Russell Street, often socialising with Kean. Source: J.F. Clarke's *Autobiographical Recollections*.

The great John Hunter (brother of William of the Great Windmill Street school) lived and lectured at number 31 Golden Square (where he had built a dissecting-room) between 1763 and 1769, and it is possible that Dermott, or even Douchez, was using Hunter's former premises.

41 John Hilton (1805–78) was demonstrator of anatomy at Guy's from 1828. He had a brilliant reputation as an anatomist, and later in life became surgeon to Queen Victoria and president of the RCS; he had the honour of performing the post-mortem on Sir Astley Cooper when the baronet died in 1841.

Hilton was the first surgeon to give a clear account of cerebro-spinal fluid; and his book *Rest and Pain* (1863), on the importance of recuperation, was the first to explore in an empirical way the benefits of rest. However, he himself shunned the notion of empiricism and the 'scientific' community, and found Charles Darwin's ideas ludicrous. Hilton believed that life, death and the spirit could never be understood in chemical or physical terms: 'All is darkness to the human understanding,' he said. Source: *A Biographical History of Guy's Hospital* by Samuel Wilks and G.T. Bettany (1892).

Hilton gave waxwork-maker Joseph Towne detailed anatomical information when Towne was producing his celebrated wax anatomical figures, which are still in the Gordon Museum at Guy's. Towne habitually worked alone in a locked room with corpses and wax, and his methods died with him.

42 5 December 1831.

43 *The Centenary History of King's College London* by F.J.C. Hearnshaw, p.293.

44 *King's and Some King's Men* by H. Willoughby Lyle, p.301.

11 At the Bailey

1 To be found in the London Metropolitan Archives, Old Bailey Sessions Roll, OB/SR609/10.

2 In *Old Bailey Experience* it was stated that some judges boasted of their capacity to get through sixty to seventy criminal cases a day; p.60.

3 Fellow lawyer Serjeant William Ballantine branded Phillips a greedy and unkind man in his memoirs, *Some Experiences of a Barrister's Life* (1882). As a child, Ballantine was taken by his father to see the trial of Bishop, Williams and May.

4 'Mr Adolphus and His Contemporaries' in *Law Magazine*, Volume 4 (1846), p.60; drunkenness among lawyers and judges was also noted in Ballantine's *Experiences*, p.54.

5 Serjeant Ballantine again. No one seems to have recorded how lawyers smelt.

6 Bodkin's copy of *Arabiniana* is in the British Library.

7 Serjeant Ballantine.

8 See footnote 12 below.

Reports from *The Times*, *Morning Advertiser* and *Globe and Traveller* are from editions dated 3 December 1831; and the *Weekly Dispatch* of 4 December 1831. The basic narrative of the trial is taken from the Old Bailey Sessions Papers, First Session, 1831, pp. 24–33. It is supposed to be a comprehensive report of proceedings, but is nothing of the sort: much is left out, and the newspaper accounts are an invaluable back-up. The staccato, elliptical nature of the Sessions Papers are evidence that much was jettisoned in publishing a formal report of trials of the day.

9 Roderick Floud's book *Height, Health and History 1750–1980* (1990) contains tables of the heights of adolescent recruits to the Marine Society – a charity that 'rescued' street boys and trained them to be sailors – and to Sandhurst Military Academy; Floud's data for the 1820s and 1830s suggests the class basis for height differentials.

10 In the late 1820s a five-year-old, who could not see over the bar of the prisoners' dock, was put on trial at the Old Bailey; he had taken a watch from the counter of a baker's shop in Ealing, thinking that his mother would like to see how pretty it was. Source: 'The Schoolmaster's Experience of Newgate' (anonymous), in *Fraser's Magazine*, June 1832.

11 William Street is today's Rockingham Street; the Alfred's Head is no more.

12 There is a striking similarity between this passage and the paragraphs in Chapter 52 of *Oliver Twist* that describe Fagin's trial at the Old Bailey:

The court was paved, from floor to roof, with human faces. Inquisitive and eager eyes peered from every inch of space. From the rail before the dock, away into the sharpest angle of the smallest corner in the galleries, all looks were fixed upon one man – the Jew. Before him and behind: above, below, on the right and on the left: he seemed to stand surrounded by a firmament, all bright with gleaming eyes.

He stood there in all this glare of living light, with one hand resting on the wooden slab before him, the other held to his ear, and his head thrust forward to enable him to catch with greater distinctness every word that fell from the presiding judge, who was delivering his charge to the jury. At times, he turned his eyes sharply upon them to observe the effect of the slightest featherweight in his favour; and when the points against him were stated with terrible distinctness, looked towards his counsel, in mute appeal that he would, even then, urge something in his behalf. Beyond these manifestations of anxiety, he stirred not hand or foot. He had scarcely moved since the trial began; and now that the judge ceased to speak, he still remained in the same strained attitude of close attention, with his gaze bent on him, as though he listened still.

A slight bustle in the court recalled him to himself. Looking round, he saw that the jurymen had turned together, to consider of their verdict. As his eyes wandered to the gallery, he could see the people rising above each other to see his face: some hastily applying their glasses to their eyes: and others whispering to their neighbours with looks expressive of abhorrence. A few there were, who seemed unmindful of him, and looked only to the jury, in impatient wonder how they could delay. But in no one face – not even among the women, of whom there were many there – could he read the faintest sympathy with himself, or any feeling but one of all absorbing interest that he should be condemned.

As he saw all this in one bewildered glance, the death-like stillness came again, and looking back, he saw that the jurymen had turned towards the judge. Hush!

They only sought permission to retire.

He looked, wistfully, into their faces, one by one, when they passed out, as though to see which way the greater number leant; but that was fruitless. The jailer touched him on the shoulder. He followed mechanically to the end of the dock, and sat down on a chair. The man pointed it out, or he would not have seen it [. . .]

At length there was a cry of silence, and a breathless look from all towards the door. The jury returned, and passed him close. He could glean nothing from their faces; they might as well have been of stone. Perfect stillness ensued – not a rustle – not a breath – Guilty.

The building rang with a tremendous shout, and another, and another, and then it echoed deep loud groans, that gathered strength as they swelled out, like angry thunder. It was a peal of joy from the populace outside, greeting the news that he would die on Monday.

The noise subsided, and he was asked if he had anything to say why sentence of death should not be passed upon him. He had resumed his listening attitude, and looked intently at his questioner while the demand was made; but it was twice repeated before he seemed to hear it, and then he only muttered that he was an old man – an old man – an old man – and so, dropping into a whisper, was silent again.

The judge assumed the black cap, and the prisoner still stood with the same air and gesture. A woman in the gallery uttered some exclamation, called forth by this dread solemnity; he looked hastily up as if angry at the interruption, and bent forward yet more attentively. The address was solemn and impressive; the sentence fearful to hear. But he stood, like a marble figure, without the motion of a nerve. His haggard face was still thrust forward, his under-jaw hanging down, and his eyes staring out before him, when the jailer put his hand upon his arm, and beckoned him away. He gazed stupidly about him for an instant, and obeyed.

Not long into researching this book, I learnt that others had also suspected that the Most Deathlike Silence passage in the report of the Italian Boy trial was the unacknowledged early work of Charles Dickens – a nineteen-year-old shorthand reporter at the time of the case. A cutting, 'Dickens and *The Times*: Traces of His Hand', is one of many smaller items collated by Dickensiana collector John F. Dexter and presented to the British Museum (and now held in the British Library). Dexter's cutting from *The Times* dates from 1933 and it discusses the similarity between Dickens's fiction and a number of police-court cases – at Great Marlborough Street and Hatton Garden – that had appeared in *The Times* one century earlier. In a handwritten note, Dexter prefaces a copy of the 1831 broadsheet *Burking the Italian Boy!: Fairburn's Edition of the Trial of Bishop and Williams, Tried at the Old Bailey. Taken in Shorthand* (which reprints the Most Deathlike Silence paragraphs in full) with the words: 'F.W. Pailthorpe gave me this pamphlet stating that it was "reported" by Charles Dickens and that he had this information from an authoritative source. The description of the prisoners on pages 21–22 bears evidence of Charles Dickens's hand.' Frederick William Pailthorpe (1838–1914) was an illustrator of Dickens's fiction in editions that appeared after Dickens's death in 1870; I have been unable to establish that Pailthorpe ever met Dickens. Pailthorpe's 'authoritative source' is unknown; but artist and caricaturist George Cruikshank (1792–1878), who provided illustrations for *Sketches by Boz*, *Oliver Twist* and other Dickens work, and who often sketched prisoners in the dock at the Old Bailey, is a strong candidate.

However, there is only anecdotal evidence that Dickens's reporting career before the spring of 1832 comprised anything other than stints in the reporters' gallery of the Houses of Parliament and at the ecclesiastical and naval court of Doctors Commons, which stood just to the south of St Paul's Cathedral, in Knightrider Street. Furthermore, while Dickens's maternal uncle, John Henry Barrow, had links with *The Times* (and is said to have helped Dickens to learn shorthand), there is no evidence that his nephew was connected to the Thunderer at any point in the earliest stage of his career; and none whatever that Dickens had anything to do with Fairburn – purveyor of inexpensive woodcut-illustrated broadsheets.

It is reasonable to assume that if such a lucky – and lucrative – break as reporting one of the crimes of the century had come Dickens's way in 1831, he would have referred to it at the time (in letters or in conversation) or in later years. In fact, direct references to the Bishop and Williams case are scarce in Dickens's journalism and non-existent in the correspondence of his that has survived. Though bodysnatchers appear in *Barnaby Rudge* and *A Tale of Two Cities*, these novels were set in the 1780s; resurrection and burking were, it seems, of comparatively little interest to Dickens in his tales of urban low life of the 1820s and 1830s.

He had an opportunity to refer to John Bishop in a letter to a friend, Henry Kolle, written in the summer of 1832, in which he invited Kolle to call in on the Dickens family, who had decided to take a short holiday in Highgate. (The letter is reprinted in *The Letters of Charles Dickens*, The Nonesuch Edition, 1938, Volume 1, p.9.) Dickens was staying next door to the Red Lion, Highgate, just yards from the house Bishop had grown up in, yet he makes no reference to its proximity, despite the fact that just eight months after the trial, that part of Highgate would have retained a ghoulish notoriety for being the birthplace of the killer.

Three years later, in November 1835, Dickens was given an entrance pass to Newgate so that he could tour the gaol, with a view to writing a profile of it. In his sketch 'A Visit to Newgate', which Dickens wrote soon after this trip to the gaol, he notes the death masks of 'the two notorious murderers' Bishop and Williams (which were almost the only objects furnishing a small ante-room), 'the former, in particular, exhibiting a style of head and set of features which might have afforded sufficient moral grounds for his instant execution at any time, even had there been no other evidence against him'. Is it just the facetious tone here that gives the impression that Dickens knew not a great deal about Bishop? Certainly, he makes no attempt to add any background information – a strong temptation, surely, if he had once had the good fortune to sit just yards from the killers and observe them in minute detail.

These arguments notwithstanding, it is possible to piece together a plausible explanation for what instinct urges: that the author of Fagin's trial scene had reported the trial of Bishop, Williams and May. Firstly, there is no need to search for evidence that Dickens had any official connection with *The Times*, or any other publication, for that matter: it is perfectly possible that the Most Deathlike Silence paragraphs were the work of a 'penny-a-line' freelancer syndicating his work to more than one newspaper. The Most Deathlike Silence appears first in *The Times* of Saturday (morning) 3 December, and then makes its way into the *Globe and Traveller* of Saturday evening 3 December, then the *Sunday Times*, the *Observer* and the *Weekly Dispatch*, all of Sunday 4th; and it then filters down to the broadsheet by Fairburn and another published by one J. Kiernan, called *The Execution of Bishop and Williams for the Horrid and Inhuman Murder of the Italian Boy*. Pierce Egan's own pamphlet, which went on sale on Tuesday 6 December, reproduces the passages too; Egan's effort simply grafts some underworld 'flash' words on to a foreword and afterword – his literary party-trick.

There is anecdotal evidence that as early as the age of fourteen Charles Dickens was attempting to sell penny-a-line journalism that he had produced on a speculative basis. Samuel Carter Hall, in his 1883 memoirs, *Retrospect of a Long Life*, recalls the boy calling in at the office of the newspaper the *British Press*, where Hall worked alongside Dickens's father, John. Charles would drop off his own reports of news that, claimed Hall, had escaped the attention of the regular reporters of the *British Press*.

John Dickens had embarked on his journalistic career in the mid-1820s. He was working as a shorthand writer and reporter when the *British Press* ceased publication in the autumn of 1826; he subsequently appears to have joined the parliamentary staff of the *Morning Herald* and then the *Mirror of Parliament*, a rival to *Hansard* set up in 1828 by John Dickens's brother-in-law, John Henry Barrow – the man with *The Times* connections. Another brother-in-law, Edward Barrow, was a newspaper reporter, and may also have offered a helping hand to the impecunious John Dickens. Charles Dickens, meanwhile, left school in 1827, aged fifteen, and worked as a lawyers' clerk for about two years, and at seventeen or eighteen began work as a freelance shorthand reporter, renting an office at 5 Bell Yard, close by the court of Doctors Commons, where he obtained most – but not all – his work; he did not relinquish this office until April 1832. By some point in 1831 Charles was also working for the *Mirror of Parliament*, alongside his uncle and father. (I have followed William J. Carlton's attempted chronology of Dickens's early career in his book *Charles Dickens, Shorthand Writer*, 1926).

Precise dates and employers (and knowing which stints of moonlighting overlapped with which bouts of more established, regular employment) are maddeningly hard to come by for Charles Dickens's very early career; and even William J. Carlton found himself flummoxed when attempting a definitive chronology for Dickens's early working life. This is likely to stem from Dickens's own attempts to make murky his early years. Dickens rarely spoke or wrote about his pre-1834 career – 1834 being the year in which he gained a full-time staff position (as parliamentary reporter) on a noteworthy publication (the *Morning Chronicle*), at a salary of five guineas a week. Presumably in reply to a specific inquiry from novelist and friend Wilkie Collins, Dickens wrote, in June 1856, an uncharacteristically imprecise and unmistakably disdainful summary of his early working life:

> I was put in the office of a solicitor, a friend of my father's, and didn't much like it; and after a couple of years (as well as I can remember) applied myself with a celestial or diabolical energy to the study of such things as would qualify me to be a first-rate parliamentary reporter. . . . I made my debut in the Gallery (at about 18, I suppose) engaged on a voluminous publication no longer in existence called *The Mirror of Parliament*. When the *Morning Chronicle* was purchased by Sir John Easthope and acquired a large circulation, I was engaged there, and I remained there until I found myself in a condition to relinquish that part of my labours. I left the reputation behind me of being the best and most rapid reporter ever known, and could do anything in that way under any sort of circumstances, and often did.

(Letter to Collins dated 6 June 1856, quoted in Carlton's *Charles Dickens, Shorthand Writer*.)

'[He] was extremely sensitive as to the possibility of any rubbish being given to the public in the form of "early writings",' wrote Dickens's sister-in-law Georgina Hogarth to H.G. Kitton, who was compiling a memorial volume of tributes to Dickens, *Charles Dickens by Pen and Pencil*. Hogarth recalled an incident when a female friend from Dickens's late adolescence proudly presented the by-now famous novelist with the manuscript of a play he had written in 1833: 'He made a bargain with her,' Hogarth told Kitton, 'by making her a present of a Christmas Book just completed, on condition that she gave up the boyish production to him, which he had the satisfaction of putting into the fire with his own hands.' Dickens wrought a campaign of ruthless destruction on his personal archive: for all the volumes of Dickens's letters that have been found and published, an even greater number were destroyed at his hands or by friends at his request. On 3 September 1860, he was observed building a bonfire in his garden and committing to the flames caches of letters and papers.

Furthermore, Dickens came to disapprove strongly of newspaper accounts of murderers in the dock, execution scenes, last dying words and official confessions. It is difficult to date with precision this change of heart – the point at which the author of such *grand guignol* passages as the death of Bill Sikes, the murder of Nancy, and Fagin's last night alive decided that criminals' final hours should not be committed to print; but it was certainly strongly felt by 1849. On 17 November of that year Dickens wrote to *The Times* to explain his disgust at public executions. (He had recently gone to Horsemonger Lane Gaol, Newington, South London, and reported on the dreadful public scenes at the hanging of husband and wife Charles and Maria Manning, condemned to death for killing a former lodger.) 'I would place every obstacle in the way of his sayings and doings being served up in print on Sunday mornings for the perusal of families,' wrote Dickens of the executed murderer. Seven years later he expanded on this theme – claiming that the way in which the press reported the final days of murderers made killers appear noteworthy, even admirable – in two articles in his magazine *Household Words*, 'The Demeanour of Murderers' (published 14 June 1856) and 'The Murdered Person' (published 11 October 1856).

A genuine change of heart, doubtless; but was it also informed by the wish to shake off a past career? The epitome of the nineteenth-century self-made man, Dickens was never generous in acknowledging sources, influences and helping hands. He wished to appear as though he had sprung from nowhere. Hence his slightly sniffy denials in response to queries about inspirations, role models and his early years. If he had indeed been part of the tribe of shabby, opportunistic penny-a-liners who made a living, and received useful introductions, at court-houses and inquests, he is very likely to have made every effort to suppress any reminders of this. Unless a letter by, or addressed to, Dickens comes to light, or a manuscript memoir from a contemporary of his early reporting years turns up, the authorship of the Most Deathlike Silence must remain, like so much in this case, a mystery.

12 A Newgate Stink

1 Reprinted in *The History of the London Burkers*.
2 'A Visit to Newgate' in *Sketches by Boz* (1836).
3 Sources for the topography of Newgate: *Facts Relating to the Punishment of Death in the Metropolis* by Edward Gibbon Wakefield; *Old Bailey Experience*; *The Hangmen of England* by Horace Bleackley (1929).
    The condemned cells stood near to where the Old Bailey's current service road abuts Newgate Street.
4 Quoted in *The Life and Work of Astley Cooper* by R.C. Brock, p.15.
5 Forty-eight-year-old Wontner had only one leg, after a fall from a horse in 1821; he would die in 1833 and his successor, William Cope, would prove incompetent.
6 *Report and Evidence of the Select Committee Appointed to Inquire into the Cause of the Increase in the Number of Commitments and Convictions in London and Middlesex*, 1828, p.307.
7 *Old Bailey Experience*, p.339.
8 Corporation of London Records Office, *Report Delivered to the Court of Aldermen by the City Gaols Committee on the Conduct of the Reverend the Ordinary Cotton*, Key Rep 1831/32, p.163.
9 If these sheets should ever come to light they would fill some of the many vast gaps in what is known of the London resurrection community.
10 In extraordinary circumstances, a 'writ of error' could overturn a verdict, but only by challenging a point of law. The author of *Old Bailey Experience* could recall only one instance in which a writ of error had overturned a death sentence; p.105.
11 The author of *Old Bailey Experience*.
12 Albany Fontblanque, *England Under Seven Administrations*, p.161.
13 Extract from *Cotton's Book of Reports and Occurrences*, copied into the *Report Delivered to the Court of Aldermen by the City Gaols Committee*, p.163.

14 Day of Dissolution

1 This is where the *Morning Advertiser*'s reporter was stationed; he only knew the execution had happened by the reaction of the crowd.

2 Bean's evidence to the Court of Aldermen, given 28 December 1831; *Report*, p.175.

3 Edward Pearson, porter to the Royal College of Surgeons, had bought refreshments for the twelve policemen on duty at Hosier Lane and along the route: four half-quartern loaves, 1s 6d; one and a quarter pound of cheese, 11d; six pints of porter, 2s. Source: the manuscript diaries of William Clift in the library of the Royal College of Surgeons, entry date 5 December 1831.

4 Calcraft (1800–79) had been in the job only two years (he was originally a cobbler), though he was never to prove proficient in turning people off.

15 The Use of the Dead to the Living

1 7 December 1831.

2 Guthrie's letter quoted by Jessie Dobson in her essay 'The Anatomising of Criminals' in the *Annals of the Royal College of Surgeons of England*, August 1951, Volume 9, Number 2, p.112.

3 Public Record Office, Metropolitan Police Outgoing Correspondence, 3 December 1831–16 March 1832, letter forwarded to Tuson from the police, MEPO 1/8/10163–12032.

4 *The Times*, 29 December 1831. Superintendent Thomas had presented, or perhaps sold, to Egan Bishop's apprentice indentures too, which Egan claimed were signed 'Thomas' Bishop; however, the killer had an elder brother called Thomas (born on 5 January 1794), and it is likely Superintendent Thomas had acquired the wrong document – or had perhaps been sold a fake memento. Need it be said that Superintendent Thomas had no right to sell these objects.

    Clift's drawing of Williams's tattoo is to be found in his diaries, housed in the library of the Royal College of Surgeons; entry dated 5 December.

5 The *Lancet*, 14 January 1832.

6 Gall, quoted by Dr Elliotson in the *Lancet*, 14 January 1832, as part of the report of Elliotson's London Phrenological Society lecture on Bishop and Williams.

    Elliotson (1791–1868) was University College London's first Professor of the Principles and Practice of Medicine, in 1832. He became a personal friend of Charles Dickens, and the two men shared an interest in mesmerism, the field that Elliotson moved on to when he had tired of phrenology.

7 Repeated on paper by John Wade in his *Treatise on the Police and Crimes of the Metropolis*, p.204.

8   This phrase is borrowed from Sir Walter Scott by John Wade in his *Treatise*, p.149.

9   *Bell's Weekly Messenger*, 11 December 1831.

10   Advertisement for phrenological casts in *The Phrenological Record* by A.L. Vago (1883).

11   According to H. Lonsdale's *Sketch of the Life and Writings of Robert Knox* (1870), quoted in Ruth Richardson's *Death, Dissection and the Destitute*, p.96.

12   *London* by Charles Knight, Volume 1, p.424; *Old Bailey Experience*, p.40.

13   Reported in the *Globe and Traveller*, 5 December 1831.

14   *New Monthly Magazine*, June 1833.

15   *Figaro in London* ran from November 1831 until December 1834, and its first editor was Henry Mayhew, future compiler of the influential volumes *London Labour and the London Poor* (1851–62). George Rowland Minshull found himself one of its targets when it reported his bad-tempered decision to gaol a vagrant mother who refused to name her child's father, even though he had deserted her; *Figaro in London* stated that Minshull himself was probably the father. But the newspaper subsequently decided that it rather liked the magistrate when he discharged a boy who had been arrested for selling *Figaro* in Leicester Square – Minshull was seen chuckling in court over the newspaper's cartoons.

16   *Hansard Parliamentary Debates*, 27 February 1832, p.836.

17   Pelham, Perceval and Hunt were speaking on 17 January 1832; *Hansard*, pp.578–83.

18   Guthrie's *Letter to the Right Honourable the Secretary of State for the Home Department containing Remarks on the Report of the Select Committee of the House of Commons on Anatomy* (1829).

19   *Hansard*, 6 February 1832, pp.1276–8.

20   As Ruth Richardson has pointed out, in her meticulous account of the passage of the Anatomy Act:

> At several crucial moments in the parliamentary progress of the [second Anatomy] Bill, when the opposition had argued persuasively, or when general discussion threatened to delay its passage, the Bill's supporters did not scruple to remind all present of the late 'enormities'. The reminder served as a way of curtailing debate by the introduction of a note of urgency, and decoyed parliamentary attention from important issues arising from the Bill.
>
> *Death, Dissection and the Destitute*, p.198.

16 How Many?

1 *Hansard*, 12 December 1831, pp.154–5.

2 The earliest reports to escape Newgate also stated that Bishop and Williams vigorously denied that pitch-plasters were used in killing their victims – surely one of the least important aspects of the case, but one that was given prominence in the Sunday papers. Perhaps it was in response to the rash of alleged burking attacks across London which, victims claimed, had involved pitch-plasters being sealed across the mouth and nose for suffocation.

3 J.C. Reid's book *Bucks and Bruisers* (1971) and Serjeant Ballantine's *Some Experiences of a Barrister's Life* are the sources of the interesting connection between Cotton and Egan. Cotton was, according to Ballantine, fond of a joke, 'well-fed', rubicund and a keen book and curiosity collector. He is said to have invited Egan to a number of banquets at Newgate/the Old Bailey.

4 If, as I suspect, *Old Bailey Experience* was written by James Harmer, then it would make sense for Cotton (Harmer's friend) to be so warmly defended, and for an evangelical rival such as Dr Whitworth Russell to be criticised.

5 Sources for Theodore Williams's misdemeanours: *Report of the Evidence, with Bill of Costs, in a Suit Promoted in the Consistory Court by the Reverend Theodore Williams, Vicar of Hendon, against James Hall, a Resident of that Parish, for Brawling at a Vestry Meeting, Held for the Purpose of Making a Church Rate* (1838) – a pamphlet in the British Library; *The Victoria History of the Counties of England: A History of the County of Middlesex*, Volume 5 (1976); and *The History and Topography of the Parish of Hendon, Middlesex* by Edward T. Evans (1890). Evans points out that Williams had a library of thousands of volumes at his vicarage in Parson Street and an unusual collection of potted conifers in the garden of the same.

   Williams died in 1875, aged ninety-one, and is buried in the graveyard of his church, St Mary's, on Greyhound Hill, Hendon.

6 *The Times*, 2 October 1839.

7 *The Sun*, 5 December 1831; reprinted in *The Times*, 6 December 1831.

8 The *Globe and Traveller*, 5 December 1831.

9 The *Sun*, 12 December 1831.

10 Extracts from Cotton's journal relating to the events of 3, 4 and 5 December 1831 copied into the *Report Delivered to the Court of Aldermen*, p.163.

11 *The Times*, 24 December 1831.

12 *Report Delivered to the Court of Aldermen*, p.163.

13 *Hansard*, 28 June 1832, p.1086.

14 *Cobbett's Weekly Political Register*, 28 January 1832, pp.258–9.
15 City of Westminster Archives at the Westminster Reference Library, St Paul's, Covent Garden, Parish Records, Letter Book, H864.
16 The *Sun*, 9 December 1831.
17 The *Globe and Traveller*, 3 December 1831.
18 The *Globe and Traveller*, 15 December 1831.
19 City of Westminster Archives, St Paul's, Covent Garden, Parish Records, Annual Accounts, 1829–54, H872.
20 The *Morning Advertiser*, 22 December 1831.
21 Public Record Office, Home Office Domestic Letter Book, Volume 67, Letter from the Home Office to Joseph Paragalli dated 10 January 1832, HO 43/41.
22 City of Westminster Archives, St Paul's, Covent Garden, Parish Records, Letter Book, H865. In addition, 'The sum of £2 was contributed by a lady, per Mr Minshull, towards these expenses whilst the proceedings were pending. . . . As the contribution was anonymous, no opportunity has been offered of thanking the donor'; H872.

Epilogue

1 Public Record Office, Hulk Returns, HO 8/31.
2 Appendix A of the *Fourth Annual Report of the Poor Law Commissioners for England and Wales* (1838), p.106; evidence of Dr Arnott.
3 Hackney Archives at the Hackney Local Studies Library, Admission and Discharge Registers of Shoreditch Workhouse, 1832–6, XP507; this is one of the few East London workhouses for which registers of inmates exist for the 1820s and early 1830s.
4 *Report from the Select Committee on Allegations Relative to the Conduct of Certain Magistrates in the Holborn Division of Middlesex in Granting Licences for Victualling Houses* (1833), p.15.
5 *The Catalogue of Dr Kahn's Celebrated Anatomical Museum* is in the British Library. Kahn, a German showman, moved his museum several times in the middle of the century, and its venues included Regent Street, Oxford Street and Coventry Street.
6 George Godwin, *Town Swamps and Social Bridges* (1859), p.23; and Hector Gavin, *Sanitary Ramblings, being Sketches and Illustrations of Bethnal Green* (1848; reprinted by Leicester University Press in 1971), pp.9–10.
7 Issues dated 1 and 8 January 1898.
8 *Baroness Burdett-Coutts: A Sketch of Her Public Life and Work* by HRH Princess Mary Adelaide, Duchess of Teck (1893).

9 'The Baroness Burdett-Coutts' by Mary Spencer-Warren, part of the 'Illustrated Interviews' series in *Strand Magazine*, Volume 7 (1894), p.248.

10 *Authentic Memoirs of the Lives of Mr and Mrs Coutts, Communicated by a Person of the First Respectability* (1819).

11 The case crops up one last time in literature towards the end of the century in George Eliot's *Middlemarch* (1871–2), Chapter 50, when the rector's gossipy wife, Mrs Cadwallader, says snobbishly of the book's heroine, Dorothea Brooke, that she 'might as well marry an Italian with white mice' as marry Will Ladislaw, and thereby lose her fortune. *Middlemarch* is set in 1829–1832, and partly concerns the efforts of idealistic young doctor Tertius Lydgate to found a new hospital in the town. Mrs Cadwallader's remark is a reference to the London Burkers case and to the scandal that doctors could find themselves linked to.

12 The complete 12-volume bound set of *The Mysteries of London* is extremely rare. However, in 1996 an abridged copy, with an introduction containing biographical material on Reynolds and reproducing some of the original wood engravings, was published by Trefor Thomas (in the Keele University Press imprint).

13 Evidence given in the *Second Report from the Select Committee on Metropolis Improvements*, 1837–8; *Report*, p.82.

BIBLIOGRAPHY

Contemporary / Primary Sources

Government papers at the Public Record Office, Kew

HO 8/31	Hulk Returns
HO 43/41	Home Office Letters
HO 59/2	Home Office Letters
HO 62/8	Daily Police Reports
HO 64/2	Petitions and Pardons
MEPO 1/8	Metropolitan Police Outgoing Correspondence
MEPO 1/44	Commissioners of Metropolitan Police Outgoing Correspondence
MEPO 1/49 and 1/50	Bow Street Magistrates' Outgoing Correspondence
PCOM 1/23	Old Bailey Sessions Papers, First and Fourth Sessions, 1827
PCOM 1/28	Old Bailey Sessions Papers, First Session, 1831, and Second Session, 1832
PCOM 2/199	The Newgate List, 1826–8

London Metropolitan Archives

OB/SR609/10	Old Bailey Sessions Roll
MJ/CC/V/003	Clerkenwell New Prison Committals Lists

Corporation of London Records Office

Key Rep 1831/32	*Report Delivered to the Court of Aldermen by the City Gaols Committee on the Conduct of the Reverend the Ordinary Cotton*

Guildhall Library Manuscripts Room

MS 7498/30	St Leonard's, Shoreditch, Marriage Registers

King's College Archives

KA/C/M2   Minutes of King's College Council Meetings

St Bartholomew's Hospital Archives

MU3   *Histories of Specimens in the Museum*, a manuscript
                          logbook compiled by surgeons Edward Stanley
                          and James Paget between 1832 and 1845

Royal College of Surgeons of England Library

Manuscript diaries of William Clift

British Museum Manuscripts Room

The Place Papers, BM Add Mss 27,789, Volume 1, ff184–6

Shropshire Records and Research Centre

P40/68 to P40/71   Parish Registers of St Leonard's Church,
                          Bridgnorth, 1803 to 1808

City of Westminster Archives

H864 and H865   St Paul's, Covent Garden, Parish Records,
                          Letter Books
H872   St Paul's, Covent Garden, Parish Records,
                          Annual Accounts, 1829–54

Hackney Archives

XP507   Shoreditch Workhouse Admission and
                          Discharge Registers, 1832–6

Reports of parliamentary select committees

Report and Evidence of the Select Committee on the Existing Laws Relating to Vagrants,
    1821
Report and Evidence of the Select Committee on Anatomy, 1828
Report and Evidence of the Select Committee into the State of the Police of the
    Metropolis and of the Districts adjoining thereto, 1828
Report and Evidence of the Select Committee Appointed to Inquire into the Cause of

the Increase in the Number of Commitments and Convictions in London and Middlesex, 1828

Report and Evidence of the Select Committee on that Part of the Poor Laws relating to the Employment or Relief of Able-Bodied Persons from the Poor Rate, 1828

Report and Evidence of the Select Committee on the State of Smithfield Market, 1828

Report and Evidence of the Select Committee into the State of the Police of the Metropolis, 1833

Report and Evidence of the Select Committee on Allegations Relative to the Conduct of Certain Magistrates in the Holborn Division of Middlesex in Granting Licences for Victualling Houses, 1833

Report and Evidence of the Select Committee on Medical Education, 1834

Second Report from the Select Committee on Metropolis Improvements, 1837–8

Fourth Annual Report of the Poor Law Commissioners for England and Wales, 1838

Hansard Parliamentary Debates

Acts

5 Geo IV c 83 An Act for the Punishment of Idle and Disorderly Persons, and Rogues and Vagabonds, in that part of Great Britain called England

Newspapers/Journals

Bell's Weekly Messenger
The City Press
Cobbett's Weekly Political Register
Figaro in London
Fraser's Magazine
The Globe and Traveller
The Hackney Express & Shoreditch Observer
The Hue and Cry (from 1828 the Police Gazette)
The Lancet
The Morning Advertiser
The Morning Chronicle
The Morning Herald
The Morning Post
New Monthly Magazine
The Observer
Strand Magazine
The Sun

The *Sunday Times*
The *Times*
The *Weekly Dispatch*

Contemporary books, articles and pamphlets

An Exposure of the Various Impostures Daily Practised by Vagrants of Every Description, London, ?1842?

Authentic Memoirs of the Lives of Mr and Mrs Coutts, Communicated by a Person of the First Respectability, London, 1819

Ballantine, Serjeant William, *Some Experiences of a Barrister's Life*, London, 1882

Brenton, Edward Pelham, *Letters to His Majesty, to Earl Grey, the Duke of Richmond, the Bishop of London, Lord Melbourne, Lord Kenyon and Capt the Hon George Elliot On Population, Agriculture, Poor Laws and Juvenile Vagrancy*, London, 1832

Burn, Richard, *Justice of the Peace and Parish Officer*, London, 1830 (22nd edition)

The Catalogue of Dr Kahn's Celebrated Anatomical Museum, London, 1871

Catnach, James (publisher), *The Trial and Execution of the Burkers for Murdering a Poor Italian Boy*, London 1831

Chadwick, Edwin, 'Preventive Police', in *The London Review*, 1829

Chesterton, George Laval, *Revelations of Prison Life*, London, 1856

Churchill, Henry Blencowe, *Arabiniana: or The Remains of Mr Serjeant Arabin*, London, 1843

Clarke, J.F., *Autobiographical Recollections of the Medical Profession*, London, 1874

Cooper, Bransby, *The Life of Sir Astley Cooper*, London, 1843

Cursory Remarks on the Evil Tendency of Unrestrained Cruelty, Particularly on That Practised at Smithfield Market, London, 1823

De Quincey, Thomas, 'The Nation of London', 1834, reprinted in *The Selected Writings of Thomas De Quincey*, ed. Philip Van Doren Stern, New York, 1939

The Diary of a Resurrectionist (by Joshua Naples?), ed. J.B. Bailey, London, published 1896

Dickens, Charles, 'A Curious Dance Round a Curious Tree' in *Household Words*, 17 January 1852
A Tale of Two Cities, London, 1859
'The Demeanour of Murderers' in *Household Words*, 14 June 1856
'A Detective Police Party' in *Household Words*, 27 July 1850
Great Expectations, London, 1860–1
The Letters of Charles Dickens (The Nonesuch Edition), ed. Walter Dexter, London, 1938

'The Murdered Person' in *Household Words*, 11 October 1856

Nicholas Nickleby, London, 1838–9

Oliver Twist, London, 1837–8

'A Visit to Newgate' in *Sketches by Boz*, London, 1836

Diprose, John, *Some Account of the Parish of Saint Clement Danes Past and Present*, London, 1868

Egan, Pierce, *Life in London*, London, 1821–8; reissued as Volume 2 of *Unknown London: Early Modernist Visions of the Metropolis, 1815–1845*, ed. John Marriott, 6 volumes, London, 2000

Evidence of the Reverend William Stone, Rector of Christ Church Spitalfields, & Others as to the Operation of Voluntary Charities, London, 1833

Fairburn (publisher), *Burking the Italian Boy!: Fairburn's Edition of the Trial of Bishop and Williams*, London, 1831

Fitzgerald, Percy, *Chronicles of a Bow Street Police Officer*, London, 1888

Fontblanque, Albany, 'The Diseased Appetite for Horrors' in the *Examiner*, 11 December 1831; reprinted in his *England Under Seven Administrations*, London, 1837

'Four Views of London' in the *New Monthly Magazine*, London, June 1833

Gavin, Hector, *Sanitary Ramblings, being Sketches and Illustrations of Bethnal Green*, London, 1848; reprinted Leicester, 1971

Goddard, Henry, *Memoirs of a Bow Street Runner*, London, 1856 (published 1956)

Godwin, George, *Town Swamps and Social Bridges*, London, 1859

Grant, James, *The Great Metropolis*, London, 1837

Grose, Francis, *Lexicon Balatronicum: A Dictionary of Buckish Slang, University Wit, and Pickpocket Eloquence*, London, 1823

Guthrie, George, *A Letter to the Right Honourable the Secretary of State for the Home Department containing Remarks on the Report of the Select Committee of the House of Commons on Anatomy*, London, 1829

Hall, Samuel Carter, *Retrospect of a Long Life*, London, 1883

The History of the London Burkers (by James Harmer?), London, 1832

Hogg, John, *London As It Is*, London, 1837

Hood, Thomas, 'Mary's Ghost' in *Hood's Whims and Oddities*, London, 1826

Kiernan, J. (publisher), *The Execution of Bishop and Williams for the Horrid and Inhuman Murder of the Italian Boy*, London, 1831

Knight, Charles, *London* (six volumes), London, 1841

MacFarlane, Charles, *Popular Customs, Sports and Recollections of the South of Italy*, London, 1846

MacIlwain, George, *Memoirs of John Abernethy*, London, 1853

'Mr Adolphus and his Contemporaries' in *Law Magazine*, Volume 4, London, 1846

Old Bailey Experience: Criminal Jurisprudence and the Actual Working of our Penal Code of Laws (by James Harmer?), London, 1833

Poe, Edgar Allan, 'The Man of the Crowd', 1840, reprinted in *Selected Tales*, ed. Julian Symons, Oxford, 1980

The Registers of St Paul's Church, Covent Garden, Volume 5, *Burials, 1752–1853*, ed. William H. Hunt, London, published 1909

Report of the Evidence, with Bill of Costs, in a Suit Promoted in the Consistory Court by the Reverend Theodore Williams, Vicar of Hendon, against James Hall, a Resident of that Parish, for Brawling at a Vestry Meeting, Held for the Purpose of Making a Church Rate, London, 1838

The Report(s) of the London Society for the Suppression of Mendicity, 1824, 1826, 1829, 1830, 1831

Reynolds, G.W.M., *The Mysteries of London* (1844–56); selections edited by Trefor Thomas into single volume, *The Mysteries of London*, Keele, 1996

'The Schoolmaster's Experience of Newgate' in *Fraser's Magazine*, June 1832

Smeeton, George (publisher), *The Stranger's Guide, or Frauds of London Detected*, London, 1808

Doings In London, London, 1828

Smirke, Sydney, *Suggestions for the Architectural Improvement of the Western Part of London*, London, 1834

Smith, J.T., *Etchings of Remarkable Beggars*, London, 1815

Vagabondiana, London, 1817

The Cries of London, London, 1839

Smithfield and the Slaughterhouses, London, 1847

South, John Flint, *Memorials of the Craft of Surgery in England*, London, 1886

Stow, John, *Survey of London*, London, 1603

Teck, Duchess of (HRH Princess Mary Adelaide), *Baroness Burdett-Coutts: A Sketch of Her Public Life and Work*, London, 1893

Vago, A.L., *The Phrenological Record*, London, 1883

Vaux, James Hardy, *New and Comprehensive Vocabulary of the Flash Language*, London, 1819

Vidocq, Eugène-François, *Mémoires*, Paris, 1828–9

Wade, John, *A Treatise on the Police and Crimes of the Metropolis*, London, 1829

Extraordinary Black Book, London, 1831

Wakefield, Edward Gibbon, *Facts Relating to the Punishment of Death in the Metropolis*, London, 1831

West, William, *Tavern Anecdotes*, London, 1825

Secondary sources

Barron, Caroline M., *The Parish of St Andrew Holborn*, London, 1979
Bickerdyke, John (pseudonym for Cook, Charles Henry), *The Curiosities of Ale and Beer*, London, 1886
Bleackley, Horace, *The Hangmen of England*, London, 1929
Brock, R.C., *The Life and Work of Astley Cooper*, London, 1952
Carlton, William J. *Charles Dickens, Shorthand Writer*, London, 1926
  'The Barber of Dean Street' in the *Dickensian*, Volume 48, Part 1, Number 301, 1952
Cobb, Belton, *The First Detectives*, London, 1957
Cole, Hubert, *Things for the Surgeon*, London, 1964
Dobson, Jessie, 'The Anatomising of Criminals' in the *Annals of the Royal College of Surgeons of England*, August 1951, Volume 9, Number 2
Durey, M.J., 'Bodysnatchers and Benthamites' in the *London Journal*, Volume 2, Number 2, 1976
Edwards, Owen Dudley, *Burke & Hare*, Edinburgh, 1980
Evans, Edward T., *The History and Topography of the Parish of Hendon, Middlesex*, London, 1890
Floud, Roderick, *Height, Health and History 1750–1980*, Cambridge, 1990
Forster, John, *The Life of Charles Dickens*, three volumes, London, 1872
Gordon-Taylor, Gordon, *Sir Charles Bell: His Life and Times*, London, 1958
Hearnshaw, F.J.C., *The Centenary History of King's College London*, London, 1928
Hewer, Richard L., *The Sack 'Em Up Men*, London, 1928
Humble, J.G., and Hansell, Peter, *Westminster Hospital, 1716–1966*, London, 1966
Ignatieff, Michael, *A Just Measure of Pain: The Penitentiary in the Industrial Revolution, 1750–1850*, New York, 1978
Inwood, Steven, 'Policing London's Morals: the Metropolitan Police and Popular Culture, 1829–1850' in the *London Journal*, Volume 15, Number 2, 1990
Kitton, H.G., *Charles Dickens by Pen and Pencil*, London, 1889
Knox, Tim, 'Joshua Brookes's Vivarium' in *The London Gardener, or The Gardener's Intelligencer*, Volume 3, 1997–8
Lyle, H. Willoughby, *King's and Some King's Men*, London, 1935
Lynam, Shevawn, *Humanity Dick*, London, 1975
Menefee, S.P., *Wives for Sale*, Oxford, 1981
Mitchell, L.G., *Lord Melbourne 1779–1848*, Oxford, 1997
Monson-Fitzjohn, G.J., *Quaint Signs of Olde Inns*, London, 1926
Moss, A.W., *Valiant Crusade*, London, 1961

'Old Stories Re-Told: Resurrection Men' (unsigned) in *All the Year Round*, 16 March 1867

Olmsted, J.M.D., *François Magendie*, New York, 1944

Pain, Wellesley, *Richard Martin*, London, 1925

Pain, Wellesley and Fairholme, E., *A Century of Work for Animals*, London, 1924

Paley, Ruth, 'An Imperfect, Inadequate and Wretched System?': Policing London Before Peel' in *Criminal Justice History*, Volume 10, London, 1989

Partridge, Eric, *A Dictionary of Slang and Unconventional English*, London, 1937

Plarr's Lives of the Fellows of the Royal College of Physicians of England, Bristol, 1930

Rae, Isobel, *Knox the Anatomist*, Edinburgh, 1964

Reid, J.C., *Bucks and Bruisers*, London, 1971

Reith, Charles, *British Police and the Democratic Ideal*, London, 1943

Richardson, Ruth, *Death, Dissection and the Destitute*, London, 1988 (reissued 2001)

Robinson, Eric (ed.), *John Clare's Autobiographical Writings*, Oxford, 1983

Slater, Michael (ed.) *Dickens' Journalism* (in four volumes), the Dent Uniform Edition, London, 1996–2000

Spencer-Warren, Mary, 'The Baroness Burdett-Coutts' in *Strand Magazine*, Volume 7, London, 1894

Sponza, Lucio, *Italian Immigrants in 19th-Century Britain: Realities and Images*, Leicester, 1988

Storey, Edward, *A Right to Song: The Life of John Clare*, London, 1982

Taylor, James Stephen, *Poverty, Migration and Settlement in the Industrial Revolution*, London, 1989

Thornbury, Walter (ed.), *Old and New London* (six volumes), London, 1879–85

The Victoria History of the Counties of England: A History of the County of Middlesex, Volume 5 (1976), and Volume 11, *Early Stepney with Bethnal Green* (1998), both published Oxford

Wilkinson, George Theodore (ed.), *The Newgate Calendar*, London, abridged version, published 1962

Wilks, Samuel, and Bettany, G.T., *A Biographical History of Guy's Hospital*, London, 1892

Zucchi, John E., *The Little Slaves of the Harp*, Montreal, 1992

INDEX

Abernethy, John, surgeon, 102, 136, 179

alcohol *see* drink

Anatomical Society/Anatomy Club, 167, 168, 190, 312n

Anatomy Act/Anatomy Bill(s) xv, 168–9, 248–51, 262, 275–6, 287, 324n

anatomy schools (*see also individually named schools*):
at London hospitals, 30, 162–3, 164–5
museums in, 161, 163–5
private, 30, 162–3, 167–8, 182, 291–2n, 293n

animal-cruelty campaigns/legislation, 134–9, 304n

Appleton, John, dissecting-room porter at Grainger's School, 62, 101, 153, 155, 178–9, 185, 196, 219, 226

apprenticeships, 76

Arabin, Serjeant William St Julien, lawyer, 188, 190, 315n

Ballantine, Serjeant William, lawyer, 315n

Barbican, 110, 130, 147

Barry, J.T., lawyer, 186, 193, 198, 199, 207

Battle Bridge (King's Cross), 34, 276

Baylis, Rebecca, lived near Nova Scotia Gardens, 200, 268, 271

Beaman, George, surgeon, 1–2, 28, 95, 96, 158, 192–3, 205, 265, 278

beggars *see* vagrants

Bell, Charles, surgeon, 35, 136, 158, 163, 171, 239, 312n

Bethnal Green workhouse, 47, 98, 122

Birdcage public house *see* pubs

Bishop, John:
appearance, 6, 7, 42, *56*, 123, *189*, 190, 209, 210, 230, *234*, 235, 238, 240
attitude/behaviour towards authority figures, 22–3, 25, 26, 41, 42–3, 59, 98, 123, 126, 210, 222, 230
birth and early years, 39, 76
bodysnatching career, 30, 36, 39, 41–3, 45, 97, 203, 227
children, 95, 98, 122, 126, 202, 204, 221, 223, 227, 256, 269, 270–2, 277
life after death, 280
perjurer, 39, 43, 238
prison record, xviii, 41–3
reputation, 41, 42, 123
theft of Mr Gardner, 43, 45
witness 'AB' at parliamentary select committee?, 36, 170

Bishop, Rhoda, 39, 51, 95, 97–8, 119, 125–6, 143, 152–4, 187, 201, 207, 217, 218, 221, 223, 226, 253, 257, 270, 276–7, 294n

Bishop, Sarah, 39, 41, 45–6, 95, 96, 97–8, 99, 119, 120, 125–6, 143, 187, 207, 221, 223, 227, 270, 276–7, 282, 294n

Black Joe Johnson, vagrant entertainer, 102, *103*

'blood money' for informers, 267

Bloody Code, The, xvi, 31, 139

Bodkin, William Henry, barrister and charity chairman, 188, 190–1, 192, 299n

bodysnatchers *see* resurrection men

bodysnatching:
    little surviving evidence, xviii, 35–6, 293n, 322n
    not a felony, 34, 250
    subject to increased police vigilance, 34–5, 41
Bow Street police office/magistrates' court, 41, 54, 55, 56, 96, 126, 169, 273, 304n, 309n
Brenton, Edward Pelham, philanthropist, 77–8, 298n
Bridewell Prison, 73, 110, 298n
Bridgnorth, 47–8
broadsheets, 240, 241, 242, 243, 244, 247, 254, 318n, 319n
Brookes, Joshua, anatomist, 162–3, 164, 167, 168, 170, 293n, 311n
Brookesian museum/Vivarium, 163, 165, 310n, 314n
Brun, Augustine, padrone, 92–5, 196–7, 198, 262, 265
Burdett-Coutts, Angela, baroness, millionairess, philanthropist, 282–4, 300n
Burke and Hare, xv, 5, 28, 57–9, 144, 168, 169, 170, 172, 174, 185, 192, 241, 245, 250, 285, 290n, 302n
burking, suspected/attempted in London, 72, 144–5, 147–8, 169–70, 172–3, 219, 308n, 325n

Calcraft, William, executioner, 232, 233–4, 235, 323n
Cannell, Ann, lived near Nova Scotia Gardens, 13–14, 120, 195
'Captain Swing' riots, 80, 299n
Carpenter, Rosina, lover of James May, 60–1, 147, 205–6
Carpue, Joseph, 10–11, 22, 161–2, 163, 167, 172, 179–80, 309–11n, 314n
carts and coaches:
    coach fares, 13, 19
    used by resurrectionists, 35, 39, 45, 52

charities, 78–9
child trafficking see padroni
children see missing children
cholera, 284–5, 288
Christison, Robert, surgeon, 192
Chunee, an elephant, 280, 311n
City of London see Corporation of London
Clare, John, poet, 173, 313n
Clare Market, 52, 188, 295n
Clerkenwell New Prison/Clerkenwell House of Detention, xviii, 42, 61, 295n
Clift, William, curator of the Royal College of Surgeons museum, 233, 234, 236, 237, 323n
Cobbett, William, xvii, 262
Coldbath Fields Prison, xviii, 42, 277, 287
Colla, Andrew, Italian artisan, 198–9, 212, 263–5, 274–5
Collins, Wilkie, 320n
Columbia Square/Columbia Market, 283, 284
Cooper, Astley, surgeon, 97, 152, 162, 163, 166, 167–8, 171, 174, 182, 193, 213, 309n, 311n, 313n, 314n
Cooper, Bransby, surgeon, 163, 166, 174
Corder, James, vestry clerk of St Paul's, Covent Garden, 5, 25, 26, 28–9, 54, 57, 71, 94, 123–4, 126, 220, 262–8
Corn Laws, 77, 298n
Corporation of London, 65, 111, 133, 137, 230, 304n
corpses:
    child corpses, 31, 176, 187
    exhibiting unusual illness/pathological condition, 31, 313n
    male preferred to female, 30, 176
    oversupply of, 21, 30, 176
    prices of, 11, 22, 27, 30, 145, 153
    scarcity of, 31, 167

Cotton, Reverend Horace, chaplain/'Ordinary' of Newgate Prison, 217, 218, 220, 221, 222, 231, 233, 252, 254, 255, 256, 258, 259–61, 307n, 325n

Covent Garden, 67, 72, 73, 84, 190, 298n
  Market, 24, 25, 29, 70, 83, 106–7, 273
  Theatre, 67
  watch-house/station house, 1–2, 5, 6, 57, 71, 122, 158, 197, 198, 202, 263, 309n, 314n

crime levels, 31, 76–7

Cruikshank, George, artist/caricaturist, 105, 133, 318

Culkin, Bridget, suspected burker, 146–8, 274

Cunningham, a runaway, 226–7, 246, 253, 256, 258, 261, 271

Curwood, John, lawyer, 186, 192, 195, 197, 200, 203

'Daft Jamie' (James Wilson), victim of Burke and Hare, 58, 185, 245, 246, 285

Dance, George, the Elder, 294n

Dance, George, the Younger, 215

dancing doll man/men, 102, 103, 105

Davis, James, dissecting-room porter at Guy's, 16, 27, 178, 195–6, 203, 205

De Quincey, Thomas, xvii, 108, 115

Dermott, George, anatomy teacher, 26, 276, 314n

detection, primitive state of, 59, 63, 66–7, 96, 98, 182

'Dicity, The' see London Society for the Suppression of Mendicity

Dickens, Charles, xviii, 36–8, 42, 54, 63, 72, 132–3, 151, 213, 246, 280, 282, 284, 297n, 300n, 304n, 309–10n, 315–22n, 323n

Barnaby Rudge, 318n
  Bleak House, xviii, 151
  Great Expectations, 132, 305n
  Nicholas Nickleby, 306n
  Oliver Twist, xviii, 10, 54, 132, 295–6n, 299n, 315–7n, 318n, 321n
  A Tale of Two Cities, 96

Dickens, John, 72, 319–20n

dissenters/non-conformists (evangelicals, Quakers, Baptists, Methodists etc), 138, 222, 254–5, 305n

Dodswell, Mary, second-hand clothes dealer, 207

Douchez, George, surgeon, 95–6, 314n

drains see sewers

drink, xviii, 10, 11, 13, 16, 20, 21, 22, 27, 45, 153, 154, 187, 194, 201, 216, 223, 224, 225, 226, 227, 256, 290–1n
  'half and half', 154, 248
  'hot' beer/'rum hot'/'egg hot', 16, 25, 156, 291n

Drury Lane, 23, 90, 126, 301n
  Theatre, 65, 67, 70, 126, 240

Duchess of St Albans/Harriot Mellon, 41, 282, 284

Duke of Sussex (Augustus Frederick Hannover), 190, 208, 212–3

Earl Grey, 65, 190, 230, 297n

Egan, Pierce, author of Life in London, 109, 237, 254, 296n, 319n, 323n, 325n

Elephant and Castle, 19, 52

Elliotson, John, phrenologist, 237–9, 323n

enclosure of farmland/commons, 77, 80

evangelicals see dissenters/nonconformists

executions/capital offences:
  figures for, 31, 128, 292n
  scenes at public executions, 229–30, 232–3, 321n

Fagin, fictional corrupter of youth, xvi, 10, 174, 315–7n, 319n
Fairburn, publisher of broadsheets, 317n, 318n, 319n
family structure, 76
fashion, bad indicator of class, 109, 302n
Ferrari, Carlo see The Italian Boy
Field Lane, 8, 9, 10, 27, 176, 272, 289
Figaro in London, 248, 249, 299n, 324n
figurinai/plaster image-makers, 2, 84–5
flash houses, 65, 66, 68, 246
Fleet River, 9, 10, 141, 286, 287–9
Fontblanque, Albany, essayist and historian, 142–3, 220
forensic medicine, primitive state of, 96, 182, 192, 235, 278
Fortune of War public house see pubs
Forty Thieves gang, the, 73
freemasons, 190
French Revolution, xvi, 79, 114

Gall, Joseph, phrenologist, 237, 239, 323n
Garibaldi, Giuseppe, 279
George IV, 65, 97, 135, 159, 306n
George public house see pubs
Gissing, George, lived near Nova Scotia Gardens, 13, 120, 195
Godwin, George, architect/sanitary campaigner, 280–1
Golden Lane, 19, 27, 31, 61, 79, 145, 205, 274
Golden Square, 176, 177, 258, 314n
Gordon Riots, 176, 301n
Grainger, Edward, 162, 166–8, 312n
Grainger, Richard, 168, 178–9
Grainger's School of Anatomy/Webb Street School of Anatomy, 16, 21, 27, 31, 39, 62, 101, 153, 154–6, 166–8, 178–9, 181–2, 185, 196, 219, 312n
graveyards:
  Enon Chapel, 52

Moorfields Roman Catholic Chapel, 25, 291n
St Clement Danes/'The Green Ground', 52, 162
St Giles in the Fields, 25, 291n
St Saviour's/Southwark Cathedral, 167
Great Windmill Street School of Anatomy, 159, 161, 169, 174, 234, 236, 309n, 314n
Guthrie, George, 166, 175, 176, 234, 236, 250, 312n
Guy's Hospital, 11, 14, 16, 19, 20–1, 26, 27, 28, 31, 39, 62, 101, 162, 166, 167, 171, 177–8, 182, 196, 208, 313n, 314n

Hackney Road, 33, 46, 117, 142, 150, 225
Hall, Mary Ann, a lover of James May, 19, 52, 206
Hanover Square, 3, 57, 198
Hanoverian era/eighteenth century, reaction against, xvi, 31, 161, 166
Harmer, James, solicitor and campaigner for legal/penal reform, 143, 150, 218, 254, 307–8n, 325n
Head, Rhoda see Bishop, Rhoda
Head, Thomas see Williams, Thomas
Higgins, Constable Joseph, a New Policeman, 60, 95–6, 98–9, 142, 202
Highgate, 39, 41, 48, 51, 80, 282, 293n, 299n, 318n
Hill, William, dissecting-room porter at King's College, 21–3, 26, 177, 180, 191, 275–6
Hilton, John ('Anatomical John'), anatomist, 177–8, 314n
Hogarth, Georgina, Charles Dickens's sister-in-law, 320–1n
Holborn, 5, 34, 59, 81, 82, 83, 84, 90, 115, 130, 295n

Holywell, Shoreditch, 12–13, 148, 151–2, 223
Hood, Thomas, author of *Mary's Ghost*, 170–2
horse-stealing, 43, 128, 130, 305n
Horsey, Samuel, sledge beggar, 102, *104*, 301n
Hoxton, 41, 149, 204, 207
Hue and Cry/Police Gazette, 74–5, 76, 116, 130
Hunt, Henry ('Orator'), Radical MP, 250, 252
Hunter, John, anatomist, 163, 314n
Hunter, William, anatomist, 96, 314n
Hunterian Museum, 163, 280

Illumination protest, the, 27 April 1831, 69, 175–6
informers *see* police
Islington, 79, 115, 116, 129, 141, 299n
The Italian Boy/Carlo Ferrari/the corpse delivered to King's College:
  Bishop's accounts of where the corpse came from, 26, 223, 224
  Brun's ambiguous identification, 92–3, 196–7, 262
  Carlo's origins, arrival in England and last known whereabouts, 92, 94–5, 196, 197, 263, 266, 269
  coroner's inquest on, 2–6, 8, 25–9, 54
  exhumed, 92–3
  Lincolnshire drover's boy/'White', 223, 253, 255–6, 258, 261, 263–4, 266
  memorialised in print and pictures, *93*, 240–6
  Paragallis' claim to have known, 3, 5, 94–5, 197–8, 262–3, 265
  physical appearance of corpse, 1, 5, 22–3, *93*, 191, 262–5
  post-mortem findings on, 1–2, 28, 62, 95–6, 191–3, 262–3, 265–6, 278

sightings in Nova Scotia Gardens of an Italian Boy, 54–5, 57, 94, 120–2, 199–201, 264, 268, 271–2
sightings in the West End, 3, 57, 93–5, 197, 198, 265
The Times's opinion on, 4–5
Italian boys/image boys in London, 2–3, 83–5, 87–91, *106*, 110, 197, 198, 300n

King of Denmark, (Magpie and Stump *see* pubs
King, John, son of Margaret, 121–2, 199, 201, 268, 271
King, Margaret, lived near Nova Scotia Gardens, 54–5, 57, 94, 120–2, 199, 268, 271
King, Martha, daughter of Margaret, 122, 199–200, 268, 271
King's College, 1–2, 20–3, 28, 35, 158–60, 179–81, 191, 234, 235, 236, 275–6, 278–9, 280
Knox, Robert, Edinburgh surgeon, 58, 136, 168, 170, 174, 185, 192, 245, 285, 313n

The Lancet, 92, 160–1, 163, 275–6, 278, 309n, 312n
laudanum, 223, 225, 226, 256, 257, 290–1n
literacy, xvii, 73, 285
Little Windmill Street School of Anatomy ('Tuson's'), 10–11, 163, 187, 311n
Littledale, Sir Joseph, judge, 190, 220
Lock, Henry, barman at the Fortune of War, 18–19, 194
London:
  affect on human health, 108, 285, 301n
  darkness of, 106–7
  fog, 134, 230, 232, 285, 306n
  gaslighting introduced, 108
  labyrinthine nature of, xix, 289

local government of, 78, 298n
monotonous streets and buildings,
106–7
population size/demography, xv, 77
self-absorbed citizens, 108, 120,
175–6
traffic noise and jams, 110, 125, 141
London Bridge, 20–1, 153, 154
London Hospital, The, Whitechapel,
162, 172–3
London Society for the Suppression
of Mendicity/'The Dicity', 78, 79,
81–3, 110, 115, 188, 299–300n

Magendie, François, anatomist/vivi-
sectionist, 135–6, 239
magistrates:
attitude towards resurrection men,
34–5
attitude towards vagrants, 78, 81,
90–1, 109, 110–2
failure to keep records, xviii, 78,
298n
Martin, Richard, MP, animal-cruelty
campaigner, 134–8
May, James:
appearance, 6, 7, 8, 56, 60, 189,
190, 209–10, 240
birth and early years, 52
bodysnatching career, 30, 52–3,
205
knew Bishop four or five years, 10,
123, 224
lodgings in Dorset Street,
Newington, 19, 27, 52, 60, 196,
202, 206, 295n
love-life, 19, 51–2, 205–6
maintains his innocence, 125, 205,
212, 219, 220, 221
previous employment, 52
reveals resurrection secrets, 219,
322n
seizure and ill health, 221, 256, 273
shunned, 12, 52, 273

and teeth of corpse, 19–20, 27–8,
60, 62, 96, 193, 194, 196, 220
writes poem in Newgate, 218–9
Mayhew, Henry, xvii, 248, 324n
Mayo, Herbert, 2, 158, 160–1, 163,
234, 235, 239, 278
medical students:
bad behaviour of, 169–70, 236, 250,
312n
badly taught/treated by hospital
anatomy teachers, 162–3, 166
number of in London, 31, 167,
312n
Melbourne, Viscount (William Lamb),
Whig Home Secretary, later Prime
Minister, 28–9, 57, 59, 65, 71, 116,
220, 252, 262, 268, 297n, 300n
menageries, 84, 163, 311n
'Metropolitan Improvements', 287–9,
307n
Middlemarch, 327n
Millbank Penitentiary, 48, 49, 50, 179,
215, 221, 222
Mills, Thomas, dentist, 19–20, 60,
196, 208, 267, 276
Minshull, George Rowland, magistrate, 54, 57, 62, 63, 68, 95, 96,
100–1, 118–21, 123–6, 136–7, 154–6,
176–7, 180, 186, 218, 265, 275,
296–7n, 312n, 324n
Miss Christy, the case of, 33, 292n
missing children/runaways, 2, 23, 29,
70, 71–3, 76, 101, 116–7, 132, 177,
219
'mobs'/riots:
in London, 69–70, 79, 170, 175–6
in the provinces, 79, 80, 169, 170,
312n
Mortimer, Robert, resident of Nova
Scotia Gardens, 119, 195, 233
The Mysteries of London, 285–7, 327n

Napoleon Bonaparte, 280, 284,
311n

Napoleonic Wars, 76, 77, 84, 114, 301n, 312n

neighbours in Nova Scotia Gardens/Crabtree Row, 13–14, 54–5, 57, 98, 101, 118–22, 195, 199–201

Newgate Prison, 40, 42–3, 48, 50, 72, 73, 188, 214, 221, 222, 307–8n, 318–9n
  condemned block, 212, 213, 322n
  conditions in, 213, 215–7
  Dead Man's Walk, 216, 231
  Debtors Door, 13, 214, 229, 231
  Press Room, 213, 215, 218, 221, 230–1
  Press Yard, 212, 213, 217
  use of aliases in, xviii, 48

Nova Scotia Gardens, xv, xix, 13, 33, 45–7, 98, 120, 142–3, 195, 201, 247, 280–2, 284, 288
  clothing found at, 99–101, 120–1, 148–50, 154, 185, 197–8, 199, 200, 202, 204, 207, 225, 227, 256, 264
  Italian boy seen at, 54–5, 57, 94, 120–2, 199–201, 268
  Number 2: 17, 46, 50–1, 101, 118–20, 122, 148, 225, 270
  Number 3: 9, 13, 17, 46, 51, 95, 98–101, 118–20, 122, 142–3, 150, 200, 223–4, 225, 226, 227, 247, 258, 269–70
  white mice at Number 3: 122, 202, 207, 227, 264, 268–9, 279

Observer, The, 252–4, 256

Old Bailey:
  Sessions House and nature of trials at, 40, 43, 48, 76, 186–8, 212, 213, 220, 231, 315n, 318n
  street, 12, 13, 38, 39, 40, 130, 223, 229

Old Street/Old Street Road, 19, 41, 61, 224, 225, 304n

Oxford Street, 3, 71, 82, 137, 162, 198

padroni/child traffickers, 88–90, 269, 300n

Pailthorpe, Frederick William, illustrator of Dickens's work, 317–8n

Paragalli, Joseph, 3, 5, 59, 92, 94–5, 100, 196–8, 262–3, 265, 267, 269

Paragalli, Mary, 3, 57, 198, 263, 269

Partridge, Richard, 2, 21–2, 23, 28, 35, 62, 71, 95–6, 158, 179–80, 191–2, 193, 234, 235, 262–3, 278–9

Paterson, Mary, victim of Burke and Hare, 58, 185, 245, 285

Peel, Robert, Tory Home Secretary, later Prime Minister, 63, 65, 267

phrenology, 237–40, 278

physiognomy, 210, 239–40, 247, 278

physiology, 136, 158, 239, 278

Pigburn, Fanny, 148–57, 181, 182, 185, 201, 219, 224–6, 245, 253, 256, 257, 258, 261, 267, 270

Pilcher, George, surgeon, 154–6, 179, 309n

Place, Francis, Radical/reformer, 69–70

Poe, Edgar Allan, 66–7, 108

police:
  attitude to vagrants, 70, 90–1, 109, 110–2, 298–9n
  Bow Street Runners, 63–4, 65, 66, 67–8
  informers, use of, 66
  Metropolitan ('New') Police, 30, 35, 53, 54, 57, 104, 109, 119, 137, 148, 277, 296n, 301–2n
  'Old' Police (constables, watchmen, Bow Street patrols and Charleys), 30, 63–5, 67–8, 111, 295–6n

Poor Laws:
  'Old' Poor Law, 80–1, 113–4
  Poor Law Amendment Act (1834) 'New' Poor Law, xvi, 104, 108–9, 113–14, 255, 281

pubs:
  Alfred's Head, Elephant and
    Castle, 19, 315n
  The Bear & Ragged Staff,
    Smithfield, 127–8
  The Bell, Smithfield, 187, 223, 272
  The Birdcage, 13, 51, 55, 120, 122,
    199, 200, 284
  The Feathers, 47, 156, 201, 224
  The Flowerpot, 153, 226, 309n
  The Fortune of War, 10, 11, 12, 16,
    18–19, 25, 27, 37, 38, 40, 43, 127,
    128, 147–8, 191, 194–5, 205, 208,
    219, 223, 233, 256, 269, 272,
    293n, 313n
  The George, Smithfield, 13, 187
  The Green Dragon, Highgate, 39,
    293n
  The King of Denmark/Magpie
    and Stump/Old Bailey watering
    house, 12–13, *14*, 39, 40, 187, 223,
    229, 232, 272
  The London Apprentice, 156, 225
  The Plough, 43, 187
  The Red Lion, Highgate, 39, 293n,
    318n
  The Three Tuns, Smithfield, 223
  The Unicorn, 2, 6, 62, 309n
Pye Corner, 38, 127

Quakers *see* dissenters/non-conformists
Queen Victoria, xvi, 190, 314n

Randall, John, lived near Nova Scotia
  Gardens, 200–1, 268, 271
Reform:
  Bills/Act, xvi, 69, 79, 175, 248
  unrest in London, 68–70, 79, 175–6
  unrest in the provinces, 79, 80
Regent Street, 94–5, 111, 197–8, 265
resurrection men:
  arrests, 35, 292–3n
  authorities turn blind eye to, 168–9,
    313n

capable of burking, 219, 262
and corrupt sextons, undertakers,
  watchmen etc, 31, 41, 152
deceiving/betraying each other, 22,
  34, 36, 152
earnings of, 30
individuals in London resurrection
  trade: Patrick Connolly, 152;
  Edward Cook, 172–3, 219, 313n;
  William Davis, 31; 'Boney'
  Dunkley, 147; Hollis, 152; John
  Jerrome, 53; George Long, 147;
  Murphy, 152; Joshua Naples,
  293n; the Shearing brothers, 147,
  274–5; Stringall, 275; Robert
  Tye/Tighe aka James Kettle/
  Cattle, 147, 274; Vaughan, 97, 152
made obsolete, 276, 287
posing as friend/relative, 33
pubs of, 10, 38–9
good relationship with dissecting-
  room porters, 21, 22, 26, 153,
  176, 177, 178
relationship with surgeons, 36,
  96–7, 167–8, 170, 174, 207
reputation for violence, 18
shunned, 12–13, 34, 39, 276–7
tools of the trade, 95–7
wives/female relatives assist/sell
  corpses' clothing, 33, 99, 207,
  313n
working conditions of, 31, 34, 96,
  293n
Reynolds, G.W.M., author of *The
  Mysteries of London*, 285, 287
Richardson, Ruth, historian, 168,
  293n, 312n, 324n
riots *see* mobs
Rippingille, Edward, artist, 173
Ross, Eliza, suspected burker, 172–3,
  219, 313n
Royal College of Surgeons of
  England, 161–2, 163, 233–4, 236,
  280, 311n, 312n, 323n

Russell, Whitworth, chaplain of
Millbank Penitentiary, 221–2, 229,
232, 254, 259, 260, 325n

Sadler Thomas, Joseph, police superintendent, 23, 28, 59–63, 67–70, 95,
98–101, 106, 112, 120, 121, 122, 123,
126, 148, 149–50, 154, 155–7, 179,
186, 193–4, 198, 199, 202, 207, 219,
262, 265, 269, 277–8, 312n, 323n
Saffron Hill, 61, 90, 141, 198, 274,
287, 288, 289
St Bartholomew's Hospital, 10, 20, 35,
38, 43, 101, 102, 123, 128, 134, 147,
162, 179, 194, 227, 233, 279, 305–6n
St Giles, 82, 289, 298n, 299n, 300n
St Leonard's church,
Shoreditch/Shoreditch church, 41,
46, 51, 53, 224, 287, 294n
St Thomas's Hospital, 39, 152–3, 156,
162, 167, 226
Select Committees:
on Anatomy (1828), 34–8, 148, 170,
174, 293n, 312n
on Medical Education (1834), 162
on the Police of the Metropolis
(1828), 67, 68, 70, 73, 110, 112,
188, 305n
on Smithfield Market (1828), 127,
133, 137
Settlement, Act of (1662) 113–4,
302–3n
Sewell, John, magistrate and evangelical, 260–1
sewers, xviii, 287, 288
sexual assaults/sex crime, 144, 148,
292n, 308n
Shearing brothers *see* resurrection
men
Shields, Michael, 8, 20, 25–6, 30, 38,
123–4, 126, 152–4, 156, 185, 194,
226, 273–4
Shoreditch workhouse, 41, 149, 277,
294n, 326n

slang terms, 10, 13, 14, 18, 31, 34, 41,
76, 109–10, 127, 130, 187, 195, 216,
290–1n
slave trade, 139
Smirke, Robert, architect, 28, 159
Smirke, Sydney, architect, 107
Smith, J.T., artist, 103, 105, 110, 115
Smithfield, 10, 28, 40, 43, 48, 127–41,
253, 255, 271
criticism of its sights and smells,
129, 130, 132–4
danger of stampedes/charges,
129–30
drovers and salesmen, 129, 130, 132,
134, 135, 137
horse market, 130, *131*, 135
ill-treatment of livestock, 134–5
knackers yards, conditions in, 133,
137, 305n
old buildings/narrow streets, 127,
129, 139, *140*, 141, 286, 289
as site of execution, 139
vagrant children in and around,
132, 226, 246
wife sales, 132
smock frocks, 6, 10, 13, 19, 23, 26, 61,
144, 190, 195, 276
Society for the Suppression of
Juvenile Vagrancy, 79, 298n
Soho, 10, 176
Somerville, Dr James Craig, 35,
174
South, John Flint, surgeon, 153, 226,
309n
Spitalfields Gang, 31, 36, 51
Starbuck, Charles, Quaker stockbroker and political lobbyist, 4,
305n
Stow, John, historian, author of *Survey
of London* (1603), 47
street sideshows/entertainers, 83–5,
86, *87*, 88–89, 91, 112–3
Stuart, Lord Dudley Coutts, MP,
90–1, 282, 284, 300n

surgeons:
  accusations of exclusiveness and
    snobbery, 161–3, 166–7
  criticised by the newspapers, 181–2
  dealings with resurrectionists, 10,
    11, 36, 167–8, 170, 174
  lack of respect for corpses, 179–80,
    250
  need to be circumspect about
    dissection, 168–70, 174–6

teeth see May
Temple Bar, 69, 111
Tim Buc Too, street-crossing sweeper,
  102, 104, 301n
The Times, 4–5, 144, 207, 240, 244–5,
  257–8, 263, 266, 290n, 317n, 318n,
  319n
Tindal, Sir Nicholas Conyngham,
  judge, 190, 203, 207–9, 212,
  219–20
Trader, Thomas, lived near Nova
  Scotia Gardens, 13–14, 120
Trueby, Sarah, the Bishops' landlady,
  45, 46, 120, 142, 201, 207, 269
Tuson, Edward, 10, 11, 162, 163, 167,
  187, 207, 234, 236, 311n
typhus, 280, 285, 288
Tyrrell, Frederick, surgeon, 163, 193,
  265

unions see working classes

Vagrancy Act (1824), 73, 76, 80, 89,
  90, 91, 104, 109, 110, 112–3, 138,
  188, 239, 269, 304n
vagrants, 70, 78–9, 81–3, 102, 103,
  104–6, 110–2, 114–5, 298n, 303n
  children, 29, 73, 77–8, 83–5, 132,
    247, 297n
  fraudulent beggars, 109–10, 302n
  rewards for arresting/fines for
    failing to arrest, 80–1
Vaughan, Sir John, judge, 190, 220

Vidocq, Eugène François, police
  informer/detective, 67, 296n
vivisection, 135–6, 174, 192

Wade, John, Radical/reformer, 109,
  110, 114, 115, 120, 303n
Wakely, Thomas, surgeon, founding
  editor of The Lancet, 160–1, 166,
  255, 309n
Walsh, Caroline, burking victim,
  172–3, 219, 313n
Warburton, Henry, MP, sponsor of
  the Anatomy Bills, 168–9, 248, 250
Ward, Edward, neighbour of the
  Bishops, 202, 207, 264, 269
weavers, xv, 30, 46–7, 70, 79, 110
Webb Street School of Anatomy see
  Grainger's
Wellington, Duke of, 65, 159, 175–6,
  248, 312n
West Street, 10, 27, 61, 290n
Whitechapel, 37, 73, 82, 129, 298, 305
Wigley, Thomas, porter, 16, 18, 38,
  190–1, 194–5, 208
William IV, xvi, 70
Williams, Theodore, vicar of
  Hendon, 123, 212, 217, 218, 219,
  220, 222, 231, 253, 254–5, 256, 259,
  260, 261, 325n
Williams, Thomas (Thomas Head):
  aliases, use of, 48, 50, 185, 236–7,
    292n
  appearance, 7, 8, 48, 50, 56, 123,
    189, 190, 209, 210, 230–1, 234,
    236–7, 238, 240
  birth and early years, 47–8, 97
  criminal career of, xviii, 30, 48, 141
  life after death, 279–80
  in Millbank Penitentiary, 48, 50,
    179, 237
  new to bodysnatching, 16, 30, 51,
    97, 203, 204, 228, 257
  previous employment, 28, 48, 50,
    98, 204

theft of William Sullivan, 33

Wontner, John, governor of Newgate Prison, 215, 217, 219, 220, 221, 255, 256, 308n, 322n

Wood, Charles, blind beggar/entertainer, 102, *103*

Woodcock family, lived next door to Bishop, 101, 118–9, 201, 205, 258

workhouses, xvi, 33, 47, 78, 109, 113–4, 180, 203, 205, 207, 276, 281, 303n

working classes:
  earnings, 30, 47
  hatred of resurrectionists, 12–13, 125–6, 152, 175, 273, 276–7
  helping each other, 81, 115–6, 175, 303n
  shorter than the middle/upper classes, 190, 197, 315n
  unions, and attitudes to collective action, 79, 115–6, 175–6, 277
  and the vote, xvi